THE FOOD BOOK

A Journey Through the Great Cuisines of the World

Melbourne | Oakland | London

Contents

Sign in the window of a Lyon restaurant.

GREG ELMS / GETTY IMAGES

France

'The French think mainly about two things – their two main meals', a well-fed *bon vivant* friend in Paris once told us, 'everything else is in parentheses'. And it's true. While not every French man, woman and child is a walking Larousse Gastronomique, eating well is still of prime importance to most people here, and they continue to spend an inordinate amount of time thinking about, talking about and consuming food.

CULINARY CAPITALS PARIS, LYON **KNOWN FOR** CHEESE, HAUTE CUISINE **IMPORTS** NORTH AFRICAN FLAVOURS **EXPORTS** 1.7 BILLION LITRES OF WINE **DEVOUR** *PAIN AU CHOCOLAT* **AVOID** SNAILS

APERITIFS

Sharing food, drink and friendship on a Parisian street at night.

GREG ELMS / GETTY IMAGES

CULTURE

The Celtic Gauls, France's original settlers under the authority of Rome from around the middle of the 1st century BC, were immoderate in their eating habits even by their conquerors' standards, consuming 'bread in a very small quantity with a great deal of meat either boiled, roasted or grilled', according to the Greek geographer, Strabo.

The Gauls favoured such 'oddities' as cranes, herons, hedgehogs and dormice, highly spiced with cumin, coriander, mint and pepper.

The Franks, successors to the Gauls, introduced a certain amount of refinement but not much was changed on the menu. Emperor Charlemagne had banquet tables laid with silver and gold goblets and plates, but the food remained primarily meat-based. Even by the time the first French-language cookbook was published by Guillaume Tirel (or Taillevent) in about 1375, menus consisted almost entirely of 'soups' (actually sodden pieces of bread boiled in a thickened stock) and meat and poultry heavy with the taste of herbs and spices, including new ones like ginger, cinnamon and cloves first introduced via Spain by the Moors.

The 16th century was something of a watershed for French cuisine. The culture of the Italian Renaissance arrived full swing during the reign of François I, who ruled 1515–47.

When Catherine de Médici, future consort to François' son, Henri II, arrived in Paris in 1533, she brought with her a team of Florentine chefs and pasty cooks who introduced such delicacies as aspic, truffles, *quenelles* (dumplings), artichokes, macaroons and puddings to the French court. French cooks, increasingly aware of their rising social status, took the Italians' recipes and sophisticated cooking styles on board, and the rest — to the gratitude of epicures everywhere — is history.

Perhaps the most decisive influence on French cuisine at this time, however, was the work of chef François-Pierre de la Varenne. La Varenne downplayed the use of spices, preferring to serve meat in its natural juices sharpened with vinegar or lemon juice. A basic tenet of French cuisine was thus born: to enhance the natural flavours of food in cooking and not disguise it with heavy seasonings.

REGIONS

Climatic and geographical factors have always been important to food in France. The hot south tends to favour olive oil, garlic and tomatoes, while the cooler, pastoral regions to the north emphasise cream and butter. Areas near the coast specialise in mussels, oysters and saltwater fish. People do eat dishes from outside their region — a *choucroute*, say, in a Marseille brasserie. But these dishes will never be as good as they are when they're at home; the ingredients and the preparation just won't be there to give them their authentic tastes.

Diverse though it is, French cuisine is typified by certain regions: Normandy, Burgundy, Périgord, Lyon, Provence and Alsace. Still others such as the Loire region, the Basque Country and Languedoc-Roussillon have made incalculable contributions to what can generically be called French cuisine.

Brittany and Normandy

Normandy stretches along the English Channel from Brittany to Picardy. The topography here is one of flat grasslands and *bocages* (small forests), interrupted by gentle hills. The climate is mild but damp, excellent for grazing and for most crops, except grapes. The region supplies roughly half of France's dairy products. Cream is an integral part of many of the region's rich, thick sauces and Norman butters are particularly sought-after. The markets of Trouville, Honfleur and Cherbourg

Tasting olive oil on the Cote d'Azur.

A goat in Normandy.

GREG ELMS / GETTY IMAGES

Onions and garlic, plaited and hanging against a stone wall.

Fishing boats line the harbour in Marseille on the Cote d'Azur.

Apples used for producing cider and Calvados.

Eating mussels, using the shell to grasp the flesh.

are crammed with lobsters, crayfish, langoustines, prawns, tiny scallops, oysters, mussels and fish. Apples are the third essential staple of Norman cuisine, and *cidre* (cider) is used extensively in cooking. Apples are also the base for the region's signature pastry, *tarte Normande*.

Brittany is also a paradise for lovers of seafood, including oysters from Cancale and the Morbihan Gulf coast; scallops and sea urchins from Saint Brieuc; crabs from Saint Malo; and lobsters from Camaret, Concarneau and Quibéron.

- The *crêpe* (wheat pancake) and *galette* (buckwheat flour pancake) are the royalty of Breton cuisine. The main difference between the two lies in the batter. A *crêpe* is made from wheat flour and is sweet. The buckwheat flour used in a *galette* is a traditional staple of the region, and the fillings are always savoury. A *galette complète* comes with ham, egg and cheese.

The Loire

The culinary heartland of the Loire, from which most other areas take their cue, is the historical region of the Touraine. The Loire region is v at its gentlest and most refined, offering harmonious landscapes, languid rivers, elegant architecture and wonderful wines such as Sancerre, Chinon and Saumur. When French people look for their common denominator, they end up at the Loire.

- The cuisine should be familiar, for it was the cooking refined in the kitchens of its châteaux in the 16th century that became the cuisine of France as a whole.
- This is the birthplace of *rillettes*, *coq au vin* and *tarte tatin*.
- France's best-known butter biscuit, *le petit beurre*, with its just-asking-to-be-nibbled tooth-combed edge originates in Nantes.

Burgundy

When the Burgundians arrived from their homeland on the shores of the Baltic Sea in the 5th century, they found a land planted with vines, grain crops and mustard. This agricultural legacy of the Romans would in time determine what and how Burgundy would eat, and the region's pre-eminent position on the trade route between the Mediterranean and northern Europe would bring prosperity. Indeed, by the 14th century, what had become the Dukedom of Burgundy was richer and more powerful than the Kingdom of France itself.

- Burgundy's cooking can be described as *cuisine bourgeoise* at its finest — solid, substantial and served in generous portions.
- Given what the Romans left behind them, it's not surprising that the 'trinity' of the kitchen here is beef, wine and mustard.
- The region's best known dish, *bœuf à la bourguignonne* (what the rest of the world calls *bœuf bourguignon*) is beef marinated and cooked in red wine with mushrooms, onions, carrots and bacon.

Périgord, Limousin and the Auvergne

Périgord, better known as the Dordogne, is a land of valleys, fields and forests, prehistoric painted caves, châteaux and, in the south, vineyards. It is one of France's main gastronomic centres and especially renowned for rich dishes made with fresh, locally grown products.

The tranquil, green hills of Limousin present the perfect image of France. The abundance of water nourishes the grasslands that make Limousin a major producer of beef as it does the region's many fruit and nut orchards.

Farther east are the higher plateaus and mountains of the

GREG ELMS / GETTY IMAGES

Hazelnuts for sale at a Parisian *épicerie* (grocery store)

Massif Central, which encompass the historical region of the Auvergne. The terrain, the climate and even the Auvergnats themselves are often described in French as rude (meaning rugged, harsh and tough), so, too, is its cuisine. *Potée Auvergnate* (a hearty soup-stew of cabbage, bacon, pork sausages and potatoes) is the speciality.

- *Confit de canard* and *confit d'oie* are duck or goose joints cooked slowly in their own fat. The preserved fowl is left to stand for months before being eaten.
- *Châtaignes* (chestnuts), once a staple food in Périgord, are now used as a flavouring; they can be stuffed in the cavity of a goose before roasting or bound into sausages and blood puddings.
- A *gigot brayaude* is a leg of lamb studded with garlic cloves and served — *à la limousine* — with red cabbage braised with chestnuts.

FEASTS

Food itself makes French people celebrate. There are special holidays where traditions — even watered down or secularised if religious — still endure.

- One tradition that is very much alive is called the Jour des Rois (Kings' Day) and takes place in early January, marking the feast of the Epiphany. A galette des rois (kings' cake), a puff pastry with frangipane cream, a little dried fève (which originally meant a broad bean but also means a plastic or silver figurine) is topped with a gold paper crown and placed on the table.
  The youngest person in the room goes below the table and calls out who should get each slice. The person who gets the slice with the bean is named king or queen, dons the crown and chooses his or her consort.

Al fresco dining in the Périgord region, Aquitaine.

GREG ELMS / GETTY IMAGES

- *Pâques* (Easter) is marked here as elsewhere with *œufs en chocolat* (chocolate eggs, often filled with candy fish and chickens) and there is always an egg hunt for the kids. The traditional meal at Easter lunch is *agneau* (lamb) or *jambon de Pâques* (Easter ham).
- At Christmas lunch, families throughout Provence eat *les treize desserts* (the 13 desserts) ranging from orange-flavoured bread and nougats to a variety of fresh and dried fruits that represent Christ and the 12 Apostles. *Fruits confits* (candied or glazed fruit) such as apricots, tangerines, plums, lemons and even melons, are popular gifts at Christmas and New Year in Provence.
- Menton, known as the warmest spot on the Côte d'Azur, celebrates its most famous product, the lemon, with the *Fête des Citrons* on Mardi Gras in February.
- Bayonne in the Basque Country honours its lovely ham with *Foire aux Jambons* (Ham Fair) just before Easter.
- The *Fête du Vin* (Wine Festival) takes place in Bordeaux in late June and early July.
- The *Fête du Thon* (Tuna Festival) held on the first Saturday in July, is a time when sports organisations set up stands and sell tuna dishes around Saint Jean de Luz.

ETIQUETTE

It's not easy to cause offence at a French table, and while there are some distinctions, manners have more to do with common sense than learned behaviour. A French table will be set for all courses at restaurants (not always at home), with two forks, two knives and a large spoon for soup or dessert. When they finish each course, diners cross their knife and fork (not lay them side by side) face down on the plate to be cleared away.

- Like other Europeans, the French hold their fork in their left hand and their knife in the right while eating; they don't cut their food and then switch the fork to the right hand as is the custom in North America.
- Never cut the bread but break it. It is quite acceptable to sop up sauces and juices with bread.
- Never cut off the tip of pie-shaped soft cheeses, such as Brie or Camembert; cut cheeses whose middle is the best part (the blues, for example) in such a way as to take your fair share of the crust; and at very formal dinners, never go back for seconds at the cheese course.
- If there are wine glasses of varying sizes at each place setting, the larger one will be for red wine (and water), the smaller for white wine.

THE MENU

A meal in a restaurant rarely consists of more than three or four courses: the *entrée* (starter or first course), *plat principal* (main course) and *dessert* (dessert). Some people choose a *fromage* (cheese) course instead of dessert.

The vast majority of French restaurants offer at least one fixed-price meal, known as a *menu à prix fixe* or *menu du jour.* Carte is the word for the menu itself; a *carte des vins* is a wine list. In some places, you may also be able to order a *formule* or *menu touristique*, which usually has fewer choices but allows you to pick two of three courses. In many restaurants, the cheapest lunch menu is a better deal than the equivalent one available at dinner. Many upscale restaurants offer a *menu dégustation* or *menu gastronomique*, which allows you to sample small portions of up to six courses.

- *Apéritif* — a pre-dinner drink
- *Dessert* — dessert

Fillet of beef with *foie gras* and truffle on top.

A chef buying herbs at a street market in Paris.

GREG ELMS / GETTY IMAGES

Fougasse, provincal olive bread on display at Carpentras Market on the Cote d'Azur.

- *Digestif* — 'digestive' or after-dinner drink
- *Entrée* — first course or starter
- *Fromage* — cheese
- *Hors d'œuvre* — cold and/or warm snacks taken before the start of the meal
- *Plat principal* — main course
- *Salade* — a relatively simple green salad with dressing

DAILY MEALS

The French tend not to fill up at breakfast. Traditionally, they start the day with a bit of baguette left over from the night before, eaten with butter and jam then followed by a cup of coffee.

- *Croissants* are eaten mainly at the weekend.
- *Café au lait* is coffee with hot milk.
- For those in provincial France, lunch remains the main meal of the day and is usually taken at a restaurant.
- The two-hour midday meal has become increasingly rare, at least on weekdays and in big cities.
- In many restaurants, the cheapest lunch menu is a much better deal than the equivalent one available at dinner.

ESSENTIAL PRODUCE

Bread

Nothing is more French than *pain* (bread); the peasants were demanding bread on the eve of the French Revolution when Queen Marie-Antoinette famously suggested they 'eat cake'. *Boulangeries* (bakeries) offer an infinite variety of breads. Most French breads are at their best if eaten within four hours of baking. You can store them for longer in a plastic bag, but the crust becomes soft and chewy.

GREG ELMS / GETTY IMAGES

A picnic taken in the Loire Valley.

Bread has experienced a renaissance in France in recent years, and most *boulangeries* also carry heavier, more expensive varieties made with all sorts of grains and cereals; you will find loaves studded with nuts, raisins or herbs. These heavier breads keep much longer than baguettes. To extend the life of them, wrap the loaf in a slightly moist tea towel.

- *Baguette* — the standard long, crispy French loaf
- *Ficelle* — a thinner, crustier version of the baguette
- *Pain* — a wider, less crispy version of a baguette
- *Pain de campagne* — a country loaf
- *Pain au levain* — traditionally made yeast bread
- *Pain de seigle* — rye bread

Along with bread, bakeries usually sell baked goods and pastries that are lumped together under the term *viennoiserie*. These include:

- *Brioche* — a small roll or cake made of yeast, flour, eggs and butter
- *Croissant* — a flaky crescent-shaped roll, and
- *Pain au chocolat* — a flat 'croissant' filled with chocolate.

Charcuterie

A list of French *charcuterie* can go on and on and on. Strictly speaking *charcuterie* (from the verb *charcuter*, 'to butcher') is made only from pork, though a number of other meats (beef, veal, chicken, goose) are used in making sausages, blood puddings, hams and other cured and salted meats. The all-encompassing word *cochonailles* (pig or pork products) now does the job that *charcuterie* used to do.

- *Andouille* — A large smoked tripe sausage cooked and ready to eat.

- *Boudin blanc* — A smooth white sausage made from poultry, veal, pork or even rabbit, which is cooked and can be served with, say, haricot beans or apples.
- *Boudin noir* — Blood sausage or pudding made with pig's blood, onions and spices and usually eaten hot with stewed apples and potatoes.
- *Foie gras* — The most celebrated pâté is made from fattened goose or duck liver. It was first prepared around 1780 as *pâté en croûte à la Clause* by one Jean-Pierre Clause, chef to the military governor of Alsace, who was impressed enough to send a batch to the king at Versailles.
- *Galantine* — Boned, stuffed and pressed or rolled poultry or pork served cold in aspic.
- *Jambon* — Ham; smoked or salt-cured pork made from a pig's hindquarters.
- *Pâtés* — Essentially mincemeat that has been spiced and baked in a dish or earthenware terrine and can be served hot or cold.
- *Rilletes* — Potted meat that is shredded with two forks, seasoned, mixed with fat and spread cold over bread.
- *Saucisse* — A small sausage that is boiled or grilled.
- *Saucisson* — Generally a large salami eaten cold.
- *Terrines* — *Pâté* sliced from the container itself.

Cheese

General Charles de Gaulle, expostulating on the inability of anyone to unite the French on a single issue after WWII, famously grumbled, 'You cannot easily bring together a country that has 265 kinds of cheese.' But his comments are well out of date; today, France counts upwards of 500.

Pan bagnat, a crunchy salad roll.

Sweet, soft doughnut stack.

Perfectly-French *baguettes* in a basket.

Local sausages at a market in Carpentras on the Cote d'Azur.

Rilletes de Tours, served in a *terrine*.

Saucisson de Lyon with wine sauce and potatoes.

French cheese is made from cow's, goat's, or ewe's milk. The milk can be raw, pasteurised or *petit-lait* (the whey left over after the milk fats and solids have been curdled with rennet). Cheese can also take on a multitude of sizes and shapes — from small and round and long and cylindrical to the shape of pyramids, hearts, bricks and large wheels. The taste of France's cheeses are as complex as its wines: sweet, nutty, earthy, salty, acid, metallic and so on. But all have one thing in common: they all undergo a process of ripening or curing.

The choice on offer at a *fromagerie* (cheese shop) can be overwhelming. But don't be daunted; *fromagers* (cheese merchants) allow you to try before you buy. This list divides French cheeses into five main groups as they might be divided in a *fromagerie* and recommends several types. As the French say, a meal without cheese is like a day without sunshine.

Chèvre or goat's milk cheese is usually creamy and both sweet and a little salty when fresh but hardens and gets much saltier as it matures.

- *Sainte Maure de Touraine* is a creamy, mild cheese from the Loire region and a good introduction to the goat family. It has a salted ash rind and a distinctive straw running through the centre.
- *Crottin de Chavignol* from Burgundy is the classic goat's milk cheese. It can get very salty after a maturation period of more than two weeks.
- *Cabécou de Rocamadour* comes from Midi-Pyrenées and is excellent in spring when the cheese is fresh and tastes of grass and milk. Cabécou is often served warm with salad or marinated in oil and rosemary.

Fromage à pâte persillée, or blue cheese, is called *persillé* because the veins often resemble parsley. *Fourme,* which now denotes a type of blue-veined cheese, was once the catch-all word for cheese in general and the origin of the word *fromage*.

- *Fourme d'Amber* is a very mild cow's milk cheese from Rhône-Alpes and a good introduction for newcomers. The consistency lies somewhere between Gorgonzola and Roquefort.
- *Roquefort*, a ewe's milk cheese is to many the king of French cheese.
- *Bresse Bleu*, a pasteurised cow's milk cheese from Rhône-Alpes has a soft rind of white mould and is creamier than most blues.

Fromage à pâte demi-dure or semi-hard cheese means all uncooked pressed cheeses.

- *Tomme de Savoie* is an outstanding cheese made from either raw or pasteurised cow's milk.
- *Cantal* is a large cow's milk cheese from Auvergne that tastes something like Cheddar.
- *Saint Nectaire* is a pressed cheese of pink or reddish colour that has a strong smell and a complex taste.

Fromage à pâte dure or hard cheese in France is always cooked and pressed.

- *Beaufort* is a grainy cow's milk cheese with a slightly fruity taste from Rhône-Alpes; one of the largest-selling cheeses in France.
- *Comté* (AOC) is a a yellowish, pressed and cooked cow's milk cheese from Franche-Comté.
- *Emmental* is a cow's milk cheese made all over France, but *Emmental Grand Cru*, arguably the best, comes from the mountains in the east.

GREG ELMS / GETTY IMAGES

A plate of Corsican cheeses.

Fruit

Spring brings *fruits rouges* (red or berry fruits) such as *framboises* (raspberries) and *fraises* (strawberries). These are followed by stone and pitted fruits like *cerises* (cherries), *pêches* (peaches), *prunes* (plums), and wonderful little yellow mirabelle plums, and later soft fruits like *groseilles* (red currants), *cassis* (blackcurrants) and *groseilles à maquereau* (gooseberries). The late summer and autumn bring *pommes* (apples), *poires* (pears) as well as *amandes* (almonds), *noix* (walnuts), *noisettes* (hazelnuts) and *châtaignes* and *marrons*, two kinds of chestnuts that can be ground into flour for baking pastries and cakes.

- The peaches and pears of the Touraine, the cherries of Auxerre in Burgundy and Céret in Roussillon, the melons of Poitou-Charentes, the sweet chestnuts of the Cévennes in Languedoc and the Ardèche in the Rhône region, and the black walnuts of Grenoble and Périgord are all eagerly awaited by fruit lovers.
- Normandy produces more apples than any other place in France and makes good use of them in its *tartes* (pies), *cidre* (cider) and Calvados (apple brandy).
- *Pruneaux d'Agen* (Agen prunes) start life as a deep purple *prune* (plum) grafted onto a mature Ente plum tree. The plums are picked between 25 August and 25 September and then dried. Most will end up as whole, juicy *pruneaux demi-secs* to be eaten plain or cooked in poultry, pork or veal dishes.

Fungi

Champignon is a general term for 'mushroom', both cultivated and wild. The ordinary *champignons de Paris* (button mushrooms) that you'll see everywhere are grown in the Île de

Punnets of blackberries for sale at a street market on Rue Mouffetard in Paris.

Pears at the market.

Punnets of strawberries.

France as well as in the Loire region. They go into soups and sauces and are cooked with meats. No cultivated mushroom can come close in fragrance, flavour and texture to the wild variety, and *aller aux champignons* (to go mushrooming) in any wood close by in autumn is a well-established tradition.

- There are literally dozens of edible types that all fall in line behinf the king of all fungi in France, the *truffe* (truffle).
- Never attempt to gather mushrooms yourself if you are not familiar with the varieties that grow in France. Staff at pharmacies are able to separate the delicious from the potentially deadly.
- *Cèp* is a large brown mushroom with thick stems and a spongy underside to the cap.
- *Chanterelle* is a pale orange mushroom with forking gills and funnel-shaped cap (also known as *girolle*).

Meat

The word for meat, *viande*, originally meant 'food' and in some regards that definition remains valid today: a meal in France is not complete without meat. The most popular meats are *porc* (pork), *veau* (veal), *bœuf* (beef), *agneau* (lamb) and *mouton* (mutton) — in that order. There are niche markets for other meats, including *cheval* (horse), *chèvre* (goat) and even *âne* (donkey), which usually ends up as an air-dried sausage. It's not that the French consume meat in vast quantities at one sitting; meat is primarily used in charcuterie, casseroles and stews. Indeed, most uninitiated Anglophones will recognise very few cuts at a French *boucherie* (butcher); T-bone steaks and roasts are nowhere to be seen.

- The best beef comes from cattle raised in Limousin, Bazas in the Gironde near Bordeaux and, in particular,

Charolles in Burgundy. A *pavé charolais*, a thick-cut steak of Charolles beef, is synonymous with good-quality meat in France. The meat should be tender and soft to the touch, veined with fat and dark red in colour.

- Ovines that graze on salty tidal marshes by the sea produce the best meat; look for lamb from Pauillac, the Cotentin peninsula in Normandy and the Vendée and Touraine regions of the Loire.
- The pigs in Alsace, Brittany and the Cantal in the Auvergne produce the best pork, and Le Mans in the Loire region is known for its excellent veal.

Poultry

Volaille (poultry) is the French term used to describe all types of winged creatures. Of these, the most popular is *poulet* (chicken), a term that encompasses any number of variations: *poussin* (very young chicken), *poule* (boiling hen), *poulet de grain* (corn-fed chicken), *poulet de fermier* (free-range chicken), *poularde* (pullet or fatted hen for roasting), *coq* (cock or rooster) and *chapon* (a castrated rooster).

- *Poulet de Bresse* is the choicest chicken available. Bred in Bresse in Franche-Comté, these *Appellation d'Origine Contrôlée* (AOC) chickens are the delight of both amateur cooks and prize-winning chefs. Easily recognised by their distinctive white plumage, bright red wattle and blue-grey legs, Bresse chickens are raised in the open for 12 weeks then spend their last fortnight fattening up on corn and milk.
- *Canards* and *oies* (ducks and geese) are widely consumed but are especially popular in Normandy and Périgord.

GREG ELMS / GETTY IMAGES

Sliced *cèpes* (mushrooms) in baskets.

Geese walking through the grass in a Normandy field.

GREG ELMS / GETTY IMAGES

Vegetables

Légumes (vegetables) were a relative late-comer to the French table; the first recorded appearance was *choux* (cabbage) at a banquet prepared by Taillevent for the king in the late 14th century. But when they did arrive, the French welcomed them with a relish that continues today. France abounds in vegetables of all types and, depending on the season, you'll find everything from the tiny purple *articauts* (artichokes) of Provence and the celebrated *rose de Roscoff*, the pink onion grown in Brittany, to the humble *potiron* (pumpkin).

- Brittany's tender *primeurs* (early spring vegetables) and the sheer variety of vegetables grown in Normandy are celebrated throughout France. Normandy alone produces some 130,000 tonnes of carrots a year.
- Provence and the lower Rhône region is well suited for growing artichokes, eggplants, peppers and salad vegetables. Provence has olives: La Picholine *olives vertes* (green olives) and *olives noires* (black olives) of La Vallée des Baux and Nyons.

SHOPPING

One of France's premier culinary delights is to stock up on delicious fresh breads, pastries, cheese, fruit, vegetables and prepared dishes and sit down for a gourmet *pique-nique* or cook a meal with friends. Most people in France buy a good part of their food from a series of small neighbourhood shops, each with its own speciality, though like everywhere more and more people are relying on supermarkets and hypermarkets.

Since each *commerçant* (shopkeeper) specialises in only one type of food, they can provide all sorts of useful tips.

- *Boucherie* — sells fresh meats but for a wider range of poultry products you have to go to a specialist.

- *Boulangerie* — France's bakeries supply three-quarters of the country's bread. Bread is baked at various times during the day, so it's available fresh as early as 6 am and also in the afternoon. Places that sell bread but don't bake it on the premises are known as *dépôts de pain*.
- *Charcuterie* — a delicatessen offering sliced meats, *pâtés*, *terrines*, *rillettes*. Most supermarkets have a *charcuterie* counter.
- *Épicerie* — literally, a spice shop, is a small grocery store which sells a little bit of everything, including fruit and vegetables. It is also known as an *alimentation générale*.
- *Fromagerie* — at a *fromagerie*, sometimes called a *crémerie*, the owner can supply you with cheese that is ripe and will almost always let you taste before you decide what to buy.
- *Marché* — a covered or open market, in a country town or the big city is the best place to buy your meat, fish, cheese and produce for a number of reasons: quality, choice, price and sheer entertainment.
- *Pâtisserie* — mouth-watering pastries are available at a *pâtisserie*. Some of the most common pastries include *tarte aux fruits* (fruit tarts), *pain aux raisins* (a flat, spiral pastry made with custard and sultanas) and *religieuses* (eclairs that resemble a nun's habit – vaguely).
- *Poissonerie* — people have such a taste for fish that fishmongers in inland cities and towns often have as a big a selection as the ones closer to the coast.
- *Viennoiseries* — *croissants*, *brioches* and *pains au chocolat* and the like are called *viennoiseries* and are usually bought at *boulangeries*.

Legumes at Agha Épicerie in Paris.

Picking cherry tomatoes in a country garden.

Decorated gourds at Carpentras Market on the Cote d'Azur.

Cave of the Societe Roquefort holding approximately 23,000 rounds of cheese.

GREG ELMS / GETTY IMAGES

PREPARATION

Utensils

The *batterie de cuisine* (kitchen equipment) and *utensiles* (utensils) you'll encounter here will be like the ones you use at home, including your basic steel, cast iron or copper pots and pans, a collection of *casseroles* (saucepans), *poêles* (frying pans), *cocottes* (casseroles), *marmites* (pots), *bassines à ragoût* (large stew pots) and so on.

- A *faitout* (or *fait-tout*) is a multipurpose pot or stew pot. Note that a *casserole* is not a casserole but a saucepan and that a *cassolette*, an earthenware dish used for baking, has nothing to do with *cassoulet*, the classic Languedoc dish of beans and preserved meat that is cooked in a *poêlon en terre cuite* (earthenware casserole).
- Pots and pans like *plats à sauter* or *sauteuses* (sauté pans), *braisières* (braising pans), *poissonières* (fish kettles) and *bains-marie* (double boilers) are designed for those who prepare elaborate dishes.
- Hand-held utensils might include a *fouet* (whisk), *louche* (ladle), *presse-ail* (garlic press or crusher), *écumoire à friture* (skimmer or slotted spoon) and a collection of *couteaux* (knives) — everything from a *couteau à éplucher* (peeling knife or potato peeler) to a scary-looking *couperet* (chopper or cleaver).
- The *planche à pain* is a bread board with a difference. Essentially a shallow wooden tray into which a wooden lattice has been fitted to catch the crumbs as you slice.
- Specialist items might include a *coupe volaille* (poultry scissors), *turbotière* (turbot poacher), *poissonière à truite* (trout poacher) or a *poêlon escargots* (snail pan).

- A *fil à Roquefort* is a wire cutter like they use in *fromageries* to slice cheese. But this one has a marble base so it's perfect for slicing such temperature-sensitive items as *foie gras*, mousses, *terrines* and *pâtés* as well as Roquefort cheese.

Techniques

There are several general types of French cuisine.

- *Haute cuisine* (high cuisine), also known as *grande cuisine* (great cuisine), is the classic cooking style of France and is typified by rich, elaborately prepared and beautifully presented multicourse meals. The aim is harmony and an appearance or artfulness and order.
- *Cuisine bourgeoise* is French home cooking of the highest quality in which the goals are bold, earthy tastes and textures.
- *Cuisine des provinces* (provincial cuisine), also known as *cuisine campagnarde* (country cooking), uses the best local ingredients and most refined techniques to prepare traditional rural dishes.
- *Nouvelle cuisine* (new cuisine), characterised by rather small portions served with light sauces and artistically arranged, was a popular cooking style in the late 20th century but has since fallen out of favour. Still, *nouvelle cuisine* has had a great influence on cooking techniques and the presentation of food in France and abroad.

DEFINING DISHES

Bouillabaisse

Bouillabaisse is Provence's most famous soup, from the French *bouillir* (to boil) and *baisser* (to lower, as in the flame). It is made with at least three kinds of fresh fish, always including

Hanging hams in a Parisian *boucherie*.

Shelves displaying kitchenware.

Making *tarte au fromage*, cheese tarts.

Waiter taking mussels to a table in Honfleur, Normandy.

GREG ELMS / GETTY IMAGES

rascasse (scorpion fish), cooked for 10 minutes in broth with onions, tomatoes, saffron, bay leaves, sage and thyme.

Bouillabaisse, which is eaten as a main course, is usually served with toast and *rouille* (spicy mayonnaise of olive oil, garlic, chilli peppers and fish broth) that some people mix into the soup but most spread on the toast.

Cassoulet

No dish is more evocative of Languedoc than *cassoulet* (a casserole or stew with beans and meat). This dish is classic *cuisine campagnarde* (country cooking) and uses the best local ingredients and most refined techniques. Of course like so many trademark dishes, *cassoulet* changes in its make-up from area to area and even from town to town. For while the *cassoulet de Castelenaudary*, perhaps the most celebrated version of the dish, cooks only pork (in all its guises) with its beans, the version from Carcassonne adds mutton, and the *cassoulet* from Toulouse, the centre of Languedoc until the 1960s, contains all of the above plus its most celebrated contribution to gastronomy, *saucisse de Toulouse* (a fat, mild-tasting pork sausage). All *cassoulets*, however, share several key ingredients: goose fat, herbs, onion and garlic and bread crumbs, sprinkled on just before it is put in the oven.

Cassoulet is labour-intensive – the beans must be well soaked to allow the germination that sweetens them, and the cooking must be long and slow to meld the flavours.

DRINKS

Aperitifs

Aperitifs often precede a meal and are meant to induce appetite. It's usually something sweet or slightly bitter, but a white Vouvray, a sweet *vin jaune* (yellow wine) from the Jura or a glass of Champagne make lovely aperitifs.

- The classic French aperitif is a *kir* (white wine with blackcurrant liqueur).
- *Pastis*, a particular favourite in the south, is an aniseed-flavoured aperitif often mixed with water. If mixing *pastis*, pour the water in first, otherwise the two won't mix properly and may take on a slightly soapy taste.

Coffee

Coffee took France by such storm in the mid-17th century that the establishments where it was served became the focal points for social life and lent their name to the lexicons of most languages. Few people in the world today would have trouble understanding the word 'café'.

- *Une tasse de café* (a cup of coffee) can take various forms but the most ubiquitous is espresso, made by forcing steam through ground coffee beans. A small, black espresso is called *un café noir*, *un café nature*, *un express* or simply *un café*. Espresso here can often taste more sour than bitter as it should.
- *Un café crème* is an espresso with the addition of steamed milk or cream.
- *Un café au lait* is lots of hot milk with a little coffee, served in a large cup or even a bowl.

Digestives

Digestives are usually ordered after dessert along with coffee. France's most famous *marcs* (grape brandies) are the highly refined, double-distilled Cognac from Charente and the earthier Armagnac from the region of the same name in Gascony.

- *Marcs* are a clever way of making use of an over-production of fruit. The grape skins and pulp left

Mackerel at a Parisian street market.

Marmitaki de thon, roasted tuna and potatoes.

GREG ELMS / GETTY IMAGES

Jarret de porc confit, pork shank confit, at Cochon A L'Oreille Restaurant, Paris.

GREG ELMS / GETTY IMAGES

Cups of sweet cider at the Creperie Val de Rance in St Malo, Brittany.

A French vineyard.

Classic French espresso.

over after being pressed for wine are distilled and made into the celebrated Marc de Champagne, Marc de Bourgogne (from Pinot noir) and Marc du Jura. A distillation of Marc du Jura with the addition of unfermented grape juice becomes Macvin du Jura.

- *Eaux-de-vie* (literally, waters of life) are distilled, usually clear brandies made and flavoured with locally grown fruits, herbs or nuts. Of the many varieties, kirsch, a cherry concoction, is the most famous. *Mirabelles* (yellow plums), *quetsches* (dark red plums) and *framboises* (raspberries) are used in Alsace and Lorraine to make some of the best *eaux-de-vie*. Calvados is an apple brandy made in Normandy that ages beautifully; poire William is a pear-based *eaux-de-vie*. The *eaux-de-vie de noix* (walnut *eaux-de-vie*) from Limousin is excellent.
- Liqueurs, produced all over France, are sweeter and lighter than *eaux-de-vie*. Most are made from grapes, *eaux-de-vie*, sugar and either fruit or the essences of aromatic herbs. Well-known brands include Cointreau from the Loire region, Bénédictine from Normandy and orange-spiced Grand Marnier made in the Île de France. For the finest fruit liqueurs, look for the words '*crème de ...*' as in *crème de cassis* (blackcurrant liqueur).

Wine

The *vignoble* (vineyard) has always been an integral feature on France's culinary map. Italy has its 'Super Tuscans', Australia has its Penfold Grange Hermitage, but no other nation makes wines like France.

The French thirst for wine goes back to Roman times, when techniques to grow grapes and process wine were introduced. Wine got a real boost during the Middle Ages when vineyards developed around monasteries; priests needed wine to celebrate mass and no doubt the monks wanted to enjoy themselves in the process.

Like all food products in France, wine production is strictly supervised by the government. Wines are divided into four categories:

- *Appellation d'Origine Contrôlée* (AOC) wines have met stringent regulations governing where, how and under what conditions they are grown, fermented and bottled.
- *Vin Délimité de Qualité Superieure* — These are good wines from a specific place or region that follow rigorous tests, though an AOC wine has stricter criteria both for wine production and tasting.
- *Vin de Pays* — Wines with this label are of reasonable quality and are generally drinkable because there are various standards that need to be met.
- *Vin de Table* — These wines are also known as *vin ordinaire* and there's only two rules governing their production: only real, authorised grapes can be used and the alcoholic content be between 8.5% and 15%.

Grape juice differs from wine in one vital way: fermentation. This is a chemical process caused by the reaction of yeast with sugar. Since yeast is found in grape skins and the fruit contains a high sugar content, grapes have both of the ingredients required. After the grapes are carefully picked and sorted, they are pressed. The pulpy juice, known as 'must', is put into vats to ferment and sulphur dioxide is added to prevent contamination.

- For *vin rouge* (red wine), the grape skins are left in the must, usually for about three weeks. The skins not only add colour but tannin, which imparts an astringent

GREG ELMS / GETTY IMAGES

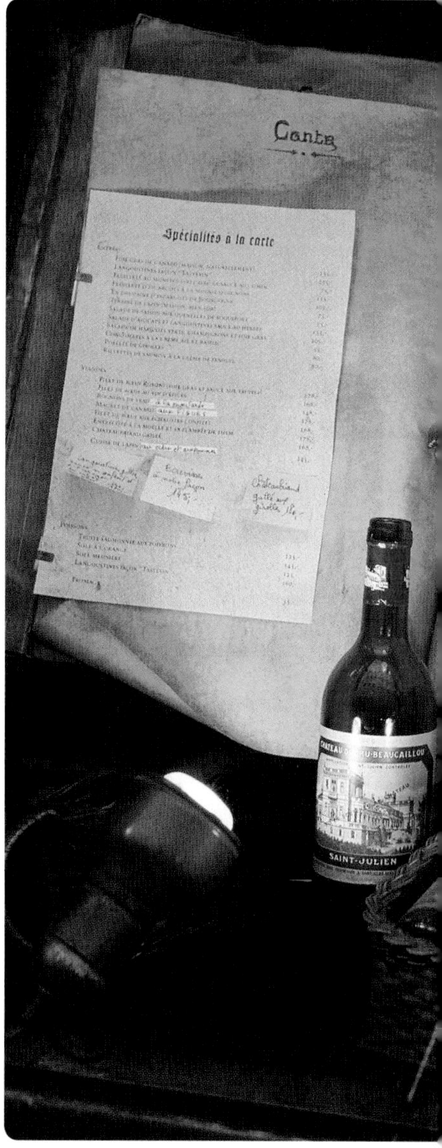

Menu display in the window of a Parisian restaurant.

taste and is an important natural preservative, allowing red wines to mature for years.

- *Vin blanc* (white wine) takes a bit longer and is fermented at a lower temperature. The earlier the fermentation of white wine is stopped, the sweeter the wine is due to the high sugar content.

After fermenting, the wine is poured into containers — usually wooden vats for the red and stainless-steel ones for the white. Red wine can be left for up to two years in the casks. Finally, the wine is either mixed from various vats to produce a blend or poured straight into the bottle.

In France, it's most often the region and the village that define wines, not the *cépage* (grape variety).

- Chablis, dry and crisp, is made from the Chardonnay grape.
- Champagne is also made from Chardonnay.
- Cabernet Sauvignon and Merlot grapes are the base for the deep, rich red wines from Bordeaux, sometimes with the less robust Cabernet Franc thrown in. The mix can vary year to year.
- Pinot noir is the grape used to make the more subtle red Burgundies. This grape variety is a fickle one and produces wine best drunk under 10 years of age.
- Syrah (known in Australia as Shiraz) is planted mainly in the Rhône Valley to make the heavy, red Hermitage wines.
- Sauvignon Blanc produces the flowery, dry whites of Sancerre and Pouilly-Fumé in the eastern part of the Loire Region.
- Chenin Blanc, mostly associated with the Loire's dry,

white Vouvray, can be used to make dry, semi-dry or sweet wine.

- Sémillion is used in Sauternes from Bordeaux. It's particularly suited for sweet dessert wines.
- Gamay is the grape used to make light and fruity Beaujolais and the younger Beaujolais Nouveau.
- The plump Muscat grape is primarily used to make sweet dessert wines in the south.

FRENCH ONION SOUP

Nothing is more Parisian than onion soup with a crust of oven-browned cheese.

Serves 6

Ingredients
225 g onions, sliced
100 g butter
1 tablespoon flour
1.5 litres beef stock
salt and pepper
12 thin slices of *baguette*
300 g Gruyère cheese

Method
Cook the onions in 60 g of butter. When they are golden, sprinkle with a tablespoon of flour. Mix well with a wooden spoon and gradually add the stock or water. Season with salt and pepper and simmer for 15 minutes.

Fry the *baguette* slices in the remaining butter in an oven-proof frying pan until brown. Top the bread with thin slices of cheese and grill for 2 minutes or until cheese melts. Ladle the soup into individual earthenware bowls and top with the bread and cheese. Serve.

GREG ELMS / GETTY IMAGES

Grapes ready to be harvested.

Delivering *foccacia* in Venice.

ALAN BENSON / GETTY IMAGES

Italy

Eating in Italy is a revelation. To sit at a dinner with an Italian is to understand where their heart is at, what is important to them. To savour hand-made pork sausages under the Pugliese sun is to see, finally, how important eating is for a happy life. And to watch the fluid movements and charming manner of a Neapolitan pizza-maker is to see that food isn't just part of Italian culture, it is the creative and fulfilling essence of its life.

CULINARY CAPITALS UMBRIA, PUGLIA **KNOWN FOR** PIZZA, PASTA, *GELATI*, COFFEE **IMPORTS** CHOCOLATE **EXPORTS** OLIVE OIL, PASTA **DEVOUR** FRESH PASTA, NEAPOLITAN PIZZA, *TIRAMISU* **AVOID** TOURIST RESTAURANTS

ALAN BENSON / GETTY IMAGES

The Sassi, one of the older districts of Matera, Basilicata.

Artichokes at the market.

Caffe corretto, espresso with grappa.

CULTURE

The country that has exported its food culture around the world (think pizza and pasta) is a surprising place. It's only within the last 150 years that Italy as we know it came into being, and even today, it feels like a collection of 20 separate countries rather than a united nation. So while the people are linked under one government, differences abound. Nowhere can that be seen more than in the food. Where else can you eat *couscous* or strudel, over 200 types of pasta, nearly 500 types of cheese and drink wine made in over 1000 styles?

Italy is graced not only with many dialects and wildly differing geography, but it's also blessed with clever cooks. A veritable roller-coaster ride of affluence and poverty has led to a *cucina* (cuisine) that is one of the most regional in the world. Add to this a sense of local pride, recognition of the seasons' bounty, and wonderful hospitality and you end up with food that has a sense of its place, its time and its origins. Not only does Italian *cucina* have a sense of those things, it's a life-affirming celebration of them.

This cultural enjoyment and immersion in food is for everybody. So, while there are world-class, fine-dining restaurants in Italy, you're just as likely to have a fantastic experience watching someone make *ravioli* (stuffed pasta) in their kitchen, as you would eating out.

Italian cuisine does not exist

Italian *cucina* doesn't exist. Spend any time among the people of, say, Umbria or Puglia and you'll hear an awful lot about Umbrian *cucina* and Pugliese *cucina*, but Italian *cucina*? Well, that's not something they know about. The geography makes for many micro-climates and the history for plenty of micro-cultures. The result is one of the most diverse, wonderful and thoroughly amazing cuisines imaginable.

This is due partly to the relatively recent unification of Italy, and partly to the dramatic differences in geography. The narrow band of land now called Italy covers 20 different regions. Some of them nudge the Austrian and Swiss alps; on a clear day Sicilia is within sight of northern Africa; Milano is closer to London than it is to parts of Sicilia; while in Valle d'Aosta, they speak French as fluently as Italian. The food in each of these places registers these geographic variances.

The Italian peninsula is dominated by rolling hills or fiercely steep mountain ranges dotted with fertile flat plains, all of which affect the way Italians eat.

History

While tribe after tribe, then empire after empire, dominated part or all of the Italian peninsula, there is one common denominator in Italian *cucina* — everyone seems to have arrived, seen the food that was here, liked it and added their own bit of pizzazz to make it even better.

- The Etruscans, the first really organised group to run the show for about eight centuries from about the 12th century BC, saw the local grain, *farro* and cultivated it.
- The Romans also used *farro*, but added wheat and spices, such as pepper and ginger, to the diet.
- The Moors' influence can be seen today in the use of *couscous* and fragrant citrus along with the use of almonds in sweets.
- The Spanish brought the Grenache grape to Sardegna, where it became known as Cannonau.
- And in between, such home-grown empires as the Genoans' and Venetians', who were rabid traders, embellished the *cucina* with ingredients brought back from travels to the near and Far East.

ALAN BENSON / GETTY IMAGES

Canola fields near Matera, Basilicata.

The Venetian Marco Polo did his bit to open up the minds and palates of what now forms Italy. He left Venezia (Venice) in 1271 bound for China as a lad on his father's 20-year foray. He came back with samples of many items, but most notably sugar, rice and spices.

But the real coup for Italian cuisine came when the former pirate from Genova (Genoa), Cristoforo Colombo, made an epic journey to find a quicker, less perilous route to India and discovered the rich bounty of the Americas. This forms the foundation of what we now know as Italian *cucina*. Before his return, *peperoni* (capsicum), *peperoncini* (chillies), *pomodori* (tomatoes), *patate* (potatoes) and *granturco* (maize) were unknown to Europe. Who can imagine Italian food without tomatoes?

The *cucina* you eat in Italy today is the result of combining foods that weren't even known about, let alone eaten, a few hundred years ago. Yet these introduced ingredients were incorporated into the local diet. The thing with Italy is that everyone has added and embellished over time, but always with an eye to what was good before.

ALAN BENSON / GETTY IMAGES

Wild asparagus.

REGIONS

Umbria

The heart of Umbrian food is the hearth. Wood fires are used for everything from *porchetta* (spit-roasted pig) to tiny birds to *bruschetta* (grilled bread appetisers) and mushrooms. In Umbria it is the pig that reigns supreme, followed closely by lamb, sheep milk cheeses, truffles and anything wild that hasn't been hunted out.

- The local *porcini* mushrooms are some of the best in the land, and the elusive *tartufo nero* (black truffle) and the *tartufo bianco* (white truffle) are both found here.

ALAN BENSON / GETTY IMAGES

Tartufo nero, black truffles.

- The pork butchers of Norcia are famed around the country, giving the name *norcineria* (signifying quality) to good butchers in Roma and beyond. Their *prosciutto* (cured ham) is saltier, coarser, but more fragrant and complex than those of Parma and San Daniele.
- About 30 minutes from Norcia is Castelluccio, set on a high plain, and home to the best lentils in Italy.
- Umbria has its own pasta, most notably *umbricelli* (sometimes called *ceriole* or *ombricelli*), and *stringozzi*. Both are made by hand with the same water-based dough. *Umbricelli* are round and string-like, but not as fine as *spaghetti*, while *stringozzi* are more squarish, but equally long.

Puglia

Pugliese food, of any region in Italy, can probably be described as the most Italian, if it's possible to say such a thing. Pugliese food represents the essence of modern thought behind Italian food — take a single ingredient and try to capture its unique character, that special something, and bring it to the fore.

- Puglia's most famous pasta is the sublime *orecchiette*, the 'little ear'-shaped pasta often still made by hand and served with *cime di rapa*, bitter turnip tops tossed with anchovies.
- The *pane* (bread) of Puglia is legendary, and some of the best bakers in Roma and Milano are of Puglian descent. By far the best *pane* are cooked in a wood-fire.
- You may also come across *taralli,* which can be like tiny circular pretzels or as big as a doughnut. They can be crispy or just crusty, but they always have a hole in the middle.
- Local sheep and cow's milk cheeses are excellent,

including *burrata*. *Burrata* is made by treating *mozzarella* (stretched water buffalo or cow's curd cheese) and placing a bit of cream inside. The outside is pure white, impeccably smooth, and when you cut it open you release strips of cheese encasing the cream.

FEASTS

Every day is a celebration in Italy. Someone always has something to celebrate, even if it's just being alive. But even more amazing is that there are so many organised festivals, many of them coming from the country's pagan past.

People on the Italian peninsula have always celebrated a harvest, some god or other, a wedding, a birth or the alignment of the sky/stars/moon. And when Christianity arrived, they simply put their new God as the figurehead. Most of these festivals were pretty wild affairs, such as the Saturnalia festival in Roman times, where a week of drunken revelry in honour of the god of disorder was marked by a pig sacrifice at the start, and a human sacrifice at the end.

Celebrations these days are more sedate affairs by comparison. But they can still be amazing, such as the snake festival of *Le Marche*. The tiny hamlet of Cocullo celebrates the feast day of San Domenico by draping poisonous (though de-fanged) snakes all over the saint's statue and themselves. Then each of the five leading snake-handlers and statue carriers get to eat a *ciambellona*, a cake in a ring-shape, which represents a snake biting its tail.

The biggest times for festivals these days centre around *Natale* (Christmas), *Pasqua* (Easter) and *Carnevale* (Carnival, the period leading up to Ash Wednesday, the first day of Lent). Religion plays a major part, along with a certain amount of superstition. For example, a piece of Christmas *panettone*

Sardine fillets on display at a market in Rome.

Roast chestnuts.

Gorgonzola being offered to a customer in Volpetti, Rome.

Prosciutto being carved in a home kitchen in Umbria.

ALAN BENSON / GETTY IMAGES

(sweet cake) eaten on 3 February (San Biagio's day) is said to ward off sore throats for the rest of the year.

The classic way to celebrate any feast day is to precede it with a day of eating *magro* (lean) because the feast day is usually a day of overindulgence in *grasso* (rich and not so lean – okay, fatty!). And while just about every festival has some kind of food involved, many of them are only about food. The general rule is that a *sagra* (feasting festival) will offer food (although you'll normally be expected to pay), and at a *festa* (festival or celebration) you may have to bring your own.

ETIQUETTE

You've heard that old myth about the Italian mamma who keeps feeding you until you're just about to burst? Well it's hardly a myth. Generosity at a meal is a sign of hospitality, so refuse at your own peril. Hearty eaters tend to be looked on more favourably, particularly by older Italians, who show genuine concern for those who are noticeably thin.

There will be more than one course at virtually any meal to which you're invited. Many families will bring out the *prosciutto* (cured ham) to carve at the table. *Salame* (cured sausages), often home-made, will be sliced and offered. A great steaming bowl of pasta is almost a certainty, then a small serve of meat or fish, to be followed by salad and fruit. Large meals may also contain a soup, a second pasta course, a *dolce* (a sweet), or all three.

At someone's home you can and should *fare la scarpetta* (make a shoe) with your bread and wipe plates clean of sauces — a sign you've really enjoyed the meal, and one that won't go unnoticed. Cutlet bones can be handled with the fingers, which can be surreptitiously licked, and small groans of enjoyment are positively welcomed. Serviettes aren't generally tucked into collars, but it's more acceptable to do so at home than out.

When eating pasta, don't be afraid to shovel it in, because if you don't, the rest of the table will probably be finished well before you. Long strands of pasta are twirled around the fork, using the pasta bowl as the base to make bite-sized morsels. Any bits hanging down are bitten through and not slurped up as is done in parts of Asia. It's okay to lower your head towards the bowl slightly and eat energetically. You will probably never be offered a spoon to eat your pasta with, as locals consider this practice quite rude.

Italians don't like people who eat with their mouth open or talk when their mouth is full. In contrast to the way they wolf down pasta, they find the North American habit of cutting the meat and then switching the fork to the right hand intriguing. They tend to understand the difference but don't consider it particularly civilised.

DAILY MEALS

Italians eat with a certain amount of gusto. This means that they tend to eat fast, they eat a lot, and they like to lubricate the meal with local wine.

The main meal of the day is traditionally *pranzo* (lunch), and while this is changing gradually because of modern work practices (such as the abolition of the siesta in some cities), the big *pranzo* is still very much alive thanks to the nature of the prima *colazione* (breakfast).

Colazione for most Italians is a *cappuccino*, or many will have an espresso, and only a few actually eat anything. If they do, the prima *colazione* of choice is a pastry. The most popular pastries are *cornetti*, similar to a croissant, but not as flaky and often filled with *cioccolata* (chocolate), *marmellata* (marmalade) or *crema* (cream).

Pranzo can be a huge meal and it was typically eaten at home. It was at least two courses — a first course of pasta plus a

Zucchini flowers.

Fresh fish at Trani harbour in Puglia.

ALAN BENSON / GETTY IMAGES

secondo (second course) — although it could be as many as ten courses. These days, office workers and those with less of an appetite may simply grab a *panino* (a sandwich, but one that uses *ciabatta*, or a roll rather than sliced bread) or *pizza al taglio* (piece of pizza) to eat while they work, particularly in the larger cities.

Cena is the evening meal, and was traditionally smaller than *pranzo*, but this, too, is changing. It used to be — and still is, to many — one course, perhaps *pizza al taglio*, maybe a pasta, or a plate of veal with some vegetables.

ESSENTIAL PRODUCE

Cereals, pulses and grains

Grains have always played a fundamental role in Italian cuisine.

- Even before there was wheat for flour there was *farro*, an ancient grain still in use today, featuring in many of Italy's regional dishes such as *pizzoccheri* (buckwheat pasta) and the huge array of thick, resolutely flavoured soups such as the *friulani orzo e fagioli*, (barley with beans in a thick broth).
- One of the most popular of all grains is *polenta*, the cornmeal staple of the north. *Polenta* served with milk was a classic belly-filler in poorer times, and is still popular with kids.
- Another grain popular throughout the north is *riso* (rice), which has given the world that classic dish, *risotto*. The best *risotti* are made from simple ingredients, such as chicken stock and mushrooms, and finished with a dollop of butter or mascarpone and freshly grated *parmigiano reggiano* (parmesan cheese).
- Dried beans are popular around the country, but nowhere as much as in Toscana. Keep an eye out for

The finished cheeses in storage.

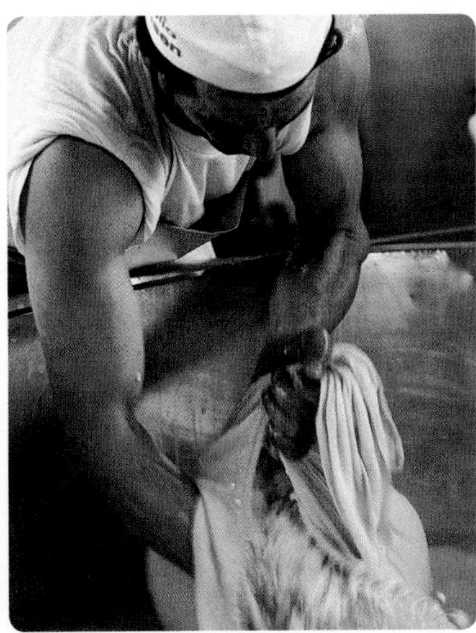
Draining the curd during *latteria* production.

Cheese in moulds.

the brown-and-white dappled *borlotti* beans and the extremely popular white *cannellini*.

Cheese

If General Charles de Gaulle reckoned he had trouble governing a country that had 365 cheeses, then it's no wonder Italy has had no luck finding a long-term leader lately, as their cheeses number closer to 450. That Italy produces so many types of cheeses is a source of great wonder, but a fact little known outside her borders.

Basically Italy can be divided into cheese regions based on the animal whose milk is used: cow, goat, sheep and buffalo. While Parmigiano and Gorgonzola have gained a name overseas, much of Italy's great cheese is simply known as *pecorino*. There exists a *Denominazione di Origine Controllata* (Controlled Designation of Origin) or DOC system for cheeses similar to that of wine to protect the origin and integrity of cheese styles. About 22 cheeses have gained DOC status. Of these, seven are from sheep.

Some of the best-known Italian cheeses include the following:

- *Asiago* — a scalded-curd cow's milk cheese with a sweetish taste from the alpine regions of the Veneto.
- *Burrata* — a delightful combination of cream wrapped in smooth, young cow's milk mozzarella.
- *Fontina* — a rich, heady, scalded-curd cow's milk cheese with a smooth texture that is used extensively in its homeland of Valle d'Aosta, particularly in the *fonduta* (a dish not dissimilar to a fondue).
- *Gorgonzola* — a particularly pungent blue cheese originally from northern Lombardia (Lombardy) but now more often made in the nearby town of Novara in Piemonte (Piedmont).

- *Mascarpone* — not really a cheese, but a cultured cream that is used extensively in desserts of the north. It's essential for the best *tiramisu*.
- *Mozzarella di bufala* — the classic porcelain white, super-fresh cheese, essential for the best pizza and a sheer joy to eat fresh.
- *Parmigiano Reggiano* — the hard cheese used all over Italy for grating onto pasta and in other savoury dishes or as a table cheese. One of the greatest of all the world's cheeses.
- *Pecorino* — the general name given to sheep milk cheeses. Most are part-cooked and have a semi-firm texture and nutty taste.
- *Provolone* — originally from Basilicata, this incredibly popular cow's cheese is made with spun curd (similar to *mozzarella*), then worked into huge squashed pear-shaped cheeses held in shape with a cord.
- *Ricotta* — this by-product of the cheese-making process is divine, and the best generally comes from sheep.
- *Taleggio* — washed-rind cow's cheese with a soft texture, an orangey skin and a mouth-filling, heady taste.

Mushrooms

If you are travelling in Italy in autumn or early winter, the *funghi* (mushrooms) alone — from the haunting, intense and intensely likeable *tartufi bianchi* (white truffle) to fresh *porcini* — can make your trip worthwhile. In autumn, cars parked in obscure parts of the countryside don't usually mean picnics or even clandestine or youthful liaisons (although they could), but are a sign that the weather is ideal for mushroom foraging.

There are several hundred types of fungi growing in the hills of Italy. Over 50 species are edible, including a few *tartufi*

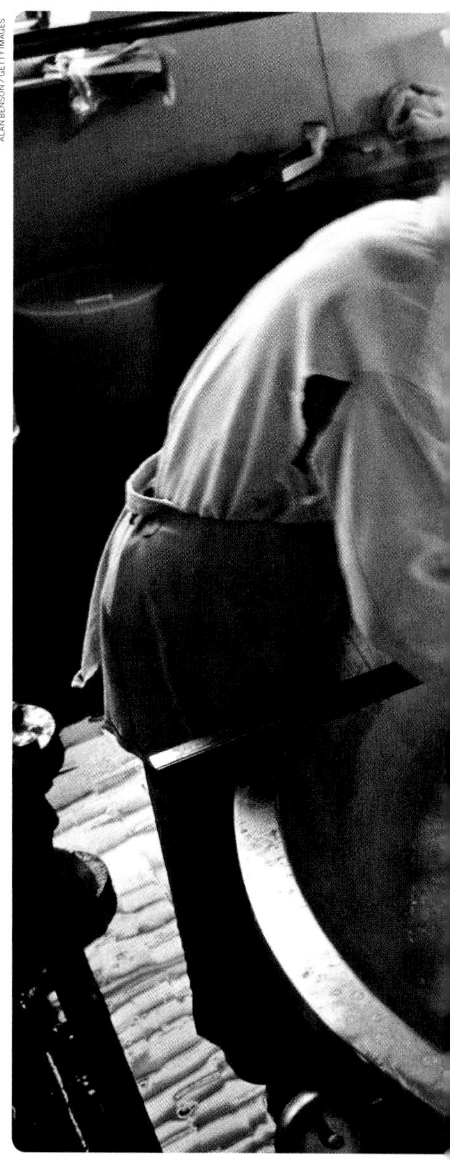
ALAN BENSON / GETTY IMAGES

Draining curd during the production of Parmesan cheese.

(truffles), the true *porcini* (*Boletus edulis*) and its related species, as well as wood blewits (*tricholoma nudum*) and other brightly coloured varieties.

Olive oil and olives

Olio d'oliva (olive oil) is surely a gift from the gods. How else can you explain something so simple, so versatile and, dare we say it, healthy?

The dullish-looking olive tree has a kind of philosophical importance to the people of Italy. It is symbolic of the Mediterranean, the climate, the culture and her people. The olive branch is the universal emblem of peace, the trunk means good luck and prosperity, and the oil is the divine essence.

Not surprisingly, then, thousands of hectares of Italian countryside are given over to the stuff. For all the hype, however, there's not really that much to it. You basically take a bunch of olives, smash them up and press them. You take the liquid that comes out and centrifuge it (or let it stand) to separate the oil from the water.

The quality of olive oil depends on the region in which the olives are grown, their variety, the ripeness at which they're picked, how soon they're crushed and the crushing method. Green olives tend to produce more bitter, yet fruitier oils; riper olives tend to lead to sweeter, milder oils. As you travel the country you will see how the oil varies, and how the food is paired with the oil. In Liguria, olive oil is sweetish and mellow with a lot of finesse; in Toscana it is more robust, greener and a bit sharp; while in Puglia the flavour tends to be more rounded, but still with a lusty, gutsy taste.

Pasta

Pasta existed in Liguria and Napoli long before Marco Polo went east. Although both regions still fight over who actually

ALAN BENSON / GETTY IMAGES

Olives on a tree.

made pasta first, Italy made it popular in the world.

Most pasta can be divided into two groups: *pasta fresca* (fresh pasta) and *pastasciutta* (dry pasta). Differences occur in the way they are made and how they are used. The size and shape of each pasta is no accident. Pasta absorb sauces differently, and each one is designed as part of a dish, so you won't see Italians putting a beef *ragù* (meat sauce) with a pasta designed for a light vegetable sauce. Each name often has a literal reference to the pasta's shape.

The more popular varieties of *pasta fresca* are as follows:

- *Bigoli* — a thick version of *spaghetti* from the Veneto, often made by hand and sometimes using wholemeal flour. Usually served with an anchovy or meat sauce.
- *Cannelloni* — large pasta sheets rolled around a filling of minced meat, eggs and spinach, covered with béchamel and baked. A dry, tubular version also exists.
- *Fettuccine* — a Roman version of *tagliatelle.*
- *Lasagne* — flat sheets used in the classic dish of the same name. The sheets are also available dried.
- *Pappardelle* — broad, flattish noodles from Toscana, usually served with a duck or rabbit *ragù*.
- *Ravioli* — formed from flat squares of pasta topped with a filling of minced meat or vegetables and another flat sheet pressed on top. *Raviolini* are the smaller stuffed pasta, and *ravioloni* the bigger.
- *Tagliatelle* — long flat strips about 5 mm (1/4 in) wide. Similar versions are called *taglierini*, *tajarin* and *tagliolini*.
- *Tortellini* — originally from Bologna, these tiny mouthfuls of meat-stuffed pasta are fashioned in the shape of Venus' belly button.

- *Trenette* — a Ligurian fresh pasta made to look like longish, thin tongues. Usually served with pesto and potato or green beans.

Following are some varieties of *pastasciutta*:

- *Bucatini* — a long pasta similar to *spaghetti*, but with a hole down the centre. The name comes from *bucato*, meaning 'with a hole'.
- *Cavatelli* — round, flat pasta discs made by squashing small balls of dough with the heel of the palm, originally from Puglia.
- *Gnocchetti* — despite sounding like it should be small *gnocchi*, this is a tiny dry pasta with a shell pattern on one side.
- *Linguine* — long flat pasta cut similar to *tagliatelle*; made without eggs. Name comes from the word for 'tongue'.
- *Maccheroni* — generally used to mean the *macaroni* we know, although the term can be applied to pasta in general or tubular pasta in particular.
- *Orecchiette* — the classic pasta of Puglia, its name derived from its shape, 'little ear'.
- *Penne* — takes its name from *penna*, meaning 'pen' because the tip looks like the nib from a fountain pen, they are smallish tubes cut at an angle. Often served *all'arrabbiat*a (in spicy tomato-based sauce).
- *Pinc*i — in Toscana this long, thick *spaghetti* is sold dried just about everywhere. Traditionally it is hand-rolled and made with durum wheat flour.
- *Rigatoni* — the name comes from the word for 'lines' and the pasta is like tubular penne but with ridges on it to help it hold more sauce.

Bigoli con ragu, pasta with bolognaise sauce.

Gnocchi with tomato sauce and basil.

Spaghetti alla vongole, spaghetti with clams.

The exterior of a *Salumeria* in Norcia, Umbria.

ALAN BENSON / GETTY IMAGES

- *Spaghetti* — 'little string' pasta originally from Roma. Best sauces include *carbonara* (egg, parmigiano and pancetta), *aglio e olio* (garlic and olive oil) and *alla vongole* (clams).
- *Stringozzi* — named after the leather cord that the locals reputedly wanted to strangle tax collectors with this is a long pasta made with hand-milled flour but cut to form squarish strands rather than round ones.
- *Umbricelli* — hand-made thick pasta typical of Umbria, made by rolling dough through the fingers. Classic accompaniment is butter and some shaved truffles.

Salumi

Salumi is a broad term that takes in all the varieties of *prosciutto* (cured ham), *salsiccia* (roughly translating as sausages) and related pig products, as well as other meat smallgoods, including salami.

It is pig that reaches its greatest heights in the *salumi* of Italy. But to list all the variations is fruitless. Often a *salame* (preserved sausage) is described simply as *nostrano*, meaning 'ours' or 'local'. This same name means it will be heavier, almost Germanic in taste in Trentino in the north; gently fragrant in Emilia-Romagna; fiery with chillies in Puglia; and positively reeking with garlic and fennel in Sicilia. There are differences even within a region.

Usually the pig would meet its maker in early December, so that any cured meats would have most of the winter to age before the weather warmed up. The pigs also tend to be in peak condition after eating well in the autumn. Specialist butchers are known to travel from village to village to help with the slaughter.

Also iconic in the landscape of Italian food is *prosciutto*. This typical Italian ham is made from raw legs of (preferably female) pigs. *Prosciutto* is quite remarkable. It must be sliced finer than paper, and its beautiful, sweet perfume starts to dissipate as soon as it is cut. The legs are salted and air-cured, usually in mountainous regions in fresh air. Each has its own character from the pigs and the curing environment.

SHOPPING

To shop in Italy is to be thrust, heart pumping and mouth watering, into the heart of Italian life. A market is an experience that drips with vitality, although the butchers' shops can be gruesome, they are still inspiring. The *caseificio* where you buy cheese can be the place where the cheese was made only hours before, and the person selling it to you may be the cheese-maker.

Italians love specialist shops — for meat, for cheese and for pastries. In fact, it seems that you can add the suffixes *-icio* or *-eria* to virtually any food product and open a shop. So if you sell lots of *prosciutto* (cured ham) you may have a *prosciuttificio.* If someone makes a lot of *confetti* (coloured, sugared almonds) then their shop may be called a *confetteria* or *confettificio*. And a store that specialises in *grappa* (the high-octane digestive drink) may put up a sign saying *grapperia*. Thankfully most stores have names that are the same nationwide.

Italy uses the decimal system and so goods are usually priced by the *chilo* (kilogram), or very often by *l'etto* (the 100 gram). Most shops close early one day a week, and not many are open on Sundays. Expect just about every food shop outside of the major cities to close for a few hours in the middle of the day for a siesta. The good thing is that they tend to stay open at least until you realise you're going to need some lunch.

At the market

Sheep-milk farmers selling *ricotta* out of the boots of cars; men with blackened hands biting the ends off ink-stained cuttlefish

ALAN BENSON / GETTY IMAGES

Salsiccia for sale in San Remo, Liguria.

before preparing them for sale; spruikers yelling, open mouths full of chipped, stained teeth ... this is a *mercato* (market) in full flight in Italy. Where Italians have a market, they have life, and the sheer liveliness of it defies the imagination.

You can hardly believe the freshness of the fish, the sweet smell of the herbs, the clamour and hubbub, the bustling, heaving humanity. *Vongole* (clams) may spray you with a fine thread of the seawater they're kept in, joke-telling stall holders jostle to have their photo taken, babies are clutched to hips, arguments are fought, lovers kiss, and all the while the buying and selling goes on.

If someone tells you a market is open every day, that means every day except Sunday. Many markets close at about 1 pm, and some don't re-open, although big ones do on most days. Saturday is usually the biggest shopping day of the week, because even workers can shop then. And a lot of extra shopping has to be done for that all-important Sunday lunch.

PREPARATION

At home

The Italian home kitchen doesn't differ much from the type of kitchen you'd find in Texas or Sydney. There's a stove (virtually always gas), a sink and very little bench space. But much of this is recent: it's only in the last fifty years or so that most homes had an oven. Before that, many would use communal, wood-fired ovens where they would roast or bake their dinner when the bread-baking had finished for the day.

The Italian kitchen tends to form the hub of the house. The lack of bench space is no problem when there's a kitchen table, which there always is. On the table you may find a simple *crostata* (fruit tart) covered with a tea towel, waiting to be devoured. You will often, and it's no cliché, find a tray with home-made pasta either drying or just sitting idle, waiting to be cooked.

People eating al fresco at an restaurant in Orvieto, Umbria.

ALAN BENSON / GETTY IMAGES

Risotto with herbs.

ALAN BENSON / GETTY IMAGES

Peas in a pod at a roadside stall in Sardinia.

Cooking al fresco

Italians love to cook outdoors and you may often see them lighting a fire when out for a picnic. The smell of wood smoke is important for so many dishes. From the simple *bruschetta* (grilled bread) of Umbria and Toscana, to the *farinata* (chickpea pancake) of Liguria, the allure of food scented with wood smoke is highly sought after.

The communal wine bars of Friuli may offer *polenta* (corn meal) cooked over an open fire (often cooked over fires indoors in winter), and at traditional *polenta* festivals you can still see well-built men stirring the meal in vast cast iron pots over open fires. Because of the cost and logistics of cooking over a fire, Italians these days bring the flames and smoke into their restaurants. There are eating houses all over the country specialising in wood-fired pizza, steaks or suckling pigs. However given half a chance, Italians will still light a fire and cook anything they can over the coals.

Utensils

The utensils of the Italian kitchen would be familiar to most people from Western countries. Rolling pins, slotted spoons, paring and cooks knives are all part of the culinary landscape. But there are a few implements that are rarely seen outside of Italy.

One has to be the polenta maker. It consists of a brass basin that sits on the stove, and a motor on top that slowly turns a paddle, taking the labour out of the constant stirring required.

The other a pasta maker. These are simple rolling machines with attachments for tagliatelle, ravioli and the like. Pasta machines are never, ever, washed, as once they have water on them, they will start to stick. Instead they are brushed clean of flour ready for the next use.

More specialised is the *spá'tzle* (dumpling) maker. *Spá'tzle* is an egg and flour paste that is so runny it can drip through the holes of a colander (one way to make them if you do not have the special tool). With the devised tool, you run a handle over what looks like a large-holed grater with very few holes. Each sweep of your hand pushes a dribble of paste through the holes and straight into boiling water underneath.

One knife that is sometimes seen in Italy is the *mezzaluna*. The name literally means 'half moon' and the knife has a smoothly curved shape with a handle on either end. Holding the handles vertically, you rock the blade from side to side and it chops everything in its path. It's particularly good for chopping herbs such as parsley.

DEFINING DISHES

Pizza

Everybody eats pizza in Italy. You'll see this staple in the curiously Germanic Alto Adige region, or sold in slices at Taormina in Sicilia (Sicily), where you can eat it within sight of a still-rumbling Monte Etna. In Napoli (Naples) where the modern pizza was born, the passion for eating it is only surpassed by its high quality. In Roma (Rome) they've made it the best fast food in the nation.

Pizza in Italy isn't the same as it is in New York or London, or anywhere else for that matter. And pizza in Napoli isn't like pizza from just about anywhere else within Italy. Taste it for what it is, rather than comparing it to the impostors that call themselves pizza all around the globe and you will be amazed at how something so simple can be so good.

There are basically two types of *pizze*: round pizza which is baked to order, and *pizza al taglio* baked in large rectangular trays and sold in slices. Don't be afraid to ask for them *caldo* (hot) as they are always reheated in grills or ovens and never in that insult to reheated *pizze*, the microwave.

ALAN BENSON / GETTY IMAGES

Shop display of olive oil pourers.

Multiple flavours of *gelati*, served in a cone and topped with sauce.

Panforte.

Pistachio cannoli.

The most delectable toppings are most often the simple ones. Perhaps *pomodoro*, just tomato, with a few basil leaves, or *patate con rosamarino*, finely shaved potato with a scattering of rosemary. Many toppings don't include cheese, and modern interpretations tend to be creative without compromising the taste. *Radicchio* (chicory) with Gorgonzola is a fine example.

Ice cream, granita and sorbet

Sicilians like to take the credit for having invented ice cream (*gelato*; plural *gelati*), which might surprise the Arabs who brought the technology to Sicily. One thing's for sure, no other nation today can boast such consistently good frozen desserts.

- *Gelati* is the most accessible, lickably soft form of ice cream and has to be tasted in Italy to be fully understood.
- *Artigianale gelati* (artisan or home-made gelato) is available at most towns of any size and the best is flavoured with real fruit or real espresso coffee.
- Other frozen sweets include *granite* (singular, *granita*), *sorbetti* (sorbets) and sometimes *semifreddi* (semi-frozen). *Granite* are slushy ices that take their name from their granular texture.
- *Sorbetti* are made from fruit and sugar, usually without egg (or just with egg white) and without dairy products.

DRINKS

Coffee and wine dominate the Italian drinks map, and not surprisingly, too, since the quality of both is impeccable, whether it be served in the local *osteria* (simple eating-house) or a fancy *ristoranti* (restaurant).

Coffee and tea

Okay, get this: coffee in Italy isn't like anywhere else in the world. It's better. So don't come thinking of *caffè (*coffee) as the stuff that comes in a bottomless cup in North America. And it isn't at all like the French *café*, despite its being made in similar machines.

The first thing to get your head around is the temperature. Coffee is served at the perfect temperature for flavour, *tiepido* (tepid). This means that the *crema*, the caramel-coloured foam on top of an espresso, preserves the aroma without being bitter.

Italians adore their *caffè*. They duck into bars for a quick fix and invariably sugar their coffee. In some areas the barista may do this for you if you don't ask them not to.

Coffee decoder

- *Caffè* — while the word means 'coffee', if used alone, it always implies the classic small espresso, which always has a dense, light brown *crema* (foam) on top.
- *Caffè corretto* — a *caffè* with a drop of strong alcohol added to 'correct' it.
- *Caffè decaffeinato* — decaffeinated coffee, available virtually everywhere in all coffee styles.
- *Caffè freddo* — a shot of coffee in cold milk.
- *Caffè latte* — similar to a French *café au lait* but not as milky or as large. It's occasionally served in a glass, and is a milkier version of the *cappuccino*, with less foam.
- *Caffè lungo* (*doppio*, *americano*) — a long coffee. While the name means 'double' it is usually the same amount of coffee grinds with extra water poured through.
- *Caffè macchiato* — an espresso 'stained' with just a dot of milk.

ALAN BENSON / GETTY IMAGES

Italian espresso being created.

- *Cappuccino* — the favoured breakfast of most Italians. A shot of espresso is topped with thick, richly foamed milk called *schiuma* (and it is sometimes dusted with cocoa).
- *Latte macchiato* — warmed milk 'stained' with a shot of coffee and usually served in a long glass.
- *Macchiatone* — a bigger version of a *caffè macchiato*, but without as much milk or foam as a *cappuccino*.
- *Ristretto (caffè ristretto)* — a 'restricted' coffee. This is the real essence of the coffee bean as it is just the first dribble of coffee that comes from the machine when making an espresso, with a very concentrated (but not bitter) flavour.

By comparison with *caffè*, *tè* (tea) in Italy is a disappointment. In bars the water comes from the espresso machine and is not freshly boiled. The tea you buy in Italy is also a bit limp in taste (even the British brands seem different), and doesn't quite do the drink justice. You can find *tè freddo* (iced tea) in bars and this is often as good as you'll find in other countries.

Digestives

To sum up the majority of Italian *digestivi* (digestives) in one word, you only need to say *grappa*. *Grappa* is the single most popular *digestivo* in the country, favoured from the alps to the isles. In its roughest form it is made from the distilled *vinacce* (crushed grape skins and stalks) from any type of grape, is extremely high in alcohol and tastes like it's made from barbed wire. At its best, *grappa* is made from the *vinacce* of high quality grapes of one variety, has a distinctive taste and is as smooth as velvet. It's always clear, and is the favourite after-dinner drink of most Italian men.

Liqueurs

There are many *liquori* (liqueurs) in Italy, often flavoured with berries or fruit. The most common are:

- *Amaretto* — an almost syrupy almond liqueur with a hint of bitterness underneath the sweetness.
- *Limoncello* — a duckling-coloured lemon drink that comes from the Amalfi coast and is now becoming more popular.
- *Sambuca* — aniseed flavoured and popular with younger drinkers.

Wine

Italy produces about a fifth of the world's wine, but it has never made the big time internationally until recently, mostly because it didn't want to. Wine, like the rest of Italy's *cucina* is not accorded any noble status. It was and remains an intrinsic, albeit enjoyable, part of life. Some critics say that Italians spend far too much time drinking the stuff, and not enough making it. Times are changing though, and wine production in Italy is certainly contracting in quantity, while increasing in quality.

Grape varieties

Estimates vary about the number of grape varieties in Italy, but the short and always correct answer to the question is 'heaps'. Italy boasts at least 1000 varieties (some suggest as many as 2000), of which about 400 are known to be in production. Many are clones of common types such as Sangiovese, while others are distinct varieties.

One thing is for sure, the grapes of a region are usually distinct to that region even if the same variety of grape exists elsewhere. This means that the wines of, say, a town such as

Glasses of chilled *Asti Spumante*.

A bottle of peach *grappa*.

ALAN BENSON / GETTY IMAGES

Oranges and lemons.

Pretty hillside vineyards near Bressanone.

ALAN BENSON / GETTY IMAGES

Barbaresco are distinctly and consistently different from those of nearby Barolo, even though both use the same grape variety, Nebbiolo (from the word *nebbia*, meaning 'fog'). Each has its aficionados.

The major players in Italian wine production today are Trebbiano and Sangiovese and their related varieties. The Trebbianos occupy over 100,000 hectares of vineyards, and are the most widely planted type in Italy. Most of the grapes end up in reasonably light but spirited white wines or in blends. Sangiovese is the most prolifically planted variety in the region of Toscana through to the central south. Like Trebbiano, it's a collection of various grapes under the one banner, but in this case it is a red grape.

Other important grape varieties include:

- the powerful red Nebbiolo, that is harder to tame to make great wine than the Pinot Nero (Pinot noir) grape.
- Barbera, the more commonly used red grape variety of the north, found particularly around Asti and Alba in Piedmont.
- the Moscato grape, used from Piedmont to Sicily, with differing results and in differing wines. The best known Moscato wine is Moscato d'Asti, one ordinary version of which used to be known as 'Spumante'.
- Sicily's great dessert wine, Moscato di Pantelleria, from the island of the same name.

Wine styles

Italy has all the major wine styles found elsewhere, plus a few more besides. There's *frizzante*, the fizzy wines. Often these can be referred to as *spumante*, the word *spuma* referring to the froth that arises as they are poured. The most famous is the Moscato d'Asti and the Veneto's Prosecco. Prosecco

Brut is a *spumante*, but it's as dry as any sparkling wine.

Red wines, the most common wines in Italy, are known as *vini rossi*, white wines as *vino bianchi* and rosé-style wines are called *vini rosati*. Along with these are *vino da contemplazione /meditazione* (wines of contemplation/meditation). One from an Eolian island off the coast of Sicilia is Passito di Pantelleria made from partially dried grapes. The result is a surprisingly lush yet not overly sweet wine with a length and character that is not really suited to dessert, or to the meal proper. It's more suited to sitting around and being enjoyed while you meditate on life and all its pleasures.

INSALATA CAPRESE

This dish uses simple produce. You need a sharp knife and plates. If you don't have plates, just put all the ingredients on really good white bread rolls.

Serves 2

Ingredients

2 large, fully ripe, vermilion-coloured tomatoes
100 g (3 ½ oz) buffalo mozarella
5–6 leaves fresh basil
fine sea salt and freshly milled black pepper
extra virgin olive oil, to serve

Method

Core the tomatoes and cut into thin wedges. Slice the mozzarella as thinly as you can. Layer the tomato and cheese slices, alternately, so they slightly overlap on the plate.

Tear the basil leaves and scatter over the top. Sprinkle with salt and pepper, and drizzle generously with the olive oil.

Serve with crusty white bread, then eat with gusto.

ALAN BENSON / GETTY IMAGES

Etruscan cellar in Montepulciano.

Perched on a hill overlooking Granada is Alhambra, a fortress and castle.

OLIVER STREWE / GETTY IMAGES

Spain

Popular images of Spain include Gypsies and *paella*, bullfights and sherry, Gaudí and *sangría*. Food goes hand in hand with history, architecture and the everyday. Spainish cuisine is a proud and adaptive melange that will surprise and intrigue; exhaust and delight — it will fill you up, make you cry for mercy, and then beg for more. *Buen provecho*.

CULINARY CAPITALS BARCELONA, MADRID **KNOWN FOR** *PAELLA* **IMPORTS** NUTS **EXPORTS** FRUIT AND VEGETABLES, OLIVE OIL, WINE **DEVOUR** *TAPAS* **AVOID** SHEEP'S TAIL

Fresh bread is delivered early on the streets of San Sebastian.

OLIVER STREWE / GETTY IMAGES

CULTURE

In Spain, a cuisine is served that vividly reflects and celebrates its culture and colourful history. Dining Spanish style means dining with the memories and influences of Romans, Moors, Aztecs, Basque fishermen, La Manchan peasants, Spanish grandees and French tourists. You'll encounter a confusion of styles, sensuality balanced by simplicity, culinary routine punctuated by indulgence, and an unerringly constant kitchen philosophy.

Simplicity and generosity

Spanish cooking is straightforward and there is never any mistaking what you are eating. 'It should taste of what it is,' goes the mantra. To disguise a food or to hide its true nature is sacrilege. Herbs and spices are used sparingly. The cook will seldom alter, mash, puree or mould a food beyond recognition, for it must also look of what it is. To these ends simplicity is prized.

And simplicity can be a very difficult thing to achieve. It takes close attention and kitchen alchemy to draw out a delicate flavour by means of fire and oil and little else. It is an easy thing, on the other hand, to destroy it. A dish of Spain is generous. You will never have to lift up a sprig of parsley to find your portion of meat. And Spanish cookery is unpretentious. Your food will not be tarted up and made to look cute, or grand, or rare and costly, or more colourful. There is no over-reliance on sauces. There is no confusion of tastes.

The Holy Trinity

Take a seat at any table in Spain and, almost without exception, you will face the Holy Trinity of Spanish cuisine: bread, oil and wine. This triumvirate is the cornerstone of Spain's culinary history. To this Holy Trinity add garlic, religion and conviviality.

Spanish fare has been described by better writers to be 'thick with garlic and religion'. And indeed garlic is infused in almost everything. There is garlic soup, bread rubbed with raw garlic and garlic sauces such as *alioli* (garlic mayonnaise). So many recipes have been brought into being by religious observance or proscription: *tarta de Santiago* (Saint James' cake) and *huessos santos* (saint's bones), just to name two.

And as for conviviality the very purpose of Spanish dining is to nourish the soul as well as the body. Dining is the time to strengthen ties between family, community and religion.

Almonds are used in *pilafs*.

The taste of crossroads

Spain has the Romans to thank for the basis of their cuisine, but other cultures, armies and importers have also imposed their own tastes. After the Romans came the Moors from North Africa. To the fields they brought the almond groves, oranges and other fruits. Sugar cane was an important Moorish import, and the reduction and distillation of sugar syrups brought about the development of perfumes, liqueurs, and medicinal tinctures. Moorish commerce provided artichokes, rice, eggplants, spinach, the reintroduction of saffron and sophisticated agricultural techniques. To the kitchen they brought the characteristic combination of various finely chopped ingredients that eventually led to such dishes as *paella*. They introduced spiced casseroles, stews, nut sauces and fruit syrups.

Freshly picked green and black olives.

The Spanish, having gradually adopted Moorish cuisine, soon encountered another rich tradition, the highly developed imperial cookery of the Aztecs. Moctezuma's kitchens had developed complex nut sauces, and they made skilful use of ingredients such as chilli, chocolate and tomato. Spanish cooks readily adopted these foods into their own culinary canon, and a wonderful early fusion cuisine arose. An inspired cook could take the best of it all, creating exciting new flavours. Take a

Cherries in a basket, Caceres.

simple example, the taste of a cup of Spanish chocolate: chocolate from the Aztecs, cinnamon from the Moors. It's the taste of crossroads.

REGIONS

The Heart of Spain

The Heart of Spain runs from north to south. From Aragón at the foot of the Pyrenees, it cuts a wide swath through the middle of the Iberian peninsula all the way down to Gibraltar. This is the Spain of Ferdinand and Isabella, and of looming castles and medieval lanes. It is the Spain of Cervantes, and of the Conquistadors; of Gypsies and Flamenco; hot afternoons and siestas; saffron and *sangría*. This is the Spain that resides in the popular imagination.

Many people call this axis of Iberia the 'Route of Roasts'. For it is roast lamb, kid and suckling pig that define this region's culinary heart. In cities such as Segovia you cannot but be aware of the roasting. The rich aroma snakes its way through the winding cobblestone streets and hangs there, an olfactory siren, beckoning locals and tourists alike to follow the aroma and find delight. The roasting is done in large wood-fire ovens called *hornos asadores*.

Meats roasted in the *asador* must be true babies. Suckling pig, lamb or kid, no more than 25 days old, are placed on a rack in a *cazuela* (earthenware cooking dish) with a little water in the bottom. The rising steam helps to tenderise the meat. The *cazuelas* must be moved around constantly in the big oven by means of long paddles, like those used in a pizza oven. The end product has skin the colour of burnished bronze and is often served still hissing from the oven. Table knives are superfluous so easily does it fall apart; you could eat it with a toothpick.

OLIVER STREWE / GETTY IMAGES

Aerial view of olive groves over the hills.

FEASTS

In addition to the feasts of the calendar, there are many other reasons and excuses for Spaniards to have a party. Birthdays, anniversaries, first communions, graduations and weddings are all celebrated with great enthusiasm. Nowadays, even a divorce is ample reason to pour the wine, say grace and tuck in.

Spaniards are also keen on marking days with saints, and nestled among the staple sweets at any *pastelería* (cake shop) are the tell-tale pastries of the saint or religious *figure du jour*:

You know it's All Saints' Day when the sweet, *huessos santos* (saint's bones) appear.

While the first Christians got wine with their bread, modern Holy Week revellers dunk their body of Christ in milk and egg to make the Easter treat, *torrijas* (French toast).

On 6 January, children celebrate the arrival of the gift-bearing three kings, and everyone munches on *roscón de Reyes*, a spongy, family-size doughnut adorned with dried fruit and sugar.

Of all the holiday seasons, Christmas is the gastronomic timepiece *par excellence*. With the first whiff of roasted chestnuts and sweet potatoes from streetside stands, you know Mary had better start scouting for a manger. Things start getting serious when supermarkets clear entire aisles to fill them with *turrón*, the quintessential Yuletide sweet.

New Year's Eve

It's *Nochevieja* (New Year's Eve) just before midnight, you are a guest in a home or restaurant, or perhaps you are on the Puerta del Sol in Madrid. Your host, or a smiling man or woman you've never seen before passes by laden with fresh grapes. You are given 12. When the clock tolls midnight, you are to eat one grape with each sound of the bell. Get it right and swallow the last grape with the last bell and you'll have good luck in the coming year. Mess up and it's sour grapes for you.

ETIQUETTE

Spanish table manners and settings are studies in simplicity. Unless you are in a very smart restaurant, you will keep the same knife and fork throughout the meal. You might also have a spoon and that will be that: no need for highly specialised surgical instruments. You will have one wine glass and one water glass, unless you also order *cava* (sparkling wine). Then you might be given a flute or a tulip for the bubbly. Your water glass will be larger than your wine glass. The message of this should be clear. The only bit of arcana to remember at the Spanish table is that you should always keep your hands in view, never let them be hidden in the folds of napery or under the table. The reason for this is unclear: it could go back to days of blood feuds and hidden daggers.

THE MENU

The Spanish menus is one of the more user-friendly. There are two genres of menu: the sitting and the standing. The standing menu is always posted on the wall of the *tasca* (tapas bar). It may be a simple printed poster, it might be a chalkboard with entries in colourful florid script. In Madrid it's common to mount a crafted wooden board, polished and fixed with slots into which smaller boards can be inserted or removed as selections change.

In the Basque country the whole thing is greatly simplified. A small notice on the wall announces that *tapas,* or *pintxos* as they are known here, are priced at so much and *raciones* (full portions) are priced at something more, usually double. The *pintxos* are all laid out upon the bar in a beautiful display of culinary abundance and all you need to do is begin eating. When you are satisfied, tell the barman how many you ate and you'll be charged accordingly. It's the honour system in much

Bunch of purple grapes.

Wild strawberries for sale.

Old woman among the vines in the countryside of Galicia.

The Four Cats cafe-restaurant, a one-time favourite hang-out of artist Pablo Picasso.

OLIVER STREWE / GETTY IMAGES

of the Basque country. All you have to do is eat, drink and pay. Then, even in the humblest little, darkest little, most out of the way little *tasca*, the Spanish niceties will be observed: your change will be presented in a little dish; never given from hand to hand or hand to bar.

Printed menus that are brought to your table are of two sorts: the *menú del día* (the day's set menu) and the *menú la carta* (a la carte menu). By law all restaurants in Spain (as opposed to *tascas*) are required to offer a luncheon known as the *menú del día*. It must consist of three courses plus bread, and water or wine. The third course is always dessert. The price of the *menú del día* is always less than if you were to order the same items a la carte. It's one of the best deals in Spain.

The *menú la carta* is also available at lunch, and it is the only one for your evening meal. It is simplicity itself, divided into food types: meat, fish, fowl, dessert and so on. In the smarter restaurants it may lead with a selection of *entreméses* (starters) but you are free to have anything you wish and in any order. Only one note of caution on the *menu la carta*: don't try to get anything not specifically listed, or cooked in some slightly different way. Spanish cooks don't like to improvise and waiters don't like to confront them.

DAILY MEALS

The Spanish begin their day simply enough. Coffee and a bit of bread or biscuit with butter or jam is enough for breakfast. And perhaps a glass of sherry or a gin and tonic. The morning tipple is an institution in Spain. Stay in Spain long enough and you will adjust your sleeping schedule to 5 hours (2 to 7 am); then 3 hours (4 to 7 pm). At 8 am on such a schedule you will find a noggin of gin or a glass of *fino* (dry sherry) just the thing.

The midday meal is the big one. It will not start until about 2 pm and might not start until later. Everyone in Spain, except waiters and cooks, sets aside their tasks and turns to the table. For the next couple of hours their world will revolve around the table and each other.

Around 9 pm the world wakes again. As you sit at your table with your *aperitivo* (aperitif), perfect strangers will pass you on the way to their table, look at you squarely and say *'Buen provecho!'* (enjoy your meal). The clatter of crystal and china offer counterpoint to the music outside. The wine is heady. The dinner may be light, the midday meal having been so substantial, but the convivium is as thick as the garlic in the *alioli*.

ESSENTIAL PRODUCE

Bread

The first branch of the Holy Trinity of Spanish cuisine is *pan* (bread). It is a symbol of continuity, prosperity, and security. Bread is the basis of any meal. It might be as simple as bread dipped in milk or drizzled with olive oil for breakfast, or part of a soup, such as in *salmorejo* (thick cold tomato soup). The Andalucían farmer's breakfast, *migas canas*, is emblematic of the most basic, minimalist cookery using bread. The hungry *campesino* soaks a dry loaf in salted water. He peels a few cloves of garlic and fries them in oil. When this is brown he adds the bread and stirs, cooking and browning until it resolves itself into toasty crumbs. To this he adds hot milk, and cooks it to a rich and savoury porridge.

Fish

With the possible exception of the Japanese there are no people more mad for seafood than the Spanish. They will eat any creature that emerges from the depths. When it comes to fish, their favourites are *bonito* (tuna), *bacalao* (cod), *sardinas* (sardines) and *anchoas* (anchovies). All fresh.

OLIVER STREWE / GETTY IMAGES

Bread for sale on a street in Barcelona.

Nothing holds a place in the Spanish heart, soul and belly like dry salted *bacalao* (cod). Even those who rarely eat it, revere it, and this has been so for centuries. So much of Spanish history is bound up in it, and fuelled by it. *Bacalao* is at the forefront of Spanish culinary consciousness.

This is remarkable when you consider that *bacalao* has never been seen, let alone caught, off the coasts of Spain. It lives in the cold waters of the northern Atlantic, off Newfoundland, Iceland, the British Isles and Scandinavia. But for centuries it has been a mainstay of the Spanish diet. At some point, Basque fishermen began to take *bacalao*, pack them in salt, and live off them while they were at sea. Eventually they discovered great shoals of them and began bringing home the salted catch.

Bacalao is delicious too, although you would not know that to look at it in its preserved state. Encrusted with salt crystals, with a whitish-grey appearance, it looks more like a geological object than foodstuff. But when soaked overnight it comes magically back to life. And during its time in suspended animation it undergoes the most remarkable changes, becoming somehow both firmer and more tender than it was when it went into its salty sleep. It barely tastes of salt, tasting richly but not pungently of the sea. The flesh separates easily but does not disintegrate into a mash between the teeth.

You can enjoy *bacalao* in any city in Spain, but perhaps the best place is in the Basque country where it still holds its sway just as strongly as ever. Even Basque atheists, all half dozen or so, love it. And everyone will pay the price necessary, regardless how high.

One of the best introductions to *bacalao* is in *esqueixada*, a salad of raw desalted *bacalao* with crushed tomatoes, olives and onions. The acid in the tomatoes takes the raw edge off the *bacalao*, revealing its flavour. *Bacalao pil-pil* is an ancient preparation with garlic, and *bacalao a la vizcaína* combines cod

The prized black *ibérico* pigs on the run in Andalucia.

Branding of the *jamon*.

Ibores, a locally-produced cheese.

with chillies and capsicums. Taste *bacalao*, and taste the soul and history of Spain.

Ham

Ham is the great culinary constant. This is what unites the Spanish. Strapped into a cradle-like frame called a *jamónera*, every bar, restaurant and *tasca* (tapas bar) in the kingdom of Spain has at least one ham for carving at any given time. More often the establishment has several hams, the skins and hooves still attached, hanging from the walls or ceilings. Stuck into the bottom of each ham is a little plastic cup resembling an upside-down umbrella to catch the slow drippings. Most average Spanish homes have a *jamónera i*n the kitchen.

Salted and semi-dried by the cold dry winds of the Spanish sierra, Spanish ham is like no other in the world. It's closest relative is the Italian *prosciutto*. But a Spanish ham is a bold, deep red, sometimes even the colour of wine. It's well marbled with buttery fat streaking through the lean like a rainbow. It smells like meat, and forest and field, and of the mushrooms and acorns and herbs that the beast has fed upon. Perhaps the most remarkable feature is its texture. It is neither tough nor tender. It is rarely fibrous, and seems to dissolve upon the tongue like rich fat chocolate.

Spanish hams are of two principal types: *ibérico* and *serrano*. *Ibérico* is from a pig indigenous to the Iberian peninsula and believed to be a descendant of *sus mediterraneus*, a wild boar. It is delicious and can be ruinously expensive. Indeed, in villages where small family operations produce *jamón ibérico de bellota* the hams can actually be the target of burglars who eschew the family jewels and heist the hams instead! Variations of *ibérico* include:

- *Jamón ibérico* — a general term for any ham from black-coated ibérico pigs.

- *Jamón real ibérico ham* — from *ibérico* pigs whose feeding in the wild is supplemented with fodder.
- *Jamón ibérico de bellota* — the king of hams, from *ibérico* pigs that have fed on acorns in the wild during the season before slaughter.
- *Pata negra* literally, black hoof — another term for *ibérico*. Spanish hams are normally shipped and hung with the hoof attached. A black hoof is an indication, though not a guarantee, that it's *ibérico* ham.

Serrano means 'of the sierra' or the mountains. It used to designate any cured ham from Spain. Nowadays it refers to hams made from white-coated pigs that were introduced into Spain from northern Europe in the 1950s. *Jamón serrano* is the term used to describe it.

Olive oil

Spain grows 262 varieties of olive, 90% of the production of which is sent to the presses for *aceite de oliva* (olive oil). At an annual production of over 600,000 metric tonnes Spain is the world's largest producer and consumer, of olive oil. Indeed it is anointed, saturated, awash and delightfully drowning in the most flavourful golden fluid under the Mediterranean sun. Olive oil isn't just salad dressing. In Spain this is the cooking medium par excellence. The Spanish use it to make desserts; to cook *patatas fritas* (fried potatoes); and to keep their skin smooth.

As with the finest French wines, the finest Spanish olive oils are most often blends. Under Spanish law a virgin oil has to meet 40 different criteria for quality and purity, and to be classified as extra virgin, its acidity level can be no higher than 1%. And under the laws of consumer demand, the product must be consistent over the years. The oil must have

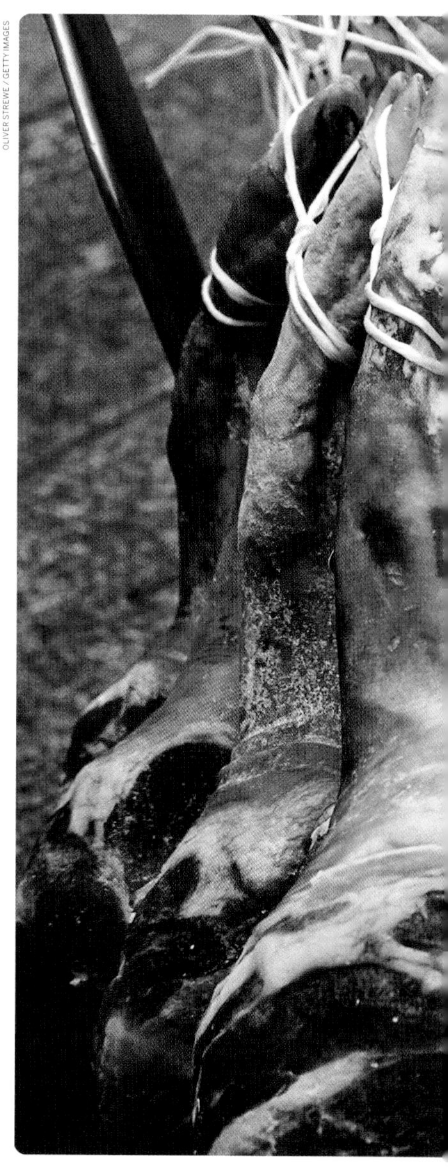
OLIVER STREWE / GETTY IMAGES

A delivery of ham in Santiago de Compostela.

a predictable taste, smell and texture, and a predictable flash point. The blending room of a larger producer will have as many as a dozen tasters working at one time to mix, taste and smell and match to create the signature oil.

Rice

Long before *paella* was put in a pan the people of the Iberian peninsula were using *arroz* (rice) to prepare dishes of ethereal quality and gustatory delight, including:

- *pilavs* with almonds, raisins or dates
- rice stews of slurp-it-up goodness such as *arroz marinera* (rice with seafood)
- baked casseroles of rice and legumes made fragrant with garlic, enriched with potatoes and blessed with the tang of ripe tomatoes
- rice and black beans combined to make the holiday dish, *Moros y Cristianos* (Moors and Christians), as well as rice for holidays, rice for work days and rice for dessert.

So how many rice recipes are there? In Valencia they tell a tale from the War of Independence — the struggle against Napoleon. A certain French general had taken many Spanish prisoners, and one Spanish cook. Smitten by her first few offerings of rice the general told her that he would free one of her countrymen for each new dish she prepared. A total of 176 Spaniards, so they say, had been freed by the time the general was relieved of his command.

Sauces

There are four basic principles in Spanish sauce making, all simple. Firstly, Spanish sauces are based on olive oil. Secondly, Spanish sauces are not thickened with flour, but with ground

OLIVER STREWE / GETTY IMAGES

Bowl of freshly-picked green olives.

nuts or bread crumbs. Thirdly, sauces begin in the mortar and pestle. Lastly, for the most part, sauce is not a discrete ingredient, but the liquid in which food is cooked.

The most important Spanish sauces include:

- *Adobos* (marinades) — marinades are the spiciest of Spanish sauces. They employ strong vinegar, garlic and oregano, bay leaves and sometimes chillies.
- *Ajo* (garlic) — these sauces came to Spain with the Romans. Soldiers, peasants, fishermen and farmers combined olive oil with chopped garlic and parsley, maybe a squeeze of lemon juice or dash of vinegar. In this guise it's called *aliño*. A more sophisticated version using raw eggs is *alioli*, which is often stirred into soups, or added to rice dishes.
- *Mayonesa* (mayonnaise) — if you see anything on the menu '*con dos salsas*', it means two ice-cream scoops of mayonnaise, one of which is coloured with paprika.

Sausages

Of the raw or cured sausages, the most common is called *chorizo*. While sausages have been made here since Roman times, the *chorizo* is the newest member of the family, dating back to only the 17th century. It has a number of well defined characteristics.

- *Pimenton* (paprika),the dried powder of the ground sweet red capsicum, along with salt, garlic and black pepper, are used to season a ground mixture of pork and pork fat.
- It is then stuffed into large or small intestine, and smoked or air cured.

- It has a bright red colour, a chewy texture, and an assertive, spicy taste reminiscent of salami.
- It will probably be the most common sausage you see in Spain.

Among the cooked sausages *morcilla* is like a Spanish black pudding, a blood sausage. This sausage is the first to be made, immediately after slaughter, as the blood is the most perishable ingredient. It is simmered in cauldrons, usually at the slaughter site, until it turns black and coagulates.

- Also in the *morcilla* recipe are pork fat, salt, and often but not always, a few spices, onion or chopped nuts.
- A very common addition to the *morcilla* is cooked rice.
- There are even morcillas that are made sweet, and are taken as either appetiser or dessert.

Sweet or savoury, its flavour is deep but not assertive. And with its pudding like texture, is so tender it melts in the mouth and hardly needs chewing.

PREPARATION

The kitchen

The kitchen is generally an unfussy affair, containing some or all of the following:

- A gas cooker with two burners, a few *ollas* (pots) for making stews or boiling water.
- Half a dozen *cazuelas* (earthenware cooking dishes) of various sizes for the casseroles that define so much of gastronomic Spain.
- The *olla* (pot) is used for what is arguably the oldest dish in the Spanish culinary canon: *olla podrida*, the rotten pot.

OLIVER STREWE / GETTY IMAGES

Sausages are among the goods for sale at this market stall in Santiago de Compostela.

Pistachios for sale by the scoopful.

Produce from J. Murria Fine Foods in Barcelona.

Tomatoes are key to many Spanish dishes.

- A porrón (a wine bottle with a long drinking spout).
- A primitive *parrillada* (grill), usually found over a fire ring outside the kitchen.
- Unique to the Spanish kitchen, and without which none would be complete are *paelleras* (*paella* pans). A true *paellera* is wide, round and shallow with no lid. Iron is the preferred material. It has two handles and may dip slightly in the middle where the oil can pool for easy frying. The shallow depth of the pan helps ensure that the rice cooks in a thin layer. People say that the cooked rice should be only as thick as *un ditet* (the width of one finger, to a height of 1½ centimetres in the pan). The trick is to maximise the amount of rice touching the bottom of the pan because that's where the flavour resides. For that reason, *paella* pans enlarge in diameter not in height.

DEFINING DISHES

Empanada

Empanada, essentially bread with a filling, constitutes the culinary 'great leap forward' from bread taken with something, to bread cooked with something. At its simplest an *empanada* is a layer of bread dough, something spread atop it, and another layer of dough laid down on that. Baked golden, you will see this ancient dish in the *tascas* and *sidrerías* (bars) of Spain. They are most commonly filled with preparations of tuna. In Extremadura the mixture is simple, in Catalunya it is spiced and enriched with tomato. In Andalucía it may contain chopped olives.

Gazpacho

Gazpacho is emblematic of Spanish cookery. It is a dish that says 'I am Spain'. *Gazpacho* is a whole family of soups, and not easy to define with exactitude. But there are three common threads that together make *gazpacho* the quintessence of gastronomic Spain. The first is that it contains the Holy Trinity of Spanish cuisine, bread, oil and garlic. The next is the presence of new world crops such as tomatoes and capsicums without which Spain would be a very different place. And the last thread is that persistent Moorish ghost that flickers and shimmers in the undercurrents of Arabian spices, nuts, and in smooth soft textures. All in all, this is liquid Spain.

Paella

Put two Spanish cooks together and you are likely get two different *paellas*. All will agree that a *paella* contains short-grain rice, garlic, parsley, olive oil and saffron. The popular image of *paella* is a pan of saffron-coloured rice bursting with shellfish, known as *paella de marisco*.

Most visitors to Spain have never had *paella*, or nothing worth the name. *Paella* should have the delicate yet pervasive aroma of saffron. It should not be 'bursting' with shellfish, or anything else. The rice is the chief player in this little gastro-drama and nothing should upstage it. One piece of meat per diner is about right. The grains of rice should be dry, plump and tender.

There are many varieties of rice, but ideally the *paella* should be made with *bomba* rice. Its distinctive starch structure causes it to open out accordion-fashion when cooked, allowing for maximum absorption while remaining firm.

The cooking dish should be shallow, allowing for optimum cooking of the short-grain rice and for maximum contact with the bottom of the pan, where most of the flavour lives. And for the final touch of authenticity, the cook should turn up the heat in the final minutes of cooking so as to brown the bottom into a crunchy, savoury crust called the *socarrat*.

OLIVER STREWE / GETTY IMAGES

Pulpo gallego from Galicia

Tapas

Tapas, the true *tapas* of Spain, are inextricably knit to the culture and soil of Spain. *Tapas* are not a collection of recipes, or the shape or size of a morsel. They are an expression of a people and their unique way of living.

The word *tapa* means lid, or top. The verb form, *tapar*, means to top or to cover. You might encounter a dish with a name like *carne tapada con queso* (meat topped with cheese). While there is some argument as to the origin of the *tapa*, most people agree that it harks back to the 18th century. Tavern keepers would place a slice of ham or cheese or bread on the mouth of a glass of sherry or other wine to keep out the dust and flies. The salt or dryness of the 'top' created thirst and thirst created profits, so a grand custom was born.

What constitutes a *tapa*? Aside from the circumstances of its consumption, anything can be a *tapa*, as long as it is small, easy to eat, and thirst-provoking or alcohol absorbing. For example a scoop of *paella* on a saucer can be a *tapa*; a hunk of bread drizzled with olive oil, a few slices of *chorizo*, a hard boiled egg, a piece of cheese, all can be *tapas*.

But commonly you will find:

- *pulpo gallego* — spicy boiled octopus
- *garbanzos con espinacas* — chickpeas with spinach
- *anchoas fritas a la catalana* — deep-fried anchovies
- *gambas al ajillo* — garlic shrimps
- *tortilla española* — a potato omelette
- and *boquerones,* fresh anchovies marinated in wine vinegar, are everywhere.
- In Madrid try *callos* (tripe), in Andalucía go for *caracoles* (snails) and in the Basque Country everything conceivable is made with *bacalao* (cod).

Basque country *tapas* served up in San Sebastian.

Mussels feature on a seafood platter.

Two bottles of Spain's finest Rioja.

Tapas are eaten at a *tasca* (tapas bar). You'll find *tascas* in every city in Spain, though they are less common in the northern Mediterranean region. Walk into a *tasca* and you will likely be astounded by the variety set before you: Shellfish on sticks, cheese and ham, slices of bread topped with whatever is to hand, individual little earthenware casseroles filled with hot dishes of clams or cod or vegetables, and lovely mayonnaise-laden morsels.

DRINKS

Chocolate

Along with coffee the most common hot beverage in Spain is *chocolate caliente* (hot chocolate). This is not the hot cocoa you are used to from childhood. This stuff is thick, like porridge. It's barely pourable from the urn in which it is kept hot throughout the morning in the *tasca* or *chocolatería*. Popular as it is in the morning, most Spaniards stop drinking it by midday. It is traditionally taken with *churros*, fried doughnut strips.

Wine

One chamber of the Spanish heart is reserved for olive oil and the other for wine. Wine is present at every meal. Spain has more acreage under vines than any nation on earth, although due to methods in use, it does not have the greatest wine production.

You'll find the wine in Spain to be 'user friendly'. It's easy to understand both on the label and in the bottle. Like their solid food, the Spaniards' liquid nourishment is straightforward and unpretentious. They do not like fussy wine any more than fussy food. They like it to taste good, smell good, and feel good going down. They do not require it to have infinite complexity over which one may linger and chat about for an hour. This is largely because they do not take wine by itself. It's part of a meal. So eat, drink and enjoy.

Almost all geographic areas of Spain grow grapes. A great deal of them, especially from central Spain, are grown for blending. Wine is pumped into railroad tank cars and shipped off to France where dealers mix it with their own common stuff and sell it as cheap *vin ordinaire*.

Rioja

Rioja is the name given to wines grown in the area lying between the Cantabrian mountain range in the north and the Demanda range in the south. It lies along the valley of the Ebro river and takes its name from one of its tributaries, the Rio Oja. Its boundaries reflect only geographical, not political considerations, as it straddles the areas of La Rioja, Navarra, Castilla y León and the Basque Country.

France has had a lot of influence in the wines of Rioja, although you should not say so to a Spaniard. However, it is undeniable that when the phylloxera blight struck France, many Bordeaux wine makers came to Rioja for a generation or two, and taught the locals a few tricks. Many believe that the Tempranillo grape came originally from France. But advancing this point of view is the surest way to open unpleasantries anywhere in Spain, and to start a fist fight in Rioja.

When hunting down wine in Rioja, it pays to be familiar with a few terms:

- *Sin crianza* refers to young wines, less than a year old.
- *Crianza* refers to red wine at least two years old, having spent at least one year in the barrel, and months in bottle. White or rosé crianza need only age for one year.
- *Reserva* is the name given to selected red wines that have the right characteristics for long aging. They require at least one year in the barrel, and must be at least three years old before sale. Wines of truly exceptional vintage are known as *gran reserva*.

OLIVER STREWE / GETTY IMAGES

Toulouse-style shopfront in Barcelona.

White grapes.

Sherry barrels.

Grape vines in Navarra.

- *Castillo* is the equivalent of chateau-bottled wine, wherein all the grapes used are grown on the estate.

Sangría

The wines of Spain were not always of the high quality we have come to expect these days. When they were good, of course, they were very very good. But when they were bad — *diablos!* But instead of wasting it, the Spanish would take the bad wine and put something into it to mitigate the taste. Sometimes it was just water, sometimes it was other wine, often it was spices or fruit juice. Over time a few recipes came into being that pleased most and offended none. To this day, *sangría* is an idea, not a chemical formula. Some people might use apple juice, or pineapple juice. Others might use nutmeg, or cloves. But a fairly standard recipe calls for citrus and cinnamon. How much of this or that to add to the wine depends on the wine: how good, how bad, how sweet, how dry. The final product should be refreshing and quaffable.

Sherry

There are three main styles of the famed Spanish sherry. *Fino* is pale, straw, or golden coloured with a sharp aroma of almonds. It is very dry and refreshing, and probably the most common tapa tipple in southern Spain. Spaniards also enjoy it taken as a table wine, and serve it with seafood and soups. *Manzanilla* is almost the same as *Fino*, but with additional characteristics imparted by the area in which it is produced, the seaside town of Sanlúcar de Barrameda. It has an almost salty finish. Said to be an embodiment of the local sea breezes, *Amontillado* is amber in colour with a deep nutty aroma reminiscent of hazelnuts and raisins. It goes well with strong cheeses and oily fish.

Pasteis de Belem, a type of custard tart, in the window of the famous Antiga Confeitaria de Belem in Lisbon.

IAN AITKEN / GETTY IMAGES

Portugal

Present-day Portugal is a cosmopolitan banquet containing the foods and moods of her near neighbours and far colonial ports — from chargrilled sardines to *bacalhau* and beer, this small country of roughly ten million makes a big mark on the culinary globe.

CULINARY CAPITALS LISBON, PORTO **KNOWN FOR** SARDINES AND SWEET THINGS **IMPORTS** FISH AND SEAFOOD **EXPORTS** PORT **DEVOUR** *PASTÉIS DE NATA* (CUSTARD TARTS) **AVOID** DEEP-FRIED PIG'S EAR

Pasteis de Belem
cada:
140$00 - € 0,70

A Portuguese vineyard is respendent in the autumn light.

Sardines served with lemon.

A hearty Portuguese lunch.

CULTURE

Portugal is perched on the extreme south-western edge of Europe and until 500 years ago was awash with the influence of the Moors from the south, Spanish to the east and British and Flemish to the north. The fearless Portuguese then took to the high seas in search of trade routes and profit from the bounty of the Orient. So you'll find plenty of seafood dishes along with the spoils of its outposts — spice and rice from the Indies, tea and silks from the Orient and corn from the Americas. Acorn-fed pork, eel stew, golden Madeira, sweet pastries from the convents and tawny port all colour the pantry picture.

Independence

The best of Portuguese food is prepared with simple cooking methods, and strongly reflects its region and proud past. It is fiercely independent of fashions and international trends, and the Portuguese have defended their right to reject an intellectual or superior approach to eating and drinking. The produce of the land and the ways it is prepared are part of a strong culture and heritage. Richly satisfying dishes should be ingested at intervals of a few short hours, for maximum enjoyment. Portuguese food eschews airs and graces and must be shared with family, friends and anyone who looks remotely like they could do with some fortitude, regardless of rank, race or rancour.

Family secrets

Restaurants tend to be family run, and when they are, they keep their recipes secret and only pass them on to the next generation of family. There are few definitive written recipes, because these aren't the kind of secrets that can be written down. This specificity also means that in a particular town (such as *Mealhada*, famous for roast suckling pig), the locals' knowledge of — and definite preference for — the way that one restaurant prepares it over another is common. But this regard for specific tastes is not as important in the cities and tourist areas. That's why, to experience the real food of Portugal, you have to get off the beaten track and be prepared to sniff out local treasures.

The Portuguese pantry

Bread, cheese, wine, pork and fish. This is what awaits you in a country in love with its ocean and the fresh produce of a dramatic landscape. It's food of — and like — the people themselves: proud, generous and well seasoned.

In the Portuguese pantry you'll find terminology, textures and tastes all tossed up in the air and assembled at random. Soup is dry. Vegetables are made into jam. Chicken is a dessert. Pies are made with bread dough. Cakes are savoury. Bread can be a biscuit. But it all tastes delicious.

REGIONS

Portugal is divided into seven mainland regions, broadly grouped under the North, Central and South, and two Atlantic archipelagos, Madeira and the Azores. Regional cuisines reflect the changing landscape as its major rivers, the Tagus and the Douro, wend their way from Spain and across Portugal to the ocean through verdant pastures and wine growing areas to the fish-rich sea. Cabbage and spicy sausage soup in Minho, slippery tripe in Porto, cured ham from Chaves, roast suckling pig in Bairrada, wines from Colares, muscatel from Setubal, Serra cheese in the Beiras, almond sweets from the Algarve and egg sweets from Aveiro.

FLY AWAY WITH YOUR IMAGINATION / GETTY IMAGES

Cafes and people at a sweet town on the River Douro.

Alentejo

What can we say? Even Portuguese people not from this region, which covers much of the southern and central parts of the country, wish they were. The baking plains, the olives and oil, the bread-based one-pot dishes, the wild boar, the sassy reds. Wines, that is. Welcome to the land of megaliths, ancient stories and whitewashed villages. Everyone loves the Alentejo, and they especially love to sup on its bounty.

There's only one important thing to remember here, and that is that pork will confront you at every repast. Oh, and bread. Bread figures heavily, not just on the table, but also in cooked dishes. In summer you'll be eating *gaspacho*, a chilled tomato and garlic soup ladled over thick slices of bread. In winter, sustenance will come from *migas* (seasoned fried bread), which you are likely to face for breakfast and possibly also at lunch. Pork is a typical version, where garlic is fried in lard (pork fat), with bread and water added. The mix all pulls together to form a solid, flavoursome 'dough' that is sliced and served hot with different cuts of pork such as spare ribs, lean meat and smoked sausage. See why a glass of wine is necessary at breakfast too?

All year round you will eat *açorda* (bread soup), which is, at base, just bread and water. There are variations of course, but you will usually taste crushed garlic, salt and aromatic herbs (coriander or pennyroyal).

You can also expect to eat:

- fried wild asparagus with scrambled eggs
- oozingly rich Serpa cheese
- carrots preserved with coriander
- rabbit fried with thyme
- eel stew fragrant with mint
- white beans cooked with fresh spring truffles

GREG ELMS / GETTY IMAGES

Bacalhau a bras: salt cod, potatoes and scrambled eg

- hare stewed with butter beans
- mullet *caldeirada* (stew)
- dogfish *açorda*
- roasted partridge
- pork and clams.

Don't worry if you eat too much — if you've covered the Alentejo, you've actually covered a third of Portugal.

ESSENTIAL PRODUCE

Bacalhau

You will not understand Portugal unless you partake of the dried salt cod called *bacalhau*. It's bound up with myth, history and mealtimes, including everyday meals and the most important celebrations on the calendar.

It used to be that Portuguese fishermen caught the cod and brought it back to be salted and dried by women in towns all along the coast. Now the fish are bought from other countries, with the best and most expensive catch from Norway and Iceland and others from Newfoundland, Canada, Denmark and Nova Scotia. However, if you're lurking about in the towns of Viana do Castelo or Aveiro at the right time, you may see what the whole coast of Portugal used to look like with different types of splayed, salted fish set in the sun to dry. The obsession goes so deep that even in Madeira, where no fresh cod is sent for salting and drying, they catch a similar local fish, prepare it in the same way and call it 'false' *bacalhau*.

Cheese

The Portuguese have kept *queijo* (cheese) simple, and many people make fresh cheese from their own milk rather than buy it. This means it can be something of a hit and miss affair, but if you have a few extra sheep and goats out the back, you may as well use them. There's not a lot of pomp and ceremony about cheese in Portugal. It's part of daily life.

Portugal's cheeses are made mainly from ewe's or goat's milk, or a combination of the two. You will eat cheese every day here, either before a meal with a bowl of olives and a glass of wine, in between meals as a snack, or in between bread as a sandwich. You may even eat it for breakfast with honey and spices. It's unlikely, with the exception of the cheddar-like cow's milk *queijo da ilha* (island cheese from the Azores), that you'll find cheese cooked into a dish.

Requeijão is the deliciously rich ricotta-like cheese made from ewe's milk whey, and it is eaten fresh as a savoury *acepipe* (hors d'oeuvre); on bread with honey for breakfast; as a dessert with caramelised pumpkin; or even hot and soupy as a nutritious lunch with bread and wine.

Common also is an offering of small chunks of *queijo de ovelha* (ewe's milk cheese) either before or after a meal, (or in between meals) with a beer or glass of wine. Rabaçal, Azeitão and Saloio are also excellent, as are Évora, Serpa and Nisa from Alentejo, and Monte from Trás-os-Montes.

Cheese rounds at the Mercado do Balhao.

Cinnamon

The Portuguese's favourite spice, *canela* (cinnamon) makes its way into almost all sweets, a quill is often used instead of a spoon to stir coffee, and it is also added to lots of savoury braised poultry and meat dishes.

Galician kale

Couve Galega (Galician kale) is from the Minho region and while kale, savoy and other types of cabbage are used all over the country, this is the crown prince. The defining ingredient in

Cakes like these are commonly eaten for breakfast.

Fresh goat cheese in a herb-infusued oil.

A fisherman watches over his sardines drying in the sun on a beach in Nazaré.

PAUL BERNHARDT / GETTY IMAGES

caldo verde (Galician kale and potato soup), it's also used in lots of other cooked dishes. You'll see people buying it by the bagful, finely shredded, at markets.

Piri piri

Brought back from Angola, this explosive little chilli, which is made into a sauce, has become a staple to add to everything grilled, especially fish and chicken. In Portugal, *piri piri* has come to be a generic reference to chilli, even though it's just one type of chilli.

Potatoes

Why do the *batatas* (potatoes) here taste so good? They're universally wonderful, nutty and sweet, and always served in generous quantities. Too many (of which there always are) are never enough. In the Algarve sweet potatoes are baked whole until their skins split, then the flesh is eaten with a spoon, or fried and sprinkled with cinnamon and sugar.

Sardines

Portugal and seafood: it's impossible to imagine them apart.

Sardines are probably the most favoured fish after *bacalhau*. You will see sardines grilling in the streets, on restaurant menus, and on family dining tables. They will be barely scaled, full of their own guts, and heads left on. Grill, squeeze some lemon over, salt and eat with your fingers. If you hear anyone saying — or selling — *sardinhas do nosso mar* around the town of Viana do Castelo, it means 'sardines from our sea'. This concept is important to the Portuguese, as they like to think of everything they eat as being local, including the fish. Eating fish from 'our sea' — meaning that stretch of ocean that's closest to home — supports local fishermen. Curiously, this is irrelevant when it comes to *bacalhau*, for which demand is so great that they'll take it from anywhere.

Smoked ham

The Portuguese love a pig and every part of the beast finds its way to the table. In some parts of the country, workers start the day with soup or slices of smoked sausage. King among the smoked pork products is *presunto* (smoked ham), every bit an equal to Italy's *prosciutto*. To make the ham:

- The whole legs are brushed with a paste that varies from region to region but always includes salt, garlic, paprika and wine.
- The meat is left to cure for several weeks between layers of salt.
- After the salt is rubbed off, the hams are suspended in the *fumeiro* (smokehouse) for up to two months.
- Once the hams are smoked they are brushed with olive oil and sprinkled with paprika and borax (which acts as a preservative), then hung to age for at least a year.

Presunto is delicious as a thinly sliced snack, in sandwiches, sliced thickly and panfried as a steak, or cut up and added to other dishes for flavour.

Sweets and pastries

Portuguese life is sweet. Sweeter than just about anywhere else. And rich. Sugar and egg yolks are the two commonest ingredients. And that's thanks to the Moors, who brought sugar cane, almonds and fruit to Portugal, and the nimble fingers of nuns, who made egg-yolk sweets as gifts.

At *pastelarias* (pastry shops) you'll find plenty of *pastéis* (pastries), while at other eateries the choice varies from the

GREG ELMS / GETTY IMAGES

Arroz doce, Portuguese sweet rice pudding.

devastatingly calorie- and cholesterol-rich conventual *doces* (sweets) to sweet rice and custards, or cakes, such as *toucinho do céu* (a rich, sweet almond and cinnamon cake), *queijadas* (tarts with a sweet, dense filling) and the famous *pastéis de nata* (technically cream, but really custard, tarts). Apart from sugar, egg yolks, oranges, almonds and lemons, cinnamon is a common ingredient, as is bacon fat or lard, especially in areas where pork products rule.

Some desserts are simply a whole egg yolk candied in sugar and wrapped in pastry, or folded in communion wafers. It is impossible to overstate the dominance of these few ingredients on the sweet scene and palate of the country.

PREPARATION

No kitchen would be complete without *pratos de barro cozido* (earthenware cooking dishes) of various sizes, some of which have a specific purpose.

Tigela means bowl, but more specifically an earthenware bowl in which individual *tigeladas* – spongy egg custards flavoured with vanilla, lemon or cinnamon — are cooked and served.

A *tacho de barro* is an earthenware casserole dish that comes in numerous shapes and sizes and of which every kitchen will have plenty, partly because they are so practical and partly because they cost next to nothing. The dishes may be sealed or unsealed, plain or brightly painted. They have the advantage of going from oven to table, and food cooked in them tastes different from when it's cooked in other materials.

Common Portuguese cooking methods include:

- *assado* — roasted
- *churrasco* — barbecued, usually on a spit or skewer (especially good for chicken)

A chef prepares *espetada*, beef skewers, in a traditional oven.

HOLGER LEUE / GETTY IMAGES

- *espetada* — skewered food (also refers to the skewer itself), especially good in Madeira
- *estufado* — stewed, also refers to the stew itself
- *frito* — deep-fried, fit treatment for just about any food you can think of
- *fumado* — smoked, as in all the sausages and pork meats but also eels
- *grelhado* — grilled, for fish, pork chops and other fast cooking cuts
- *nas brasas* — charcoal grilled, for sardines, and sausages such as *chouriço* and *linguiça* (a longer, thinner version of *chouriço*)
- *no forno* — baked in a woodfired brick or stone oven.

DEFINING DISHES

Galician kale and potato soup

Caldo verde (Galician kale and potato soup) can be had all over the country but is best in Galicia because it is where the correct cabbage comes from; other regions may make it with shredded kale or other types of cabbage instead of the dark *couve galega*. It's suitable for breakfast, lunch and dinner and scarcely a menu is without it.

Soups and stews

What's the difference between a soup and a stew? In Portugal, sometimes not much. The Portuguese are masters and mistresses of fuelling themselves on the smell of an oiled broth, which they thicken with bread to make *açorda* (bread soup). All the soup soaks into the bread, which becomes squishy and flavoursome, and sometimes it is thickened even more with a beaten egg, or is enriched with sausage or seafood. So it's like a stew without the long, slow cooking. Two of the best known versions are:

- *açorda de marisco*, with prawns, mussels and baby clams, from Estremadura, and
- *açorda à Alentejana*, a bread soup made with garlic, olive oil, broth, greens, poached eggs and aromatic herbs like coriander or pennyroyal.

The soup category of a menu can include:

- the famous *caldo verde* (Galician kale and potato soup), mentioned above
- the ubiquitous and delicious *canja* (chicken broth, just in case you need restoration) or *papas* (a gruel, as in 'of pork') and
- *gaspacho* (cold tomato and onion soup), which is popular in the south and is frequently served with grilled sardines. Unlike its northern cousin it is not often pureed, so it's like a wet salad.

The soup section also contains *sopa seca* (dry soup), which is neither a soup nor dry. It's more like a hotpot with bread. The point is that a soupy kind of dish can be light enough to sustain a model without threatening her livelihood, or substantial enough to feed a troop of farmhands.

Refogado

Refogado or *cebolada* is the typical flavour base for lots of traditional soups, stews and braises. It's basically a generous splash of olive oil and a cascade of finely chopped white onion slowly cooked until it is a molten, golden mass. Then garlic, bay leaves and maybe some tomatoes are added and it's all cooked some more. This intensely flavoured puree then infuses an entire dish of beans, rice, seafood or meat with wonderful

Caldo verde, Galician kale soup.

Chorizo

STEPHEN WALLS / GETTY IMAGES

Gaspacho, cold tomato and onion soup.

depth. It's somewhat confusing having two names for the one item, but technically speaking the process is called *refogado* while the onion mix itself is *cebolada*.

Suckling pig

In the town of Mealhada, it seems suckling pig is the only dish on restaurant menus, and people travel for miles to get it. The whole sucking pigs are rubbed with garlic, lard and salt, staked with a thick metal rod and roasted in a woodfired oven. Served simply with bread and wine, the skin is papery, golden and crisp and the flesh underneath meltingly good. It is eaten hot or cold, on site or as a takeaway.

DRINKS

Wine

So what's so good about Portuguese wine? For a start, some of the country's grape varieties are among the oldest on the planet, and many simply don't exist anywhere else. Secondly, the Portuguese also worked out how to make average wine into superlative fortified wines: the generic Madeira and port, and the branded Moscatel de Setúbal.

Portugal doesn't reliably label its wine by region or grape. If you're used to looking for the characteristics of a particular grape variety, or a blend, you'll be lost for reference points in Portugal: the grapes taste so uniquely of themselves they can only be compared to other Portuguese wines. Authorities are attempting to get agreement between producers on what to call the same types of grape.

In general, the most interesting wines are reds, port and Madeira, then *vinho verde* (light sparkling wine) and muscat. And the most interesting thing to do with them is consume them with food at every meal: that's what they're made for. Despite the complexity of wine types, you'll only be asked to

WITTELSBACH BERND / GETTY IMAGES

A taste of history: Madeira wine from 1977.

nominate *vinho tinto* (red wine) or *vinho branco* (white wine). Colour is the only distinction made.

Fortified wines

Any wine that has been fortified with alcohol to stabilise and strengthen it is called a fortified wine. Portuguese examples include the branded Moscatel de Setúbal and the generic Madeira wine and port wine.

Madeira

Some have said that no drink, no foodstuff of any kind, shares the apparent immortality of old vintage *vinho da Madeira*, so if your kind host offers you an aperitif with four score on it, revel in the knowledge that you're drinking from the cup of history.

Madeira is made from any of four so-called 'noble' grape varieties, including *Sercial* (dry and light), *Verdelho* (medium and golden), *Boal* or *Bual* (medium sweet and dark gold) and *Malvasia* (sweet and chestnut brown), which is called *Malmsey* when sold. *Terrantez* is a rarer style that falls somewhere between *Verdelho* and *Boal*.

Madeira may also be classified by age as well as by grape variety. Vintage is dated and made exclusively from one of the noble grape varieties. It has a minimum ageing period of 20 years in wood and two years in the bottle. Extra Reserve is made from 85% noble grape wines and aged for a minimum of 15 years. Special or Old Reserve must be over ten years old and Reserve at least five.

Port

Although the high alcohol wine (around 20% alcohol content) *vinho do Porto* (port) is named after the town of Porto, the action begins about 100 kilometres upstream in the vineyards of the middle and upper Douro. The vineyards stretch a further 100 kilometres or so east to the Spanish border. The wine is made at the source from up to 40 different grape varieties. It is then fortified with brandy or, more accurately, neutral grape spirit, which arrests fermentation and leaves the wine naturally sweet but still with plenty of alcohol.

Barrels were traditionally then floated down the Douro to Porto on ancient, high-tillered wooden boats that remain now only as a curiosity, having been supplanted by the less picturesque but probably more efficient road tankers.

As port has always been made for export (especially for the insatiable Brits), the Portuguese actually don't drink as much port as you might think for a product that was conceived on their turf.

Aguardente

The brandy-like spirit *aguardente* will threaten your health in the most seductive way. It's a type of brandy, except it can be made from just about anything, and sometimes is. The unidentifiable home-made type is best avoided — it will almost certainly make you sick.

Brandy is a spirit distilled from fruit and, in the case of cognac, from wine. This makes it more expensive than grain-based spirits. While the best *aguardente* is said to rival cognac, it's potent. Virgin visitors may be shocked to see grandmothers knocking back a shot of 50% proof *aguardente* before breakfast, but rest assured its purpose is strictly medicinal and the bottle will remain untouched until tomorrow. Other brandies to try include *bagaçeira* (grape-skin spirit), *aguardente de figo* (fig spirit) or *ginjinha* (cherry spirit).

Beer

Portuguese *cerveja* (beer) is both strong (over 5% alcohol) and inexpensive. It's also wonderfully refreshing. It's best in

GREG ELMS / GETTY IMAGES

Piri piri, red-hot chilli pepper sauce.

draught rather than bottled form. The best place to get a beer is a *cervejaria*, or beer house, where you'll find snacks as well. There's plenty of beer in *tascas* (cheap eateries) and restaurants too, but look out if you decide to either begin or end your meal with a beer — looks of fascination and horror will accompany your choice because, of course, you should be drinking wine with your food. Beer is for drinking at all other times of the day, preferably with a nice and salty deep-fried pig's ear.

PIRI PIRI SAUCE

You could just go out and buy a bottle of the red hot chilli sauce, *piri piri*, but where's the fun in that? Far better to make your own, and pass it around the table. That's what happens in *tascas* (cheap eateries); a large jar of house-made *piri piri* with a long handled spoon is passed from diner to diner to spread over whatever is before them. Don't even think about eating your *frango no churrasco* (char-grilled chicken) without it.

Makes approximately 2½ cups

Ingredients

1 cup finely chopped red birds-eye chillies (remove seeds if you can't stand the heat)
6 garlic cloves, finely chopped
2 teaspoons sea salt
½ cup white wine vinegar
1½ to 2 cups extra virgin olive oil

Method

Put all the ingredients in a large jar, close the lid tightly and give the lot a mighty shake. Leave it in the fridge for a week, give it a good stir then start using it on whatever you like.

Two men walk down a country lane with a pack of happy hunting dogs in Wales.

ROBERT VAN WAARDEN / GETTY IMAGES

British Isles

British cuisine is based on local, seasonal produce. Simplicity, frugality and quality are at its heart. This is a country where basic meals were designed to sustain workers through the week; the saying 'waste not, want not' would be familiar to many households. It is that respect for the most humble of ingredients that shapes modern British cuisine and rewards the adventurous eater.

CULINARY CAPITALS LONDON, LUDLOW **KNOWN FOR** ROAST BEEF, BEER **IMPORTS** SPICES **EXPORTS** WHISKY, SEAFOOD **DEVOUR** STILTON CHEESE, WELSH LAMB **AVOID** DEEP-FRIED MARS BARS

Snug in a pub in Belfast, enjoying lunch at the Crown Liquor Saloon.

Scotch egg, mustard and beer.

LAURIE NOBLE / GETTY IMAGES

Scottish razor clams for sale at a London market.

CULTURE

Immigrants and emigrants have long influenced British cuisine. Britons went out into the world to stake out the British Empire and returned with exotic fruits, vegetables, sugar and spices. Famously a nation of meat eaters, it wasn't until the 16th century that the potato arrived by ship from the Americas. But cross-fertilisation began with the Romans, who introduced grapes to the island. In subsequent centuries, British cuisine evolved distinct local accents and now has voices from around the world.

REGIONS

Britain may be a small island but it is an intensely regional place. How local ingredients are grown and prepared is determined by tradition, topography and climate.

Scotland

The top third of Britain is as close to wilderness as Britain gets, with clean, fast-flowing rivers, and rugged island groups off the coast. Several iconic products have evolved here, not least whisky (always without an 'e' in Scotland), Arbroath smokies and the *haggis*. Scottish rivers support populations of wild salmon, and the abundant water, filtered in places by thousands of years of peat, is also used in the distilling industry. The art of preserving salmon, and fish from the North Sea landed at Scotland's ports, has been refined in community smokehouses. Arbroath on the east coast, specialises in the smoked haddock known as Arbroath smokies. The fish are cured in salt and then smoked; the salmon is traditionally cold-smoked and the smokies hot-smoked at more than 60°C.

- The flaked flesh of an Arbroath smokie can be used in *Cullen skink*, a Scottish soup of smoked fish, potatoes, onions and cream. The name comes from the port of Cullen on the Moray Firth; '*skink*' is the Gaelic for soup or broth.

- *Haggis* is the archetypal peasant food, utilising all the bits of a sheep left over after the meat has been stripped away. The heart, lungs and liver are finely chopped, mixed with oatmeal, onion and spices, including cloves and pimento. The mixture is stuffed into a sheep's stomach and boiled. The *haggis* is served with mashed neeps (turnips) and tatties (potatoes).
- Only the hardiest grains survive in the Scottish climate: oats and barley are the pick of the crop. They're widely used in lieu of wheat flour and rice. Pearl barley is added to soups. Oats are found not only in *haggis* but also oatcakes (brittle savoury biscuits), porridge (eaten in Scotland with salt instead of sugar), and the Scottish dessert cranachan, an amalgamation of oatmeal, cream, honey, whisky and fresh raspberries, which thrive here.

The food of Scottish lore: *haggis*.

Wales

The Welsh landscape shapes the small principality's cuisine. Bulging out from the west of Britain, this is a land of rivers, valleys and hills. The Atlantic coastline is long and respite from sea-soaked cliffs is provided by broad, sandy beaches. The climate is famously wet and windy. Few vegetables thrive here except the leek, a national emblem, so the Welsh have become adept at cajoling food from the most challenging circumstances.

- Along the south coast of Wales, a delicate green-purple seaweed called *laver* is collected. The thin fronds are similar to those used in Japanese *nori*, except this seaweed is boiled for several hours and then pulped to form a paste called laverbread. It can be served as

Welsh rarebit.

VISITBRITAIN/BRITAIN ON VIEW / GETTY IMAGES

A shepherd and his dogs rounding up sheep on farmland in the hills of the Brecon Beacons in Wales.

a side dish, with seafood such as scallops or cockles (small local shellfish), or alongside lamb or mutton.

- *Bara brith is* Welsh bread, made from currants and candied peel.
- Lamb is the key product of Wales. Various breeds were created to thrive in the harsh conditions here. With the sea air and salt marshes, Welsh lamb has earned a reputation for unmatched flavour.
- Welsh cheese is made from cow, goat and sheep's milk. A well-known Welsh cheese is crumbly Caerphilly, which is used in Welsh rarebit; a thick sauce of cheese, cream, egg yolk, stout and mustard grilled on toast.

The North

England's northern counties of Lancashire and Yorkshire, Northumberland and Cumbria and everywhere in between, are where the island's uplands begin. The North was a place of manual labour, where things were made during the Industrial Revolution. Designed to get calories into hard-working bodies as cheaply as possible, the local food has few frills. But the region boasts many iconic dishes. In the east, which is dominated by fishing ports such as Grimsby, seafood is paramount. Kippers (herring) are cured in the smokehouses of Craster and, to the south in Whitby, potatoes meet local fish in the deep-fat fryer for a portion of perfect fish and chips.

Move inland to Yorkshire (the county that lends its name to the batter pudding that accompanies a traditional roast lunch) to find Harrogate teas, York ham, Yorkshire tea cakes and rhubarb from the 'rhubarb triangle' between Bradford, Leeds and Wakefield. Yorkshire is geographically blessed with open moorland where grouse are raised to the north, and green fields of grazing sheep in the Dales to the south.

LARA HATA / GETTY IMAGES

Some say it's the national dish: chicken *tikka masala*.

- Lancashire hot pot was a dish designed to simmer on the stove all day before the miner, farm labourer or mill worker came home.
- Black pudding, part of a family of blood sausage that includes French *boudin noir* and Spanish *morcilla*, is a speciality of the North West, especially those from the town of Bury.
- From the sand flats of the North West, Morecambe Bay's brown shrimps are potted in butter with spices (nutmeg or mace, cayenne pepper), salt and lemon.

Some of cities of the North — Bradford, Leeds and Manchester — are home to large immigrant populations from the Indian subcontinent, making for a curious marriage of British tastes and subcontinental spices, such as the tomato and coriander-sauced chicken *tikka masala,* or the *balti* which is cooked and served in a thin metal dish. They would not be recognised in India, Pakistan or Bangladesh; these dishes have evolved independently in Britain since the 1950s.

The East

The flat, fertile fields of England's eastern flank are where much of the country's crops and vegetables are grown. Potatoes, cabbages, onions and other vegetables flourish in oft-flooded Lincolnshire. The county also lends its name to the sage-flavoured Lincolnshire sausage. The coastline of eastern England curves out to encompass Suffolk and Norfolk, which together comprise East Anglia.

- Both counties are famed for the seafood that is harvested close to their coast. Whole crabs from Cromer in Norfolk are boiled and served with samphire, a wild vegetable that grows along East Anglia's shingly shore, or sea spinach (or beet).

- Norwich is home to the vivid yellow Colman's mustard, one of a number of iconic British condiments (as well as Worcestershire sauce, horseradish sauce and tomato ketchup). Mustard has been part of English cuisine since Roman times or perhaps earlier.
- In Cambridge, a dessert of burnt cream is credited to Trinity College (Trinity cream), although it's closely related to *crème brûlée* and *crema Catalana*. Double cream, egg yolks and sugar are simmered in a pan and left to cool overnight, before a sprinkling of sugar on top is caramelised.

The West Country

Where the West Country begins has long been a source of debate. Strictly, it comprises the counties of Devon and Cornwall, favourite holiday destinations for generations of families and famed for cream teas, fudge and Cornish pasties.

- The pastures of this temperate corner are extremely green, resulting in rich cream and butter; the cream teas feature clotted cream served with scones and a dollop of strawberry jam.
- The coastline, crowded with inaccessible coves and small fishing ports, is noted for its seafood; those Cornish scallops and other shellfish that aren't shipped straight to restaurants can sometimes be bought at the dockside. Local catches of fish include red mullet, sardines and mackerel.
- Fish features in the Cornish speciality stargazy pie, from the village of Mousehole. Fillets of small fish are laid in a dish and covered with a sauce of white wine, fish stock, onion, bacon, cream, parsley and egg; a pastry lid is placed on top and decorated with the heads of the fish.

The beloved Lea & Perrins Worcestershire Sauce.

Large steak pastie with bowl of crinkle chips.

British summertime: scones served with jam and cream in the garden.

Plate of fish and chips with a side of ketchup.

CULTURA/DIANA MILLER / GETTY IMAGES

The Southwest of England embraces the nearby counties of Dorset, Somerset, Gloucestershire and Herefordshire.

- The region's rich milk is used in cheddar cheese, which originated in the Somerset village of Cheddar; the cheese was matured in the cool limestone caves nearby.
- Somerset produces cider from its numerous orchards.
- Gloucestershire's famous Old Spot pigs are among the finest in the world, and can be cooked with cider or apples from Somerset.

London and the South

The capital has long been at the epicentre of British cuisine.

- From the 17th century, oysters, probably from Whitstable in Kent, were served from barrels on London's street corners — they were a cheap street food then.
- The first fish and chip shop was opened in 1860 in the East End of London by a young Jewish entrepreneur named Joseph Malin.

With its place at the heart of the nation's trade, London also received the tastiest finds from around the world during the 17th, 18th and 19th centuries: sugar and spices were unloaded at East End wharfs and tomatoes, potatoes, pineapples and other commodities all excited Londoners before they filtered out to the rest of the country.

Along the south coast, the sea and the warmer climate make for a varied basket of produce.

- Kent is the county of hops, an ingredient of beer.
- To the west, the counties of Sussex, Berkshire and Hampshire also produce sheep and pigs.
- From Hampshire, Alresford's watercress, the peppery

variety with large leaves, was regularly delivered by train to London.

FEASTS

Christmas and Easter are the most significant festivals of the year. At Christmas it is usual for a turkey to be roasted and served with a huge range of vegetables, including Brussels sprouts. Following that, a fruity Christmas pudding is steamed. Most families bake mince pies (originally made from meat but now from dried fruit and spices) and a Christmas fruitcake that lasts the length of the festive season.

Cake also plays a part in Easter celebrations: Simnel cake made with sultanas, currants, candied fruit, dried peel and mixed spice is eaten on Easter Sunday. On Good Friday, hot cross buns are eaten buttered.

Each of Britain's regions has special occasions when a local dish takes centre stage.

- In Scotland, *haggis* is traditionally served on Burn's Day in January, in honour of the Scottish poet Robert Burns.
- In Wales, on St David's Day in March, a broth of bacon on the bone, well-marbled lamb neck, cabbage, potato and leeks called *cawl* is ladled out.

THE MENU

A typical British menu has three courses: a starter, main course and dessert. More expensive restaurants may offer a tasting menu that can feature six or more smaller courses. The greatest dilemma is whether to follow the French style of serving cheese before dessert (thus keeping savoury and sweet flavours separate) or serve cheese after dessert like the British — a preference largely attributed to the the way the bombastic flavours of Stilton and cheddar cheese marry so well with the

TETRA IMAGES / GETTY IMAGES

The classic English breakfast.

fortified wines the British developed in the 18th century.

In the 1990s, some of Britain's pubs, traditionally places where the quality of the beer took precedence of over the food, began serving more refined meals. This was the precursor to what is now called Modern British cuisine; simple but tasty food that taps into the traditions of seasonality and local produce. Today, with the revival of small-scale craft breweries, a more casual approach to dining out, and a growing appreciation of good food, the lines between restaurants and pubs are blurred.

The best restaurants are not exclusively located in cities; the town of Ludlow in the Cotswolds supports several world-class restaurants.

DAILY MEALS

'Breakfast like a king, lunch like a prince and dine like a pauper': this remains a land of three square meals a day where breakfast in particular is the mainstay of the working week. The meal has regional variations and its exact composition is the cause of much debate, but the basic components of eggs (fried, poached or scrambled) and bacon (fried or grilled) are shared. It's typically served with a mug of tea.

- Along with the bacon and eggs, a full English breakfast adds a combination of the following ingredients to a platform of toast or fried bread: grilled tomatoes (halved), fried mushrooms, baked beans and sausages.
- In Scotland and northern England a slice of black pudding may replace the sausage and a potato (tattie) scone may be added.

Britain's lunch has changed the most because of the shift from working in fields and mines to offices. For rural workers, lunch would have often been a variation of the ploughman's lunch:

The traditional English roast dinner, complete with Yorkshire puddings and gravy.

EMMA GUTTERIDGE / GETTY IMAGES

a hunk of fresh-baked bread, a wedge of local cheese, a homemade pickle or chutney, and an apple, all wrapped in a square of cloth.

The Cornish pastie, a half-moon-shaped envelope containing diced meat, swede and potato, also derives from where Britons used to work: in the tin mines of Cornwall miners would hold the crimped edge of a pastie, eat the filling and discard the now-dirty handle.

At weekends, Sunday lunch would often be the central meal of the week, a chance for families to gather around the table. The meal would be based around a roast chicken or cut of meat such as a shoulder of lamb or joint of beef. Leftovers would be used during the week in dishes such as cottage pie (beef topped with potato) and shepherd's pie (lamb topped with potato).

ESSENTIAL PRODUCE

Beef

British cuisine is built on strong foundations. Britain has the world's most extensive range of native breeds; no other nation has developed or exported as many different varieties of livestock. Cattle are no exception: British breeders created the blueprint for some of the most successful — black Aberdeen Angus from Scotland, russet-coloured Hereford and the shorthorn. Most, if not all, British beef is grass-fed, which benefits the animal's quality of life and the flavour of the meat. Angus beef, in particular, has the marbling of fat that meat-lovers seek out for roasts.

- The prime cuts are the rib, top rump, sirloin and fillet.
- The fillet is also the star of the dish Beef Wellington, where it is wrapped in pastry with an insulating layer of chopped mushrooms, white wine and cream.
- Rose veal is the meat of young male dairy calves.

Cheese

More than 700 cheeses are made in England, most are strongly identified with a place. Cheddar is the most widely produced cheese and accordingly, it has the greatest variation in quality; it doesn't enjoy Protected Geographical Indication (PGI) status. A good cheddar should be creamy and nutty but also savoury and tangy. Farmhouse cheddars are aged nine months or more. Stilton, the archetypal blue-veined cheese, can only be made in Derbyshire, Leicestershire or Nottinghamshire. It's at its best at Christmas, having been matured for at least ten weeks. A longer maturation brings a deeper, more mellow flavour. The blue veins are the mould *penicillium roqueforti*.

Apple crumble is a much-loved dessert in Britain.

Fruit

Apples are the most British of fruits, not least because they grow happily in the climate. There are more than 2300 varieties of apple in Britain, with evocative names like Egremont russet. It was in about 1825 that Richard Cox created his orange pippin, still one of the tastiest British apples — spicy, aromatic, sweet but tart.

- Bramley apples are sharp and should be cooked either in savoury dishes or in desserts where sugar is added, such as apple pie.
- Plums grow well in Britain and are cooked in tarts, crumbles, jams and chutneys.
- Soft fruits such as raspberries, blueberries, currants and strawberries are essential summer eating with cream.
- Wild blackberries are common and are picked in August and September and made into jams or fruit crumbles by topping cooked apple and blackberry with a mixture of butter, flour, oats and sugar and baking.

Plums.

Blackberries grow thick and wild in the British countryside.

Game

On the 12th of August the moors of Scotland and northern England resound to the sound of shotguns: it's the first day of the season for shooting red grouse. These medium-sized birds are native to Britain but are now reared specifically for the shooting season. They feed on heather, which gives them a distinctive flavour. Due to the expense of joining a grouse shoot, the birds are rarely seen in shops. Once plucked, the bird is wrapped in fatty bacon and roasted quickly at a high heat. Grouse is not the only game bird prized in Britain — woodcock, quail, partridge, pheasant, wood pigeon and various wildfowl (duck mainly) are all eaten.

On four legs, venison is the largest wild animal consumed in Britain. Several types of deer range across Britain from the largest red deer on Scottish mountains to roe deer in southern woodlands. Game meat is typically very lean so roasting a fillet is quick; cuts such as shoulders and haunches can be pot-roasted or casseroled.

Lamb

British lamb is highly regarded across Europe; like its cattle, Britain has the largest range of native sheep breeds in the world, stemming from the Victorian desire to perfect specific breeds for specific locations.

- In Wales breeds like the Welsh Hill Speckled were bred to live on mountains.
- So were the Ronaldsay in Scotland, which graze on salty grasses and heathers and produce a prized meat.
- A revival of nose-to-tail eating — where every bit of an animal is used — has seen greater interest in offal, such as lamb's kidneys, which are used in the pastry-covered steak-and-kidney pie.

DUNCAN WHERRETT / GETTY IMAGES

A greengrocers shop in Derby.

Seafood

For a long time much of Britain's finest seafood was shipped straight to Europe's restaurants — Scottish langoustines went to France, monkfish and hake to Spain. But there's still more seafood that is pulled from the cold waters around the island and worth trying.

- Crustaceans include brown crabs (also known as common or edible crabs) that are cooked by plunging them into boiling water, then the meat is picked from the shell and fat claws.
- There are also prawns and langoustines, and shrimp that are eaten straight from a pot.
- Eels were once a common food, caught in the River Thames and served in a pie with mash in London's East End cafes. It's a very rare dish now, as are jellied eels.
- Cod remains the nation's favourite fish. Once so common that it was a cheap and ubiquitous source of protein, cod is much more of a deluxe choice today.

Vegetables

Britain's sharply defined seasons mean that there are different vegetables at their best throughout the year.

- Among the first vegetables to poke their heads above the ground are asparagus spears. These are a treasured arrival in early to mid-May; the green stems and purple heads, eaten as freshly as possible, are lightly steamed or cooked on a griddle and served with a knob of butter.
- The white flowers of wild garlic plants line lanes and woodland paths of southern England in April and May.
- By June and July, broad beans and peas are starting to appear, followed by cucumbers and courgettes.

- The first of the Jersey Royal potatoes, originally from the Channel Island of Jersey, are also unearthed in June and July, their small size and sweet flavour making them perfect for summer salads.
- From October onwards many root vegetables, including celeriac, parsnip and salsify are ready.
- Above the ground, traditional winter green vegetables are Brussels sprouts and kale.
- Rhubarb, although a vegetable, is treated as a fruit and stewed with sugar or baked in a crumble.

SHOPPING

All but the most modern towns have a market square, which would have been in use several times a week. That tradition has been superseded by less frequent farmers' markets, which are as close as most people get to buying local produce direct from the source.

Similarly, most high streets used to have several bakers and butchers, but today's British towns are lucky if they have one of each. The supermarket — some chains of which are excellent and others awful — has taken over.

DEFINING DISHES

Bakewell tart

From the town of Bakewell in Derbyshire's Peak District, this dessert is sometimes considered a tart, sometimes a pudding; the difference is that puff pastry is used for the pudding and shortcrust for the tart. The case is lined with a layer of raspberry jam and then filled with a mixture of sugar, butter, ground almonds and egg yolks. It can be served with cream or custard.

Rhubarb for sale at the market.

Raspberry Bakewell slices.

Woman holding Brussels sprouts harvested but still on the stalk.

Victoria sponge cake.

A pile of fruity Eccles cakes.

Lemon shortbread biscuits.

Cakes

North to south, Britain is a nation of cake-lovers.

- In Scotland, shortbread is a hard, buttery biscuit and Dundee cake is a rich fruit cake.
- In the north of England, Eccles cakes are small, flat, sugary, currant cakes; tea cakes are more of a bun, while parkin is a sticky, gingery, spicy cake.
- Further south, lardy cake is a speciality of Wiltshire and the southwest. It's a dense, doughy cake with lard and dried fruit, coated in sugar.
- Across the border in Wales, Welsh cakes are flat, fruity scone-like cakes that are cooked on a griddle.
- In London, the Chelsea bun is a similarly fruity snack but it has the addition of cinnamon and other spices.
- The Victoria sponge, named after Britain's 19th century queen, is a a classic sponge, sandwiched together with jam and/or cream.

Fish and chips

The classic image of British food is of newspaper wrapping fat, golden chips and a piece of deep-fried cod or haddock.

- A fillet of fish is dunked in a batter of beer, flour, milk and egg, then swiftly submerged in bubbling hot oil for five or more minutes. What should emerge is the still-moist fish encased in a crispy golden armour.
- Serve with twice-cooked chips, which have been deep-fried at a medium heat then finished off at high heat.

Fruit fool

The glut of summer fruits — strawberries, raspberries, red and black currants — is responsible for a trio of simple desserts.

- Fruit fool is basic but delicious: raspberries and strawberries are briefly poached with sugar then folded into whipped cream.
- Eton Mess adds pieces of meringue to the recipe.
- Summer pudding is slightly more complex: raspberries, red currants and sugar are stewed with sugar and a little water for a couple of minutes until the juices run, then poured into a pudding basin that has been lined with slices of white bread. The top is covered with more bread and a weighted plate compresses the lot as it is refrigerated overnight and the juices soak through the bread. It is served with double cream.

Lancashire hot pot

Cheap cuts of hill-reared lamb, covered with a layer of sliced potatoes that turn golden and crispy, are simmered slowly in a pot with carrots, leeks and onions. After several hours, the lamb will fall away from the bone. The hot pot, like all one-pot meals, is a practical recipe to sustain hard-working people.

Roast beef

So closely associated with the British that the French nickname them 'les rosbifs', roast beef has been a cornerstone of British cuisine since the 18th century, when it appeared in plays and paintings. The tradition was to roast a large cut of beef on Sunday and eat the rest of it during the week — which perhaps explains the British taste for condiments. The meat would have been roasted over an open fire for several hours. Today, lean cuts such as top rump, sirloin and fillet are roasted in an oven for less time, although cuts on the bone benefit from longer and slower cooking. The best beef is hung for at least a couple of weeks to deepen the flavour. It is served with roast potatoes, vegetables (carrots, perhaps red cabbage) and Yorkshire

Two pints of bitter.

puddings. Horseradish sauce made from the root of the horseradish plant, a member of the mustard family, adds a little heat to the dish.

DRINKS

Beer

Beer was an essential daily drink in medieval Britain, as there were few sources of clean drinking water. Some would say little has changed since, except the beer itself. For a drink with so few ingredients — water, hops, yeast and malt — it can be found in innumerable permutations, from light, zesty, summer ales to dark, heavy, bitter stouts.

- Bitter is a mostly mild, amber-coloured beer that is served at room temperature.
- Pale ale was a response to clear European lager and emphasises the hops; it's typically served chilled and in varying strengths.
- India Pale Ales (IPA) were generously hopped beers that were high in alcohol by today's standards. In the 18th century, when Britons were running the British Empire in India and the West Indies, these beers proved not only popular but also survived the long sea voyages more successfully, thanks to the extra hops and alcohol.
- London porter, which sustained the work of London's street and river porters in the 18th century, is a dark, strong, bitter beer made with roasted malt. Stout is thought to have evolved as a stronger version of porter, although the differences between the two are debated.
- Today Britain retains the Imperial measurements of pints (568 millilitres or 20 fluid ounces) and half-pints to serve beer.

Tea

The cup of tea is a do-it-all drink: warming, cooling, refreshing, comforting. Yet it has only been a classless panacea since the 19th century, prior to that it was drunk in city coffeehouses, where it was known as China tea.

Tea and coffee arrived in Britain courtesy of seafaring European explorers. Imports from the East India Company soared in the 18th century, as plantations in India and Sri Lanka (Ceylon) were established. It was at this time that tea became more of any everyman's beverage. Most tea drunk in Britain is black tea, and the quality varies from nondescript teabags to high quality single-estate leaves.

A plate of oysters and a pint of stout in a bar.

Wine

Grapes were grown by the Romans in Britain centuries ago, when the climate was warmer. But it wasn't until the 1980s that the first of the current crop of wineries realised the potential of southeast England's chalk slopes. Vines were planted and today the region around Sussex, Kent and Hampshire produces good white wine and excellent sparkling wine.

Fortified wines — port from Portugal and sherry from Spain — were favoured by Britons, who financed the industry.

Whisky

Scotland's greatest export is the water of life — or *uisge beatha* in Gaelic. Whisky can be made from malted barley or malted barley with other grains, and is either blended or from a single distillery. Single malt whisky is the most refined option. There are more than 100 Scottish distilleries in five regions: Highland, Lowland, Islay, Speyside and Campbeltown. Each has its own characteristics, often stemming from the quality of the local water and climate. Whiskies can be astringent, smoky, floral, or even sweet in taste — a sniff will reveal the whisky's character.

A nice cup of tea at an outdoor cafe.

Whisky tasting in Lothian, Scotland.

Afternoon tea at Dublin's famous Bewley's Cafe.

OLIVER STREWE / GETTY IMAGES

Ireland

Ireland has always been blessed with a wealth of staples and specialities. It's what to do with these riches that has baffled generations of Irish mothers. But a new wave of cooks is creating a refined, distinct and contemporary Irish cuisine. There's little innovation involved: it's more a confident return to tradition. Simplicity is the watchword, and the finest local ingredients the inspiration.

CULINARY CAPITALS DUBLIN, CORK, BELFAST **KNOWN FOR** IRISH STEW, SODA BREAD **IMPORTS** POTATOES, TEA **EXPORTS** GUINNESS, BEEF **DEVOUR** ANYTHING WITH CREAM **AVOID** TRIPE

Bewley's
Bewley's

Colourful houses on a misty day in Bantry.

OLIVER STREWE / GETTY IMAGES

CULTURE

The first farmers, the basic genetic stock of the Irish, were Stone Age settlers who arrived in Ireland around 4000 BC. They provided the foundation for the country's culture and agricultural economy, clearing vast tracts of forests in order to grow crops and raise animals.

Perhaps the most important introduction into Ireland was that of the potato, apparently planted in Walter Raleigh's garden in Youghal, around 1585. By the 17th century, Ireland had a mish-mash of culinary traditions left by foreign invaders. Those with power and position enjoyed a wealth of riches including meats, dairy produce, orchard fruits and whiskey. Meanwhile the peasant classes – most of the people on the island – still existed on a diet largely unchanged since medieval times. Dairy produce, or 'white meat' as it was known, was vital to their survival.

Once the Irish scrambled to become 'modern' but now – as a young, thriving nation – it can afford to be introspective once again. Thoroughly European and with nothing to prove, the people are returning to their traditions. This pride can be seen on the table better than in any other part of Irish life.

ETIQUETTE

Conviviality is the most important condiment at the Irish table. Meal times are about taking the load off your feet, relaxing and enjoying the company of your fellow diners. There is very little prescribed or restrictive etiquette. In fact, the only behaviour likely to cause offence could be your own haughtiness. The Irish will happily dismiss any *faux pas* but if they think you have ideas above your station, they'll gleefully bring you back down to earth. As long as you bring warmth, good cheer and a friendly word, you'll be welcome at any Irish table.

ESSENTIAL PRODUCE

Potatoes

Even today, potatoes feature in at least one daily meal, and the average person eats a whopping 140 kg of them annually.

- Many of Ireland's most famous dishes call for, or assume, the inclusion of potatoes. Irish stew would be soup without them, and bacon & cabbage minus the potatoes just wouldn't do.
- In spring, signs advertise 'New Potatoes' all over the place, and people talking excitedly about them, cursing the last season and handling the new tubers like precious stones.
- You would think that, of all places, the land most closely associated with the spud would have the best range and highest quality in the world. But there are surprisingly few varieties, the most popular being *Kerr's Pinks, Records, King Edwards* and *Golden Wonders*.
- Such is the demand in Ireland, that even though the country produces half a million tonnes of tubers a year, they actually import them – mainly from Italy and Cyprus – between seasons.

Vegetables

With the revival of interest in Irish cuisine, a new generation of cooks is unlocking the potential of fresh veggies. You'll still find vegetable mush served up at times, but also crunchy, crispy and tender garden delights such as glazed carrots, buttered leeks and cabbage, cauliflower drenched in a tangy cheese sauce, baked parsnips, and asparagus with hollandaise sauce.

Depending on the season you can get excellent local produce. If you are driving around the country, keep an eye out for hand-written road signs announcing fresh fruit and vegetables for

A large white pig in a field in County Cork.

Freshly-picked carrots in a basket.

A handful of *Kerr's Pinks* potatoes.

sale. Buying at source is the best opportunity to get the freshest, particularly berries, and a pit-stop could turn into a culinary adventure.

Pork, Ham & Bacon

The pig is the only farm animal native to Ireland and has been vital to the Irish diet since the Middle Ages when the prime cuts were reserved for the local nobility while the riff-raff fought over the scraps. Hardly surprising then that sausages, puddings and other assorted by-products of pork became popular very early on and continue as Irish staples today.

The leg of the pig is known as ham, and everything else is called bacon. Large hams are particularly popular at Christmas to complement the traditional turkey, but all types of bacon are eaten year-round. Cooked ham is hugely popular as the base filling for the ubiquitous sandwich, often accompanied by little more than a slice of cheese or a spread of mustard.

Another traditional pigmeat is the *crubeen* (pig's trotter) which used to be eaten with soda bread or in pubs.

Beef

Tripe, from the stomach tissue of slaughtered cattle, used to be a popular Saturday night dish because it was good for absorbing alcohol. It is still quite common and available throughout the country.

More palatable beef preparations you're likely to come across include Gaelic steaks (fried beef steaks with a shot of whiskey added to the juice), spiced beef (a traditional preparation especially popular around Christmas) corned beef, beef & Guinness stew, the timeless shepherd's pie (which, despite its name, is always made with beef in Ireland), steak and onions, and the Sunday institution, roast beef.

A fishing boat moored at Ballycotton in County Cork.

Lamb

Lamb remains one of the few truly seasonal foods in Ireland. Lamb is at its best in summer when it has fed on plenty of grass but still retains its tenderness. From autumn, the meat tends to be tougher but it has a more full-bodied taste. In late summer, look out for Mountain Lamb from Connemara and Kerry. Unlike its lowland cousins, this lamb roughs it on hilly, rocky regions and feeds on the heather and rough grasses which grow there. The result is a sweeter, even more distinct and delicious lamb.

Fish

Much of the fish available is farmed and the difference in taste and texture between wild and farmed fish will have you reaching for your rod. But there are still treats to be had without having to play with worms.

- Kippers, herring which has been split, cured and smoked are widely used for brekkie and as starters.
- Salmon, especially smoked, is one of the delicacies most associated with Ireland and has been the delight of visiting gourmets and anglers for centuries.

Dairy

Unless you come from a climate similar to Ireland's you'll hardly recognise the range of dairy produce, all of which has a fullness and richness of flavour that is unsurpassed. This is thanks largely to the oft-cursed rainfall which gives Irish cattle a plentiful supply of healthy grass.

- Milk — still one of the most popular meal-time drinks, and Ireland's favourite cow, the familiar black and white Friesian, is the breed responsible. Around Cork and Kerry, be sure to sample the local produce

A leg of lamb studded with rosemary and ready to be roasted.

Cashel Blue made in County Tipperary.

Olive oil loaf and wheaten bread.

as it has an unparalleled richness. Munster is the emporium of Ireland's dairying tradition and Cork was established in the 19th century as the centre for the export of dairy produce.

- Cream — Irish cream is a treat to behold. Rich, thick, luscious and full of flavour, it will probably be unlike any other cream you've tasted before. It comes almost exclusively in one grade with a fat content of 40%.
- Butter — Irish people eat a lot of butter and they produce more than eight times what they use. The distinctive gold foil of *Kerrygold* butter can be found in supermarkets all over the world, shining like a beacon to Irish ex-pats longing for the natural flavour of their homeland. Such mild creamery butters are the most common, but there are also some sublime country, or farmhouse, varieties available from small specialist producers.
- Cheese — A current revival in cheesemaking is being sustained by a reputation for a distinctive style, quality and taste in Irish farmhouse cheeses. Producers are dotted around the country but located particularly in the lush dairy lands of the midlands, and the Atlantic coast of Cork and Kerry.

Bread

There are still some excellent traditional-recipe breads made around the country, most notably in Belfast where soda breads, farls and scones have remained as staples.

The most famous Irish bread, and unquestionably one of the tastes of Ireland, is soda bread. Because Irish flour is so soft it doesn't take well to yeast as a raising agent. In the 19th century, bread soda (bicarbonate of soda) was introduced for leavening bread, and combined with buttermilk it makes a superbly light-textured and tasty bread. It was easy to make in the home; it could be mixed in minutes, baked, cut and ready to eat within an hour. It was the perfect match to Ireland's hearth cooking and was made in a cast-iron pot, known in Ireland as a pot stove. The pot stove would be covered and buried in the fire, where it was turned regularly to ensure that the heat was evenly distributed.

DEFINING DISHES

Black Pudding

Black pudding is a traditional Irish food making a sensational comeback to popularity in some of the country's top kitchens. It is made, traditionally, from pig's blood, pork skin and seasonings although these days beef by-products are usually used. The most famous version, and the one given credit for the black pud gourmet revolution is from Clonakilty in Co Cork. White pudding is a version without the blood which is made from the remaining offal pieces of the pig and various cereals.

Cakes

Although bread is the cornerstone of the country's baking tradition, cooks are equally adept at knocking up cakes, scones and biscuits. The Irish like nothing better than sitting down for a cup of tea, a natter and something sweet (perhaps to counter their ribald exchanges). Traditionally, Mums would always have scones, buns or cakes on hand to accommodate unexpected guests. Those with time, and the knack for baking, maintain this tradition and you'll be regaled with a range of baked goodies: rich fruit cakes, dusty scones, a bewildering array of seed cakes, fruit tarts or pies (rhubarb, apple, pear, blackberry), shortbread (adopted from Scotland), whiskey cakes, fluffy sponge cakes and virtually any kind of treat which can hold luscious Irish cream.

Tea and biscuits at Assolas Country House.

A basket of fruit scones at Ballymoc House.

A pear tart in preparation.

The Traditional Irish Breakfast

Perhaps the most feared Irish speciality is the traditional fry of bacon, sausages, black pudding and eggs that is the second part of every B&B deal in the country. In spite of the hysterical health fears, the fry is still one of the most common meals in the country. While time constraints mean it's not eaten daily, it is a weekend luxury for most people, particularly as an accompaniment to the Sunday newspapers and a hangover.

The fry can be eaten at any time of the day, and is often even served as the main meal with, maybe, a lamb chop added to make it more substantial, as if that were necessary. Leftover potatoes can also be sliced and added – that is, if you can stomach any more spuds.

Irish Stew

The composition of this one-pot wonder is a matter of passionate, and almost comical, debate between purists. Most say it was originally made with mutton which was the only meat available year-round. Others, particularly in the North, used spare pork ribs in their Irish stew. Beef was also included and noted historians say kid was the original meat. Potato is a given, but carrot is the vegetable of contention. Many kitchens add it for colour and extra flavour while the purists baulk at the idea, saying it spoils the simple flavour of the dish. What is certain is that it was originally a peasant dish, made up of whatever ingredients were readily available.

DRINKS

Drinking in Ireland is much more than a social activity: it's the foundation on which the culture is built. This explains why, through centuries of poverty and oppression, the Irish have retained a reputation for hospitality and good humour.

OLIVER STREWE / GETTY IMAGES

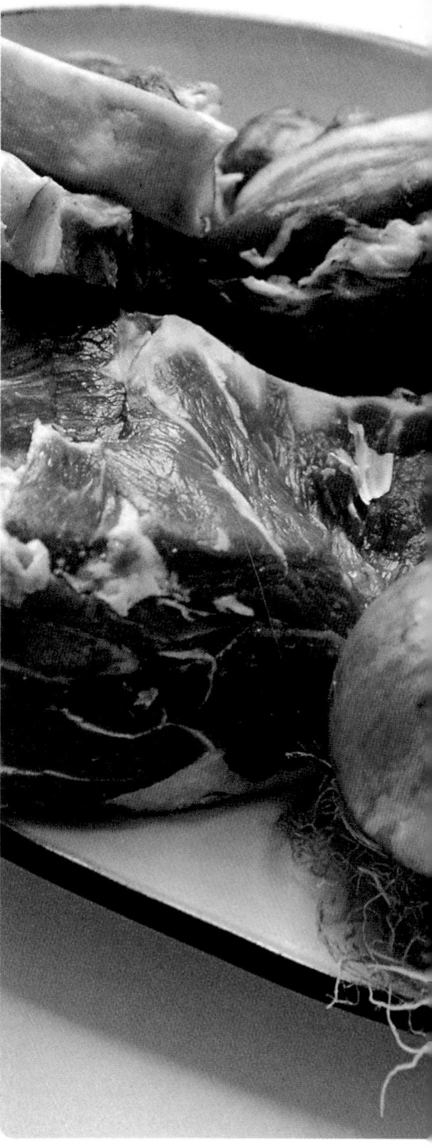

Ingredients for Irish stew.

Tea

When it comes to refreshment, tea is king. Predictably, the Irish drink more of it, per capita, than any other nation in the world. Over 10,000 tonnes of leaf are imported each year which works out to an average of almost four cups of tea a day for every man, woman and child.

The drinking and sharing of tea is inextricably linked with Irish sociability and it is the first expression of hospitality. As soon as you cross the threshold of any Irish home, once initial introductions have been exchanged, you'll be offered tea. It's about sharing, accepting and getting to know one another.

Whiskey

There are almost 100 different types of Irish whiskey. If you're in an Irish family's home outside of Ireland you could well be offered Jameson, the most popular Irish whiskey in the world. If you're in Ireland it could be Powers Gold Label, the choice of the nation. But if you're in Munster, it will probably be Paddy and if Ulster is your oyster then it will definitely be Bushmills.

Stout

Of all of Ireland's drinks, the 'black stuff' is surely the most celebrated. Even though there are two other major stout producers in Ireland, the Guinness name has become synonymous with the drink.

As Irish pubs are the focus of the country's social existence, stout is the fuel that drives it. Unlike whiskey, stout has always been a sociable drink, to be enjoyed with company in a pub and very rarely drunk at home.

Stout, the drink and the word, embodies something of the Irish spirit; confident, strong and resilient. Guinness itself is quintessentially Dublin, reflecting the vigour and verve of the capital. Brewed in Ireland since the 18th century, it is now one of

A big cold beer in Shanagarry, County Cork.

The Guinness factory in Dublin.

A bottle of whiskey distilled in Ireland.

the world's favourite drinks. More people would know the black emblem with the golden harp than the tricolour of Ireland's national flag. Guinness is drunk in 150 countries and counting, it is brewed all over the world from Australia to Nigeria, and an estimated four million pints of it are consumed every day.

Liqueurs

After whiskey and stout, Ireland's next greatest alcoholic achievement is their range of liqueurs.

Baileys was the original Irish Cream Liqueur and, even though it has only been produced since the early 1970s, it is a great ambassador for Irish booze as it's the world's leading cream liqueur. Carolans, its main rival, has been making a very similar product, with honey, since the late 1970s. Most pubs will stock both. They are the perfect way to round off a meal or a night out and, contrary to widespread perception, you can get drunk on the stuff. They are 17% proof, and must be drunk on the rocks.

Hot Toddy

Even the worst case of the sniffles won't deter Irish people from drinking. When they feel the hint of a cold coming on, they reach for a hot toddy. Simply put, it's a combination of boiling water, cloves, a teaspoon of sugar (optional), lemon and whiskey. It works! It warms you up, clears congestion and keeps the worst cold symptoms at bay until you leave the pub.

Irish Coffee. Stories of origination abound but the most common one credits Joe Sheridan, a barman at Shannon airport, with the creation of Irish Coffee in the 1940s. Landing in the bracing cold, shivering passengers used to approach Sheridan looking for an alcoholic drink and something warming. He hit upon the winning blend of Irish whiskey and piping hot coffee, topped with rich cream. It was just the trick then, and still is today.

Trout cooking on an outdoor fire.

PHILIP LEE HARVEY / GETTY IMAGES

Sweden

Sweden has come a long way from its days of all-beige fish and potato platters. Immigration has introduced fresh flavours to the meatballs-and-mash menu, while a new wave of young chefs has been experimenting with traditional ingredients and time-honoured local techniques. The result is the much-fêted New Nordic cuisine, with a passion for the homegrown and the seasonal that takes Swedish cuisine to an acclaimed new level.

CULINARY CAPITAL STOCKHOLM **KNOWN FOR** MEATBALLS **IMPORTS** MEDITERRANEAN INFLUENCES **EXPORTS** VODKA **DEVOUR** *KANELBULLAR* (CINNAMON BUNS) **AVOID** *SURSTRÖMMING* (CANNED HERRING)

Cooked crayfish, bounty from the Swedish seas.

Meatballs with potatoes and lingonberries.

Moose meat sizzling on a grill.

CULTURE

Seafood and meat (including game) form the core of the typical Swedish menu, along with the ever-present potato. The term *husmanskost* is used to describe a sort of everyman's cuisine: basic, unpretentious and traditional. The most famous example of this is, of course, Swedish meatballs. Other classic *husmanskost* dishes include pickled and fried herring, *gravadlax* (cured salmon) and *pytt i panna* (a potato hash).

While new-school Swedish nosh thrives on experimentation, it also retains firm roots in Sweden's culinary heritage. Even the most avant-garde chefs admire simple, old-school *husmanskost*, and many seek to acknowledge its influence while putting an innovative twist on it.

Traditional food-preserving techniques (curing, smoking and pickling, for example) have found favour in the kitchens of New Nordic chefs. The prevalence of preserved grub harks back to a time when Swedes had little choice but to store their spring and summer harvests and hunting prizes for the long icy winter.

REGIONS

With a north-south expanse covering more than 1500 kilometres, latitude and climate have played a key role in regional flavours.

- The north — Methods of preserving food (drying, salting, smoking) take some cues from the indigenous reindeer-herding people of the Arctic north, known as the Sami.
- The coast — The country's lengthy coastline provides an abundance of treasure, especially dotted along the southwest coast, around Sweden's second city of Gothenburg. Here, the shellfish (oysters and mussels) are first-class, as are the shrimp and crayfish.

- *The south* — Sweden's southernmost region, Skåne, has a milder climate and fertile, black-soil fields. It's often dubbed 'Sweden's larder'. Apples, asparagus and new potatoes are harvested here; wine production is a surprising recent addition.
- *Gotland* — The island of Gotland is home to food producers heading in new directions. The Burgundy (black) truffles harvested here now grace menus throughout northern Europe, and visitors can join a truffle hunt in October and November.

Frying new potatoes at the 'Potato Day' festival.

FEASTS

Midsummer's Eve

The biggest party of the Swedish calendar, Midsummer starts on the first Friday after 21 June, with Midsummer's Eve marked by the raising of the maypole, followed by lots of singing and dancing. A typical Midsummer menu features pickled herring alongside boiled new potatoes with fresh dill and sour cream. The traditional accompaniment is a cold beer and aquavit. Dessert is the first strawberries of summer, served with cream.

Kräftskivor

Swedes celebrate (or mourn) the end of summer with *kräftskivor* (crayfish parties), where folks wear bibs and party hats while eating buckets of crayfish and drinking aquavit (and singing drinking songs). Similar parties take place in parts of the country with *surströmming* or eel, but the drinking element remains consistent.

Julbord

Christmas cranks out the *julbord*, a particularly gluttonous version of the *smörgåsbord*. Added to the usual delicacies are

Pieces of pickled herring.

Midsummer's Eve celebrations include dancing around the Maypole on Aspo Island.

seasonal gems like baked ham with mustard sauce. *Julmust*, a sweet dark-brown soft drink, and *glögg,* warm spiced wine, are also Yuletide staples. The best accompaniment to a warm cup of *glögg*, available at kiosks everywhere in winter, is a *pepparkaka* (gingerbread biscuit).

ETIQUETTE

Generally speaking, for Swedes, dining is ritualised and taken quite seriously, even down to the afternoon coffee break *(fika)*. Food is often considered a celebration of the traditions that hold Swedish society together.

Toasting (saying *'skål'*) is something of a formal ritual, too. Don't take a drink until your host has given a toast. When toasting, make eye contact before sipping (wine) or gulping (aquavit), then nod to others before putting your glass down.

DAILY MEALS

Breakfast for locals is a simple affair along the lines of coffee and muesli, but hotel buffets will go the whole hog: various types of bread plus traditional *pålägg* (toppings), stretching from cheese to sliced meat, pickled herring and Kalles caviar (an iconic caviar spread in a tube).

A hearty lunch has long been a mainstay of the workforce, with cafes and restaurants serving a weekday, fixed-price lunch special called *dagens rätt*. It's one of the cheapest ways to sample quality Swedish cooking. The *dagens rätt* usually includes a main course, salad, bread, cold drink and coffee.

ESSENTIAL PRODUCE

The 3200 kilometre-long coastline and clear, cold waters make for an abundance of high-quality fish and seafood. Wild game forms a large part of Swedish cuisine, particularly in the

LEHNER / GETTY IMAGES

Classically Swedish: smoked salmon and *gravadlax* served on rye bread with dill and a squeeze of lime.

country's north. Traditional Sami cooking relies heavily on reindeer; elk (moose) is also quite common.

Fresh, richly flavoured berries are the signature taste of Sweden's short, intense summers. Blueberries, wild strawberries, cloudberries, lingonberries, rowanberries and elderberries are among the varieties foraged in forests and fields. In autumn, foragers turn their attentions to wild mushrooms.

If you follow the lead set by locals, you'll be rewarded with some surprisingly good flavour combinations. Lingonberries and cloudberries add flavor to a number of Swedish savoury dishes. Horseradish and dill are key enhancers, too. Pairings of food and beverage are important: there's no crayfish without singing and aquavit; no *sill* (pickled herring) without strong cheese and ale; there's no coffee without cake — or, heaven forbid, vice versa.

DEFINING DISHES

Gravadlax

Gravadlax (or *gravlax*) is salmon cured with a dry rub of salt, sugar and dill. It is usually served as an appetiser, thinly sliced and accompanied by a dill and mustard sauce, either with crispbread, rye bread or boiled potatoes.

Kanelbullar

The most ubiquitous sweet treats are *kanelbullar* (cinnamon buns). Several bakeries and cafes offer slight variations, lacing the bun with anything from chocolate to crushed pistachios. Soft and doughy at their best, they're a popular staple for *fika*, the Swedes' adored coffee-break ritual.

Meatballs

A certain flatpack-furniture giant may have helped popularise Swedish *köttbullar*, but every Swedish family has its own

Cardamom buns for sale at the market.

Chanterelles are found in Swedish forests.

A bowl of Baltic herring.

recipe. There are generally a few consistent rules: the meat is ground beef (sometimes mixed with pork and veal), flavoured with allspice and blended with milk-soaked breadcrumbs (giving the balls a soft consistency). The meatballs are generally small in size, and eaten with boiled potatoes, creamy brown sauce and lingonberry jam.

Pytt i panna

Classic *husmanskost* includes *pytt i panna* (literally 'small pieces in a pan'), a potato hash that includes onion and diced meats (ham, sausage, bacon), topped with sliced beets and a fried egg — it's the king of Swedish comfort food. The dish is often abbreviated to *pytt* and occasionally called '*hänt i veckan*' ('happened this past week'), reflecting its origin as a dish made with leftovers. These days, however, *pytt* is such an institution that you can buy pre-cubed meat and potatoes from the supermarket.

Surströmming

Surströmming is a canned, fermented Baltic herring traditionally eaten in August and September. It is served in *tunnbröd* (soft unleavened bread like a tortilla) with boiled potatoes and onions, all washed down with aquavit. It's so pungent it's usually eaten outdoors. It's an acquired taste, sure, but it does have a legion of hardcore fans, mostly in northern Sweden.

Smörgåsbord

The best way to explore the flavours of Swedish cuisine, from the sublime to the ridiculous, is to partake in a traditional *smörgåsbord*.

The *smörgåsbord* (from the words *smörgås*, meaning sandwich, and *bord*, meaning table) stems from 18th-century traditions. It became internationally known at the 1939

NICHOLAS PITT / GETTY IMAGES

Fried herring, new potatoes and lingonberry sauce.

New York World's Fair, and the waistbands of overexcited diners have been groaning ever since.

All-you-can-eat buffets are a bastardised form of the true *smörgåsbord*, and to better understand the latter, it's handy to know about Swedish concepts like *ordning och reda* (tidiness, good order), and *lagom* (meaning 'just right', neither too much nor too little, everything in moderation). For successful *smörgåsbord* navigation:

- Start with the herring dishes, accompanied by boiled potatoes, crispbread and sharp cheese, and washed down with an aquavit.
- Grab a clean plate and move on to the more substantial fare — the *gravadlax*, eel, smoked salmon, salads, egg dishes and *charcuterie*.
- Clean plate again, and it's on to the hot dishes: meatballs, spare ribs, roast beef and *Janssons frestelse* (Jansson's temptation), a rich potato-and-onion casserole loaded with cream and anchovies.
- Finally, leave space for cheese, fruit and sweets.

DRINKS

- Coffee is the unofficial national drink, seemingly drunk in gallons during *fika*.
- Sweden's trademark spirit is *brännvin*, of which Absolut Vodka is the most recognisable example.

Aquavit is distilled from potato or grain, and spiced with caraway and other flavours like dill, anise, fennel, coriander and cardamom. It's usually downed in one gulp from a shot glass, and considered essential at festive gatherings to wash down the likes of pickled herring and crayfish.

Pavement bars and cafes in the city of Bergen.

PETER ADAMS / GETTY IMAGES

Norway

Norway is the quiet achiever of the Scandinavian cohort. Sitting pretty at the very top of Europe, Norway has magnificent mountains and *fjords*, and basks in its enviable living standards and oil-generated wealth. In northern climes, where the winter night may last for months on end and the summer sun barely sets, the seasons wholly dictate what's for dinner.

CULINARY CAPITALS OSLO, BERGEN **KNOWN FOR** REINDEER **IMPORTS** PIZZA **EXPORTS** SALMON, COD, JARLSBERG CHEESE **DEVOUR** CLOUDBERRIES WITH CREAM **AVOID** *LUTEFISK* (JELLIED DRIED COD)

ENHJØRNINGEN
SJØBODEN

Fish from Norway's plentiful waters hanging out to dry.

Cherries.

Basket of *krumkake*.

CULTURE

Mainland Norway covers a north-south range of over 2500 kilometres. Its elongated shape and fjord-riven coast results in one of the world's longest and most rugged coastlines, measuring some 25,000 kilometres. Add to this an estimated 50,000 offshore islands and you will understand why Norway has an age-old fishing tradition and celebrates vast seafood riches.

A large portion of the country lies above the Arctic Circle, including the subpolar archipelago of Svalbard. Food at these latitudes was once about simple subsistence: any animal in the vicinity was fair game, and every skerrick of the beast was put to good use (meat, hide, oil, bones). Traditional preserving techniques saw the bounty stretched to cover lean times.

Over time, agriculture and farming have seen the menu broaden, but there's still a strong tradition of simple foodstuffs sourced from the sea, the forest and the lake. There is little room for sentimentality about eating from the top of the food chain, hence the appearance of whale and seal on Norwegian menus.

Still, it's often claimed (and backed up by authoritative research surveys) that Pizza Grandiosa, a brand of frozen pizza, is in fact Norway's national dish. More than 20 million units of Grandiosa pizza are eaten each year, by a population of 4.7 million!

FEASTS

The star dish of Christmas dinner (celebrated on Christmas Eve) varies by region. *Ribbe* is a clear national favourite — it's roasted pork belly, accompanied by *sauerkraut* and boiled potatoes. *Pinnekjøtt* is the Yuletide dish of choice on the west coast; these cured and sometimes smoked mutton ribs are steamed for several hours, traditionally on a bed of birch sticks (hence the name, which translates as 'stick meat'). It's paired with mashed swede and potatoes.

You'll invariably find *lutefisk* (jellied dried cod), *rømmegrøt* (a rich porridge) and a cornucopia of sweet biscuits: tradition dictates that seven different kinds of Christmas cookies *(småkaker)* should grace the festive table.

The almost-universal Christmas drink is *gløgg*, or mulled wine, that blends raisins, almonds, ginger, cloves, cardamom and other spices. Aquavit helps keep the mood elevated.

ESSENTIAL PRODUCE

Fishing and aquaculture (fish farming) are the foundation of Norway's coastal economy. In fact, the country is the world's second-largest exporter of fish (after China).

Needless to say, fish and seafood here are outstanding. Fish grow more slowly in cold water and their flesh develops a firmer structure, with more flavour than fish in warmer waters. Salmon *(laks)* remains blissfully cheap in this notoriously expensive country. Other local freshwater specialities include brown trout (only in the south), perch and Arctic char; ocean fish include cod (*torsk* or *bacalao*; often dried), herring, haddock and mackerel. Shrimp, lobster and crab are also harvested.

Roast reindeer meat is one of the tastier local ruminants; elk is also popular.

Long summer days provide perfect, flavour-enhancing growing conditions for the country's main fruit-growing region, around splendid Hardangerfjord, near Bergen. Strawberries, plums, cherries, apples and other orchard fruits proliferate.

Eat this... ***Gudbrandsdalsost*** is a brown cheese made from the whey derived from goat's milk or cow's milk. It has a slightly sweet flavour and is traditionally cut into wafer-thin slices and eaten on bread or crispbread for breakfast.

Fish hanging out to dry.

A board of traditional cheeses.

Blue mug full of *molter*, or cloudberries.

DEFINING DISHES

Fårikål

When a dish has its own national day (the last Thursday of September), you know it's cemented a spot in local lore. September is the month when Norwegian farmers bring their sheep down from summer grazing pastures, and this simple casserole of mutton and cabbage stewed with whole peppercorns is a favourite autumn treat. It is traditionally served with boiled new potatoes, lingonberry sauce and crispy flatbread.

Fiskesuppe

It's no surprise to find fish prepared a hundred ways in Norway — *fiskeboller* (fish balls) and *fiskegrateng* (fish au gratin, usually made with any leftover white fish, macaroni and *béchamel* sauce) are beloved, as are fish soups, and there are countless recipes. One of the soup classics originates from Bergen: it's a velvety mix of cream, fish (haddock, halibut, cod, sometimes salmon), potato and julienned root vegetables.

Lutefisk

Pungent *lutefisk* is dried cod made almost gelatinous by soaking it in lye solution. This 'fish jello' remains inexplicably popular among the Norwegian communities of North America, and is enjoying greater popularity at home. *Lutefisk* is usually enjoyed around Christmas time, served with plenty of butter, plus *lefse* (flatbread) and side dishes of bacon, mushy peas and potatoes.

Rømmegrøt

A beloved local delicacy, rustic *rømmegrøt* is a rich, smooth porridge made slightly tangy from the use of natural sour cream. It's sprinkled with sugar and cinnamon and features an 'eye' of butter dolloped in the centre of the bowl.

YVETTE CARDOZO / GETTY IMAGES

A pretty bowl of soup served in a Bergen restaurant.

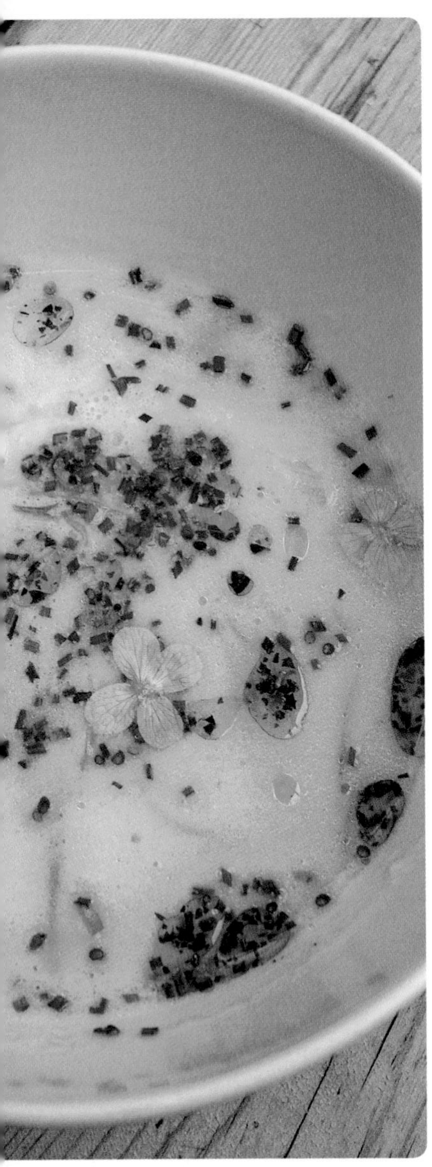

Multekrem

The quintessential Norwegian dessert, *multekrem* is made from cloudberries and whipped cream.

- Amber-coloured *molter* (cloudberries) look like raspberries, taste musky and exotic, and are nicknamed 'highland gold'. These fruits are highly prized and considered a delicacy.
- They're difficult to cultivate and are ripe for picking for only a few weeks of the year (from about mid-July). They grow one per stalk on open swampy ground and withstand temperatures as low as -40°C.
- As their season is so short it is most common to find cloudberries in jam or compote form (which can then be used for a dish such as *multekrem*).
- *Multekrem* is traditionally served with *krumkake* (conical waffle cookies) at Christmas.

DRINKS

In a list of per-capita coffee consumption, Nordic nations take five of the top six spots. Finns top the table, with the Norwegians in second place: they down a hefty 9.9 kilograms per person per year.

The national spirit is aquavit (or *akevitt*), a potent dose of Norwegian culture distilled from potatoes and flavoured with caraway. Perhaps the most esteemed version is Linie Aquavit. The *linie* (line) of the name refers to the equator, because each barrel is shipped around the world, from Norway to Australia and back. The makers claim that the perpetual rolling, the ocean air, and the changes in temperature and humidity all go toward improving the taste. Bottles of Linie Aquavit bear the name of the ship involved, its route and the amount of time the barrels have aged at sea.

MICHAEL TALALAEV / GETTY IMAGES

Aamanns, herring board.

Denmark

Interesting things are afoot in Danish kitchens, not least the culinary movement that's got the food world raving: New Nordic cuisine. Born in Copenhagen, this style of cuisine passionately embraces local and seasonal produce. In the last decade, the Danish capital has been transformed into a dining dynamo.

CULINARY CAPITAL COPENHAGEN **KNOWN FOR** DANISH PASTRY **IMPORTS** MEDITERRANEAN AND ASIAN INFLUENCES **EXPORTS** BACON, BEER, BUTTER **DEVOUR** HOT DOGS **AVOID** PICKLED HERRING IN CURRY SAUCE

Evening dining by the canal in Nyhavn.

Seafood with white asparagus and shrimps.

AMIEL JEAN-CLAUDE / GETTY IMAGES

Gourmet hot dogs in the Danish capital.

CULTURE

Chief responsibility for the spotlight now shining Copenhagen's way lies with the city's young chefs, many of whom have apprenticed with some of the most influential chefs in the world.

These young guns have taken their experience and combined it with a passion for Denmark's raw ingredients — its excellent pork products, game, seafood, root vegetables and wild berries — and a reverence for the seasons. They have then cast their net wider, to encompass ingredients from the whole Nordic region — produce that is unique to, or thrives in, the often-extreme Nordic climates, landscapes and waters.

Modest, often-overlooked ingredients such as pulses and grains are being rediscovered, and food historians consulted. Foraging in the wilderness for herbs and plants is also popular. Ingredients are skillfully prepared using traditional techniques (curing, smoking, pickling and preserving) alongside contemporary experimentation.

But, for all the excitement over New Nordic cuisine, it would be misleading to suggest that the entire Danish nation is in the grip of a fervent foodie revolution. It isn't. Rather, things are changing slowly but surely, as is the Danish way.

To sample local flavours, in coastal areas look for a traditional *røgeri* (smokehouse), where you can buy inexpensive seafood. Classic Danish home cooking can be found in a traditional *kro* (inn), while a *bageri* (bakery) is a sure bet for quality bread and pastries.

FEASTS

The Danes do Christmas *(jul)* with an abundance of their trademark *hygge* (cosiness) — candles, festive decorations and twinkling lights hold the wintry darkness at bay. The biggest festivities are on Christmas Eve where the centrepiece of the traditional dinner is roast duck or goose, served with red cabbage and potatoes. On 25 December, the leftovers make for an excellent buffet-style *koldt bord* lunch (*koldt bord* literally means cold table).

Another Christmas Eve tradition is rice pudding. Hidden inside the pudding is a single whole almond, and the person who finds the almond in their bowl gets a prize.

Traditional Christmas sweets include *brunekager* and *pebernødder* (two types of spice cookies) and *klejner* (deep-fried knotted dough). *Æbleskiver* are small, spherical pancakes which are traditionally served with *gløgg* (mulled wine) in the lead-up to Christmas.

ESSENTIAL PRODUCE

Danes love to get some pork on their fork — they consume more pork than any other nation, in the form of *leverpostej* (liver pâté), *frikadeller* (meatballs) and various incarnations of roast pork and pork chops. Danish bacon is a major export item, as is Danish butter, particularly the iconic brand Lurpak, both of which delight tastebuds while threatening to harden the arteries further.

With so much coastline, fish and seafood play a vital role in the local cuisine. Herring *(sild)* is a staple; salmon *(laks)* is common. The Danes are great fish-smokers; you'll find smokehouses preserving herring, eel, shrimp and other seafood around the country's coast. The most renowned are on the island of Bornholm.

The dense, fibre-rich dark rye bread *(rugbrød)* is beloved, and forms an essential component of the Danish open sandwich, or *smørrebrød*. Root vegetables are ubiquitous (hello potatoes), while fresh berries in abundance herald the welcome arrival of summer.

Pastries for sale at LagKagehuset.

Roast pig at Horsens Middelalder Festival.

Rye bread with jams on a cutting board.

DEFINING DISHES

Danish pastries

In Denmark the sweet pastry known elsewhere in the world as a 'Danish pastry' is called *wienerbrød* ('Viennese bread', ironically), and nearly every second street corner has a bakery *(bageri)* with oodles of varieties. As legend has it, the naming of the pastry can be traced to a Danish baker who moved to Austria in the 18th century, where he perfected these treats of flaky, butter-laden pastry. True to their collective sweet tooth, Danes eat them for breakfast.

Flæskesteg

The Danish version of roast pork could easily qualify as the national dish. It always comes with a fine layer of salty crackling, and is traditionally served with *rødkål* (red cabbage) and *brunede kartofler* (boiled new potatoes caramelised in butter and sugar). *Flæskesteg* with *rødkål* makes for a fine *smørrebrød* topping, too.

Hot dogs

The Danes' favourite fast food is a *pølse* (hot dog) from one of the *pølsevogne* (sausage wagons) dotted around town, all churning out precisely the same frankfurters, buns and dressings. Late at night, after a couple of beers, a hot dog covered with fake mustard and ketchup can be damned hard to resist (the Danes eat more than 135 million of them annually).

Rødgrød med fløde

For a lesson in how you will never pronounce Danish words like a Dane, ask a native to pronounce *rødgrød med fløde*, then you try it yourself. Yes, it's unpronounceable, but it's also delicious — it's a traditional summertime dessert of stewed red berries with cream.

JOHNER IMAGES / GETTY IMAGES

Delicious Danish pastries.

Smørrebrød

Sushi and sandwiches have changed the way Danes snack just as they have everywhere else in the Western world, but the locals still hold a place in their heart for the traditional lunchtime Danish open sandwich, or *smørrebrød*.

The basic *smørrebrød* is a slice of bread (usually rye) topped, for example, with roast beef, tiny shrimps, pickled herring, liver pâté, or fried fish fillet, and finished with a variety of garnishes (the final sculptured product often looks too good to eat). In the laws of *smørrebrød*, smoked salmon is always served on white bread, herring on rye bread.

Smørrebrød is served in many restaurants and cafes at lunchtime, although it's cheapest in bakeries or specialised *smørrebrød* takeaway shops found near train stations and office buildings.

DRINKS

Danes are prodigious producers and consumers of beer. Carlsberg Breweries, based in Copenhagen, markets the Carlsberg and Tuborg labels and is one of the world's largest breweries. Still, in the past decade, bored with the liquid diet from the major producers, Danes have developed a growing taste for microbrews and craft beers. There is also a fledgling wine industry.

The most popular spirit is the Aalborg-produced aquavit *(akvavit)*. There are several dozen types, the most common of which is made from potatoes ad spiced with caraway. In Denmark aquavit is swallowed straight down as a shot, usually followed by a chaser of beer. Be sure to make eye contact with everyone during a toast: *'skål'* is the word for 'cheers'.

Bratwurst sausage with mustard on a roll.

THOMAS WINZ / GETTY IMAGES

Germany

German food is a tale of need and excess. It is comfort cuisine, born of cold winters and peasant kitchens. Beer and wine are a given — thrown back with gusto by appreciative diners as part of a rousing symphony of grill-crisped *bratwursts*, dumplings the size of snowballs, mountains of *sauerkraut* and dollhouse-sweet marzipan. The climax: Black Forest gateau soaked in strong cherry schnapps. '*Guten Appetit!*'

CULINARY CAPITALS BERLIN, MUNICH, FRANKFURT **KNOWN FOR** BEER, *SAUERKRAUT* **IMPORTS** DONER KEBABS **EXPORTS** *PRETZELS*, MARZIPAN **DEVOUR** BLACK FOREST GATEAU **AVOID** BRAIN SAUSAGE

Man sporting traditional hat in the Hofbraeuhaus, Munich.

Strudel for sale at the Christmas market.

Currywurst, curried sausage.

CULTURE

Germany's historic patchwork of semi-independent principalities and city states is reflected in its gastronomic culture, a melting pot of strong regional cuisines. Germanic tribes cultivated wheat and barley, and made beer — a drink deemed barbaric by the Romans, who planted vines. The Romans cultivated ivory-white asparagus (considered an aphrodisiac) and preserved vegetables in salt. They began eating pork instead of horse meat, and soaked meat in red wine to transport it to other settlements. The spice routes of the Middle Ages introduced cloves, ginger, cardamom and other exotic spices to Bavaria — the perfect excuse for Bavarians to start baking gingerbread, cinnamon stars and other sweet cookies and breads.

REGIONS

Berlin

The German capital dishes up an edgy fusion of cuisines. It offers world-class international fare, but it keeps a firm grasp on its indigenous kitchen too — cabbage and pea soups are winter classics.

- *Currywurst* (curried sausage) — Berliner exoticism: cooked pork sausage sliced and drowned in a fiery sauce of ketchup or tomato paste, paprika and curry powder. Served at fast food stalls, on a flimsy paper plate with a toothpick.
- *Eisbein* (pork knuckle) — Roasted or boiled pig's leg served with potato, sauerkraut and a purée of mushy green peas, onions and bacon.
- *Hoppelpoppel* — Posh scrambled eggs bind meat strips and potato.

Bavaria

No part of the pig is spared in the rural southeast where recipes are passed between generations and Lederhosen, beer halls and romantic castles abound. Fodder here is super hearty; a timeless antidote to the Bavarian alpine winter.

- *Leberkäse* (liver cheese) — Beef, pork, bacon and onions baked like a cake, served warm in slices on bread rolls with mustard.
- *Nödel* (dumplings) — Iconic staple ranging from potato *Kartoffelklösse* (potato dumplings) and *Leberknödel* (liver dumplings) to *Semmelknödel* (bread dumplings).
- *Nürnberg Lebkuchen* — A soft and chewy gingerbread with nuts, fruit peel and honey.
- *Schweinebraten* (pork roast) — Bubbling meat juices and crackling of unmatched crispness are features of this family dish, served with red cabbage and bread dumplings.
- *Schweinshax'n* (pork knuckle) — Another roast with crispy skin and meat so tender it falls off the bone.

Lebkuchen, gingerbread-style cakes.

Stuttgart and the Black Forest

Nestled in the country's bucolic southwest crook, cuisine here is as rich and earthy as its forested source. Crystal-clear streams brim with brook trout *(Bachforelle)* and dairy cows graze on pastures woven between rolling hills and deep valleys. Asparagus *(Spargel)* is harvested in April and autumn celebrates the grape harvest on sloped vineyards around Stuttgart.

- *Spätzle* — Swabian pasta: these egg-based noodles are served with cheese as a main or served plain as a side dish to meat and fish.

Swabian grilled noodles.

Al fresco dining at Staufenberg castle.

- *Maultaschen* — Ravioli stuffed with wild garlic, ground meat, onion and spinach.
- *Schwarzwälderschinken* — Dry-cured ham with a smoky aroma.

Frankfurt and Southern Rhineland

Moving north to Saarland, food becomes spicier. France is not far away and fried goose liver, *cordon bleu* and *coq au vin* are common. The hilly banks of the Rhine and Moselle rivers are synonymous with grapes, and wine inevitably ends up being used in the kitchen.

The countryside around Frankfurt, city of modern skyscrapers and old apple-wine taverns, produces outstanding cured hams traditionally smoked over juniper berries.

- *Rheinischer Sauerbraten* — Beef marinated in sweet and sour vinegar, then braised.
- *Saumagen* — Stuffed pork belly, faintly like Scottish *haggis*.
- *Sulperknochen* — Piggy trotters, ears and tails.

Hamburg and the North

North Germany's seafaring fare finds culinary inspiration in the Baltic and North Seas. Towards Scandinavia, Nordic staples like rollmops and herring (raw, smoked, pickled or rolled in sour cream) woo gourmets. Mecklenburg-Western Pomerania has a penchant for sweet and sour.

- *Grünkohl* (kale) is a natural winter staple here — the leafy green vegetable thrives on frost.
- *Labskaus* — Minced salt herring, corned beef, pig lard, potato and beetroot from Hamburg, served with gherkins and a fried egg.

Labskaus with fried egg and gherkin.

- *Grünkohl mit Pinkel* — Combines steamed kale with pork belly, bacon and *Pinkelwurst* (a spicy pork, beef, oat and onion sausage from Bremen).
- *Aalsuppe* (eel soup) — Sweet and sour soup swimming with eel, garnished with bacon and vegetables, and spiced with apricots, pears or prunes.
- *Lübecker Leckerli* — Honey-ginger biscuits from Lübeck, the Unesco-listed town of Gothic red bricks famed for its marzipan.

FEASTS

Oktoberfest

A booze-up like no other, originating in 1810 as a party to celebrate the marriage of Ludwig I. Over six million people from all over the world flock to Munich for 16 days in September to drink vast quantities of *festbier* — blonde festival beer brewed especially for the event by Munich's six breweries. Drunk from a 1-litre stein in the juicy company of roast ox or suckling pig, it is German culinary nirvana.

DAILY MEALS

Breakfast (*Frühstück*) is big — a buxom spread of breads and bread rolls, cheese, cold cuts, yoghurt and muesli, perhaps a boiled egg and, often, quark, a yoghurt-like curd cheese used thickly spread on bread for breakfast (also used in potato dips, salad dressings, sauces and cheesecakes the rest of the day).

The main meal was traditionally lunch, but these days it is invariably dinner — ensuring an appetite for that most sacred of German afternoon rituals, *Kaffee und Kuchen* (coffee and cake). This highly civilised tradition sees coffee and cake served mid-afternoon around at table, and all partake at a leisurely pace.

ESSENTIAL PRODUCE

Bread

Not just a staple but a cultural icon *brot* (bread) reaches its climax with the loopy-shaped *brezel* (pretzel). Soft yeasty dough is dunked in a salt bath and sprinkled with rock salt (or sunflower, poppy or pumpkin seeds) before baking. Lore says it was born in 15th-century Swabia when a baker was asked create a pastry through which the sun could shine thrice.

German bread comes in hundreds of varieties and sizes, often mixing wheat and rye flour. Brown is more common than white. Mini-breads (*kleingebäck*) and bread rolls (*brötchen* in the north, *semmel* in Bavaria, *wecken* in southern Germany) can be plain, covered in poppy seeds (*mohnbrötchen*), studded with sweet raisins (*rosinenbrötchen*), or sprinkled with salt (*salzstangel*).

- *Schwarzbrot* — Emphatically German, 'black' rye bread is dark brown and moist; it can be stored for months.
- *Bauernbrot* — 'Brown' bread is sour in taste and divine with a slab of butter.
- *Pumpernickel* — Rich and intense, this black rye-flour bread is steamed instead of baked to create its trademark moistness.
- *Dresden Stollen* — Christmas isn't Christmas without this spiced fruit bread-cake from eastern Germany, served generously dusted with icing sugar. The best secret is the ball of marzipan hidden away inside.

Handkäse mit musik (literally 'handcheese with music') is a hard round cheese marinated in oil and vinegar, topped with *Ebbelwoi/Apfelwein* (apple cider) and served in Frankfurt taverns.

German cultural icon, *brezel*, or pretzel.

Poppy seed sticky buns.

FRANS SCHALEKAMP / GETTY IMAGES

Schmalz, schwarzbrot and *schnaps.*

Barbequed meats at the Stuttgart Beer Festival.

MICHAEL DEFREITAS / GETTY IMAGES

Potatoes

Germans have consumed piles of *kartoffeln* (potatoes) ever since they arrived from South America in the 16th century.

- *Kartoffelsalat* (potato salad) — The perfect partner to smoked fish, here cold boiled potatoes are cut in chunks and mixed with mayonnaise. Pickles, mustard, garlic, onions, bacon, apples, leeks and cucumbers are an optional extra.
- *Schupfnudeln* (potato noodles) — Mashed potato is bound with flour and egg to create these finger-thick noodles, briefly boiled before being pan-fried to a golden crispness.
- *Reibekuchen* or *Kartoffelpuffer* (potato pancakes) — Potato dough is shaped into rounds, fried and served with onions as a savoury treat or with cinnamon and sugar for dessert.
- *Kartoffelklösse* (potato dumplings) — No roast dinner is complete without dumplings. Mashed-potato balls are dropped in boiling salted water; when they rise to the top, they're cooked.

Sausages

Born out of necessity to waste not, the humble sausage *(wurst)* was peasant food in medieval Germany. What better way to disguise and package less appetising animal parts? Centuries later it is a noble and highly respected element of German cuisine, with strict rules determining its authenticity – and its contents.

Germany's dazzling 1500 sausage varieties, typically served with bread and a sweet or spicy mustard, fall into three types:

- *Rohwurst* — a fresh sausage made from raw minced meat

- *Kochwurst* — blood or liver sausage made from cooked ingredients), and
- *Brühwurst* — a scalded or parboiled sausage like the eponymous Frankfurter or *wiener* in German.

All on its own is the *bratwurst,* which is different in every region – there are at least 50 types. Some are raw, some are scalded, and their preparation ranges from boiling in beer to oven-baking with apples and cabbage or grilling. The finger-sized *Nürnberger Rostbratwurst* is served by the dozen or half-dozen. Northern Bavaria's *Mainfrankische Meterbratwurst* is a monster of a sausage crafted in 1 metre lengths.

Blutwurst is blood sausage or black pudding, also called *rotwurst. Leberwurst* is liver sausage, and garlic is a key ingredient in the *knackwurst*. Bavaria produces white, rubbery veal sausages *(weisswurst)* and Saxony dishes up brain sausage *(bregenwurst).*

PREPARATION

Technique

New German cuisine might cast a fresh, lighter spin on century-old dishes, as chefs shift the focus to more local, seasonal ingredients. Yet ancient techniques derived from the basic need to survive the bitterly cold winter in northern Europe live on.

- *Pickling* — An ancient art used to preserve vegetables for winter and essential to German *sauerkraut.* Pickled by lacto-fermentation, the cabbage is shredded, mashed to unleash its natural juices, salted, covered and left to ferment.
- *Kasseler* — The process of smoking meat then leaving it to ripen in salty brine has been used in Germany since the 19th century.

Black Forest gateau.

* *Eintopf* — For centuries there has been no simpler way to make a stew than by chucking all the ingredients into *ein Tof* (literally 'one pot').

DEFINING DISHES

Black Forest gateau

Schwarzwälder kirschtorte is the ooh-la-la of German cuisine, devoured with passion since the 19th century. The ferociously rich gateau from the Black Forest gets its punch from the boozy *kirschwasser* (cherry schnapps) soaking through four layers of chocolate sponge, cream and cherries. Morello cherries and chocolate shavings are the icing on the cake.

Curried sausage

Currywurst was only knocked out of a fast food stand in Berlin in 1949, but this infamous dish created from a simple *bratwurst* and curry powder (obtained from a British soldier stationed in the city) fast became a national dish. Eating it al fresco or on the move, out of paper or plastic, is the only acceptable way.

Sauerkraut

Sauerkraut is pickled cabbage and a side dish few outside Germany can really fathom. Pickled white cabbage is shredded, spiced (perhaps with juniper berries or caraway seeds) and simmered. *Rotkohl* is the red-cabbage version.

DRINKS

Beer

Nothing is more deeply ingrained in the German psyche than the hallowed tradition of beer. The *Reinheitsgebot* (purity law) passed in Bavaria in 1516 demanded breweries use just four

Waiter with a fistful of beer.

Bratwurst with *sauerkraut*, Bavaria.

Vineyard.

ingredients: malt, yeast, hops and water. And while no longer a legal requirement, many German brewers continue to conform to it — to outstanding effect:

- 1,300 breweries and 11 monasteries produce 5000 different beers.
- Bottom fermentation accounts for 85% of German beers, notably: hop-flavoured Pils (pilsner), most Bock beers (strong with 7% alcohol) and Bavaria's strong and malty, slightly sweet Helles (pale lager).
- Top fermentation is used to brew the few German stouts; Berlin and Bavaria's fruity Weizenbier/Weissbier (wheat beer); and Cologne's pale strong-flavoured Kölsch are served in small glasses (200 millilitres), called Stangen (literally 'sticks').

Wine

For decades the name of German wine was sullied by the cloyingly sweet taste of Liebfraumilch and naff image of Blue Nun. No more. Respectable, new generation wine-growers include Dönnhoff (award-winning Rieslings), Weingut Meyer-Näkel (Germany's best Pinot noirs) and Wittmann (raved about Rheinhessen Silvaner and Rieslings). Wine growers work 1000 square kilometres of vineyards in 13 official wine-growing areas, mainly on the Rhine and Moselle riverbanks.

Drink this... Alcohol-free does exist. Beer-coloured, non-alcoholic ***fassbrause*** (literally 'keg brew') is an enticing mix of fruit, spice and malt extract, made in Berlin and ***wostok*** is a storybook-scrumptious, eucalyptus and ginseng-flavoured lemonade.

Belgian waffle, with strawberries, chocolate and cream.

JESSE WARREN / GETTY IMAGES

Belgium

Don't dismiss Belgium's food as a paler shade of its neighbours, even if France and Germany are next door. Over the centuries, savvy Belgian chefs have borrowed the best ingredients and techniques from European invaders to create a kitchen buzzing with creativity. The Belgian obsession with food ensures the perfect complement to a glass (or two) of aromatic honey-brown beer.

CULINARY CAPITALS BRUSSELS, ANTWERP, LIÈGE **KNOWN FOR** BEER, CHOCOLATE **IMPORTS** FRENCH, DUTCH AND GERMAN FLAVOURS **EXPORTS** ENDIVES **DEVOUR** CHOCOLATE PRALINES **AVOID** TESTICLE STEW

Waiter serving beer in Brussels.

Dried sausage.

Gift box of Belgian chocolate truffles.

CULTURE

The Romans, Vikings, Spanish, Austrians, French and Dutch all left an indelible footprint on Belgian cuisine. The Romans cultivated the precursor of the modern Brussels sprout, a thriving crop in ancient Rome. When plague broke out in the Middle Ages, St Arnold convinced locals to drink beer — boiled, hence clean — instead of stream water. At that point it was little more than barley soup that fermented spontaneously at times, but monks later added honey and spices. Medieval condiments, mustards, vinegar, dried fruits and fresh herbs from the monastery garden remain the spice of life in Belgian cuisine. At the end of the 19th century, Belgian chocolate makers started shipping cocoa beans over from their newly acquired African colony, Congo.

REGIONS

Brussels

As capital of the European Union, Brussels blends several disparate identities into one enigmatic core — in and out the kitchen. Cuisine is cosmopolitan and café culture is king in this rich gourmet city. Some typical dishes include:

- *Stoemp* — Boiled potatoes mashed with vegetables, served plain as a side dish or with sausage or ham as a simple meal.
- *Choesels* (testicle stew) — A vintage dish with balls, consumed from the late 19th century until World War II.

ETIQUETTE

There is a vast range of bars, cafes and restaurants to visit. Bear in mind that the finer the restaurant, the more French (and *haute*) the cuisine.

- Originally a place where beer was *brassée* (brewed), brasseries are casual places to dine today.
- Grab fries 'to go' at a *fritkot/friture* (chip stand), served piping hot in a paper cone with a generous dollop of thick mayonnaise, *samurai* (chilli mayonnaise), *sauce andalouse* (mildly spiced 1000-island dressing) or other flavoured sauce.
- Forget cutlery during mussel feasts. Eat with your fingers, using an empty mussel shell as a pair of tweezers to pluck out the mollusc from each shell.
- *Frieten/frites* (chips) in Belgium are not French fries — Belgians swear they invented them, chopping floury Belgian Bintje potatoes into finger-sized sticks and double-frying them in beef fat to attain an unmatched crispness and taste.

French-style meatballs.

ESSENTIAL PRODUCE

Chocolate

Belgian chocolate is among the world's best — Belgian chocolate makers insist on 100% pure cocoa butter. The star is the praline, a bite-sized chocolate shell with a soft centre created by pharmacist Jean Neuhaus in Brussels in 1912. (Dip tablets in chocolate to disguise their medicinal taste, what a wonderful idea!) The first pralines seduced with a simple cream filling. A century later, Belgian pralines seduce gourmets with specialist beans and endless innovative flavours.

Boudin blanc (white sausage) and *boudin noir* (black sausage) are made from pork (occasionally chicken or veal), to which copious amounts of milk or blood is added to colour. Nothing beats *andouille*, a rich sausage built from intestines and stomach parts.

Slices of *boudin noir*, black sausage.

Steak fries, usually served with plain or flavoured mayonnaise.

Endive

Belgian endive is prized. The nation's archetypal vegetable is crisp and cream in colour, with a sweet but faintly bitter taste. Wrap the shiny tight-leafed cones in ham, smother in cheesy white-sauce and oven-bake to make the classic dish *gegratineerde witloof/chicons au gratin* (endive gratin).

DEFINING DISHES

Filet américain

This is a Belgian brasserie staple: not a steak but *steak tartare* aka a mound of high-grade, raw minced beef spiced with finely chopped shallots, capers, parsley, seasoning and a raw egg yolk. Tabasco and ketchup are optional extras.

Meatballs

Scoffed at a little while ago as something a 1950s housewife would dredge up when the pantry was bare, *ballekes* (meatballs) are gourmet hot again. Larger tennis ball-sized *boulettes* from Liège swim in a fruity meat gravy.

Moules frites

Nothing is more iconic than a mountain of pot-steamed Belgian mussels served in their shells with fries. Mussels are harvested from the North Sea from September to February.

Waffles

Belgium's signature snack eaten hot off the griddle is traditionally dusted with icing sugar, although anything goes these days – chocolate, warm fruit, syrup, you name it. Brussels waffles are crispy, rectangular and deeply indented. Liège cooks use a more bready, cinnamon-spiced dough and favour rounder edges.

Classic Belgian meal: *moules frites* and cold beer.

DRINKS

Beer

Wine *(wijn/vin)* is the standard accompaniment to fine dining. But when it comes to Belgian tradition, beer is king.

Beers range from hoppy golden to honey brown and amber red. Many are served in their own uniquely embossed and shaped glass designed to enhance individual taste and aroma. Artisan breweries experiment with historical recipes and seasonal variations to create unique craft beers.

Key mainstream styles:

- *White beers (witbier/bière blanche)* — Thirst-quenching wheat beers, typically cloudy, flavoured with hints of orange peel and cardamom. Brewed in the Flemish town of Hoegaarden since the Middle Ages.
- *Lambic and fruit beers* — Southwest of Brussels in the Senne Valley, mysterious airborne micro-organisms allow the spontaneous fermentation of lambic beers. Sharp and acidic when young, they mature in a barrel for up to three years, and are then mixed with fresh fruit.
- *Amber ales* — A *bolleke* (stemmed spherical glass) is the only way to drink Antwerp's De Koninck, an amber-coloured ale with caramel, toasted malt and spicy notes.
- *Golden ale* — Refreshing and hoppy are terms that characterise this paler version of amber ale. La Chouffe, brewed since the 1980s by the Achouffe brewery in the Ardennes, is a perfect example.

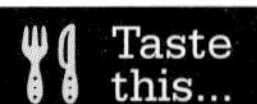

The historical precursor of gin, ***jenever*** is an archetypal Dutch-Flemish spirit flavoured with juniper berries. It is always drunk straight, but sweetened fruit versions ease the initiation for first-timers..

A cow completes the pretty alpine picture.

ADRIAN ASSALVE / GETTY IMAGES

Switzerland

Europe's land of Heidi is the land of hearty meals — and the best cuisine in this alpine country is as much about extraordinary setting as culinary extraordinaire. Autumnal game and alpine-dried meat on a farm with cud-chewing cows; an *après-ski* fondue and star-lit sledge ride home; a sweet cream cornet in a log chalet beneath glacial peaks: this is the alchemy that gives Swiss food its soul.

CULINARY CAPITALS ZURICH, GENEVA **KNOWN FOR** BIRCHER MUESLI **IMPORTS** COCOA BEANS **EXPORTS** 103.897 TONNES OF CHOCOLATE IN 2012 **DEVOUR** *ZUGER KIRSCHTORTE* (CHERRY CAKE) **AVOID** HORSE MEAT

Vineyard nestled in the mountains in Wallis.

Iconic Emmental cheese, sausage and bread.

Fried fish and shrimps.

CULTURE

The Romans planted fruit orchards, cultivated herbs and tamed wild vines. A bunch of different rulers tilled the land under the Holy Roman Empire to unwittingly sow the seeds of Switzerland today — a landlocked nation with four languages, three powerful neighbouring cuisines and an overwhelmingly diverse gastronomic tradition. Cooks in the French-speaking west take cues from France. Ticino kitchens in the south turn to Italy. And much of central and eastern Switzerland looks to Germany and Austria for culinary inspiration.

REGIONS

Lake Geneva and Vaud

French-speaking Switzerland is laced around the western tip and northern shore of Europe's largest lake. Some typical dishes include:

- *Filets de perche* — Enter Swiss fish and chips: perch filets seasoned, floured, pan-fried in butter and served with *frites* (fries).
- *Taillé au greubon* — A crisp savoury pastry from Vaud traditionally made after the family pig is slaughtered in November; pig fat is dried, cubed and thrown into this devilishly delicious loaf.

Valais

This salacious beauty embraced by the Matterhorn and fertile Rhône Valley is a blue-blood Swiss hybrid: the west speaks French, the east speaks German. Fine wine and glorious cheese unite the two in matters of cantonal pride.

- Gold-leaf autumn days usher in the bountiful grape and chestnut harvests.

- Silky black Hérens cattle produce world-class beef.
- Valaisan farmers spice and salt their best beef, hang it for five to 16 weeks, press it and slice it wafer-thin to make *viande séchée* (dried meat).

Ticino

Switzerland meets Italy in Ticino's kitchen where polenta, pasta and *risotto* are consumed with Italianate gusto. Perch, whitefish and *salmerino* (a cross between salmon and trout) are plentiful in lakes, and in the forest — chestnuts, game and mushrooms. Common dishes include:

- *Brasato* — Beef braised in red wine.
- *Capretto in umido alla Mesolcinese* — A tangy kid-meat stew, spiced with cinnamon and simmered in red wine.
- *Cazzöla* — A meat casserole served with cabbage and potatoes.
- *Cicitt* — Long, thin goat's meat sausages.

Polenta is a popular staple.

Graubünden

Germanic influence is keenly tasted in this eastern canton where Swiss-German speakers traditionally live in the mountains. Venison, chamois and wild boar are staples, and cuisine is alpine hearty. Drum roll: dumplings and strudels! Specialities are:

- *Bündnerfleisch* — Seasoned, air-dried beef or game.
- *Spätzli* — A cross between a pasta and dumpling.
- *Pizokels* — Stubby globs of boiled wheat and egg noodles, seasoned with parsley and baked with cheese.
- *Maluns* — Potatoes are soaked for 24 hours then grated, roasted in butter and flour, and flavoured with apple compote or cheese.

Pizokels with cheese, a speciality of Graubünden.

Swiss cheesemaker at work.

DAILY MEALS

Heidi may be fictional but her alpine lifestyle isn't. Dining around the Swiss table is all about storybook feasts in snowbound log chalets and wild picnics mid-hike in meadows ablaze with springtime flowers.

- Bircher muesli, sometimes with a dollop of cream, is often for breakfast.
- Lunch is from noon, and dinner as early as 6.30pm in German-speaking cantons.
- French-speaking Switzerland goes with the French *entrée* (starter), *plat* (main course) and dessert; most restaurants offer a daily meal at fixed price.
- Order wine in multiples of *déci* (100 ml).
- Don't drink water with fondue because it coagulates the warm cheese in your stomach. Opt for a dry white Fendant wine from the Valais.

ESSENTIAL PRODUCE

Cheese

Not all Swiss cheese has holes. *Emmental,* the hard cheese from the Emme Valley east of Bern, and *Tilsiter* from the same valley, both do. But there is no hole in sight in most of Switzerland's 450 other cheese types.

- *Gruyère* is a hard cheese from Gruyères, near Fribourg.
- *Appenzeller* is a stinky cheese used in tasty, strong-smelling dishes in Appenzeller, in the northeastern part of the country.
- *Sbrinz* is Switzerland's oldest hard cheese and is ripened for 24 months.
- *Tête de moine* (literally 'monks' head') is a hard,

AMIEL JEAN CLAUDE / GETTY IMAGES

Pretty and perfect Swiss chocolates.

nutty-flavoured cheese from the Jura, usually cut into flowery curls.

- *L'Etivaz* is a seasonal cheese made on high-altitude summer pastures in the Vaud Alps. Shepherds traditionally heat the morning's milk in a copper cauldron over a wood fire in century-old *chalets d'alpage* (mountain huts).

Sausages

Travel east and the *wurst* (sausage) becomes the focus of culinary veneration.

- *Cervelat* is the original Swiss sausage consumed both sides of the *Röstigraben*. A mix of minced pork, beef and spice is encased in beef intestines, smoked, then boiled or grilled.
- *St Galler bratwurst* is a white pork and veal sausage from St Gallen.
- *Les atriaux* are pork, liver, parsley and spices rolled in elongated balls, wrapped in pig fat, pan-fried and served in a white-wine gravy to those in French-speaking Switzerland.
- *Saucisse aux choux Vaudoise* are pinky-red sausages from Vaud, stuffed with pork meat, pork rinds and blanched cabbage.

Swiss chocolate

No country is more synonymous with silky smooth chocolate, and it comes in all shapes and sizes, Matterhorn and Swiss army knife included.

Switzerland established its chocolate reputation in the 19th century. Zürich businessman Heinrich Escher brought drinking chocolate back from Brussels in 1697, but Swiss manufacturing of the solid variety only began in 1819 when François-Louis Cailler (1796–1852) opened a chocolate factory near Vevey on Lake Geneva. Philippe Suchard (1797–1884) followed in 1850 with a factory on Lake Neuchâtel.

Few chocolate bars are as iconic as Toblerone, created by the Tobler family in Bern in 1909. Its unique triangular chunks, so the story goes, were inspired not by the Matterhorn mountain peak but by a line-up of Parisian cabaret dancing girls.

But the real Swiss chocolate kudos go to Henri Nestlé (1814–90) who invented condensed milk, Daniel Peter (1836–1919) who put the milk in the chocolate, and Rodolphe Lindt (1855–1909) who refined chocolate-making with 'conching', a rotary aeration process that gives chocolate its melt-in-the-mouth quality.

Oh, and the Swiss (aka Nestlé in 1930) were also responsible for the creation of white chocolate.

Crêpes with chocolate sauce.

DEFINING DISHES

Fondue

The main French contribution to the Swiss table: diners dip cubes of crusty bread into a pot of melted cheese. A classic fondue recipe melts equal amounts of Emmental and Gruyère cheese with white wine and a dash of cherry-flavoured kirsch liquor.

Raclette

Switzerland's other signature alpine dish sees a half-crescent slab of tangy raclette cheese screwed onto a specially designed 'rack oven' that melts the flat top side. As it melts,

Taste this... Everyone loves ***la religieuse***, the crispy cheese crust left on the bottom of the fondue pot or side of the raclette cheese when its salted skin sizzles. Traditionally the host's honoured guest gets the lion's share.

Rösti, a popular potato dish.

Raclette, melted cheese with condiments.

Fondue Savoyarde, three-cheese fondue.

CAROLINE MARTIN / GETTY IMAGES

cheese is scraped onto plates for immediate consumption with boiled potatoes, cold meats and gherkins.

Rösti

The star of German-speaking Switzerland rösti is so iconic it has a cultural divide — between French-speaking and German-speaking Switzerland — named after it. The term *'Röstigraben'* literally means 'rösti rift'. Potato is shredded, mixed with mushrooms, bacon bits and other seasonal ingredients, and baked in a woodfired oven.

DRINKS

Wine

The bulk of Swiss wine production takes place in the French-speaking cantons of Vaud and Valais. Merlot accounts for 90% of Ticino wine production.

- Terraced vineyards corset the steep hillsides in the Lavaux wine region, a Unesco World Heritage Site and source of fine whites like Calamin and Dézaley.
- The wonderful Valais reds use the Humagne rouge, Syrah, Cornalin and Pinot noir grape varieties. *Salgesch* reds are innovative and exciting.
- Fruity rosé Oeil-de-Perdrix (literally 'Partidge's Eye') is the tipple along Lake Neuchâtel and western shore of Lake Bienne, Mittelland.

Rivella is a soft fizzy drink made with lactose. It was created in the 1950s and remains unique to Switzerland — all export attempts have failed. Red label is original, blue label means reduced-sugar, and green label is mixed with green tea.

Diners enjoying lunch at a cafe in Krakow.

ALAN COPSON / GETTY IMAGES

Poland

'Eat, drink and loosen your belt.' So goes a favourite Polish aphorism, which gives a good indication of how this country's food works. The cuisine is heavy on meat and game, thick soups and starchy sides. Polish cooks have perfected the art of comfort food, meaning it's rich in calories and strong on flavour.

CULINARY CAPITALS KRAKOW, WARSAW **KNOWN FOR** CABBAGE ROLLS **IMPORTS** TROPICAL FRUIT **EXPORTS** RASPBERRIES **DEVOUR** GINGERBREAD **AVOID** JELLIED COWS TROTTERS

Poland's famed dumplings, *pierogies*.

Beetroot, a favourite Polish vegetable.

Chocolate *babka* cake with icing sugar.

CULTURE

Polish food relies on local ingredients such as potatoes, cucumbers, beets, mushrooms, buckwheat and apples, reflecting the country's long agrarian tradition. Most traditional dishes originated with peasants and hunters, who depended on salt for preservation, root vegetables for sustenance and layers of fat for warmth. To this day, harsh winters and short growing seasons mean that fresh produce is in short supply; fruit and vegetables are often pickled or preserved. Pork is the most common meat, but this carnivorous country consumes any animal it can, especially in the form of sausages and stews. Poles have an opportunistic side too, taking advantage of the wild foods that grow in fields and forests. A favourite pastime is gathering mushrooms and berries, which find their way into dishes in uniquely Polish ways.

REGIONS

Regional cuisine is a product of geography, as cooks utilise the bounty of the local land, with obvious influences from neighbouring countries.

Wielkopolska and Silesia

More than other part of Poland, these western regions depend on the humble potato and the aromatic onion.

- The region is well known for *pyzy* (potato dumplings stuffed with meat).
- Often considered typical `Polish' cuisine, the favoured preparation of roast duck with apples originates in Wielkopolska.
- A regional speciality, creamy onion soup is often topped with homemade noodles or crunchy fried onions.

- Irresistible *kluskie slaski* (Silesian dumplings) are made from potatoes and often served with bacon.

Małopolska

Małopolska is the source of many foodstuffs that share the name of the region's cosmopolitan capital, for example, Krakowska sausage and Krakowska duck (with buckwheat and mushrooms).

- Małopolska claims many specialities that also show up in Austrian cooking, such as *kotlet schabowy* (schnitzel) and apple strudel.
- The Tatras' cool mountain air and shepherding culture have resulted in some unique specialities in Podhale. Most noteworthy, the sheep's milk is used to produce a variety of delicious cheeses, a Highlander tradition since the 15th century. *Bundz*, *bryndza* and *oscypek* are all mild sheep cheeses that are formed into various different shapes, then brined and smoked, with delectable results.

FEASTS

All good Catholics engage in some form of pre-Lenten festivities, at least one day of feasting before the 40 days of fasting that lead up to Easter Sunday. In Poland, the preferred pre-Lenten pastry is the irresistible *pączek*, a fried doughnut that is filled with jam and sprinkled with sugar. Poles line up outside their favourite bakeries for *pączki* not on the Tuesday but rather the Thursday before Lent. By starting their consumption on *Tłusty Czwartek*, (Fat Thursday), they have the whole weekend to eat doughnuts, instead of just one day.

Celebrate Easter with a rummy, fruit-sweetened *babka*, a yeast bread that is rich with eggs and butter. The spongy sweet

IAN TROWER / GETTY IMAGES

Smoked cheese for sale in Krakow.

treat is round, with an open centre and the traditional way to celebrate the end of Lent. The blessing of the parish priest makes it even more delicious.

DAILY MEALS

Polish breakfast (*śniadanie*) is similar to its western counterpart and may include bread and butter, ham and eggs, and coffee or tea. A late lunch (*obiad*) is traditionally the most important and substantial meal of the day, and includes several courses. The evening meal (*kolacja*) often consists of sliced meats and salad or – even lighter – a pastry and a glass of tea.

While restaurant dining is not unusual, the more popular and affordable alternative is called a *bar mleczny* (milk bar). A holdover from the communist era, this is a cheap, self-serve cafeteria, subsidised by the state, which provides simple, wholesome meals for the working class. The 'milk' part of the name reflects the fact that a good part of the menu was based on dairy products. Nowadays, there are plenty of simple, cafeteria-style eateries that have been updated for the modern diner on a budget.

Menus are normally split into sections, including *zakąski* (hors d'oeuvres), *zupy* (soups), *dania drugie* or *potrawy* (main courses), *dodatki* (side dishes), *desery* (desserts) and *napoje* (drinks). The price of the main course doesn't normally include side orders such as potatoes, chips or salad; these must be chosen from the *dodatki* section.

Poles usually prefer their alcohol straight up. The exception is a sweet treat known as ***tatanka*** (buffalo) or ***szarlotka*** (apple pie), which is *zubrówka* (bison grass vodka) mixed with apple juice.

ESSENTIAL PRODUCE

Bread

Chleb (bread) has always meant more than sustenance to Poles. It's a symbol of good fortune and is sacred to many; some older people kiss a piece of bread if they drop it on the ground. Traditional Polish bread is made with rye, but bakeries nowadays turn out a bewildering array of loaves, including those flavoured with sunflower, poppy and sesame seeds, raisins and nuts.

Pork

While Poles eat chicken, lamb and pretty much any other meat, the main event is almost always pork (*wieprzowina*). Although Polish cooks have invented some delicious and unique ways to prepare pork, it is most commonly eaten as breaded pork chops (*kotlet schabowy)* or succulent roast loin of pork (*schab wieprzowy).* For something a little more adventurous, try *golonka,* which is boiled pig's knuckle, usually served with horseradish and *sauerkraut*.

Sausage

Sausage (*kiełbasa*) is normally eaten as a snack or part of a light lunch or dinner, served with a side of brown bread and mustard. It's usually made with pork, though other meats, like beef, veal and even bison, can be added to lend a distinctive flavour. The sausages are generally seasoned with garlic, caraway and other spices. The most popular type is *wiejska kiełbasa,* a thick cylinder of pork, spiced with garlic and marjoram. Other popular varieties include *kabanosy* (thin pork sausages that are air-cured and seasoned with caraway seeds); *krakowska* (usually thick and seasoned with pepper and garlic) and *biała* (thin white sausages sold uncooked and then boiled in soups).

WITOLD SKRYPCZAK / GETTY IMAGES

Sausages are in plentiful supply at this food stand during the Christmas season in Krakow.

SHOPPING

Nowadays, Poles do most of their shopping at Western-style supermarkets, which are open long hours and carry all manner of local and imported products. Smaller speciality shops such as bakeries and butchers cater to more specific needs. In every city centre, there is at least one large market, or *bazar*, where vendors hawk fresh produce, fresh-baked breads, slabs of meat and hunks of cheese, as well as home-made trinkets, tacky souvenirs, cheap clothes and more.

Traditionally, Polish kitchens contained a wood-fired oven, which contributed to a rich, smoky flavour in many Polish dishes. Nowadays, the wood-fired oven is less common, but smoked meats and fish are often incorporated into recipes to enhance the smokiness of the meals. A cast-iron casserole and a double boiler are essential for cooking soups, stews and sauces.

Looking into a food shop in Gdansk.

DEFINING DISHES

Bigos

Usually translated as 'hunter's stew', *bigos* is a tasty tangy melange of cabbage, meat and vegetables. It is popular in Poland, the Ukraine and Lithuania and for centuries Polish cooks have harboured their own secret recipes for this hearty dish. As such, there are no fixed ingredients for this clean-out-the-pantry meal: it is usually made with both *sauerkraut* and fresh cabbage; the mixed meats might include pork, bacon and

Is it a bagel or is it a pretzel? Neither. Or both. The ***obwarzanek*** is an irresistible, round, doughy snack, that's usually topped with poppy seeds, sesame or salt. They are sold from carts on the streets of Krakow, though they are occasionally found elsewhere.

Pretzel stall on a Krakow street.

Cabbages are a key ingredient in Polish cuisine.

Cabbage rolls, a staple and iconic food of Poland.

HARALD WALKER / GETTY IMAGES

sausage, although a true hunter's stew will also include venison or other game meat. Mushrooms, tomatoes, apples or dried plums enhance the flavour, as do pepper and other spices. The only hard and fast rule for making *bigos* is that it must simmer on the stove for several hours, preferably on two or three consecutive days.

Pierogi

Pierogi (or 'Polish raviolis') are square or crescent-shaped dumplings made from dough and stuffed with tastiness. They are usually boiled and then served doused in melted butter. The most popular variety is *ruskie (*Russian) *pierogi* stuffed with cottage cheese, potato and onion. Otherwise, they might be stuffed with meat, cheese, *sauerkraut* and mushrooms, or berries.

Soup

Rye is the staple ingredient in what will likely become a staple order of yours: *żurek.* This soup has a distinctive tart flavour, which is the product of fermented rye flour mixed with meat (usually sausage, bacon or ham) as well as onion, mushrooms and sour cream. It's often accompanied by a hard-boiled egg or *kiełbasa* (Polish sausage) and served inside a hollowed-out loaf of bread. *Żurek* is a traditional Easter food, although it is eaten all year-round.

Stuffed cabbage rolls

Fill your tummy and comfort your soul with *gołąbki*, or stuffed cabbage rolls, made from ground pork and beef mixed with rice or barley and enveloped in a cabbage leaf, then baked until tender. According to legend, the Polish-Lithuanian army ate *gołąbki* before defeating the Teutonic Knights and taking Malbork Castle, in a turning-point battle of the Thirteen Years War.

DRINKS

Beer

There are several brands of locally brewed Polish *piwo* (beer); the best include Żywiec, Tyskie, Okocim and Lech. Beer is widely available, usually a lager. Making a Polish-style shandy, they sometimes flavour their beer with fruit juice, usually raspberry juice, and drink it through a straw.

Vodka

Poles love their *wódka* (vodka) – only the Russians drink more per capita – and make some of the best in the world. While drinking habits are evolving, vodka remains the drink of choice when it comes to holidays, special occasions, and other times when only vodka will do. The most popular type of vodka is *czysta* (clear) vodka, which is served chilled and drunk neat. Poland is most famous for its *żubrówka* (bison vodka), which is flavoured with grass from the Białowieża Forest on which bison feed (or as local wags have it, 'on which bison peed').

Sliwowica

Fiery and fruity, *sliwowica* is a potent plum brandy that is produced and consumed in great quantities in Poland and around Eastern Europe. Made from the ripe fruit and crushed pits of Damson plums, the juice is distilled and aged to perfection. Polish drinkers have long produced their own home-brewed versions of *sliwowica* (which are still the best, purists claim); but this is becoming rare, as production is regulated and has moved to community and commercial distilleries.

Although there are variations in production methods and drinking traditions, some things are consistent: it is usually served chilled but not on the rocks; and in true Polish style, it's not sipped, but rather knocked back as a shot. *Na zdrowie!*

VLADIMIR SHULEVSKY / GETTY IMAGES

A Polish speciality, *bigos*.

BIGOS

Serves 6

Ingredients

1 cup pitted prunes
30 g dried mushrooms
80 ml cooking oil
1 kg mixed meat, such as Polish sausage, pork shoulder, beef chuck or wild boar, cut into cubes
1 onion, chopped
1 small head fresh cabbage, chopped
500 g *sauerkraut*
1 bay leaf
125 ml dry red wine
Rye bread and sour cream to serve

Method

Place the prunes and mushrooms in a bowl and cover with boiling water. Leave to steep for 30 minutes.

Meanwhile, heat half the oil in a large frying pan over a high heat and cook all the meat (except the sausage) in batches until the meat is browned and sealed. Set aside.

Sauté the onion and cabbage in the remaining oil in a large cast-iron casserole. Once softened, add the *sauerkraut*, the reserved meat (including uncooked sausage), and bay leaf.

Add the mushrooms and prunes with their soaking liquid. Mix well, bring to a boil, then simmer gently over a low heat for 1 to 1½ hours.

Add the wine and simmer for another hour or two. Remove from the heat, cover and place in a cool place overnight.

Reheat the following day and, if possible, simmer for another hour or two.

Serve with rye bread and a dollop of sour cream.

Waiter attending on guests at the Karpatia Restaurant in Budapest.

INGOLF POMPE / GETTY IMAGES

Hungary

Hungarian cuisine reflects the richness of a country at a crossroads, incorporating exotic eastern flavours and ingredients and tried-and-true western cooking techniques. Although meat is the centrepiece of Hungarian cooking, the country's mild climate yields a bounty of fruits and vegetables, not to mention fresh and full-bodied wines.

CULINARY CAPITALS BUDAPEST, EGER **KNOWN FOR** GOULASH **IMPORTS** EXOTIC FRUITS AND VEGETABLES **EXPORTS** *TOKAJ* WINES **DEVOUR** COLD FRUIT SOUP **AVOID** *KARCAG* (EVERY LAST BIT OF THE LAMB STEW)

Brightly-coloured candy.

Christmas butternut squash cake.

Mint and pea soup.

CULTURE

The quintessence of Hungarian cooking originates from a time when the nomadic Magyar people depended on herding cattle and sheep for their livelihoods. Meat-heavy dishes were prepared over an open fire while the herders tended their flocks. To this day, long-simmering soups and stews play a prominent role in the national cuisine. In fact the 'four pillars' of Hungarian cooking are four delicious soups or stews, each with its own distinctive flavouring.

Over the years, Hungarian cooks adopted elements from east and west. The Ottoman era saw the introduction of stuffed vegetables, rice pilafs, dark coffee and — most importantly — paprika. Under the Hapsburgs, schnitzels, sausages and irresistible sweets were incorporated into the national cuisine.

FEASTS

The food of choice for a Christmas feast is the traditional *töltött káposzta* (cabbage roll) — pickled cabbage leaves stuffed with minced pork meat. This dish is served in various forms throughout Eastern Europe, but the Hungarian version always contains ground paprika and is topped with a dollop of sour cream.

For both Christmas and Easter, Hungarians prepare a poppy seed or walnut roll *(bejgli)*, a rich pastry with a sweet nutty filling. A chocolate-covered fondant candy, *szalonsukor*, wrapped in colourful foil, is used to decorate the Christmas tree and sate the sweet-toothed.

ETIQUETTE

Hungary offers many options for dining out, from a butcher's shop hawking fried sausage to a self-service cafeteria or buffet. Many restaurants in Hungary evoke the atmosphere of a country inn, with rustic decor, folk music and hearty home-cooking. In recent years, chefs have begun to open restaurants with more contemporary decor and international influences.

DAILY MEALS

- *Reggeli* (breakfast) can vary widely, sometimes just a coffee and a plain bread roll, and sometimes a more elaborate affair with cheese, cold cuts, eggs and toast.
- *Ebéd* (lunch), eaten at around 1 pm, is traditionally the main meal.
- *Vacsora* (supper) is less substantial, often just sliced meats, cheese and some pickled vegetables.

ESSENTIAL PRODUCE

Paprika

Nothing defines the national cuisine more than sweet and hot paprika, which has been spicing up Hungarian soups and stews since the 16th century. It was the Turks in Buda who first grew the peppers and ground them into a piquant spice. Nowadays, the colour and taste of paprika ranges from sweet, red *különleges* to spicy, brown *erős*.

Vegetables

Fresh salad is available when lettuce is in season. Otherwise, veggies are likely to be pickled, or *savanyúság* (literally 'sourness'), which can be anything from mildly sour-sweet cucumbers and pickled peppers to very acidic *sauerkraut*.

- A *főzelék* is a sort of casserole where peas, green beans, lentils, vegetable marrow or cabbage are fried or boiled, and then mixed into a roux.
- Eggplant, peppers and cabbage are often stuffed with minced meat, rice and onions for a tasty and filling dish.

Smoked products from the famous *Mangalicsa* pig.

Slices of Hungarian salami.

Paprika, sausage and local wines for sale at a store in the Lake Balaton region.

PREPARATION

The most traditional Hungarian food preparation takes place in a cauldron called a *bogrács*, which is placed over an open fire. The ingredients benefit from a long, slow simmer, which is crucial to breaking down the tougher cuts of beef and thickening the *potage*.

DEFINING DISHES

Csabai Kolbász

For centuries, the Hungarian peasants that inhabit the region around Békéscsaba have been producing the famous paprika-flavoured sausage called *Csabai kolbász,* characterised by its spicy taste and reddish colour. The pork-stuffed intestines go through a time-tested process of drying and smoking, traditionally in an open chimney fuelled by sweet corn cobs or stems. The result is a delightfully piquant and chewy meat product, usually served on bread or alongside green peppers.

Fisherman's soup

This spicy fish soup (*halászlé*) originates from the regions around the Danube and Tisza rivers. While exact recipes are carefully guarded secrets, the key ingredients are evident: fish — usually carp or mixed river fish — and plenty of hot paprika. Traditionally, the fish soup is prepared in a kettle on an open fire, right on the river bank. The soup is served straight from the kettle, along with bread and a white wine spritzer (*fröccs*).

Goulash

The national dish of Hungary, goulash is a thick soup of meat, vegetables and potatoes, generously spiced with paprika. In Hungarian, *gulyás* means 'herdsman.' For centuries, sheep and cattle herders have prepared the hearty soup in a cast-iron

PAUL POPLIS / GETTY IMAGES

Hungarian goulash in a cooking pot.

kettle and allowed it to cook on an open fire while they are out tending their animals; many believe this is still the only proper way to do it. Of course, there are probably as many variations on goulash as there are cooks in Hungary. Some popular add-ins are noodles, *sauerkraut*, vegetables and kidney beans.

DRINKS

Brandy

According to popular wisdom, any fruit that can be used to make jam will also make a tasty *pálinka,* or fruit-flavoured brandy. Plum, apricot and pear are the most popular. *Pálinka* is served just below room temperature, in a tulip glass, and should be swirled, sniffed and savoured, just like a fine wine.

Wine

Hungary is proud of its wine tradition, which was started by the Romans and further developed by the monastic orders that settled in the hills. The most famous wine region is in the country's northern reaches in the foothills of the Zemplén mountains. Here, long, warm autumns create the conditions for noble rot, the grape fungus which causes the concentrated sweetness of Tokaj dessert wine. It was Louis XIV of France who dubbed this elixir the 'wine of kings and the king of wines'. Hungary's best-known table wine is Egri Bikovér, also known as Bull's Blood. This full-bodied red originates from the Eger region, which also produces highly regarded Olaszreisling, Chardonnay and Pinot noir.

Partake of strong coffee and lively scuttlebutt at one of Budapest's historic coffee houses. Indulge in rich, decadent tortes, such as ***dobos torta***, a layered chocolate and cream cake with a caramelised brown sugar top.

Tins of Russian caviar.

PHOTOLIBRARY / GETTY IMAGES

Russia

While sparkling wine and salty caviar represent Russia at its most extravagant, the national cuisine is largely based on simpler fare that is robust, filling and delicious. Steaming soups and chilled vodka go a long way to seeing one through the cold, dark winter.

CULINARY CAPITALS MOSCOW, ST PETERSBURG **KNOWN FOR** VODKA, *BORSHCH* **IMPORTS** GOURMET FOODSTUFFS **EXPORTS** CAVIAR **DEVOUR** *BLINI* **AVOID** MULITCOLOURED MUSHROOMS

CAVIAR
113 gm (4 oz)
net wt
MALOSSOL
Produced and packed for export
CASPIANCAVIAR BALYKCORPORATION
KASPRYBA ASTRAKHAN
Produced and packed in Russia only for export
RUSSIAN CAVIAR
net wt
56,8g (2 oz)
KIROV FISHING FACTORY
•CASPRYBA• ASTRAKHAN
MALOSSOL

Collecting wild mushrooms is a popular activity.

Lingonberries, abundant in summertime.

Locals swimming in the Volga River.

CULTURE

According to an old Russian proverb, '*Shchi* (cabbage soup) and *kasha* (porridge) is our nourishment.' This saying emphasises the important role played by soups and grains in sustaining generations of peasants. Known as *krestyanskaya* or 'peasant' fare, Russia's traditional food remains firmly based on the ingredients gathered, grown and prepared by rural cooks over the ages: fish, poultry, potatoes, mushrooms, berries, grains and garden fruits and vegetables.

During the tsarist period, the Russian upper classes took their cues from Europe, for example, speaking French and English amongst themselves. France, especially, was considered the epitome of high culture, an estimation reflected in Russian food. Grilled fish and meats, usually topped with rich sauces, are the essence of *haute-russe* cuisine.

REGIONS

Russia's culinary influences are as sprawling and eclectic as the country's vast territory, with regional dishes taking a prominent place in the national cuisine.

Volga

The mighty Volga River influences every aspect of culture in this region, including cuisine. Culinary highlights have origins in the region's rich tapestry of peoples and cultures, especially Bashkiria, Tatarstan and Udmurtia.

- *Lapsha* is a noodle soup that originated in Tatarstan, but is now widespread throughout Russia. Long, round-rod noodles are boiled in chicken, mushroom or milk broth for a hearty, satisfying meal.
- A common sight in the Volga region is rows of *oblyoma*, hanging out on the line. Dried and salty, this tasty river

fish is a local's favourite, especially (and usually) when accompanied by beer.

Caucasus

Cuisine in the Russian Caucasus is heavily influenced by the surrounding countries, especially Georgia. Caucasian cooking uses ground walnuts as an integral ingredient, which yields a distinctive rich, nutty flavour. Also inherited from Georgia is the spice mixture *khmeli-suneli*, which combines coriander, garlic, chillies, pepper and savory with a saffron substitute made from dried marigold petals.

- This is the region that invented *shashlyk*, or grilled lamb kebabs, which now appear on menus around the country.
- The Ossetian version of a *pirog* is a sinfully delicious pizza-like pie that is stuffed with meat, cabbage, or beets and cheese.

Siberia and the Far East

Fresh fish, game meat and sustaining starches define the cuisine in the northeastern regions.

- Siberia is most famous for its *pelmeni* (dumplings), and you'll find local variations in all the major cities across the region.
- Lake Baikal is home to the *omul*, a delicious cousin of the salmon, which is often dried or added to a hearty fish soup, *ukha*.
- Further east in Buryatiya, and throughout the Russian Far East, you'll often encounter the steamed, palm-sized dumplings known as *manti*. Two or three make a good, greasy meal.

KEREN SU / GETTY IMAGES

Local Uelen people drying salmon.

FEASTS

Roughly translated as 'butter week', *Maslenitsa* is the traditional festival that takes place in the week leading up to Orthodox Lent. The food of choice for this week-long feast is *blini*, thin pancakes that are filled with caviar, cheese, mushrooms, meats and sweets. In pagan times, the round shape of the pancake was symbolic of the sun, and so an appropriate way to bid farewell to winter.

For Easter Sunday, Russians bake the saffron-flavoured buttery loaf *kulich*, on which is spread the Easter cheesecake known as *paskha*, a delicious mix of *tvorog* (cheese curd), egg yolks, sugar, butter, sour cream and vanilla.

ETIQUETTE

Visitors to a Russian home can expect to be regaled with stories, drowned in vodka and served enormous amount of food on tiny plates. Once the festivities begin, it is difficult to refuse food or drink — guests are sure to go home stuffed, drunk and happy.

Dining with friends or strangers inevitably involves copious amounts of toasting. Traditionally, the first toast is always offered to the ladies present, while the second tributes the host. After that, toasting can get creative, often involving long, heartfelt speeches. Guests are also expected to offer a toast — be prepared!

THE MENU

- Most formal Russian meals commence with an elaborate spread of *zakuski*, or appetisers, often leaving little room for the main course. This tradition dates to the earliest of days in Russia. Due to unpredictable

The traditional Russian Christmas dish, *kutia*.

weather and poor roads, a host never knew when to expect his guests, so he always kept a table set with *zakuski* ready to accommodate tired and hungry travellers when they arrived. Most menus offer a mind-boggling array of salads, in addition to delicacies like *blini* and caviar.

- Rich soups, offered as a first course, or *pervaya blyuda*, may well be the pinnacle of Russian cooking. There are dozens of varieties, often served with a dollop of sour cream. Most are made using meat stock. The most common soups include *borshch*, *shchi* (cabbage soup), *okroskha* (sour cucumber soup), and *solyanka* (a tasty meat soup with salty vegetables and hint of lemon).
- The second or main course, or *glavnaya blyuda*, can be poultry, meat or fish, and is usually served with a side of potatoes.
- Many Russian desserts make use of the fruits and berries that are available in the short summer. The most famous is *sharlotka*, a kind of apple cake, but all manner of cakes and pastries fill the bakery shelves. Such sweets are most often eaten at teatime. Ice cream (*morozhenoe*) is a favourite sweet treat, and Russians eat it year-round, even in the coldest months of winter.

DAILY MEALS

The midday meal is traditionally the largest meal of the day. During Soviet times, it was customary for employers to provide this meal, so most workers would sit down to a big satisfying lunch in the company canteen. Nowadays, there is no such thing as a free lunch, but Russians still tend to take a break from their workday for a filling noontime meal. Most members of the workforce go out to lunch with their colleagues, taking

A farmer loosens his potatoes with a pitchfork.

Pretty berries in jars at the market.

Pierogi with *sauerkraut* filling.

advantage of 'business lunch' specials (usually three courses for a fixed price), affordable all-you-can-eat buffets or modern incarnations of the company cafeteria.

At dinner time, too, restaurants are packed with patrons, eager to sample the ever-changing array of dining options, from old-fashioned *haute russe* to contemporary fusion.

ESSENTIAL PRODUCE

Berries

Wild berry gathering is a favourite Russian pastime. Bilberries, lingonberries and wild strawberries pop up each summer, cranberries and blueberries in the autumn. *Yagodi* (berries) are often used to fill sweet dumplings and pastries.

Bread

Delicious, doughy bread is served at nearly every Russian meal. While white bread is not uncommon, the more typical Russian variety is a vitamin-rich sour rye, often flavoured with coriander or caraway seeds.

Mushrooms

Russians know their mushrooms: *lisichki* (chanterelles), *veshenki* (oyster mushrooms), *belyi gribi* (porcini) and *ryzhki* (orange milk mushrooms) are common finds for the forager. Any mushroom hunt is an excuse for a picnic — vodka and campfire included. The hunt provides the raw ingredients for

The classic salad ***seld pod shuby***, or 'herring in a fur coat', is a colourful conglomeration of salted herring, covered with layers of boiled potato, carrot, beetroot, onion and mayonnaise. It's terrifically neon-coloured and unexpectedly delicious!

an array of Russian specialities, such as mushroom barley soup and mushroom julienne.

Vegetables

Long winters and short growing seasons mean that Russian cuisine is dependent on root vegetables like potatoes and beets. Russian salads rely on ingredients that keep through the winter: the closest thing to a leafy green is cabbage.

SHOPPING

Gone are the days when food shopping required waiting in a different line for each food item. Nowadays, most shoppers buy their food at western-style supermarkets, full of pre-packaged foods and western brands.

Alternatively, farm-fresh foodstuffs are on display at the local market (*rinok*), a busy, bustling place, full of activity and colour. Tables are piled high with multicoloured produce, home-made cheese and jam, golden honey straight from the hive, vibrantly coloured spices pouring out of plastic bags, huge slabs of meat and slippery, silver fish posing on beds of ice.

The opulent Yeliseev Grocery Stores in St Petersburg are not practical for everyday shopping, but fun for special occasions and souvenirs. In the 19th century, this successful trading house was known for selling the finest goods and supplying the royal court. The gorgeous Style-Moderne buildings reflect the grandeur of the pre-revolutionary period, with caviar and other upscale delicacies for sale within.

PREPARATION

Food preparation in Russia is largely determined by the country's marked seasonality, meaning that the growing season is short and the winter is long. Fresh produce does not

PATRICK HORTON / GETTY IMAGES

A pomegranate juice salesman waits for customers at Sochi Market.

Classically-Russian soup: *borshch*.

Blini served with red caviar.

Pelmeni, traditional Russian dumplings in broth.

last long, so vegetables are often pickled or preserved. Berries and other fresh fruit are canned as compote or jam to last the winter. Fish is salted and dried; meat is made into sausages. Before the wide availability of canned, frozen and imported products, every effort was made to ensure that nutritious, satisfying foodstuffs were available until spring — a practice that continues in these more plentiful times.

DEFINING DISHES

Borshch

Borshch is the classic Russian soup: ruby hued and steaming hot, it's a warming blend of beetroot, carrot, cabbage and garlic. The soup may be vegetarian or meaty, with the addition of anything from sausage to chicken hearts. It's always served with a dollop of sour cream and a sprinkle of fresh dill. In summer, vegetarian beetroot soup served cold *(svekolnik)* is a refreshing alternative.

Caviar

Caviar was once the food of Russian imperial luxury, reserved for tsars and nobility. Russians spread the fish roe on buttered bread or *blini*, and wash it down with a slug of vodka or a toast of sparkling wine. The most highly prized is from the roe of the Caspian beluga, but sterlet, ossetra and sevruga sturgeon also yield caviar. Unfortunately, due to overfishing, sturgeon populations have declined drastically in recently years, driving up prices and threatening the fish with extinction. Fish-friendly travellers might consider sticking to 'red caviar' (salmon roe) until the sturgeon is in a better place.

Pelmeni

When Mongolian invaders stormed across the Siberian steppe in the 13th century, they packed their saddle bags with *pelmeni*, or dumplings, which made a high-energy snack for hard-working horsemen. This nourishing comfort food has been a staple of Russian cooking ever since. Traditional *pelmeni* are crafted from an egg-and-flour based dough, and filled with a blend of beef, pork and lamb mince. A few minutes' hearty boil cooks the dumplings. Then they are served in a clear broth or heaped in a deep bowl with plenty of sour cream and a sprinkle of dill.

Salo

The aptly named 'fatback' is the layer of fat on the back of a pig. Cut a slab; cure it with salt, pepper and garlic; store it for a few months in a wooden barrel; and you've got the Russian and Ukrainian specialty *salo*. It might be used as an ingredient in soups or sausage, but most often, it is smothered onto a wedge of black bread and eaten raw, as an accompaniment to vodka or spirits. It's enough to make health-food fiends wince. But if you can get past the idea of eating pure pig fat, it will make you salivate for more. The rich meaty flavour and melt-in-your-mouth texture of the fat are enhanced by the earthiness and chewiness of the rye bread.

DRINKS

'Drinking is the joy of the Rus. We cannot live without it.' With these words, Vladimir of Kyiv, the father of the Russian state, is said to have rejected abstinent Islam on his people's behalf in the 10th century. Alcohol has played a prominent role in Russian culture ever since.

Beer and wine

These days, beer sales outstrip those of traditional vodka. The market leader is Baltika, while fine microbreweries have opened in Moscow, St Petersburg and other cities. Wine is also

Bottles of Russian honey ale.

A street vendor sells *kvas*.

becoming more popular, although it is not really produced locally. Russians drink sparkling wine, or *Sovietskoe shampanskoe*, to toast special occasions and to sip during intermission at the theatre.

Tea

Russians make tea by brewing an extremely strong pot, pouring small shots of it into glasses, and topping the glasses up with hot water. This was traditionally done from the *samovar*, a metal water urn with an inner tube filled with hot charcoal. Modern *samovars* have electric elements, like a kettle, which is actually what most Russians use to boil water for tea these days. Putting jam in tea instead of sugar is quite common for those who like it a little sweeter.

Vodka

The word 'vodka' is the diminutive of the Russian word for water, voda, so it means something like 'a wee drop'. Vodka is normally served chilled and straight up. One person makes a toast, then everyone clinks glasses and knocks it back. Chase with a lemon or a pickle (if necessary). Women can usually get away with sipping, but men will be scoffed at if they don't knock back at least the first round.

Kvas is a mildly alcoholic, fermented, rye-bread water. Cool and refreshing, it is a popular summer drink that tastes something like ginger beer. In the olden days it was dispensed on the street from big, wheeled tanks. The ***kvas*** truck is a rare sight these days, but this cool, tasty treat is available by the bottle.

Georgian woman selling bagels in the street

STEVEN WEINBERG / GETTY IMAGES

Georgia

According to myth, God called all of the nations together so that he could portion out the world among them. The Georgians were absent because they were having a grand feast. God came looking for them later, and asked why they'd been absent, and they replied that they'd been toasting his honour. God, pleased and flattered, gave Georgians the land he'd been saving for himself: the ruggedly beautiful, fertile place that Georgians call Sakartvelo.

CULINARY CAPITALS TBILISI, KAKHETI **KNOWN FOR** *SUPRAS* (FEASTS) **IMPORTS** CHINESE FOOD **EXPORTS** WINE **DEVOUR** GIANT MEAT DUMPLINGS **AVOID** 'GEORGIAN SNICKERS' (GRAPE SWEETS)

Adjarian food from the southwest, like Georgian food generally, often makes use of pomegranate as a sauce with meats.

Khachapuri, stuffed bread.

The food market at Batumi.

CULTURE

From its sublimely perched old churches and watchtowers dotting fantastic mountain scenery to its green valleys spread with vineyards, Georgia is one of the most beautiful countries on earth and a marvellous destination for adventurous eaters. Bordered by the Caucasus Mountains to the north, which form the border with Russia, and the Black Sea to the west, this small country — just the size of West Virginia — contains a tremendous range of geographical and climatic diversity, and a deeply complicated history has given Georgia a rich culinary heritage. Georgian cuisine has been influenced by its neighbours over the years — you see Persian ways of using fruit to flavour meat stews, and nuts to thicken, flavour, and enrich sauces, for example — but Georgian cooking is still utterly its own, bold and lusty, full of stark, striking contrasts and sophisticated seasoning, but also unfussy, with an emphasis on fresh, pure flavours.

REGIONS

Tbilisi

Tbilisi, the bustling capital of Georgia, is a melting pot, with the cuisine of every region of Georgia represented. (You'll also find Chinese, Russian, Thai, Mexican, French, and Italian restaurants, but you're much better off honing in on what Georgia does best — Georgian food).

- Look for *sakhachapure* — eateries specialising in the many varieties of Georgian cheese-filled breads.
- Stuff yourself on *khinkali*, Georgia's signature, fist-sized dumplings at *sakhinkle* (dumpling houses). *Sakhinkle* also usually offer a full menu of traditional Georgian dishes, and are a great place to sample the full range of Georgian cuisine.

Kakheti

The lowlands of the Kakheti region, in eastern Georgia, offer a Tuscany-like landscape of rolling hills. Pomegranate trees thrive here, as do figs and persimmons. This is Georgia's premier wine-producing region, and a very good time to visit is during the *rtveli* (grape harvest) from about 20 September to 20 October, when grapes are picked and pressed, to the accompaniment of feasts, musical events and other celebrations. Speciality dishes include:

- *Mtsvadi* — Skewered cubes of meat, often pork or lamb, are popular throughout Georgia, but they're especially good grilled over coals made from old grapevines, as they are prepared in Kakheti. They're served lightly dressed with pomegranate juice or tossed with raw red onions and a spicy tomato sauce, or sometimes with a marvellously tart plum sauce called *tkemali* for dipping.
- *Churchhkela* — During the grape harvest, strings of walnuts and hazelnuts are dipped in a gummy, sweet paste of reduced grape juice. Nicknamed 'Georgian Snickers', you'll often see these treats, which look like knobbly candles, hanging at roadside stalls or markets.

ETIQUETTE

For Georgians, food and drink are central. Happily for the hungry traveller, guests are considered blessings so hospitality and sharing a meal are the very stuff of life. If you find yourself invited to partake of food at someone's home, do — as good as Georgian food is in restaurants, it comes fully to life when shared with Georgians at a traditional *supra*.

Supras (meaning, literally, 'tablecloth', for the way the food covers the table) are celebratory meals, involving structured toasts, wine, song, and *lots* of food. They are the epic, convivial feasts central to Georgian culture. They might involve two people

Young baker forming bread in Kazbek.

or two hundred, but if there's an occasion to celebrate, and wine and food to share, there's a *supra* in the making.

ESSENTIAL PRODUCE

Bread

Bread is an essential part of the Georgian table.

- In most of Georgia, but especially in the eastern part of the country *tonis puri* or *chotis puri* (fine white wheat breads), are baked in a tall cylindrical oven known as a *tone*. A fire is built in the bottom of the oven; once it dies down to coals, bread dough is slapped against the inner walls, which capture and radiate heat. It has a crisp exterior crust and a white, fluffy crumb.
- *Mchadi* (corn bread patties) are also common in Western Georgia. They are often paired with *lobio*, a wonderful stew of beans simmered with walnuts, herbs and spices.

Cheese

By and large, there are two traditional cheeses made in Georgia, both of which are often served as table cheeses and used in cooking.

- *Sulguni*, a smoked, melting cheese that tastes like a cross between a gouda and mozzarella, is a popular table cheese that's often used to stuff grilled vegetables.
- *Imeruli,* a hard, very salty, cheese that's made in a saltwater brine, is usually eaten at the table.

Fruit

Georgia has a wealth of fruits; which are enjoyed fresh, preserved in jams, and used to flavour meat dishes.

- Pomegranates are used as garnishes and pomegranate juice is used in marinades.
- Sour plums are boiled with herbs to make *tkemali*, a tart plum sauce, and brined in salt water then incorporated into savoury meat stews.
- Kartli, the province where Tbilisi is located, is famous for its fruit: impossibly sweet peaches and apples, gooseberries, currants, plums and sweet and sour cherries abound.

Poultry

Chicken is the most commonly used bird, but turkey is also a great favourite, and is often served in special-occasion dishes.

- *Tabaka* is a whole, flattened chicken, cooked under a brick. It has a shatteringly crisp skin and a highly spiced, garlicky sauce.
- *Katmis satsivi*, a cold dish of chicken or turkey in an unctuous ground walnut sauce and marigold sauce, is a very special dish, traditionally eaten at New Year's.

Spices

Thanks to the country's historic placement on the spice route, Georgian cooks employ a huge range of spices in their cooking. Georgians favour certain ones, which give the cuisine its distinctive flavour:

- Marigold flower petals are dried, ground, and used as a spice that's sometimes called 'Imeretian saffron'. They imbue dishes with a wonderful golden color and a subtle, thyme-like flavour.
- Summer savory, or *kondari*, is harvested in the highlands of Svaneti and used dry in many spice mixtures.

Khinkali, pleated dumplings of great popularity.

Dried marigold petals are a common flavouring.

Herbs and radishes at the food market in Batumi.

- The leaves of another highland herb blue fenugreek, *utskho suneli*, are used dried and ground.

Vegetables

Though Georgians love meat, vegetarians will find a lot to love in Georgia; vegetables are the cornerstone of Georgian dining.

- *Pkhali*, dishes made from cooked and finely chopped vegetables of every description, are seasoned with ground walnuts, fresh herbs, and spices;
- Sliced lengthwise and slathered with a garlicky walnut paste, Asian eggplants form the basis of Georgia's most popular dish: *badrijani nigvsit*.
- Red kidney beans, known as *lobio*, are stewed or served in a cold salad, seasoned with ground walnuts, coriander, and herbs.

DEFINING DISHES

Badrijani nigvsit

This dish of fried eggplant topped with a garlicky walnut paste and scattered with pomegranate seeds is very popular.

Khachapuri

Each region of Georgia has their own style of cheese bread or *khachapuri*; wonderfully buttery, calorific stuffed breads that come in all shapes and sizes. Look for:

- *Khachapuri Acharuli* from the western region of Ajara: a canoe-shaped bread overflowing with molten cheese and topped with butter and a runny egg (you tear off the crust and dunk it in the cheese and egg).
- *Khachapuri Imeruli* from Imereti are round, flat pies with melted cheese on the inside only.

BOB GIBBONS / GETTY IMAGES

Blue fenugreek is used as a spice.

- *Khachapuri penovani* are square breads, neatly folded into four quarters, with cheese (or other fillings, such as mashed potato or mushrooms) inside a filo-like crust.

Khinkali

Khinkali, pleated dumplings classically filled with spiced meat, are a Georgian specialty that are often presented, with great fanfare, towards the end of a feast. You can also find them at *sakhinkle* (dumpling houses) where you can order versions stuffed with mashed potato, mushrooms, and farmer's cheese and mint, by the dozen. Don't eat the topknot, and when eating, take care not to spill the hot juices within.

DRINKS

Wine

Georgia is home to one of the world's most ancient winemaking cultures — around 500 of the world's 2000 grape varieties are Georgian and 38 of these are still used in commercial production. Georgian wine used to taste sweet to Western palates as Russia, long the primary importer of Georgian wines, favoured sweeter styles. Russia's ban on Georgian wine imports in 2006 changed that. Today Georgian winemakers are producing wines with Western and Asian markets in mind, using modern technologies.

Qvevri wines

Georgia is home to a unique tradition that stretches back thousands of years: Grapes are crushed, then fermented with their skin-on for several months in buried earthenware vessels called *qvevri*. Prolonged contact with the skins produces wines that are rich in tannins, lending depth and dryness to the overall result. These wines are typically very inexpensive, and are sold in plastic containers.

Tables set for lunch in Mykonos.

NATALIE WINTER

Greece

The cuisine of Greece is western history right in your mouth. It is a cuisine created by people who have long known the greater world and its gifts, but equally its hardships. And so it is a cuisine whose practitioners have learned to extract the last ounce of nutrition, as well as the last iota of pleasure from every ingredient.

CULINARY CAPITALS ATHENS, THESSALONIKI
KNOWN FOR GREEK SALAD **IMPORTS** NUTS
EXPORTS CURRANTS, OLIVE OIL, FETA CHEESE
DEVOUR *SPANAKOPITA* **AVOID** TOO MUCH OUZO

BAR
BAR

Octopus hanging out to dry.

Iconic Greek sweet treat, *baklava*.

The white and blue of a Greek fishing village.

CULTURE

Greek cookery is unpretentious. Food is not tarted up and made to look cute, grand, rare or costly. There is no over-reliance on sauces, no confusion of tastes. You can be sure that whatever you order it will taste of what it is. Plus olive oil.

The basis of Greek cuisine is the Holy Trinity of grain, olive and wine served at every meal as they have been since antiquity. Apollo had three granddaughters: Spermo (Grain), Elais (Olive) and Oeno (Wine). These three are still the Greek equivalent of the kitchen gods. And as deity continues to play a mighty role in the Greek kitchen, the kitchen plays a mighty role in Greek life. The Greeks imbibe the spirit at every meal. The menu is informed by the religious calendar. Ancient Greeks dined with nymphs and sprites; their contemporaries dine with saints. The bread of the table is also the bread of life and the heavens.

Greek cuisine is Mediterranean soul food, comfort food, good in the mouth and good in the belly. It is uncomplicated and undemanding yet very giving; the culmination of 3500 years of experience in the kitchen, as well as untold years of want and poverty. It is the food of a nation that has long reached out to the world, as well as the food of a community isolated by harsh climate and terrain.

Greece is the largest Christian community in the Middle East, and Greek cuisine is both worldly and homely, sacred and profane. If you travel much in this part of the world, you'll find many commonalities at the table. Bread and olives are a constant presence, as are sweets made with honey and nuts. The music sounds familiar and the coffee is just as chewy. This is explained by the fact that the whole of the eastern Mediterranean is of a piece. It always was. Conquerors come and go, but the common crops remain.

FEASTS

In Greece, history, religion and identity are intrinsically entwined, and this is no more evident than in the nation's celebratory foods. Every morsel is laced with symbolism, from Christmas biscuits to the spit-roast lamb of Easter. Even the fasting days of Lent have culinary attraction.

Koliva, symbolising the circle of life.

Sweets for the deceased

In Greek culture, death is marked by special foods, with the wheat dish *koliva* being the most important. After the church service, *koliva* is what mourners are served because it symbolises the cycle of life. in Greece, women have always been responsible for death rituals, and in accordance with this, *koliva* is prepared by old women, grandmas or aunts. If a family is bereft of a *koliva*-maker, one is contacted through the church. Once the order is placed, the *koliva* will appear on the day of the funeral.

To make *koliva*, soft-boiled wheat kernels are mixed with dried fruit, pomegranate seeds, sugar and nuts. The fruit symbolises joy and sweetness; the pomegranate seeds, fertility. The mixture is placed on a silver platter in the shape of a mound, covered with icing sugar and studded with almonds to form the shape of a cross. The main ingredient, wheat, is a symbol of the resurrection of Christ: 'Unless the grain of wheat falls into the earth and dies, it remains alone, but if it dies, it bears much fruit.' (John 12:24)

Artichoke leaves.

Easter

This is the big one, the most important time in the Greek calendar. People plan for it through the entire year. And after 40 days of abstinence they are ready for it.

- On Good Wednesday, housekeepers call on their local

Greek men at a cafe.

priests to have the eggs and flour blessed. These ingredients will form the basis of the sacred breads of Easter.

- On Good Thursday, preparations start in earnest: the sacred breads are baked, scented with mastic, sweet spices, honey, rosemary, bay — whatever the bountiful earth provides can find its way into Easter bread, cakes and biscuits.
- Good Thursday is often called Red Thursday, and every household will prepare red-dyed Easter eggs. Eggs have always been symbols of renewal and continuity, and the red dye symbolises Christ's blood. These eggs are given as gifts, baked into breads and wielded vigourously in knock-out tournaments following Easter mass.
- Good Friday is a national holiday on which absolutely no work may be done. On this day no meat or dairy will appear on the table. And no olive oil or fruit juice, nothing that has to be crushed or deformed, in memory of the tortures Christ's body went through. On this day no one will hammer a nail or hang laundry in memory of his sufferings.
- Good Saturday is the day to slaughter the Easter lamb. In most parts of Greece it will be dressed and prepared for the spit. In the Dodecanese it will be stuffed with rice or bulgur, nuts and raisins, then trussed and placed in the communal oven to roast ever so slowly until the next afternoon. With the innards of the lamb people make *mayiritsa* (lamb's offal soup).
- Easter Sunday is the main event. The menfolk will dig a pit, kindle a fire within and have the lamb turning on the spit by mid morning. Women will keep them supplied with coffee, water and little things to nibble,

ALAN BENSON / GETTY IMAGES

Purple eggplant at the market.

and tell them that at noon they will bring them wine or ouzo. By about 11 o'clock the men will decide that it's noon somewhere in the world and that's good enough for them. The spirit of Dionysus is soon felt across the land. By mid afternoon the lamb is cooked and so are a few of the men.

DAILY MEALS

Our parents and government nutritionists have drilled us in the catechism that breakfast is the most important meal of the day. The Greeks haven't heard of this. Most Greeks think of breakfast as a cigarette and a cup of coffee. If there's time, two cigarettes. The best recourse is to take to the streets. The pie shops are open early and the range of cheap, delicious *pites* (pies) is astounding. Street vendors all over the country sell *kuluri*, a bagel-like ring of baked dough studded with sesame seeds, and one of the most common and popular breakfast foods in the country.

Lunch is the big meal of the day. It does not start until about 2 pm or later. All in Greece, except waiters and cooks, set aside their cares and come when called to table. There will be *mezedhes* (a selection of small dishes) including olives, octopus drizzled with oil and vinegar, stuffed vine leaves, dips, spreads and innumerable other culinary bits and bobs.

There is no succession of courses. Food is brought to the table as it is ready. Salad will usually come first, but that is because it is ready first. Vegetables will be a part of every meal. Then there may be more substantial fare such as fish or a meat dish such as *musaka*, thickly sliced eggplant and mincemeat arranged in layers, topped with béchamel sauce and baked. For the next two to three hours the world revolves around food and each other. Everyone eats and drinks and talks and laughs. Life happens in Greece when all are at the table.

Dinner is in the evening around 10 pm, never earlier than 9 pm. Everyone will come again and repeat the lunch ritual, though with a somewhat reduced calorie intake.

ESSENTIAL PRODUCE

Bread

In Greece, *psomi* (bread) is not merely the staff of life, it is life and birth and death, and all that transpires in between. It marks the seasons and the ages. There is a bread for your name day. There is a bread for Easter. There is a bread for Christmas, for fast days, feast days, birthdays and days of remembrance. There is oven bread, pan bread and pot bread. Wheat, barley and corn bread. Bread in a hundred shapes. Holy bread, profane bread, sweet bread, sour bread. And, by jingo, you can get that lightweight aerated sliced thin stuff we have at home if you really want it.

Since the day bread was first made in Greece, it has been imbued with sanctity, mystery, magic and superstition. Eating a special star-shaped bread called *fanouropsomo* will help your wishes to come true or help you to find lost treasures. A pregnant woman traditionally hides a crust under her pillow to ensure a healthy baby.

Perhaps the best-known Greek bread is *pita*. That stuff you buy at your local supermarket, or have filled with salad or *falafel* bears little resemblance to *pita* in Greece. Yes, it's round and flat, but that's where the resemblance ends. Greek *pita* is thick, often wholegrain and absorbent. It does not split in the middle so that you may stuff food into it. It is pliable and folds easily so that you may fold it around a tasty filling.

Feta cheese

Feta is the national cheese of Greece. Foreigners and Greeks alike think of *feta* when they think of Greek cheese. We don't

Freshly baked bread.

ALAN BENSON / GETTY IMAGES

Militinia, Aegean cheesecake.

Loaves line the shelves at a bakery.

Dakos, a dish of rye bread, *mizithra* (cheese), tomatoes and olives.

Goat milk is widely used in dairy products.

Greek honey is unique and very popular.

know how long Greeks have made *feta*, but the oldest-known record dates back to Venetian rule in the city of Chandia (Hania) on Crete. No surprise at the name, then, for the word *feta* is the Italian word for slice.

All *feta* is made from sheep's milk, though it may contain up to 30% goat's milk. Most *feta* comes from mountainous areas, where pesticides and other agricultural chemicals are rare. However, in this high environment, grazing is limited so the flocks have to cover great distances in order to be able to feed adequately. This presents a double advantage for the cheese. Because of the wide grazing pattern the sheep feed on a wider variety of plants, and they transmit their characteristics to the milk. And, because the sheep are constantly in motion they don't get fat, hence their milk is less fat, thus the cheese is less fat and has its characteristic dazzling white colour. *Feta* made outside Greece must be chemically treated in order to achieve the same whiteness.

People eat *feta* in innumerable ways:

- as part of the well-known Greek salad
- baked into pies
- crumbled on omelettes
- stuffed into fish
- dredged in flour and fried to make *saghanaki.*

But perhaps the best way, the true *feta*-lover's way, is to lay a thick slab on a plate and drizzle it liberally with olive oil. Maybe a pinch of fresh oregano. Take this with a piece of stout Greek bread and a glass of *ouzo*, and you'll have a uniquely Greek moment to savour.

Honey

The original and quintessential Greek sweetener is *meli*

(honey). Greek honey is unique, and you'll realise this as soon as you see it. It is darker than most commercially available honey, yet possesses a clarity such that you can almost see through it, like stained glass. You will know when you smell it; its aroma suggests flowers and fields. Most importantly you will know it when you taste it. It's flavour is more intense yet less sweet. It is full in the mouth yet doesn't cloy. You are persuaded that you are eating not a sweet, but a perfect natural food that happens to be sweet.

Olives and olive oil

Elyes and *eleoladho*, the olive and its liquid gold, are more than food. The olive is both the symbol and the substance of Greek-ness.

It has been used in religious rites since pagan days, and as you read this, a priest is baptising a child and anointing it with olive oil, which may have been scented with rosemary or rose petals for the purpose. When that baby grows up, grows old and then dies, it will be laid to rest in a grave lined with olive branches, for the olive is the symbol of rebirth as well as life. It is also a symbol of victory, of peace, and of plenty.

- The olive is medicine, the olive is soap and the olive is hope. Hippocrates dressed wounds with olive oil, and Christian Greeks used it as a poultice for sores.
- Olive oil is mixed into the cement used to build churches.
- Fisherfolk pour it on the waves to smooth them so they can see the fish below.
- It fuels the lamps that illuminate icons in churches.
- It is even a colour.

When you go to the market, you'll see olive oil not in small glass bottles measuring 1 litre, but in large jugs and jerry cans, casks

ALAN BENSON / GETTY IMAGES

A bowl of *kalamata* olives, cheese and glass of red w

and flasks. The Greeks consume more olive oil per capita than any other people: 20 litres annually. Greece is the third largest producer of olive oil, and the largest producer and exporter of extra virgin olive oil. Of all the trees in Greece, 80% are olive trees, and at last count there were more than 127 million.

There are hundreds of olive varieties, but most Greek olive oil is pressed from the smaller variety of *kalamata*, which is unique to Greece. The larger *kalamata* olives are used as table olives.

Both green and ripe *megharitiki* olives are also used as tables olives. When green they are the standard 'cracked' olive, so called because each one is individually cracked with a blow from a stone. As with the slit *kalamata*, this lets in the brine. When ripe they are dry salted. *Stafidholyes* are the easiest olives to recognise and to prepare. They look like giant raisins because the fully ripe black fruits are harvested then sun dried until they become wrinkled. Then they are lightly salted and packed, or immersed in oil.

Salads

Greeks would be bereft without *salata* (salad).They have eaten it since ancient days and little has changed in the ways it's prepared. *Horiatiki salata*, variously translated as country or village salad, is what we have come to know as Greek salad. Like so much of Greek gastronomy, what goes into Greek salad is widely open to interpretation.

The original was nothing more than a slab of feta and some sliced onions dressed with oil, and that alone is an excellent dish. Taken with bread and a little rough red wine it's a Greek ploughman's lunch. On good days our ploughman might add a few olives to the dish, and in summer a slice of tomato or cucumber. He might even add a few drops of his home-made wine vinegar. He would not use lettuce.

Nutty and chewy nougat.

Spoon sweets, in this case a tiny pear.

Bougatsa, or custard pie.

Spoon sweets

As the name suggests, *Ghlika kutalyu* (spoon sweets) are sweet preserves served in a spoon. They are not just candy, nor something to spread on a piece of bread and eat as a snack or with an afternoon cup of tea, they are an essential part of Greek hospitality, itself an essential of part of Greek culture. In ancient times, strangers who called on the homestead were always given cool water to drink and something to eat, often a dried fig. But that stranger might be a saint in disguise, sent by God to test your heart. Even if there were no sugar in all the world and all the bees flew away, the Greeks, both high and low, rich and poor would have something up their culinary sleeve with which to purchase a good report in heaven.

Presentation is as important as taste in spoon sweets. You can see this immediately. The colours are vivid, the fruit without blemish, the syrup shimmering. If the fruit is cut, it's cut into pleasing and interesting shapes. Bergamot peel is cut into ribbons and rolled into little bundles. Bitter orange segments are geometrically perfect, varieties of fruit are chosen for their complementary colours and shapes.

The elaborate services of crystal or silver further attest to the aesthetic importance of the spoon sweet. In Constantinople there was an entire industry dedicated to their production. The custom is for your host to pour you a glass of water, and let you take a spoonful of the sweet and place it on your saucer. First you drink the water. Then, little by little, barely more than licking the spoon, you eat the sweet. When you're finished you put the spoon in the glass. If your visit is to continue, you will then be served coffee. Spoon sweet services are often heirlooms. Even poor families treasure them and will keep them locked up in hope chests or steamer trunks, awaiting the day a saint or other stranger arrives.

Suvlaki and yiros

Grilled meats can be had all over the land. Pork, lamb, chicken and even beef are available grilled on skewers or from huge vertical or horizontal spits. Perhaps the most famous of the grilled meat pantheon is *yiros*, from the Greek verb 'to spin'. In the north of Greece it is sometimes known as *doner*. Whatever you call it, you'll always know it when you see it. At first glance it appears to be a great haunch of beef turning on a vertical spit. But look closer and see that the haunch is actually about one hundred thin slices of meat tightly stacked in a tower about one metre high and thrust through with the spit. The man turns it by hand, a quarter turn at a time. He lets the fire side of the meat cook for a minute or two, then turns it again. Between turns he deftly slices off paper thin shavings of perfectly cooked meat.

Another grilled meat favourite is *suvlak*i, which is basically cubes of meat on a skewer. It is cooked over a charcoal or gas grill then dusted with oregano and served as is.

The famous *yiros*, this one with pork.

Vine leaves

Even fresh off the tree, *klimatofilo* (vine leaves) have a tangy and cleansing taste. Packed in brine, perhaps with a dash of lemon or vinegar, they are as appetising as oysters, delicious to look at and pleasant to smell. Their most common assignment is to hold packets of aromatic rice in *dolmadhes*. Although *dolmadhes* need not include rice, as fava beans, chickpeas, fish, and almost anything can become a *dolma* if it is wrapped in a tasty leaf and is small enough to eaten by hand. It gets extra points if it goes well with *ouzo*.

Carving pork *yiros*.

Yoghurt

Yaurti (yogurt) in Greece is something to swoon over. Normally made from sheep's milk, Greek yogurt is thick, rich, fat and

ALAN BENSON / GETTY IMAGES

Pickled vine leaves for sale at the market.

flavourful. More often than not, the Greeks eat it plain at any time of day, as a snack, side dish or dip. They bake it into pies. On Crete they serve it with fried potatoes, a strange yet addictive combination. The Cretans also use it in cooking rabbit and hare. Greek yogurt also makes *tzadziki* something more than a mere vehicle for garlic.

Yaurti is a common breakfast food, featured on the menus of virtually any taverna open in the morning. Have it with thyme honey and your mouth will remember it forever.

SHOPPING

At the market

Modern shopping may have arrived in Greece, but the smells and sounds of traditional, colourful commerce can still be found. The Greeks like modernity. As they say, 'Ours is not that culture buried in the ground.' Yet there are institutions that never die.

The spirit of the *agora* (market) has never gone away. You'll hear its echoes on the islands where small farmers set up shop with a pair of primitive scales under a palm tree. Gypsies in old trucks pull over to the side of the road and sell their goods to passers by. Peddlers come to the ferry docks to sell bread, sweets and local produce to passengers. Fisherfolk still land their catch on the ancient pier and sell to all who come. And once a week in many city neighbourhoods, a farmers' market convenes. It may be upscale and elegant as in Kolonaki in Athens, it may be sprawling and vast, teeming with gypsies and Albanian refugees as in the centre of Thessaloniki; it may be small, humble and convivial as in Nafplio.

Something fishy

The Greeks have a curious relationship with the sellers of fish. Fishmongers are generally regarded as liars, cheats,

ALAN BENSON / GETTY IMAGES

Morning catch of fish.

mountebanks, charlatans, frauds and all-round bad apples. Even ancient comedies portray this popular attitude toward the fishmonger. When you go to the market they are assumed to be offering you yesterday's catch, artfully presented to look and smell like freshly caught fare. The wise shopper is urged to take nothing for granted, to probe and pinch each potential purchase, to look it in the mouth and in the eye (the seller as well as the fish) and to accept nothing but the freshest, plumpest, prettiest fish or go elsewhere.

The market taverna

All the grand markets of Greece have a taverna situated right next to the butchers. This is a very old custom, and wise. Unless you are a vegetarian the smell of fresh meat will eventually induce hunger. By about 6 pm the butchers and most of the merchants have closed up shop, but the taverna still hums with business. People come for a coffee or a drink after work. Around 9 pm the early diners arrive, and so begins the dinner service that will last for as long as anyone is hungry. The food is on display at the front. No menu needed to select mussel pilaf, cheese-stuffed squid, *yemista* (stuffed vegetables), grilled octopus, fish and *suvlaki*.

It's a family operation. Mother, aunt and daughter work the grill, the men serve, constantly passing on orders to the kitchen hand, receiving the ready viands. The pace gets manic yet they hold it together. The party begins around 2 am when revellers begin filtering in. Music begins to pulsate. A few selections are contemporary, but most of it is Greko-pop, a modernistic rendition of Middle-Eastern music. Soon the women are dancing with each other. It's a sort of belly dance, replete with flailing scarves. The men are sitting, drinking, talking, eating. They will eat, drink, sing and dance here in the marketplace until they can do no more.

DEFINING DISHES

Baklava

It's hard to mention Greek sweets without mentioning this. It is a staple of the dessert table throughout the Middle East, and there are few variations on it. *Baklava* is *baklava* whether in Athens or Beirut or Cairo. Layers of *filo* dough, well buttered or oiled, are alternated with layers of chopped nuts, and perhaps raisins or currants. They might or might not be dusted with cinnamon or cloves or allspice. The whole thing is baked and then soaked with sugar syrup or honey. As simple as it is, it can be hauntingly delicious.

Kataifi.

Mezedhes

What constitutes a *meze* (appetiser)? Theoretically anything can be served as a *meze* as long as it is small and goes well with *ouzo*. Of course 'small' and 'goes well' are definitely open to interpretation, especially in Greece. Perhaps the most common type of *meze* would be dips or spreads such as *taramosalata* or *melidzanosalata*. Even though these translate as carp roe salad and eggplant salad, they are not salads as we known them. Other popular *meze* include:

- *dolmadhes*, tangy vine leaves stuffed with aromatic rice preparations or with ground meat
- smoked or salted sardines
- *feta* or other cheese
- grilled octopus
- pickled vegetables and vegetable fritters
- fried peppers
- cured olives.

What most *mezedhes* have in common is that they are salty, piquant or otherwise assertive on the tongue. This is so they

Zucchini flowers stuffed with cheese.

Cans of anchovies.

Cooking lunch on an open grill at the Taverna Kokkalis in Stamata.

Lunchtime preparation at a pie shop.

Banana chillies at the market.

can stand up to the *ouzo*, the traditional *meze* tipple. Many *mezedhes* can be eaten by hand. The spreads and dips are eaten by scooping them up with a crust of bread.

Moussaka

Musaka (moussaka) is the best known of Greek dishes outside Greece: a casserole commonly made of layered ground lamb and sliced eggplant covered with a thick topping of *béchamel* sauce is cooked to a golden crust. Like most Greek recipes, it can be made with other ingredients such as ground beef, zucchini, squash or potatoes. Many Greek scholars believe that *musaka* was introduced by the Arabs when they brought the eggplant to Europe.

Pies

Pites (pies) are among the most common of daily fare in Greece. Most often pites are made with filo dough, but certainly not always. They can be filled with anything and everything, and they are. They can be home-made monsters cooked by *yaya* (grandma), but the ones you'll see most often are just big enough to fit in your hand. Favourites include *tiropita* (cheese pie) and *spanakopita* (spinach pie). But also look for *pites* stuffed with zucchini, eggplant, tomato, meat or things you won't be able to identify — but they will all be tasty.

Filo dough, the basis for most *pites*, is a paper-thin dough of flour and water, often containing a small amount of olive oil. The word *filo* means 'leaf', and it's used in many layers which calls to mind the leaves of a book. It produces a pie crust that's flaky, very flaky. So flaky that you should not eat *pites* sitting down as by the end you'll be covered with *filo* flakes. So do as the Greeks: eat them while walking to work or to appointments or just strolling about.

DRINKS

Retsina

Retsina is arguably the oldest continuously produced wine in the world. If you should go walking through a pine forest in Attica, you'll see the resin being collected. The harvesters use an axe to cut away a small oval of bark to expose the wood. They then hang a container and the resin slowly oozes in. The winemaker adds the resin to the wine as it ferments. Some independent producers making it at home use chips of pine wood, or even pine cones, instead of resin.

Travellers have denounced *retsina* for centuries. Merchants and ambassadors to Constantinople have written, very feelingly, that the resin was so strong it took the skin off their lips.

The usual grape for *retsina* is the white Savatiano, but any wine can be *retsina*, even red, even champagne. And be aware that Savatiano is not always made into retsina. If a wine contains resin, it will be so labelled. *Retsina* goes very well with Greek food (especially seafood) and it makes a fine aperitif. It is cleansing on the palate, stimulating to the salivary glands and good for digestion.

Ouzo

Made from distilled grapes, *ouzo* may have many flavourings (including mint, fennel and hazelnut) but chief among them is always aniseed. And no matter what the distiller may add, there is always a touchstone to let you know that it's the real thing: when you add water to *ouzo* (which is the proper way to drink it) it turns a milky white. Although they are always flavoured with aniseed, no two *ouzos* are alike, and it can be difficult to keep track. Many people say that the island of Lesvos produces the best *ouzo*. Common brand names are Mini, Aphrodite and Metaxa.

Drinks on a table in an *ouzeri*.

Bringing coffee to the boil.

Bottles of *retsina*.

Sweet tea on offer at a street market in the Bosphoros.

GREG ELMS / GETTY IMAGES

Turkey

Turks are passionate about food — they write love songs to yoghurt, ballads about fish sandwiches and poems that imagine battles between pastry and *pilav*. Turks have fun with food too. Their ice cream is so supple it can be used as a skipping rope, a to-die-for eggplant dish is called 'the priest fainted' and plump meatballs are dubbed 'woman's thighs'.

CULINARY CAPITAL ANATOLIA **KNOWN FOR** KEBABS, TURKISH DELIGHT **IMPORTS** RICE **EXPORTS** DRIED FRUIT AND NUTS **DEVOUR** *BAKLAVA* **AVOID** TRIPE SOUP

Buildings and illuminated minarets in Sultanahmet.

Sweet pastries.

Elderly man drinking tea.

CULTURE

When purists talk about Turkish food, they mean *saray* (palace) cuisine, developed in the massive, extravagant kitchens of Istanbul during Ottoman times. But even at the empire's height, most Turks didn't have access to the astounding variety and sheer quantity of food available to the wealthy — not everyone was eating whole sheep and buckets of saffron-infused pudding. Eating and drinking in Turkey has always varied according to heritage, wealth and region.

The central principles are the same though, rich or poor, east or west. Food and drink sustain the body and the spirit. Eating should be joyful but it should also be respectful, both celebration and thanks. Meats, vegetables and grains are prepared in unfussy ways to foreground their essential nature. Herbs, spices and sauces are partnered with foods without overwhelming them. There is an enthusiasm for seasonal produce but meats, fruits and vegetables are also preserved so they can be eaten out of season.

Technique and tradition

The mark of a good traditional cook in Turkey isn't creativity, it's skill: their *yufka* (*filo* pastry) is a mere membrane, their kebab tender, their *sarma* (roll-up dish) well-formed, their *pilav* (rice dish) fluffy, their *ayran* (yoghurt drink) smooth and light. You don't experiment with what is perfect, you just realise it to the best of your ability. Though many procedures are delicate, the cook needs to be deft rather than fussy; sometimes elbow grease and grunt is the way to epicurean heaven.

Until recently, cooks tended to absorb cooking techniques and combinations from the people around them, rather than from cookbooks or recipe exchanges. Old recipe books here read more like herbal medicine treatises, prescribing particular foods for various ailments rather than teaching how to cook. These days, a concern to preserve old dishes within Turkey and to introduce Turkish food to an international audience has made writing recipes down more common.

REGIONS

At its widest, Turkey stretches 1700 kilometres west to east and a strapping 1000 kilometres from the Black Sea south to the shores of the Mediterranean — plenty of room for markets, menus and what-mother-knows-best to shift and change.

Southeastern Anatolia

Southeastern Anatolia is hot, rugged and proud, and so is its food. The local cuisine is imitated all over Turkey but it's worth making the effort to try it on home turf. If it sprouts, ripens or grazes, chances are it's here: sheep, cows, wheat, lentils, chickpeas, onion, sugar, sesame, melons, peppers, spinach, nuts, olives, pomegranate and plums are all featured.

Regional highlights include:

- Malatya, the apricot centre of Turkey. The fruit, dried and fresh, is rushed to every corner of Turkey where people ask for it by name. Malatya's *pestil* (dried fruit pulp sheets or strips) and *kume* (*pestil* rolled up with nuts inside) are the best in Turkey — how so much big flavour can be packed into such little strips is a mystery.
- *Fıstık* (pistachio) is the glaring star of this region. *Fıstık* trees love hot weather and arid soil — just like the land around Antep and Siirt. The tasty nuts fetch a tidy sum, keeping these communities housed and fed. People in Antep naturally use the nuts in a plethora of dishes, such as *meze* (hors d'oeuvre), meat and rice dishes and most of the region's killer desserts.

GREG ELMS / GETTY IMAGES

Fruit and nut seller at the Balyk Pazar Market in Istanbul.

- *Çig köfte* (spicy mince kneaded with bulgur for three or four hours, wrapped in a lettuce leaf and eaten raw with a squeeze of lemon) is one of those 'you've got to try it if you're in the area' dishes.
- Diyarbakır is so enamoured of its watermelons that it holds a festival in their honour in late September.

FEASTS

Birth

The traditional tipple for celebrating the birth of a baby is a boiled sugar drink with red chilli pepper, cinnamon, rose-water and sometimes lemon juice. The drink is dyed red, these days with artificial colouring, but traditionally with crushed cochineal, a Central American insect brought to Europe by the Spanish. The sherbet is served to all guests who visit the house and also sent in decanters wrapped with red tulle to close relatives and neighbours. If the baby is a girl, the lid of the decanter is also wrapped in tulle; if it's a boy, the lid is left unwrapped. If left to cool, it will crystallise and can be cut into a diamond-shaped candy.

Marriage

Marriage celebrations are the most extravagant of all. These days even modest weddings may take a few days. The bride's family hosts an evening wedding feast (usually on a Saturday night) during which the bride sneaks off, gets married, but then returns to the fold. The next day, the groom's family holds a feast, welcoming the bride into their household.

Before consummating the marriage, the bride and groom nibble on some unsalted chicken, which is thought to bring blessings of good fortune to their union. It's also believed that the first nuptial food remains in the stomach for digestion in

GREG ELMS / GETTY IMAGES

Catching up with friends at the Old Bazaar in Istanb

the afterlife, so it's obviously of importance what is eaten.

This basic structure of the wedding is amended, appended, truncated and elongated, according to wealth and regional variations. Upscale weddings incorporate trotters day — the lucky bride is sent a dish of delectable sheep's feet by her husband on the day after the wedding.

Death

Funeral ceremonies occur as soon as practical after death, the next day if possible. Semolina *helva* is delivered by the bereaved to neighbours and friends the day after a death and again 40 days later. The *helva* may be made communally by women gathering to lament the passing of the deceased. In this case, the stirring spoon will be passed around the circle of mourners and whoever has it will lead the reminiscing.

ETIQUETTE

At the sofra

Meals usually take place around a regular table and chairs but some households still use a traditional village *sofra* (low round dining table). When eating at a *sofra:*

- Diners sit on the floor, on carpets or cushions.
- The traditional posture is to sit with one foot tucked under your bottom and the other one bent so your foot is flat on the floor. It's also acceptable to sit cross-legged.
- People may look aghast if you put your palms on the ground for support — it's thought the devil can enter through them!
- A tablecloth extends far beyond the *sofra's* perimeter, acting as a communal napkin — you drape it over your lap and it's gathered up at the end.

After the food is served and the blessing said, everybody digs in. Courses follow hot on each other's heels, partly because it's considered slothful to linger and rude to keep someone waiting. If someone's finished their soup, the main dishes will be brought out. If someone's finished their mains, the dessert will arrive. The underlying directive seems to be: get it all on the table! Let's eat! Naturally, the cook will appreciate your praise, but the best way to show your enjoyment is by eating.

Knife, fork, spoon

Until the 20th century, eating utensils were a spoon and a piece of bread. Now the standard table setting is a fork and spoon. Knives aren't rare but they aren't often necessary as most food is plated in bite-size portions.

During Ottoman times it was the custom for travellers to carry their own spoons about with them, lessening the burden on their hosts. Spoons became a prestige item, carved from wood or wrought from metal, embellished with elaborate designs. The most precious spoons were carried in embroidered cases.

DAILY MEALS

Eating in Turkey is as much about social interaction as it is about sustenance. Definitely, the connection between food and function is strong and meals are deliberately hearty to generate the energy necessary for hard rural work.

In Ottoman times Turks ate two meals a day, one in the late morning and one in the evening. Now three meals a day is the norm. The day starts with *sabahları* (morning food) or *kahvaltı*,(breakfast). A *Türk kahvaltı* (Turkish breakfast) consists of bread, white cheese and honey or jam at minimum. Usual augmentations are cold boiled eggs, tomato, cucumber, olives and sliced meat. Even though *kahvaltı* suggests coffee

GREG ELMS / GETTY IMAGES

Teas and spices for sale at the Spice Bazaar in Istanbul.

Simit, a common breakfast snack.

Meze waiter on the go in an Istanbul restaurant.

Boy selling bread from a cart at a street market.

— *kahve* means coffee — it's tea that is served as a matter of course at breakfast. Soup is also a common breakfast food.

The food eaten for the three daily meals regularly cross over. *Öle yemei* (lunch) might be the same cold spread as breakfast or it could be the more substantial kinds of foods that are eaten for *akam yemei* (dinner). This typically means soup, salad, vegetable dishes, grilled meat, *pilav* and fruit for dessert. If lunch is a big meal, dinner may revert to breakfast-style bread-cheese-olives, probably with the addition of *sarma* (wrapped dish) or some other *meze* (hors d'oeuvre). There is a traditional late afternoon cakes session which includes *börek*, *poaça* (buns) and coffee.

ESSENTIAL PRODUCE

Many of Turkey's core foods come directly from nature: apples so crisp they're almost too loud to eat, a simple meat sizzle, herbs which seem to fling flavour at you from the markets.

Bread

Living on *ekmek* (bread) in Turkey would be no problem at all. You could have:

- a sesame-studded *simit* (bread ring) for breakfast
- crusty bread and cheese for lunch
- a spicy meat *lahmacun* (Turkish pizza) drizzled with lemon for dinner and a syrup-soaked cream-topped rusk of bread for dessert.

Ekmek is the general term for bread of any sort but these days spongy white sourdough loaves are ubiquitous; *pide* (flat bread) is basic homemade village fare, as well as a pouch for *döner* and a base for pizza. *Lava* (thin crispy bread) is yeast-free but it balloons exuberantly when cooking. The chewy *simit* (bread ring) is sold in every plaza and on just about every street corner in Turkey. Turks are inclined to eat their bread plain, in between mouthfuls of food or with a little salt.

During Ramazan (the fasting month), normal loaves are sold in the mornings, but *pide ekmek* with *çörekotu* (black cumin seeds) is sold in the afternoons so hungry people have something special with which to break the day's fast.

Cheese

If it's got an udder, Turks have milked it and made *peynir* (cheese). Early nomadic herders discovered cheese was the most practical dairy food, being transportable, storable and nourishing. It could even be matured on the go, drained in skins hung from saddlebags on the march and slung over branches at the nightly camps.

Shopping for cheese in the markets is overwhelming — the bigger stalls are veritable expos, displaying all shades of white, yellow, round, square, stringy, plaited and smoked. When you're looking for the cheese that pleases, you will need to consider its age, saltiness, shape and origin. Home pastures make a big difference to the taste: the opiated output of Afyon's cows is quite different from the wot-you-lookin-at ruggedness of Erzurum's goats.

The flagship Turkish cheese is *beyaz peynir* (white cheese), usually made from sheep's or goat's milk and, during production, *beyaz penir* is left in brine for at least six months. This cheese is served at the slightest provocation for breakfast, lunch, sit-down snacks and *meze*.

Fruit syrup

Pekmez (fruit syrup) is boiled, thickened fruit pulp and it's a core food in Turkey. It's most commonly made from grapes but pomegranate, apples, quince and even rosehip can be enlisted to make this gorgeous glop.

GREG ELMS / GETTY IMAGES

Purple figs at a street market in Istanbul.

It's traditionally made by piling grapes in a stone trough and stamping on them with bare feet. The juice is drained, sieved through muslin and poured into a huge tin-lined copper pot. A square pit is dug, a fire lit and the pot is boiled up for the whole day. Thickener is added which in some villages means carefully chosen greyish soil. Once the mixture is viscous as high grade oil, it's put into jars and sealed.

Though *pekmez* looks and acts a bit like molasses, it's much more versatile. It's eaten with bread as a sort of jammy dip, poured over *baklava* or ice cream and is popular with kids.

Gozleme

Gözleme (filled *filo* pastry) is common all over Turkey, though different regions tend to make it in different shapes and with different fillings. The classic is stuffed with spring onions, parsley and cheese. *Çökelek* or any other white crumbly cheese will do fine. Mince meat, spinach or mashed potato are also possible fillers. A mix of yoghurt, milk and oil is brushed on the *yufka* to seal it, and also to give it a bit of sizzle when it's dry fried on a wok. In markets women in traditional dress sell *gözleme*, making the dough, then doing the filling, folding and grilling on the spot.

Meat

Et (meat) appears in most main meals, though it's usually itsy bitsy rather than hunka hunka — there isn't much sitting down to a rump steak. More often, flesh is cut in small pieces or minced and cooked with vegetables.

Coronary carers will note from the crackle and spit that fatty meat is prevalent. Sheep's tail was traditionally used to procure frying lard — especially in the east — though these days vegetable oil is more common. People in cities eat more meat than their country cousins, even though villagers are the

Kokoseg, roasted sheep intestines, on a spit over burning coals.

ones raising animals. Many villagers sell their livestock and live mostly on fruit, vegetables and cereals. Generally, less meat is eaten in summer, when lighter dishes are preferred.

Just about every bit of the animal is eaten: organs, head, feet, nether regions. Economy was the initial reason, but it does seem that Turks have a taste for the spooky bits.

Meat in Turkey is killed *halal*, that is, in accordance with Muslim law — a prayer is said, the beast's throat is cut, rapid death ensues and the blood is drained from the body. Lamb, mutton, beef and chicken (and less commonly, goat) are used in similar ways around the country, depending on availability. Beef is more common along the Black Sea, lamb tends to preponderate along the Aegean and east of the centre. Chicken is popular everywhere.

Pastry

Turks must be genetically bound to love pastries by now – they've been eating them since the nomads of Central Asia called a prototype *börek* (pastry dish) 'bura', after Bura Khan of Turkestan. *Böreks* are distinguished by their filling, cooking method and shape: they are square and cheesy, cigar shaped and meaty, plain and moist, pointy and potato chunky. Most people buy *börek* by the slice from their local *pastanesi* (pastry shop) and eat in with an *ayran* (yoghurt drink) for a quick breakfast, or grab a box to augment the perfect picnic platter.

Preserved fruit

Konserve meyveler (preserved fruit) is a big deal — it's dried, bottled, jarred and jammed. Drying fruit might be as simple as bunging some figs on the roof and letting the sun do its work or it could be a bit more involved. Before apricots are dried, they are split, the stone cracked and the sweet almond-shaped kernel is removed and tucked back inside the fruit. Drying fruit could also mean pounding it into submissive strips of *pestil* (dried fruit pulp sheets or strips). You'll see sheets of *pestil*, most often made from grapes, figs or apricots, hanging up in delicatessen windows all over Turkey. When *pestil* is rolled up with nuts inside, it becomes the succulent, flavourful, energy-rich *kume*.

Rice

Pirinç (rice) is used in soups, stuffings, puddings and, most gloriously, in *pilav*. It's one of the few foods that Turkey doesn't grow much of but counts as an intrinsic part of its cuisine.

Rice rises to its full potential in a good *pilav*, coaxed lovingly by an expert hand into a juicy cloud, suspended flirtingly between firmness and flounce. The reputation of a housewife and the career of a chef can stand or fall on their *pilav*. The essential quality is fluffiness: each grain of rice should stand alone, proud and independent, moist and glistening without being wet or oily. Producing a clumpy or gluggy *pilav* is a cause for great shame.

Soup

Soup is for breakfast, soup is for lunch, soup is for dinner. *Çorba* (soup) starts the meal and soup is a meal in itself. Soup is carefully planned and soup is a slapdash sopping up of leftovers. Soup sets you up for a day in the fields and brings you down after a night on the town. Soup is for life, Turkey's silent call to prayer and all its prayers answered.

Soups are generally served lukewarm, though in eastern Turkey it's not unusual to have your soup arrive stone cold.

Turkey's most famous soup is a pungent slurp-fest made from chopped lamb's tummy. It's not to everyone's taste, but if you can stomach it, a visit to the *ikembeci* (tripe soup eatery) is an essential element of any carnivore's visit to Turkey.

Tomato *salca paste* in plastic bags.

Sade pilav, a simple rice dish.

Dried fruit, nuts and sweets at the Spice Bazaar in Istanbul.

Yoghurt

When a country starts writing love songs to *yourt* (yoghurt), you know you're looking at a nation of dairy queens. One eastern Mediterranean town produces yoghurt so alluring, that its praises have been immortalised in a folk song which roughly translates as 'Oh, Silifke yoghurt, who gave birth to you? The mother who gave birth to you will be my mother-in-law.'

Yoghurt is made from sheep, goat or cow's milk and is drunk as *ayran* (yoghurt drink), spooned up as *cacık* (yoghurt salad), dolloped in soup, sauces and desserts or simply eaten as a snack. *Kanlıca,* a Bosphorus suburb on Istanbul's Asian side, is famous for its yoghurt, delicious with a sprinkling of *podra* (icing sugar).

At the markets, you'll encounter two main sorts of yoghurt. The first is *sıvı tas* (the runny first pressing) used to make *ayran* and *cacık*. The second, *süzme* (a thicker yoghurt that has been sieved to extract moisture), is used in cooking and to make herby spreads.

SHOPPING

At the market

Markets are bustling, vibrant places with a lot of by-play and theatre as well as a profusion of wonderful food. The cheese seller solemnly offers you a morsel to try. The strawberry man presses glistening fruit into your hand with a secret agent smile. The watermelon vendor yells '*Kesmece*!' ('I can cut it!'), implying that this melon is so good, he'll prove it by hacking it to bits on the spot.

There are two main types of market. The first is the purpose-built market, with shop-like stalls. These are open between five and seven days a week, and are found in sizeable towns and cities. The second is the outdoor market, set up in a street or plaza once or twice a week, and found in just about every

Delivery man with an armful of bread rolls, Istanbul.

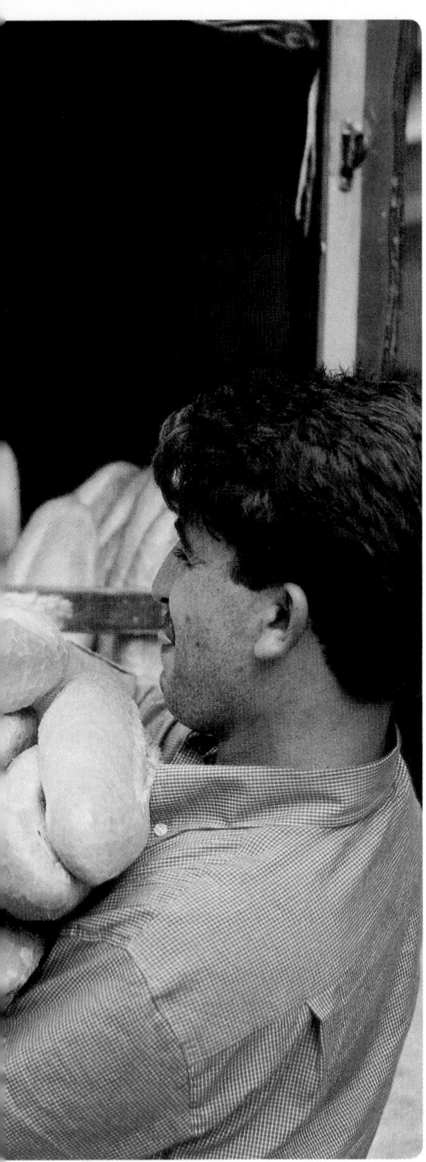

village or town. Big towns may have three or four such markets, each one in a different location.

Some markets have no apparent logical layout: a T-shirt seller is set up next to a pile of potatoes which are next to a pots and pans vendor who is hard up against a fish van. Others are more ordered: the cheese and olive sellers cluster together, the spice and nut sellers are in a row, the fish and meat sellers are set up in a line of refrigerated kiosks. A part of the scene may be devoted to livestock: goats stinking up a trailer, chickens clucking, lambs bleating, all available for inspection and sale.

Bakery

Also called an *ekmekçi*, the *fırın* (bakery) provides the divine dough that fuels the human engine: it has an almost sacred air. Most bakeries churn out bread from before dawn to lunchtime, supplying corner stores and roving vendors, as well as selling direct to the public. The core item is springy crusty sourdough loaves that tumble from the ovens at regular intervals.

Pastry and sweet shops

Pastanes and *baklavacı* (pastry shops and sweet shops) are delectable torture chambers that draw in the unsuspecting by the skin of their sweet teeth. In a flash, the hapless victim has stocked up on calories from here to Friday but is still batting the eyelids at the gooey treats in the window.

Pastanes (pastry shops) sell *kuru* pasta (dry pastry) such as biscuits and cookies perfect for snacks, picnics and gifts as well as *ya pasta* (moist pastry), the cakes and syrup-soaked wonders will have you swooning. Usually there will be tables where you can sit down and eat, and drinks (certainly tea and perhaps coffee) will be available. Some early openers also serve a simple cold breakfast. Though many *pastanes* also sell *baklava*, true devotees get their layered lovelies from the specialist *baklavacı*.

PREPARATION

Making pide

In most Turkish families the kitchen is a female domain, a social space for women as important as coffee houses are for the men.

In summer, women make a batch of *pide* every week or so but in winter they tend to prepare a large quantity communally and store it for use throughout the colder months. This involved operation takes place over two days.

- On the first day, a salty dough is made from brown flour and laid out on a cloth sheet. Another sheet is laid over the top and the dough is kneaded by people walking over it. (This is especially popular with kids.)
- The trampled dough is left overnight and the next morning it's wrenched into baseball-sized spheres.
- Each women sits with her legs under a *tahta* (wooden slab table) to roll the dough balls into big, flat circles.
- The *pide* is cooked quickly on a wok over a grape-wood fire, then piled up and stored for winter.
- Just before meals, a batch of dry *pide* is sprinkled with water and heated, making it pliable again.

DEFINING DISHES

Baklava

The prince of pastries, the swooniest sweet thang — our own ode to baklava would be passionate and unreserved. It doesn't feel right to pull the stuff apart unless it's with tooth and tongue, but let's dive in, strictly in the interests of science. *Baklava* is layers of *yufka* (*filo* pastry), folded over, rolled around or otherwise fondling a filling of nuts, *öbiyet* (a butter and sugar cousin of sherbet) or *kaymak*. The whole lot is

GREG ELMS / GETTY IMAGES

Woman cooking, adding filling to *gozleme* in the Taksim district of Istanbul.

Round *baklava* for sale in Istanbul.

Raki, served with water.

Kebabs smoking on the grill.

drowned in syrup. *Baklava* is most often eaten as a snack with coffee during the day, but Turks also save a corner of the tummy for after dinner visits to the *baklavacı*.

Kebab

Just about anything you can poke a skewer at will be an essential component of some little Turkish town's proprietary kebab. They can be made with cubed meat, minced meat, vegetables, even plums and chestnuts. But kebabs don't even have to be cooked on a skewer — just about anything that's got anything to do with meat and isn't cooked with water can end up being labelled a kebab.

The *İskender* (or Bursa) *kebabı* is relatively elaborate: it's comprised of *döner* lamb served on a bed of crumbled *pide* and yoghurt. Two different sauces, first a tomato and then a burnt butter sauce are poured on at the table.

Lahmacun

Lahmacun is a type of pizza, most often topped with ground meat, onion, chilli and parsley. Other possible toppings include cheese, meat pieces and sausage. The classic *lahmacun* is oval and as long as a goalie's foot, though restaurants may make palm-sized portions.

Each region has its own way of making a *lahmacun*. When you're not doing it dainty, *lahmacun* is eaten as follows: slice it into strips, drizzle it with lemon, daub it with chunks of tomato, roll it up and eat it with your fingers. Once it's finished, you eat the debris off your hands and arms. It's also possible to eat *lahmacun* with a knife and fork, but its not as much fun.

Meze

Meze (hors d'oeuvre) is an event rather than a type of dish. It's an evening gathering of family and friends for drinking, chatting and leisurely grazing on nibbles and tidbits. The defining feature of *meze* is that people are there to partake of it: there's no prescription for what must appear on the table. Typical *meze* dishes include different vegetables *zeytinyağlı* (cooked in olive oil) accompanied by garlic yoghurt, bulgur salad, pastrami, *lakerda* (sliced and salted tuna fish), carrot salad and *fava* (mashed broad bean salad). *Meze* dishes are usually served cold, and many can be prepared a day in advance.

Turkish delight

Plain *Lokum (*Turkish delight) is just the beginning. You'll see it mixed with all sorts of different nuts, dried fruits, *kaymak* (cream) and coconut. *Sakız* (mastic) can be added to make a chewier delight; this addition also makes it easier to make *lokum* rolls. Some towns are known for their particular *lokum* invention: Safranbolu, inland from the western Black Sea coast, is known for its colourful roll ups, often coated with desiccated coconut.

DRINKS

Drinking here is a truly social activity, a way of meeting people or having an excuse to sit down and watch the world pass by. As well as omnipresent tea, there's the famed aromatic coffee or, for a different buzz, the Turks make tasty beer, wine, as well as their flagship firewater, *raki*.

Ayran

Ayran is a yoghurt drink, made by whipping up yoghurt with water and salt to the consistency of pouring cream. It's refreshing, healthy and goes well with meat and pastry dishes or just as a thirst quencher.

The traditional vessel for making *ayran* (and butter) is a *yayık*, a big cigar-shaped wooden tub suspended on strings so

GREG ELMS / GETTY IMAGES

Lahmacun, famed Turkish pizza.

Poppy-seed *lokum*, or Turkish delight.

that it can be swung back and forth for churning. The *yayık* is still used in villages, especially for occasions when a large quantity is needed, but these days a blender or whisk is much more common.

Tea

Today Turkey grows much of the tea it consumes, most of it on the steep, steamy hills east of Rize, near the Black Sea coast. Keen tea-heads eulogise the rich Rize crop but there are a lot of other varieties of tea if you fancy a change.

The most important thing to remember is that there is always time for a cup of tea. Everything else is mere detail. You'll be offered tea just about every time you stop moving: waiting for a bus, visiting a friend, shopping.

- Tea is served in a delicate tulip-shaped glass on a saucer holding two cubes of sugar.
- Most Turks will stir both cubes into the tea – some even ask for a third.
- Strong Turkish tea does mellow out with a bit of sugar, but apple or herbal tea is lovely unsweetened. Once you've added sugar, stir your cup vigorously, then put the spoon on the saucer.
- As soon as you finish your cup (and often before), you'll be offered more tea.

Presents in your pie. During Ramazan (the fasting month) little gifts, trinkets and coins are hidden in children's evening fast-breaking böreks, though one imagines kids need no special incentive to eat after fasting all day.

Busy chefs prepare dinner for the crowds at the night market in Jemaa el-Fnaa square.

IZZET KERIBAR / GETTY IMAGES

Morocco

It's all in the hands. There is a magic in Moroccan food, and it comes from the women who make it, from secrets passed on like a sign language, by mothers and grandmothers. These secrets can't be told, only felt through fingertips, and observed over time.

CULINARY CAPITALS FEZ, MARRAKECH **KNOWN FOR** *TAJINE, BASTILLA* **IMPORTS** SPICES **EXPORTS** CITRUS FRUITS **DEVOUR** SWEET PASTRIES AND MINT TEA **AVOID** THE SHEEP'S HEAD SERVED ON *COUSCOUS* AT A FEAST

Colourful produce at the medina in Marrakech.

TIM E WHITE / GETTY IMAGES

CULTURE

Moroccans are proud of their food. It is invested with all the mythic, religious and ritual significance that a rich culinary tradition attracts. Each major dish has a story or a festival attached, and the preparation and sharing of meals is regarded as one of the most important pillars of a society that has, as its central energy, a strong sense of family and tribe.

Few cookbooks can do justice to the complexity of Moroccan food; knowledge comes from a deeper source. Traditionally, when a young bride went to her new husband's house, she brought with her a heritage of lore learned in the kitchen. Older Moroccan women rarely give precise measurements for ingredients — feeling and watching, combined with such intangibles as mood, weather, seasons and what's available that day at the *souq* (market) form their expertise.

Spice and simplicity

Moroccan cooks use spices with a heady harmony. Cinnamon, coriander, saffron, mint, cumin, ginger and pepper — the heart of Moroccan food lies in the spice shop. Redolent with tantalising fragrance, colourful, hearty and warm, a typical Moroccan dish orchestrates flavours with a deft touch. Strong, velvety flavours form an unmistakeable theme.

Moroccan food is quite simple, a fusion of whimsy and practicality depending on the ingredients and the occasion. Basic themes are few — long, slow cooking of stews and braises with sauces created by reduction; grills; salads of cooked vegetables; bread and cakes from local grain; fruit. Distinguishing characteristics come through the sophisticated use of spices — not for heat, but for fragrance and complexity, interleaving the dish with infinite drama and detail. This is where creativity comes in as each cook tells her own tale.

Culinary influences

Moroccan food is a window on the history of this fertile land. Despite wave after wave of invaders and the innovations they left behind, Moroccan culture has adapted to the times, without losing its own integrity.

First, there were the native Berbers, whose methods survive today. The tribes ate what they farmed, bartered or took. Many cooking pots and utensils are Berber in origin: the *tajine*, used to make the stew type dish named after it, and the *mejmar* cooker used to hold charcoals, could be carried anywhere by semi-nomadic families allowing good food to be made in the most rustic of circumstances.

Later, there were two influences on the development of Moroccan cuisine: the Arab influence drawn from its Persian heritage and the influences flowing back into Morocco from Spain.

Trade routes followed the ebb and flow of battles, and Morocco became a major spice user. When Islam ascended, the desert Arabs were more than ready to leave their tents and partake in the delights of the Persian caliph's court, which they had overthrown. The existence of a rich and ambitious court was crucial to the development of Moroccan cuisine as it exists today. While the rich and fertile countryside was able to support the production of good meat, vegetables, fruit, olives, nuts and dates, it was the sophistication of the courts in the major imperial cities of Fès, Meknes, Marrakesh and Rabat that developed the lavish culinary tradition.

Another major influence on Moroccan food came with the refinements developed in Spain, or al-Andaluz as it was known to the Moors. The Moors brought a higher consciousness to the culinary arts, as well as specific dishes such as *paella* (a saffron-flavoured rice dish) and some *tapas* (appetisers), which you can still find today in the coastal regions of Morocco's north. The increased production and use of olive oil is another

Fish are landed at Essaouira's port.

Cinnamon sticks at the Spice Bazaar.

Vendor offers up the head of his *mechoui*, whole spit-roasted sheep, for sale at an outdoor restaurant in Djemaa El-Fna.

good example of a Spanish preference finding its way into Moroccan culinary culture.

Later still, the Ottoman Turks introduced another historical layer. They brought grills and barbecues to Morocco's culinary repertoire.

More recently the French colonised Morocco in 1912, leaving 44 years later. They left behind certain pastries and desserts, ice creams and confectionery, wine, and the combining of grills with raw salads.

FEASTS

Aid el Kebhir

Aid el Kebhir is held to celebrate the sacrifice of Abraham. During the weeks before the holiday, sheep are fattened for the feast. They can be kept in kitchens, on rooftops, or in small garden plots before being slaughtered, mid morning on the day of *Aid el Kebhir*. This task is performed by the head of the household or sometimes a neighbourhood butcher. Every family, rich or poor, aims to have at least one sheep for this occasion. The quality of the beast may depend on the affluence of the family, but not to have a sheep is a sign of piteous poverty.

Every part of the lamb is used over the four-day festival, allowing cooks to cover a spectrum of Moroccan meat dishes:

- brochettes are made from liver
- *kefta* balls are made from minced portions
- *tajines* are made from cuts of neck, shoulder and thigh
- *dewwahra* – innards and tripe – are simmered in a spicy sauce
- the steamed head of the sheep is the crowning glory of the *couscous*

ANTARES71 / GETTY IMAGES

Sweet and succulent honey *tajine*.

- *mruziyya,* the rich *tajine* of lamb, prunes and almonds is also served and some of the meat is preserved in *khli'*
- the lamb's brains are washed, cooked and combined with herbs and spices in a salad.

Mashwi

Perhaps one of the most famous methods of preparing meat is the Berber lamb feast, Mashwi. It is, essentially, a barbecue. A whole lamb is roasted on a spit above the glowing charcoals of a fire, built in a pit dug especially for the occasion.

The cleaned lamb is brushed inside and out with a mixture of butter, salt, pepper, cumin and sweet paprika, which is reapplied every 15 minutes or so throughout the cooking process. Cooking can take up to four hours. This method of 'dry-marinating', typical to many Moroccan grills, allows the lamb to develop a crisp golden crust while the meat inside remains delectably tender. Mashwi is accompanied by a mixture of salt and often *kwahh* — lamb and heart kebabs.

Marriage

Marriage is a festival in which gastronomy plays a major role. Wedding festivals traditionally lasted a week with numerous receptions. Today, they usually last a day, often with a feast in the afternoon, a dinner and an evening party that goes until dawn.

Marriage is placed under divine protection and must appear under the most favourable auspices. For the ceremony and the meals, milk, honey, dates, sugar loaves, bouquets of mint and marjoram, rose and orange-flower waters are used — auspicious symbols of purity, sweetness, prosperity and happiness.

Already a week before the wedding, the mother will offer the future bride dishes that 'no ladle has stirred' so that her marriage will be peaceful and untroubled.

The couple's first day together begins with the breakfast

ceremony, with the mother of the bride sending breakfast trays to the young newlyweds and their guests. The menu consists of *sfenzh* (doughnuts), milk, rice pudding and sheep's heads.

Before and after the wedding, the bride visits the *hammam* to purify herself. On her return, her parents send her trays of food with mint tea, coffee flavoured with orange-flower water and cinnamon, *krachels* — small, sweet bread rolls flavoured with aniseed and a sprinkling of sesame seeds, soft boiled eggs and roasted almonds. These foods are supposed to help the bride regain her strength.

ETIQUETTE

Eating with hands

In a country where eating with hands is a time-honoured tradition, hand-washing is an extremely important part of etiquette. Everyone is expected to wash their hands before a meal.

The cook will present the meal, and leave. Your host will then pronounce, '*bismillah*' (in the name of God) which should be echoed by everyone. At this point, you may start eating.

The most important rule at the table is to eat only with your left hand. It may help to surreptitiously sit on your right hand, which can only be used for picking up bread or passing other dishes. Furthermore you should only eat with the first two fingers of your left hand, using your thumb as the pincer (three in total). Using more digits is a sign of gluttony.

Giving alms

In Morocco, *couscous* grain has strong religious and emotional significance. Because of its place at the centre of the cuisine, it is connected with one of the major tenets of Islamic law, the giving of alms. Eaten mainly at the midday meal on Friday, the Moslem day of rest, a plate of *couscous* is taken to the local mosque and distributed among the poor after the meal. Many

JEAN DU BOISBERRANGER / GETTY IMAGES

Muslim men sharing a meal in Marrakech.

Woman cooking *trid,* flat bread, on a *ferrah*, jug.

Lamb brochettes with *couscous* and yoghurt.

Bread at the door in the town of Chefchaouen.

mosques insist the poor are invited into the homes of the locals. Cooks are expected to serve the alms *couscous* in exactly the same way they would serve their own family — to make an inferior *couscous* for the poor is frowned upon.

ESSENTIAL PRODUCE

Bread

In a culture where eating with hands is the norm, bread is used to soak up sauces and to help pick up food. It is often eaten with mint tea and a few olives, or grilled and topped with fresh butter, olive oil or argan oil from the argan tree, honey, or a special mixture called *amelou*, a delicious spread of argan oil mixed with almond paste and honey.

In most houses, bread is made fresh every morning. Loaves are marked with a family seal before being taken, usually by a child on the way to school, to one of the communal wood-fired ovens that abound in each district. The bread is baked, ready for the main midday meal. Children collect the bread on their way home from school, and the sight of happy kids skipping home with loaves wrapped in brightly coloured tea towels are enduring reminders of Morocco.

Butter

Moroccan preserved butter, *smen*, inspires opinions as strong as its flavour — some people cannot abide it, while others swear that it's a unique delicacy. *Smen* is added to many Moroccan dishes, and in the mixture of ingredients, loses a great deal of pungency. However, dishes made without *smen* feel like they are not quite authentic because *smen* is yet another Moroccan taste that stamps a characteristic mark.

Zebda is a butter that is made in the spring from curdled milk. Fresh milk is left to stand for two or three days in an earthenware jug, and then churned in a *khabia* (a special ceramic jar) until the milk separates. *Zebda* is used fresh for cooking or made into *smen*. The remaining buttermilk, *Iben*, is highly prized and drunk with sweet *couscous* at banquets, or at breakfast with pancakes.

Couscous

Couscous is synonymous with Moroccan food. It is the defining national dish. *Couscous* is both the basic ingredient — a semolina found in varying forms all over North Africa and native to the region — and the name of a dish, which is the semolina topped with a rich stew.

Moroccan *couscous* is usually served as one composite dish. It is perfumed spiced and fragrant, but not hot. The dish can include any number of elements from meat and seasonal vegetables, to dried fruit and nuts. It can be sweetened with sugar and cinnamon (called *seffa*, this dish is especially popular with children and is served with a glass of milk) and yoghurt for a snack or dessert.

Dates

In a nomadic culture spawned in the desert, it is not surprising that the date has become something of a sacred fruit. Highly nutritious, delectably sweet, easy to harvest and transport, the date was the staple food of the Arab Islamic warriors who swept into North Africa, just as it sustained Berber and Saharan tribesmen.

- Originating in the fertile plains of Mesopotamia, the date palm now flourishes all over Morocco.
- Plantations are found all over Morocco, including the renowned palmeraie of Marrakesh.
- There are over 30 sorts of date in Morocco, categorised according to weight, juiciness, size and shape. But size

KODIAK GREENWOOD / GETTY IMAGES

Dates, nuts and sweet tea on a petal-strewn platter.

is not everything, and some of the smaller ones are sweeter and more succulent.

- The religious significance of the date is heralded by its daily presence during Ramadan, when the fast-breaking soup, *hrira*, is traditionally eaten with a handful of dates.
- In Berber areas, dates and a heel of bread may be the only accompaniments to a mint tea break.
- Children are given dates for Mouloud, Mohammed's birthday; and also to celebrate the end of Ramadan.

Flower water

Flower water made from bergamot flowers and roses is used widely in Moroccan cooking, giving preserves, drinks and sweet patisseries their characteristic flavour.

- Flower water is made in spring time, when flower buds are seen heaped in large, fragrant piles, on huge wicker baskets throughout the markets of Morocco.
- About six kilograms of flowers are required to distill about 10 litres of water.
- After distillation, the water should sit for about four or five months to mature before being used.
- Good flower water is used sparingly, otherwise it tends to overwhelm other ingredients.

Fruit

Because of its warm climate, Morocco is a fruit-lover's paradise. Moroccan farmers excel especially in the production of citrus fruit — different varieties of oranges, lemons and grapefruits are grown almost all year round, almost half of which is exported. Dates, melons, almonds, olives, plums,

A Berber man holds an open pomegranate, displaying the edible red seeds inside.

Onions and garlic at the market.

Dried red chillies.

peaches, apricots, apples, quinces, pomegranates, figs and grapes supplement the diet of much of Morocco's population.

Garlic

Moroccan garlic is small and pink, with a sweeter, more fragrant perfume than its European counterpart.

- It is usually grated rather than chopped into dishes.
- It can also be pulverised with a mortar and pestle and mixed with salt into a paste. Cooks often rub this paste into poultry flesh and then rinse it off before cooking.
- Garlic is used in most salads and often in *tajines*, highlighting the delicate fragrance of coriander, cinnamon and cumin with its warm aroma.

Preserves

Preserves are one of the cornerstones of Moroccan food, as one would expect from a cuisine that is fundamentally seasonal. The community of Jewish-Moroccans was said to have developed the art of preserving to a high level. In fact the Jewish quarter in a Moroccan town is actually called *melha*, meaning 'salt'.

There is no doubt that the addition of preserved ingredients creates some of the defining flavours in Moroccan cuisine. Take preserved lemons, a common feature of a tajine or salad. The lemons impart their characteristic sharp tang and silky texture to the rich sweetness of many dishes.

Sauces

There are four basic stocks or 'sauces' in the Moroccan repertoire, and these stocks are really the basis of the entire Moroccan culinary pantheon. Most recipes are based on the use of one or other of these stocks. To understand how to prepare each is to understand the nature of Moroccan food. Each cook in Morocco then varies the ingredients to achieve their own special dish. The four Moroccan stocks are:

- *mqualli* — a yellow sauce based on saffron and oil with ginger
- *mhammar* — a red sauce based on paprika, cumin and butter
- *qadra* — mqualli with onions and pepper
- *msharmal* — a red sauce, with elements of the other three sauces permitted.

To further simplify the idea, Moroccan sauces are either yellow because of the addition of saffron, or red because of the addition of paprika.

Vegetables

Vegetables grow well in Morocco, and while the imperial and banquet dishes make little use of vegetables, they are common in domestic cuisine.

- Some vegetables, such as the thorny but delicious wild artichoke, are regarded as great delicacies. It grows prolifically around Fez, where it is prepared with great patience. It's said only Fassi women have enough patience and finesse to prepare it, while Casablancan women are too independent and impatient to wrestle with it merely for the sake of pleasing their men.
- Another renowned vegetable delicacy, one of the only imperial dishes in which vegetables are celebrated, is the famous dish, *couscous* with seven vegetables. This traditional Fassi dish plays on the number seven — seven vegetables and preferably seven spices — which Arabs regard as lucky.

PAUL HARRIS / GETTY IMAGES

Traditional Moroccan *tagine*.

SHOPPING

At the market

Anyone who wants to experience the real life of Morocco must visit the *souqs* (markets) that punctuate every village, town and city. Here, all of the myriad threads of Moroccan culture converge, from the simplest and most rustic country *souq* to the grand theatre of the famous market square in Marrakech.

The typical Moroccan *souq* has it all. Donkeys awkwardly make their way through alleys of beckoning merchants and streams of shoppers. The mouthwatering smells of food cooking compete with the sharp tang of citrus fruit being squeezed or the softer scent of rose petals displayed in great shallow wicker baskets. Peddlers shout songs about their wares. Visitors pause to gaze at great piles of dates and figs and almonds.

The head of a camel is displayed along with other of his former attributes — haunches, fillets and neck — next to a crate of cheeping, lively yellow chicks. Pastel-coloured nougat studded with almonds is stacked carefully in slabs like coloured terrazzo.

The spice *souqs* in the towns show the great and colourful variety of spices used in the everyday cooking of Moroccans. Bright red paprika and cayenne peppers, soft-hued ginger, yellow turmeric, dusty sticks of cinnamon, pale seeds of cumin and greenish seeds of aniseed are heaped in great tubs to be measured out into hand-twisted envelopes of paper.

PREPARATION

Tajine

A *tajine* is the most important utensil in the Moroccan kitchen.

- The *tajine* is made from earthenware, and should be cured before use

Earthenware pots used for cooking *tagine*.

- The pointed lid is glazed on the outside and unglazed on the interior
- *Tajines* come in various sizes, from tiny to feed one or two, to a huge feeding up to 20
- They are inexpensive, but once seasoned, are jealously guarded by their owners
- The plate of the *tajine* is quite shallow, with a grooved lip to take the lid snugly. It is important that the plate and top fit together well as *tajine* cooking is long and slow
- Every sized *tajine* has an accompanying *mejmar*, a cooker which sits underneath filled with charcoal.

Couscoussier

Another kitchen stable, this two-part metal steamer — usually aluminium — is used for making *couscous*. The upper part of the *couscoussier* is called the *kaskahs*. It is perforated with holes to allow steam to come through from the lower and larger part. Both parts have handles on either side and the *kaskahs* has a lid. The two parts should fit snugly together.

DEFINING DISHES

Bastilla

Moroccans are accomplished pastry makers. One of the most spectacular and renowned of Moroccan dishes is *bastilla*. For many aficionados, a discussion of Moroccan food begins and ends with *bastilla*, the extraordinary dish of multi-layered flaked pastry leaves, interspersed with shredded pigeon or chicken meat, moistened with a mixture of two dozen eggs gently curdled in a lemony onion sauce and studded with almonds. The whole is topped with a generous layer of cinnamon and sugar.

Apart from the opposition of sweet and sour flavours and the richness of the ingredients, the outstanding feature of *bastilla* is the *warka* pastry used to make the dish. It's said that a cook is not really a cook in Morocco until she masters the making of *warka*, which demands a deft touch, and above all, patience.

Making pastry

Making *warka* is a painstaking process. Imagine the finest, translucent leaves of pastry. Imagine squatting for hours over a hot pan and tap-tap-tapping a ball of wet dough in unending circular patterns. Imagine the vigilance and persistence needed to produce over forty sheets for each pie, which is about 30 centimetres in diameter.

The *warka* is prepared on the base of a *tobsil* (a large, low, circular pan which is heated by upending it over charcoal or a gas flame). Often, in restaurants, the *warka*-maker can be seen seated on a rolled carpet in the corner of the kitchen with her t*obsil* braced over what appears to be a bunsen burner, working away quietly with a meditative intensity. The *tobsil*, turned over, becomes the receptacle in which the *bastilla* is prepared.

Modern versions of *bastilla* include the use of seafood and a sweet version oozing with a custardy milk and diced almonds.

Doughnuts

As with doughnuts the world over, the Moroccan variety — called *sfenzh* — are best eaten hot, straight from the deep fryer. Almost every street has a *sfenzh* vendor, who threads his wares onto a shred of palm frond, knotted into a handle with which the buyer carries them off to enjoy with mint tea or coffee.

Kebabs

Meat kebabs can be found all over Morocco and are one of the

Pastries sold at the bakery in Chefchaouen.

Bread in piles at the Djemaa el Fna market.

Street vendor selling pastries.

Kebabs and other traditional foods cooked in an open market stall.

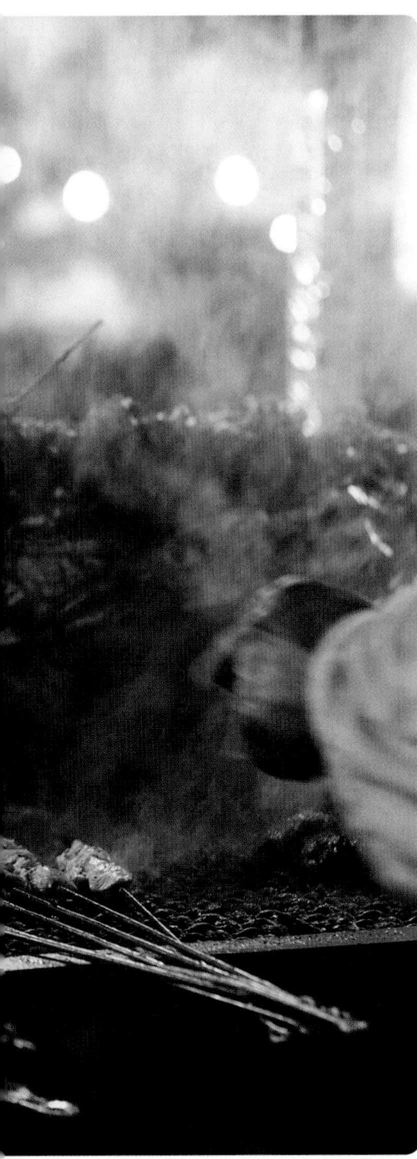
GARY YEOWELL / GETTY IMAGES

most common street foods on offer. You'll find *kefta kebabs* at almost every roadside stall. *Kefta* balls are formed from finely minced lamb which is mixed with spices (cumin, paprika, onion, salt and pepper, parsley and sometimes coriander) and moulded into small, sausage-shapes then threaded end to end on a skewer and grilled over glowing charcoal.

Commonly on offer, also, are cubes of lamb meat, which are alternated with cubes of fat to help the meat brown and sizzle. These lamb *kebabs* are known by their French name *brochette*.

All *kebabs* are served enveloped between the wings of a generous serving of bread and a choice of sauces, the most common being spicy tomato or *harissa*, topped off by sprinkling a mixture of salt and cumin over them.

Shermoola

In addition to the stocks in which most food is slowly simmered, Moroccans also use a distinctive marinade, called *shermoola*. This marinade is mainly used for fish and often as a marinade for cracked green olives. It's also occasionally used with poultry and meat.

Shermoola is a mixture of parsley and coriander leaves, onion and a variety of spices including garlic, hot red pepper, sweet paprika, cumin and sometimes saffron and ginger. These ingredients are blended with olive oil, lemon juice and salt. Sometimes, preserved lemons are chopped roughly through the mixture.

To prepare fish with *shermoola*, cooks rub it into the fish at least a half an hour before serving. Once marinated, the fish is either fried (after being rolled in flour) or cooked slowly in a *tajine*.

Tajine

After *couscous*, the *tajine* is Morocco's most renowned dish. *Tagine* refers to a method of cooking as well as a conical-lidded pot in which the dish *tagine* is prepared.

Essentially, *tajines* are stews of meat and vegetables sometimes with the addition of fruit and nuts, cooked very slowly in their stock in a glazed terracotta pot, the dish's namesake, over a charcoal fire.

Methods of preparation vary. In some regions meat is marinated and sealed before adding water. It is also sometimes rubbed with herbs and spices before cooking, allowing it to absorb a variety of flavours.

DRINKS

Almond milk

After mint tea, *sharbat bil looz* (almond milk) is probably Morocco's best-known native beverage. It is traditionally drunk at festivities and celebrations such as weddings but can sometimes be found in restaurants and cafes. Almonds are not cheap, and a considerable number are used in almond milk, increasing its value and status.

Tea

Moroccan tea is always deeply infused with mint. The fragrance of sweet, *na'na'* (mint) tea is an essential element in the heady, spiced scent of the Moroccan culinary experience.

The staple ingredients are everywhere. Every day fragrant, heavily laden carts of mint are towed in from the provinces behind tiny donkeys, to be sold in the *souqs* of every city, town and village. Mint is grown all over Morocco, but flourishes in mountainous regions, where the combination of cold weather and hot sun nurtures especially good plants. The type of mint used for Moroccan mint tea is spearmint, or *mentha viridis*.

In the south, saffron is sometimes added to mint tea. Saffron, the basis of many Moroccan sauces, grows abundantly in the area around Taliouine, and when the crocus flower (from which

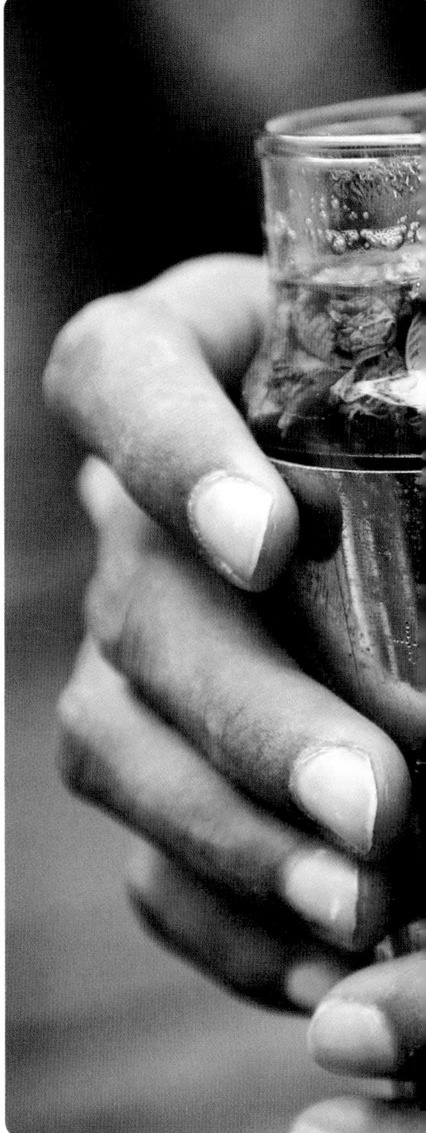

KIMBERLEY COOLE / GETTY IMAGES

Glass of mint tea in Fes Medina.

saffron threads are harvested) is ready, saffron tea is often made. In this tea, a teaspoon of saffron threads are added to the hot water and left to brew with the mint. Sometimes the saffron is used without mint (but plenty of sugar as usual). A highly prized and expensive ingredient, it is not used widely.

Tea etiquette

Tea accompanies meals and most social or business exchanges in Morocco. It can be served, on its own, or with a selection of Moroccan *patisseries* (pastries) and biscuits for morning or afternoon tea.

The tea ceremony is hedged about with a number of special accessories and rituals.

- Mint tea is always served in small, decorative glasses, and is often topped with a sprig of fresh mint.
- It is always served from a teapot in the 'Manchester' shape, inherited directly from the British heavy-bellied form, with a conical lid. This teapot is called a *barrahd*.
- When served ceremonially at a 'tea party' or before a meal, the *barrahd* appears on a four-legged silver tray called a *siniyya,* surrounded by *rbaia*, octagonal silver boxes, which hold the mint, sugar and tea.
- The hostess lifts off the intricately embroidered veil, which always covers the tray when it is not in use and, sitting cross-legged in front of it, proceeds to mix the ingredients. After the tea has brewed for some minutes, she stirs it once or twice, and pours a stream of liquid from a great height into one of the pretty glasses beneath.
- This first glass is always examined and poured back into the pot. Then all glasses are filled with the same high-handed, flourishing pour, and mint is added to each.

Man carrying Egyptian flatbread at Birqash Camel Market near Cairo.

PHILLIP HAYSON / GETTY IMAGES

Egypt

Egyptian food is hearty, honest peasant fare, full of the fresh flavours of the land. Food knits family and society together here and worries can be resolved — or at least accepted — after a good meal. *Bi-l hana wa-shifa* (literally 'with health and gratification') the Egyptians say before eating. For a meal cooked with love is more appreciated than the fanciest *haute cuisine*.

CULINARY CAPITALS CAIRO, ALEXANDRIA **KNOWN FOR** *FALAFEL*, *FUUL* **IMPORTS** WHEAT **EXPORTS** DATES **DEVOUR** *OMM ALI* (BREAD PUDDING) **AVOID** *MOLOKHIYYA* (LEAF STEW)

Street vendor placing lamb skewers on top of *tabbouleh* in pita bread as he prepares *shwarma*.

Glasses of hibiscus tea.

Falafel, an icon of Egyptian cuisine.

CULTURE

Much of today's Egyptian diet is as ancient as the land. *Hamam* (pigeon) was feasted on by the Pharaohs, the fields of the fertile Nile Valley provided them with bread and the workforce that built Giza's pyramids was paid partly in onions. At its heart, Egypt's modern cuisine is Middle Eastern. Meats and poultry are usually grilled, vegetables often stuffed, and a simplified rustic form of *mezze* (starter dishes) appears frequently.

Various foreign conquerors and communities also left their mark on the menu here. *Shakshouka* (an omelette-style breakfast dish) and *tagens* (clay pot stews) have their roots in Morocco, while the large Greek community that lived in Egypt up until the mid-20th century were probably responsible for the nation's favourite comfort food *macaroni béchamel* (an oven-baked pasta dish similar to the Greek *pastitsio*).

ESSENTIAL PRODUCE

Bread

Signifying its importance, the Egyptian Arabic word for bread is *a'aish* which is also the Arabic word for 'life'. Bread has been found inside Pharaonic tombs at Saqqara and has been the backbone of the diet since people here first began harvesting grain.

- *A'aish beladi* is a small pita-style loaf made from a combination of plain and wholemeal flour.
- *A'aish shammy* is a large, thin, circular bread made from plain flour.
- *A'aish merahrah* is a circular flatbread made from maize flour and ground fenugreek seeds.

Grains and Pulses

Lentils, chickpeas and *fuul* feature heavily in Egyptian cuisine.

All three pulses are commonly used in stews, tagens, and soups. *Roz* (rice) is a popular staple, first introduced to the diet in the 7th century, and now grown in the lower Nile Valley. It is eaten as a side dish, in stews, and is often found Egyptian desserts.

- In Egypt *fuul* is used as the main ingredient of *falafel* (known as *ta'amiyya* in Egypt) unlike the rest of the Middle East which uses chickpeas.

Bread with tomatoes and yoghurt.

Fruit and vegetables

Despite arable land constituting only 3% of the country, the Nile Valley and Nile Delta regions produce a vast amount of fruit and vegetables. Aubergines, onions, green peppers, cabbage, courgettes, okra, and tomatoes are all commonly found in produce markets throughout the country. Many vegetables are served stuffed (called *mahshi*) with a filling of rice and ground meat.

Egyptian fruit consumption is seasonally defined. *Tofa* (apples) and *bortuaan* (oranges) may be common year-round but cherries, mangoes, prickly pears, melon and pomegranate all enjoy their particular moment in the sun throughout the year.

Molokhiyya (mallow) is a leafy green first eaten by the Pharaohs and is something of a delicacy in Egypt.

Shwarma meat stand.

Meats, poultry and seafood

Throughout Egyptian history meats have been consumed sparsely and are a luxury item, not eaten every day at home. When meat is on the menu both *kebab* (chunks of skewered, char-grilled beef, lamb or chicken) and *kofta* (char-grilled minced meatballs) are popular. Seafood is commonly reserved to the coastal areas; the Red Sea, Sinai Peninsula, and Alexandria.

- *Shish tawooq* — char-grilled chicken kebab.

Fish served with rice and flatbread.

- *Hamam* (pigeon) — this Egyptian speciality is usually served roasted and stuffed with cracked wheat (known as *hamam mahshi*).

DEFINING DISHES

Fattah

In this popular dish, chicken, rice and bread are soaked in a garlic-vinegar sauce and then oven baked inside a clay pot.

Fiteer

Flaky layers of filo pastry are baked in an oven and graced with a variety of toppings. At its simplest the *fatatri* (fiteer cook) just adds honey but savoury toppings of olives, cheese, red peppers, and tuna transform this dish into 'Egyptian pizza'.

Fuul Mudammas

This classic breakfast dish consists of slow-cooked, mashed *fuul* usually mixed with tomatoes, onions, garlic, and lemon juice.

Kushari

Kushari, Egypt's favoured fast food, is regarded by many as the national dish. From early morning to late at night, dedicated *kushari* shops ladle portions from mammoth vats to a never-ending stream of customers. A completely vegetarian feast, *kushari* is a blend of noodles, rice, black lentils and chickpeas smothered in a tangy tomato sauce and topped off by fried onions, garlic-vinegar and spicy chilli sauce.

Kushari was a late-comer to the Egyptian table. It evolved in the 19th century when Egypt - though theoretically part of the Ottoman Empire - was ruled by the British. It is thought that the Indian rice and lentil dish *khichri* was brought by British travellers to Egypt and served as the inspiration for this dish. Italian settlers then added the pasta, and the Egyptians

NICO TONDINI / GETTY IMAGES

Basbousa, Egyptian semolina cake.

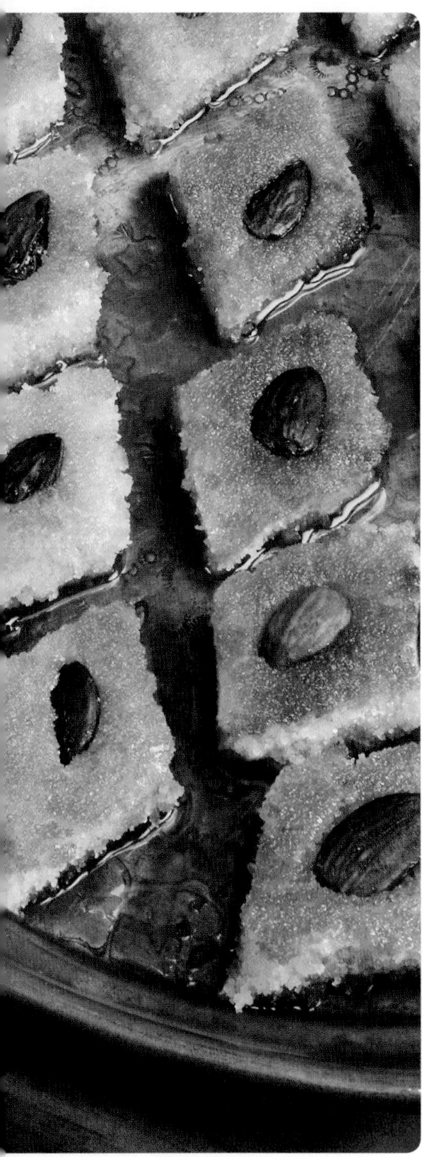

tweaked the recipe further adding tomato sauce, chickpeas, onions and garlic-vinegar.

Lisan al-usfur shorba

Otherwise known as bird-tongue soup, this soup is, perhaps confusingly, not made from tongues at all. It's main ingredient is *orzo* pasta (rice-shaped pasta) which looks like tiny tongues.

Molokhiyya

This stew of dried mallow leaves is made by simmering the leaves for many hours to a glutinous consistency, and then adding coriander, garlic and butter.

Omm Ali

This opulent bread pudding is made from layered filo pastry stuck together with lashings of coconut, sultanas and ground nuts, and smothered with cream. Some say this dessert was created by 'Omm Ali' after she beat love rival Ayyubid Empress Shajar al-Durr to death with a *hammam* (bathhouse) slipper.

DRINKS

Tea and Coffee

Nothing sums up free time in Egypt more than the social institution that is the *ahwa* (coffeehouse). Both *shai* (tea) and *ahwa* (Arabic coffee) are consumed in dizzying quantities nationwide. *Shai* is strongly brewed and typically served sweet, with the leaves floating in the bottom of the glass. *Ahwa* comes in tiny glasses, with ground coffee sludge at the bottom.

Karkadai (hibiscus) a juice made from boiling dried hibiscus flowers. A speciality of Upper Egypt, it is considered summer's most refreshing drink.

Vendor selling *ka'ik* bread from his bicycle.

TIM BARKER / GETTY IMAGES

Lebanon

So obsessed with eating are the Lebanese that even their country's name came about because of it: the snow-covered mountains inland reminded them of the pure whiteness of *laban* (yogurt). Food is more than fuel to the Lebanese. Big occasions call for long hours sweating over a hot stove and mealtimes are to be savoured; the table lingered over as the last mouthfuls of Mediterranean flavour are mopped up with a piece of bread.

CULINARY CAPITALS BEIRUT, ZAHLE **KNOWN FOR** HUMMUS, *BABA GHANOUGH* **IMPORTS** WHEAT **EXPORTS** SPICES **DEVOUR** *KIBBEH, MANEESH ZAATAR* **AVOID** *GHAMMEH* (STUFFED LAMB INTESTINES)

The pictureqe harbour at Tyre, the fourth largest city in Lebanon, and one of its major ports.

Hummus.

Confectionery from the capital, Tripoli.

CULTURE

At its core Lebanese cuisine takes its inspiration from the Middle Eastern flavours and cooking techniques seen throughout the Arab region. Flatbread, chickpeas, yogurt, and grilled meats were the staple diet of nomadic Bedouin tribes who first roamed the land. But across antiquity, and into the modern-age, the Lebanese menu has absorbed influences from a kaleidoscope of cultures.

In the medieval period, when the trading tentacles of the Arab empires stretched far into Africa and South Asia, new foods and flavours were constantly arriving at Lebanon's door. Aubergines (so central to today's cuisine) were first seen then in the marketplaces, and the Persian *mezze* spread was introduced from Iran. The Ottoman era brought more innovations in taste. The Turks popularised stuffing vegetables as a serving style, swapped goat for lamb as the meat of choice and delivered the honey-soaked, nut-encrusted wonder that is *baklava* to the table to tantalise the Lebanese sweet-tooth. The French era of dominion after World War I added croissants and *haute cuisine* techniques to this culinary fray.

Both Mediterranean and Middle Eastern, soaked in the flavours of east and west, today's menu gives a nod to Lebanon's role as an empirical crossroads.

FEASTS

Ramadan

The ninth month in the Islamic calendar is marked by fasting during the day and feasting at night.

- *Breaking the fast* dates and *amarr ad-din* (apricot nectar drink) are the traditional way to begin breaking the fast in the evening.
- *Iftar* is the sunset evening meal. Eating can begin as

soon as the first notes of the *maghrib* (evening call-to-prayer) have been heard. Liberal amounts of sweet pastries such as *baklava* are consumed after the meal.

- *Sohour* is the pre-dawn meal. It must be eaten before the *fajr* (sunrise call-to-prayer) begins.

Christmas

French influences have soaked into the food traditions of Christmas in Lebanon.

- *Bûche de Noël* (Yule Log) and *marron glacés* (candied chestnuts) are common celebration foods at this time.
- *Meghli,* rice pudding infused with cinnamon, anise, pine nuts and pistachios, is a traditional Lebanese Christmas dish.

Kofte, grilled minced lamb on skewers.

ESSENTIAL PRODUCE

Bread

Khobs (bread) binds together every meal. Traditionally it played the role of cutlery at mealtimes, as it was used to scoop mouthfuls of food from shared plates.

- *Khobs Arabi* — small pita-style loaves which puff up when baked.
- *Saj* — a large, paper-thin bread, cooked on an inverted metal platter.
- *Tannour* — a thick bread, similar to Indian tandoor, baked in a stone oven.
- *Meshta* — round loaves studded with seeds and herbs.

Courgettes fried with walnuts.

Dairy

Dairy products in the form of *laban* (yogurt) and *jebneh* (cheese) form a central part of the diet. Yogurt is served at

Mamoul, rich semolina cookies.

most meals, as a salad accompaniment or stirred into stews and soups. The most typical form is *labneh* (strained yogurt). Cheeses are traditionally made from raw goat and ewe milk.

- *Ambaris* — an aged cheese formed by allowing milk and salt to curdle in a clay pot over many months.
- *Shanklish* — round balls of cheese coated in *zaatar* and left to dry.
- *Jebneh khadra* — boiled goat cheese preserved in brine.

Grains and pulses

Chickpeas and lentils have been cultivated in the Middle East since the Neolithic Era and today are still an essential component of many dishes. Rice is the most common grain, first brought into the diet during the medieval era through the trade routes of the Arab empires in Asia. Various forms of cracked wheat also play an important role in the Lebanese larder.

- *Bulgur* — made from hulled wheat grains, bulgur is the core ingredient of many salads including Lebanon's famous *tabbouleh*, as well as soups and stews.
- *Freekeh* — grown in southern Lebanon, the wheat is picked when still green and burned and dried giving it a subtle smoky flavour.
- *Semolina* — the millfeed of durum wheat, semolina appears in desserts and biscuits and is used in the North African inspired *couscous* known as *moughrabieh*.

Meat and poultry

Although grilled meat in various kebab forms rules the roost in restaurant meals, at home the Lebanese eat meat in more moderate portions. Goat is the traditional meat of Lebanon but has been surpassed in the modern-age by lamb. Chicken is the most frequently eaten meat due to its relative affordability.

YEOWATZUP / GETTY IMAGES

Khobs Arabi, a local pita-style bread.

- *Kebab* is all-encompassing name for any skewered and char-grilled meat.
- *Kofte* is kebab ground meat formed into balls, skewered and then char-grilled.
- *Shwarma* is compressed meat sliced from a large rotating skewer. A typical Arabic street food.

Seafood

With its long strip of Mediterranean coastline and plentiful rivers, fish and other seafood is often featured on the dinner table. Both freshwater fish such as carp and *samak nahri* (trout), and sea fish such as *sultan ibrahim* (red mullet) are popular.

- The Litani River, Nahr Ibrahim (also known as the Adonis River), and Qaraoun Lake supply most of Lebanon's freshwater fish.
- The southern city of Tyre is renowned for its seafood.

Vegetables and fruit

Spring heralds the arrival of *farawla* (strawberries) and *mishmish* (apricots) while summer means juicy *teen* (figs), citrus fruits such as *bousfeir* (Seville oranges), *remenn* (pomegranates), and *tout* (mulberries).

Most of the nation's vegetables are grown in the fertile soils of the Bekaa Valley. Tomatoes, cucumber, olives and parsley all play important roles in traditional Lebanese cuisine. Common vegetables such as courgettes, peppers and aubergines are often stewed or stuffed full of spiced rice.

- *Ajami apricots* — an Iranian variety renowned in Lebanon and grown in the Bekaa Valley.
- *Olives* — Lebanon's most extensive olive groves are found in the northern Akkar region.

DEFINING DISHES

Maneesh Zaatar

Lebanon's favourite food-on-the-run, this flatbread is liberally doused in *zaatar* (a spice mix of thyme, sumac, sesame seeds and salt) and olive oil and then baked pizza style. It's often served rolled up with parsley and chunks of *torshi* (pickled vegetables) inside.

Mezze

Lebanon's most famous dishes all hail from the *mezze* spread. The culinary classics of *hummus bi tahina* (known simply as hummus in non-Arabic countries), *tabbouleh* (herby salad of finely-chopped parsley, tomatoes, and bulgur), and *baba ghanough* (mashed aubergine dip) are staple *mezze* dishes now well-known worldwide.

Other common dishes on a Lebanese *mezze* menu are *falafel* (fried chickpea balls), *fattoush* (salad of tomatoes, cucumber, mint and fried flatbread wedges), and *kibbeh* which within Lebanon is often referred to as the national dish. There are as many variations of *kibbeh* as there are *mezze* dishes but at their simplest *kibbeh* is a lamb and bulgur meatball, usually deep fried. One famous mezze delicacy is *kibbeh nayeh* (raw *kibbeh* balls, similar to steak tartare).

Some lesser known dishes of the *mezze* spread include *fatayer* (small pastries stuffed with cheese and spinach), *warak enab* (grape leaves stuffed with rice), *makdous* (aubergines stuffed with garlic and walnuts), and stewed *bamia* (okra).

Mezze is meant to be eaten straight from the serving plates using the never-ending supply of fresh flatbread to scoop food. A typical *mezze* is served in stages with dips and salads arriving first, followed by the hot dishes.

MAISANT LUDOVIC / GETTY IMAGES

Vegetables, cheeses and olives, preserved in jars, for sale in a Beirut shop.

Lemons stuffed with sardine, olive and pine nuts.

Fatayeer, little spinach triangles.

Tabbouleh, made from *quinoa*.

All the quintessential tastes of the Levant are summed up on the table in a feast of bite-sized portions which is made to be shared.

Muhalabiyyeh

This semolina milk-pudding is topped with pistachios and lightly flavoured with delicate orange blossom syrup.

Saleek

This hearty winter dish of slow-cooked meat, infused with cardamom, and rice is cooked with milk and the spice, *mastic*.

Sfiha

These bite-sized open pies that hail from Baalbek with a centre of lamb's meat doused in pomegranate syrup are traditionally prepared and baked by the butchers of the town.

DRINKS

Wine

Viticulture was first practiced by the Phoenicians and the indigenous grape varieties of *obeideh* and *merwah* are some of the oldest in the world. Taken back to Europe by the Crusaders, they are possible ancestors of the Chardonnay and Sémillon grapes. Lebanon's modern industry began in the mid-19th century with the French Jesuit Fathers of the Bekaa Valley who recognised the potential for wine making in the region's chalky-clay soils. There are about 30 wine producers in Lebanon today, most still based in the Bekaa Valley.

Drink this... ***Arak.*** An anise-flavoured alcohol distilled from obeideh grapes. The clear liquid turns milky white on contact with water, which is where its nickname 'lioness' milk' comes from.

Shoppers peruse the spices at a night market in Tehran.

PAUL NEVIN / GETTY IMAGES

Iran

The fact that words such as saffron, pistachio, spinach, orange and eggplant have come to English from Persian says much of the heritage and influence of Iranian cooking. Iranians take pride in their subtly spiced and delicately flavoured cuisine, and great joy in gathering for convivial, communal meals. Hospitality is a keynote of the Iranian character — all the better when the food is this good!

CULINARY CAPITALS ESFAHAN, SHIRAZ **KNOWN FOR** DELICATE SPICING **IMPORTS** TEA, RICE, SUGAR **EXPORTS** CAVIAR, SAFFRON, **DEVOUR** *DIZI*, *FESNJAN CHICKEN* **AVOID** *KALLE PACHE* (AN OFFAL 'CONFECTION')

Young men smoking water pipes at teahouse under Sto Se bridge.

PHIL WEYMOUTH / GETTY IMAGES

CULTURE

Lying at the heart of Eurasia, linking the Middle East and east Asia, Iran throughout its venerable history has been a blend of cultures par excellence. Iran has seen the rise and fall of empires, the coming and going of conquerors and concubines, prophets and poets, mystics and merchants. In classical antiquity, Persia (as it was then known) was a great civilisation and rival to the ancient Greek empire. Later from Arabia there came a new faith, Islam, which blossomed artistically and philosophically under the guidance of the cultured and highly literate Persians. And all the time, Silk Road caravans moved both ways across the Iranian plateau, bringing rice, tea, silk and paper from furthest Asia, and sending faiths, philosophies and learning from the Mediterranean westward. Throughout all of this, shaped by their environment and historical currents, the Iranians have developed rich and elaborate cultural and artistic traditions, a love of poetry and song, and a tradition of hospitality second to none.

REGIONS

Central Plateau

The high-altitude, desert interior of Iran where the capitals of former empires stand and where the great trading cities of the Silk Road were established appears arid and sparse to the untrained eye. Yet this land is surprisingly fertile, so with the ebb and flow of peoples, culinary traditions evolved, absorbed diverse influences and fused with the abundant, fresh, local ingredients — fruits, grains, spices and herbs, meat from herds and the hunt — to create the distinctive cuisine of modern Iran. It was in the former capital of Shiraz that the Syrah grape was first fermented to make the punchy red wine so popular today; the city was also home to several of Iran's greatest poets — perhaps not coincidentally. Some dishes from the area are:

- Tabriz *kufteh* — oversized meatballs consisting of minced lamb, flavoured with herbs and stuffed with various ingredients including sultanas, walnuts or dried apricots.
- *Gaz* — a nougat-like sweet stippled with pistachios or almonds; the most famous (and delicious) *gaz* is made in Esfahan.

Persian Gulf

With its steamy, tropical climate and proximity to the Arabian Peninsula, Iran's Gulf reveals different culinary influences from the interior provinces. Here dates, mango pickle, coriander and fennel are widely used; as this is a coastal region, fish and seafood feature prominently. The local Bandaris, so named because they live in *bandars* (ports), are ethnically Arab and they favour spicy cuisine, many dishes zinging with hot chillies as in Arabian and Indian cooking. Bandari seafood highlights include *chelo meigu* (battered prawns with rice), spiced calamari and crab.

Caspian Sea

The Caspian littoral is the favoured holiday destination for well-to-do Tehran sophisticates. The humid, often rainy shore of the inland sea offers respite from the heat of the interior. This is the only place in Iran where you'll encounter rice paddies, and the Caspian is the source of Iran's highly prized caviar, the roe of the mighty sturgeon. You won't find caviar featuring in local cuisine, however; virtually all of it is exported. A local dish that does make use of the fish is the sturgeon *kabob*: a Caspian take on the ubiquitous *kabob*, where the rich meat of the sturgeon is cooked on metal skewers over hot coals.

A bright mound of saffron for sale at the bazaar.

Pistachio nuts, an important ingredient in Iran.

KAMRAN JEBREILI / GETTY IMAGES

A man shows off a sturgeon fish at a factory in Anzali port.

FEASTS

No Ruz is the Iranian new year, celebrated on 21 March, the spring equinox. Dating back to pre-Islamic times, this is the most important holiday in the Iranian calendar. Along with well-established rituals celebrating the arrival of spring, such as growing beds of fresh *sabzi* (sprouts), it also features particular foods. On the first day of the holiday *kuku-ye sabzi* (herb omelette) and *sabzi polo* (rice with green herbs) are eaten, often with white fish. The green herbs and eggs evoke the essence of spring: rebirth and new life.

On the final day of the two-week holiday, families gather for elaborate, outdoor picnics. There are no specific No Ruz dishes here, but the *sofreh* is spread on a hillside or meadow, fires are lit and a lavish spread will be put on — a communal affair highlighting the conviviality that is central to the Iranian character, and the importance of family and sharing food.

ETIQUETTE

The concepts of silver service and grand table settings are foreign to Iranians. Instead, a *sofreh* (long tablecloth) is placed on the floor or on a *takht* (a kind of day bed) and diners gather around and sit cross-legged (shoes are removed inside the home). Individual portions are an oddity, rather a range of dishes is set out on the *sofreh* to be shared, each person choosing what appeals then passing dishes on to the assembled gathering. Most meals begin with a simple salad of fresh ingredients to be followed by small tasting dishes (pickles, cheese, dips, all accompanied by fragrant *nun* bread), gradually building up to heartier fare such as *khoresht* (stews, often featuring imaginative combinations of meats, vegetables, fruits and spices) or *kabobs*, all of which inevitably come alongside mounds of rice and more freshly baked *nun*.

Fish caught from the Caspian sea.

DAILY MEALS

The day begins with a simple breakfast, generally just lashings of tea, *lavash* (soft, thinly layered flatbread), feta or clotted cream and jam. In winter, hearty soups may also be lapped up to start the day. The main meal of the day, lunch, will definitely feature lots of rice topped with a variety of savoury delights including *kabobs* or *khoresht*. Dinner generally features similar dishes to lunch. Throughout the day any excuse is reason enough to enjoy a cup of tea, usually amid company, and sweet treats are consumed at all hours.

ESSENTIAL PRODUCE

Fruit

The sun-drenched Iranian plateau produces sweet and plump fruits in abundance. Fresh fruit is presented as a simple and cleansing dessert course. Delectable fruit-infused sherbets, sorbets and juices offer respite from the Iranian heat, while the imaginative use of fruits in savoury *khoreshts* (stews) are part of what makes Iranian cuisine so intriguing, for instance lamb with quinces or chicken with barberries.

Of all the fruits that Iran produces, it is, arguably, the pomegranate that gives the local cuisine its most distinctive edge. In a pomegranate salad, black olives, shallots and ground walnuts sit alongside the fleshy crimson granules of the fruit, while pomegranate molasses and pomegranate juice make their way into a range of *khoreshts*, and the tart, blood-red juice of the fruit is also enjoyed as a refreshing drink.

Meat

For all the diversity in Iranian cuisine and the abundance of fresh fruit and vegetables that appear in the Iranian diet, meat still takes pride of place in the majority of dishes. Lamb is a highlight, harvested from fat-tailed herds that seek out sweet forage across the rugged landscape. Chicken features prominently, too, but beef is less common. You may also encounter dishes containing roasted duck, goose or quail.

Rice

Rice (*chelow*) is a central component of virtually every Iranian meal, and is consumed in vast quantities. Classic *chelow* is parboiled, then mixed with oil and melted butter and steamed to create deliciously light, fluffy and aromatic rice. The same technique also creates *tahdig*, a crunchy, buttery rice crust at the bottom of the cooking pot that is highly prized by Iranians. Rice also appears in a range of *polos* (pilafs), dishes steeped in stock or melted butter and featuring vegetables, herbs and spices, or laced with such surprises as barberries, rose petals or sour cherries.

A farmer with his produce.

Vegetables

Iranians may have a strong carnivorous impulse but that is not to say vegetables and other fresh produce is neglected. Fresh salads begin many meals, fresh herbs garnish many a *kabob* or *khoresht*, as do many vegetables that also make their way into *polos* and omelettes. A favourite vegetable is the redoubtable eggplant, which may be baked and served with yoghurt, incorporated in *khoresht* with chicken or lamb, or simply stewed with tomatoes and onions until silky and sweet.

SHOPPING

Iranian cooking places an emphasis on fresh and seasonal ingredients, so canny shoppers head to bazaars and street markets to pick and choose from produce brought to market fresh from the fields. Supermarkets may be increasing in number in modern Iranian cities, but discerning chefs still

Pile of eggplants for sale at the market.

Iranian woman selling *nun* bread in Kerman.

Boiled beets for sale at a street stall.

TIM BARKER / GETTY IMAGES

prefer to deal one-to-one with market greengrocers and butchers to spell out their particular needs and get expert advice on the plumpest quinces or the most pungent *somaq* (sumac).

PREPARATION

Iranian chefs don't use any particular utensils or techniques that are out of the ordinary, but they are guided by a philosophy that informs the creation of recipes and menus and it is unlike anything else in the world.

This philosophy, which has its roots in the Zoroastrian religion that was founded in ancient Persia, aims to balance the intrinsic 'hot' and 'cold' qualities of individual ingredients: such balance makes for pleasurable eating (and healthy eaters). Being 'hot' or 'cold' has nothing to do with the actual temperature or spiciness of particular foods; instead the perceived heating or cooling effect of each ingredient is taken into account. 'Hot' foods are said to quicken the metabolism and heart rate; 'cold' food supposedly having the opposite effect.

During the winter months 'hot' foods will feature highly on menus, but during the baking heat of summer, 'cold' foods will be in favour. Similarly, people of a 'hot', passionate disposition are advised to eat 'cold' foods, while those who are sluggish or timid should go for 'hot' menu items.

Just how foods are classified as 'hot' or 'cold' is rather opaque, however. Wheat, sugar, sweets, dried fruits, fresh herbs, apples and most meats are 'hot', while fish, yoghurt, watermelon, rice, radishes and coffee are 'cold'. While there may seem no rhyme nor reason to this, rest assured that Iranian chefs take these factors into consideration to produce balanced — and universally delicious — meals.

DEFINING DISHES

Baghlava

Baghlava (known as *baklava* in other countries) assumes many forms across the Middle East. The Iranian version of this nut-filled layered pastry delight often features ground almonds scented with cardamom and comes drenched in rose water.

Dizi

A combination soup-stew, *dizi* (also known as *abgusht*) resembles hearty workman's fare, but is universally loved. Served in a heavy bowl with a pestle and soup spoon, it has its very own way of being eaten, too. First the broth is drunk, then the remaining chunks of lamb, potatoes, beans and chick peas are ground into a paste and mopped up with bread.

Khoresht

Hearty *khoreshts* (stews) generally have meat on the bone as a core ingredient so that long, slow simmering and the liberal addition of stock brings out the richest and smoothest of flavours and textures. The delicate and dexterous addition of spices, fruits, pulses and grains creates wholesome and pleasing meals that are subtle on the palate. Lamb *khoresht* may be grainy with lentils and perfumed with cinnamon and cardamom, or sweeter from the addition of prunes and honey. The delights of the *khoresht* remain relatively unknown outside Iran, however.

Kabobs

The *kabob* is the dish that conventional wisdom associates with Middle Eastern cuisines, and indeed the *kabob* is the most common way of preparing meat in Iran. But don't for a second imagine that Iranian *kabobs* are the same as those grease-

WAYNE WALTON / GETTY IMAGES

A baker in Fuman displays a tray of cookies.

laden parcels called kebabs that are eaten after late-night drinking bouts in the West. Here *kabob*s are prepared with skill and care; choice cuts are individually seasoned, skewered and grilled over hot coals. When the meat is golden-brown yet still succulent, the *kabob* is served up in fluffy bread or on a mound of pillowy rice, coated with a dusting of pungent *somaq* (sumac) and accompanied by grilled tomatoes, chopped onions or a bowl of yoghurt.

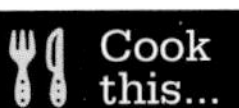

KUBIDEH KABOBI

Serves 6

Ingredients
500g lamb or beef mince
1 onion, finely chopped
1 garlic clove, finely chopped
1 tablespoon turmeric
salt and pepper
1 tablespoon sumac
6 long, metal skewers
flat bread or rice to serve

Method
Preheat a barbecue to high (or use a grill pan over a high heat).

Place mince, onion, garlic and turmeric and in a bowl and season. Use your hands to mix thoroughly, ensuring onion, garlic and turmeric are evenly distributed.

Take a handful of the mixture, roll out into a flattened sausage shape and slide the skewer through the meat lengthways. Ensure the meat mixture is distributed evenly along the skewer.

Place the skewers on the pre-heated barbecue or grill pan. Cook for 2 to 3 minutes each side, or until golden-brown.

Dust each kebab with sumac, then serve on flat bread or rice.

Hibiscus flower leaves, to be used in tea, drying on rooftop in Masuleh.

Tea, sweetened with *ghand*, is the national drink.

Chubi Bridge Tea House in Esfahan.

*Kabob*s come in various forms. *Kubideh kabob* is made of minced lamb with onions and bread crumbs and may be dressed with a squeeze of lemon. *Kabob-e barg* (literally 'leaf *kabob*') consists of thin slices of lamb or beef, *juje kabob* is skewered chicken that has been marinated in anything from lime juice to yoghurt, while *fille kabob* is the king of all *kabob*s, tender chunks of lamb fillet grilled to sizzling perfection.

Mirza ghasemi

Mirza ghasemi consists of mashed eggplant, garlic, tomato and egg cooked up into a smooth, creamy gumbo and served with rice. Done well the eggplant will betray a hint of sweetness and the garlic bring a delightful pungency.

Roast chicken with fesenjun

Rarely served in restaurants but a highlight of home cooking, *fesenjun* is considered by many to be the show-stopper of any Iranian chef's repertoire and is a dish usually reserved for special occasions or honoured guests. It's a tangy combination of ground, roasted walnuts, simmered with tomatoes, pomegranate molasses, turmeric and cinnamon. This sweet and sour concoction is poured over roast chicken with a dash of lemon. Exquisite!

DRINKS

Alcohol

Iran may be where Shiraz originated, but you would be hard pressed to find a glass of it these days in the Islamic Republic. Alcohol is tolerated for the Armenian (Christian) minority, but it is strictly forbidden for the Muslim majority. Nonetheless, a black market exists, both for local home-distilled fire water and for contraband imports. A regime-approved alternative is 'Islamic beer'; it has 0.0% alcohol.

Sadhu drinking tea.

IZZET KERIBAR

India

India is a vast and varied land, a bewildering tapestry of contrasts that every year lures millions of visitors, each pursuing the traveller's holy grail, 'the real India'. By far the best way of cutting to the heart of this astonishing culture is by exploring its deliciously protean gastronomy.

CULINARY CAPITALS DELHI, PUNJAB, TAMIL NADU
KNOWN FOR CURRIES, SPICES, OUTRAGEOUS SWEETS
IMPORTS SUGAR **EXPORTS** SPICES, TEA, CHILLIES
DEVOUR PICKLES, *POORIS* **AVOID** FOOD POISONING

PEPSI

Celebration of the Holi Festival in Mathura.

PETER ADAMS

CULTURE

If cooking were painting, India would have one of the world's most colourful palettes. When you consider the palm-fringed beaches of Kerala, the snow-capped peaks of the Himalaya, and Rajasthan's shimmering Thar Desert, you can't help but lick your lips at the prospect of such regional diversity. But India's geographical range is both a blessing and a curse. While it brings bounty to some, it wreaks misery on others.

Indian cuisine is an elusive thing to define or grasp, but despite its mind-boggling variety of techniques and ingredients there are enough fundamentals to help us identify it. One is the masterful use of spices shared by every Indian cook. There is a wealth of items in the Indian spice box with which cooks create a spectrum of tantalising flavours, from the sweetest to the most sour and everything in between. They achieve this by treating each spice individually, and by combining them in various masalas (spice blends).

The basis of every Indian meal is grain: rice in the south, and wheat in the form of *roti* (the generic term for bread) in the north. Each is generally eaten with *daa*l (the generic term for lentils or pulses; dishes made with these), *sabzi* (vegetables) and pickles. Depending on circumstances, fish and meat may be added. Beyond these staples, the diversity of Indian foods is limited only by any cook's circumstances and imagination.

Soul food

Most profoundly, food in India is integral to spiritual advancement. Regardless of creed, Indians share the belief that food is just as important for fine-tuning the spirit as it is for sustaining the body. Modern culinary practices have their roots in the Ayurveda, the ancient science of life, health and longevity. The Ayurveda classifies foods according to their positive or negative energies as well as their medicinal qualities. Many people say they only turn to Ayurveda in times of illness but its principles are ingrained in daily life and cooks seem to have an instinct for the art.

The strong association between spiritual purity and vegetarianism ensures the majority of Indians are vegetarian, even though meat (with the exception of beef) is not strictly taboo in Hinduism. Buddhists and Jains adhere to *ahimsa* (the philosophy of non-injury), but the Hindu view tends to equate vegetarianism with personal spiritual advancement, not the welfare of animals. Even those who eat meat hold vegetarianism in high esteem.

Religion is the most important aspect of Indian life, and food its most precious resource. Certain foods are deemed pure or sacred and may feature prominently in temple ritual. In the Hindu pantheon each deity has its own favourite dish. Krishna, for example, is passionate for dairy products. Ganesh, the elephant-headed god so popular with us tourists, is rarely depicted without a bowl of *modak* (sweet rice-flour dumplings). Any food which is first offered to the gods then shared among devotees is known as *prasad*.

While food is revered and used in worship in India, this is not an austere food culture. On the contrary, food is joy and celebration. You can hardly make it through a week here without getting caught up in the excitement of some looming festival, which will be marked with special feasts and dishes.

REGIONS

India is divided into 29 states, each a culturally distinct entity with unique customs, language and cuisine. As though 29 states weren't enough, each comprises myriad ethnic groupings. The cauldron of Indian cuisine overflows with such an immense variety of dishes that no Indian could taste them all in a lifetime.

JULIAN LOVE

A vegetable stall in Old Delhi.

Punjab

Nestled in the shadows of the Pindari Ranges and irrigated by five major rivers, the state of Punjab is a lush green bowl of prosperity. Though it occupies only 1.5% of India's landmass, Punjab is one of the richest states and its people earn double the Indian average. This is partly down to nature's bountiful blessings, but also due to the industrious and resilient character of its cheerful people, who are mainly followers of Sikhism. You'll be familiar with Punjabi food because many of its staple dishes have come to represent Indian food internationally.

An integral part of Punjabi cooking is the *tandoor* (clay oven), open at the top and fired by charcoal below. Originally introduced by the Turkish invaders, the *tandoor* can now be found at every restaurant front and in the courtyard of many homes. To watch fresh *naan* being made in a *tandoor* is a poetic experience. Enormous mounds of dough are kept ready, covered by a damp cloth. A small ball is broken off and expertly patted into an oval shape between the palms. This is deftly stuck onto the side of the glowing-red tandoor wall. In the twinkling of an eye the dough puffs up and becomes speckled with brown patches. Every cook knows the magical moment when the bread is ready, and out it comes with the help of an iron spike. This very same tandoor turns marinated meats into a gamut of *kabab*s: *sheekh* (mincemeat on iron skewers), *tangri* (plump chicken drumsticks), *boti* (spicy bite-sized bits of boneless lamb), chicken *tikka* (succulent chunks of chicken on skewers) and of course the ubiquitous *tandoori* chicken, which goes in whole.

South India

You'll find sour dishes in every South Indian meal, believed to offset the large quantities of chillies which are used to cool the body in these warmer climes. The curry *patta* (curry leaf) is

GREG ELMS / GETTY IMAGES

Cooking the crepe-style dish *masala dosa*.

commonly used, along with mustard seeds and *hing* (asafoetida). The combination of these three ingredients creates a typical flavour, and anyone from the rest of India could taste it blindfolded and exclaim, 'Ah, South Indian food!'

Dosas, a large family of freshly fried fermented rice-flour crepes, are a South Indian breakfast speciality that can be eaten at any time of day, either as a full meal or substantial tiffin. The *dosa* is an icon of Indian food, now enjoying popularity all over the world in restaurants, homes and street stalls. To make the batter for *dosa*, rice and lentils are soaked and ground separately; the rice into a slightly granular paste and the black lentils into a light foamy one. The two are combined and left to ferment, usually overnight. The thick batter is poured over a hot griddle, drizzled with oil around the edges, and cooked on one side for a minute or until tiny holes begin to appear on the surface. The *dosa* is served with a bowl of hot, orange *samba*r and another bowl of mild coconut *chatni* — the practice of Yin and Yang at its best.

FEASTS

India seems to be in a perpetual state of celebration. There's always some community celebrating a harvest, a god's birthday or an auspicious date in the Hindu calendar. Personal celebrations like birthdays take a back seat in the pantheon of occasions, and the most important events are those shared by the whole community, young and old, rich and poor.

Holi

Holi is the most boisterous Hindu festival and falls on the full moon in the Hindu month of Phalgun (usually around March). It's a time when people join nature in casting off their winter coats and rejoice in the arrival of spring. People greet each other with colours, everything from a gentle smearing of coloured powder on someone's cheek to a deluge of dyed waters tipped over their heads.

It's also an occasion to celebrate nature's bounty, and an abundance of special foods are prepared for the feast, including:

- *karanjis*, crescent-shaped flour parcels stuffed with sweet *khoya* (milk solids)
- *malpuas*, wheat pancakes dipped in syrup
- *barfis*, fudge-like milk sweets
- *pedas*, multicoloured pieces of *khoya* and sugar.

Many traditionally celebrate Holi with generous quantities of *bhang* (cannabis) mixed up with vegetables and fried into *pakoras* or drunk in *lassis*. With the riot of colours and half the town in a state of *bhang*-enhanced exhilaration, this will be one of the most memorable festivals you'll ever witness. It's celebrated mainly in the north because southerners don't have much of a winter to get through.

Jalebbis, deep fried morning sweet.

Diwali

Diwali, the festival of lights, is the most widely celebrated national festival, and takes place during October or November. The name is derived from the Sanskrit word *deepavali* (a row of lamps), and families set out lanterns on every available surface and float flickering candles down rivers. Shops are decked out in mercilessly bright lights, creating — literally at times — an electric atmosphere. After sunset, landscapes are awesomely illuminated, providing a twinkling welcome to Lakshmi, the goddess of wealth.

Houses and business premises are renovated, decorated and given a fresh lick of a brightly coloured paint leading up to the festival. This is the most upbeat Hindu festival; everyone is in buoyant mood, dressed in their best clothes, exchanging gifts

Sweets for sale at the *Diwali* Festival.

Offerings to the gods at the Festival of Chhath.

'The Great *Pani Puri* Seller' on Chowpatty beach in Mumbai.

GREG ELMS / GETTY IMAGES

and feasting. Of course, there would be hardly be a festival if it weren't for sweets, and consumption reaches festive frenzy during *Diwali*. Some regions have *Diwali*-specific sweets such as the delicious *anarsa* (rice-flour cookies) in Mumbai.

Navroj

While Parsis are small in number, many people celebrate *Navroj*, the Parsi New Year, because Parsis are popular, generous and gregarious hosts. They are passionate about food, and it plays a starring role in all their occasions. Fish, mutton, chicken, nuts, spices and fruit are bought the day before and cooked up into lavish spreads. The first meal of the day is traditionally *ravo* (semolina, milk and sugar) or *sevai* (milk pudding with vermicelli), after which each family visits the fire temple.

Lunch can consist of any number of items, including *pulaos* with nuts and saffron, fish masalas, mutton or chicken curries, and *daal*. *Falooda* (the sweet drink made from milk, vermicelli and rosewater) is made in every home and pressed on visitors. Parsis are always supportive of the community's poor and on this day children pass on food and gifts to remind them to always share with others.

ETIQUETTE

The honoured guest

Indian hospitality can be overwhelming and it's always extended with warmth through the medium of food.

The ancient Sanskrit idiom *atithi devo bhava* (a guest is equal to God) underpins this philosophy and whether your hosts live in a lavish mansion or a mud-brick hovel, they will do their utmost to make you feel welcome. In affluent homes they might throw an elaborate banquet; meat-eating rural families might slaughter a chicken in your honour; and few hosts will let you leave before you've at least had *chai* and something sweet.

When your host offers you food or refreshment, it's normal to decline a couple of times before letting yourself be persuaded. You won't be expected to bring anything, but sweets or fruit are always appreciated. If you cannot accept an invitation, it's best to avoid an outright 'no' as Indians may consider it impolite. Best to do as the locals do. Even if you're going to be flying home at the time, just say 'I will try'.

THE MENU

The only difficulties you will have with menus are trying to decipher the colourful Indian–English terms ('spaced lamb stew' anyone?) and getting through the whole thing before you keel over from starvation. Some menus are like books but you should think of them more as catalogues full of possibilities rather than lists of what the kitchen can supply.

Outside the big hotels, most restaurants don't have menus for lunch, when there are only vegetarian and non-vegetarian *thalis*. Cheaper places specialising in just one or two dishes won't have any menus at all, but if he can't tell you himself, the waiter will send for the best English-speaker in the vicinity to describe each dish. Otherwise, you'll be able to see the dishes being prepared and just point to whatever takes your fancy.

Only the big hotels will serve meals in courses. All other places bring the food out as soon as it is ready, even if you think you've ordered courses.

Street food

It's on the streets where you'll find India at its vital best and revolting worst; it's most colourful and drab, meditative and unrelenting. India is laid bare in the theatre of its thoroughfares and visitors are casts in the show. These streets are a banquet for the senses. You won't like some of the courses but the

GREG ELMS / GETTY IMAGES

Golguppas, puffs of crunchy fried dough.

tastes, smells, sights, rhythm and atmosphere of street cooking will be an experience never forgotten.

As all human life takes place on the streets, it's only natural that it should also be sustained here. Whatever the time of day, people are boiling, frying, roasting, peeling, juicing, simmering, mixing, or baking some class of food and drink to lure passersby. Snacking is second nature to Indians and most eat from street stalls at some time. They don't snack to tide them over between meals, they snack because they love the food and it puts the pep back in their step.

Such is the popularity of eating on the street that many establishments cook outside their front door and, while there may be rows of empty tables out back, diners scramble for available space on the kerb. Other street vendors cook outside their homes, roll rickety old *thelas* (carts) to regular spots, or keep wandering looking for the prime location. Anything that can be whipped up in the open air and eaten in a jiffy is street food, and the range is staggering.

Deep-fried fare is the staple of the boulevards, and you'll find:

- *samosas*, deep-fried pyramid-shaped pastries filled with spiced vegetables and less often meat
- *aloo ki tikki*, mashed potato patties
- *bhaji*, vegetable fritters in varying degrees of spiciness
- *pooris*, deep-fried bread
- *kachoris*, corn or lentil savoury puffs
- mouthwatering *dosa*, fermented rice-flour and lentil crepes, originated in the south but are served up by discerning vendors throughout India, along with the other southern specialities of *dosas*
- *idlis*, spongy cakes made of the same batter as dosas
- *vada*, fried salty doughnuts.

Traders ply the North East Express at Mughal Serai Station in Varanasi with a flurry of snacks and trinkets.

The snack *kachoris* served on a leaf plate.

A stack of cooked *pappadams* at a street cafe.

In the north, and in most Muslim areas, you'll find *kababs* pounded into mouthwatering submission, doused in smooth curds and wrapped in warm bread.

In season, cobs of roasted corn are hard to resist and you can't visit Mumbai without sampling *pao-bhaji* (spiced vegetables with bread) and *bhelpuri*.

Popular 'modern' items include omelettes, hard-boiled eggs, and even regular old sandwiches (especially tomato, cucumber and green chutney).

Platform food

One of the thrills of travelling by rail is the culinary circus that greets you at every station. As the train arrives the platform springs into a frenzy. Roving vendors accost the trains yelling and scampering up and down the carriages; bananas, omelettes and nuts are offered through the grills on the windows; and platform chefs try to lure you from the train with the sizzle of fresh *samosas*. Frequent rail travelers know which station is famous for which food item, and indulge their appetites accordingly. Lonavla station in Maharashtra is famous for *chikki* (nut and *jaggery* toffee), Agra for *petha* (crystallised gourd), and Dhaund near Delhi for *biryani* (fragrant steamed rice with meat or vegetables). In the bigger stations, platform vendors are either contracted rail staff or licensees so they have to comply to certain standards.

ESSENTIAL PRODUCE

No matter how simple or complicated the expression, Indian cuisine stands or falls on the quality of its ingredients. The astonishing variety of Indian food is shaped by geography, climate and the cook's insistence on using the freshest, seasonal produce available.

Breads

While rice is paramount in the south, wheat is the mainstay in the north, where a variety of wheat breads are served with virtually every meal.

There are countless variations of bread and even staples like *chappati* are made according to different recipes, depending on the region, neighbourhood or household. Most breads are unleavened and made with *atta* (whole-wheat flour) although *makki* (cornmeal), *bajri* (millet), and *jawar* (barley) are also used. Bread is made fresh for every meal.

- *Roti/chappati,* the simplest and most common Indian bread. *Roti* is made with whole-wheat flour and water, and although always round, *roti* sizes can vary dramatically.
- *Poori,* this delicious North Indian snack is a disc of dough that puffs up when deep fried. The disc is skilfully spun into a wok; after a few seconds of deep-frying it puffs up like soft, crispy balloon, and is eaten with various stewed meats and vegetables.
- *Kachori,* this is like *poori* only the dough has been pepped up with corn or, which also makes it thicker. Popular in North India, *kachori* makes for a substantial snack at any time of the day.
- *Phulka,* literally 'puff', this is a mini *poori*, made with whole-wheat flour, and cooked on a naked flame.
- *Paratha*, unleavened, fried, flaky *paratha*, when combined with any North Indian sauce, makes for a delicious morning snack. *Paratha* is often jazzed up with a stuffing of *paneer* (fresh cheese) or grated vegetables for a substantial on-the-spot snack.
- *Naan,* this tear-shaped favourite originated in the

FOTOSANJAY / GETTY IMAGES

A big plate of golden *samosas*.

Middle East, but Punjabis opened their hearths to *naan* and subsequently introduced them to the world. True *naan* has to be cooked along the walls of a *tandoor*. Laced with garlic, *naan* is difficult to resist; filled with *paneer*, impossible.

- *Bhatura,* this Punjabi speciality is a deep-fried version of *naan*, and is popularly eaten with spiced chickpeas.
- *Shirmal,* versions of this flaky unleavened bread can be found throughout Muslim India.
- *Rumali,* means, 'handkerchief'. It is a large superfine whole-wheat bread that is thrown like a pizza base. You're most likely to find *rumali* in the Muslim communities, where they are popularly eaten with *kababs*.
- *Kulcha,* this soft, round leavened bread is native to Hyderabad, and is a mainstay of Indian restaurants around the world. It's delicious when filled with onion, spices, vegetables or meat.

However it is made or served, bread is always eaten with the fingertips of the right hand only (and some dexterity is required to remain composed while breaking bread with one hand). Small pieces of bread are broken off and wrapped around morsels of food, and eaten. At the end of a meal, most people use the leftover bread to mop up the remains.

Chillies

Indian food without chillies would be like a rickshaw driver without gumption: hardly conceivable. Even so, the Portuguese introduced chillies here less than 500 years ago. India is now the world's largest producer, exporter and consumer of these smarting little suckers.

You can buy chillies fresh, dried, flaked, powdered, pickled,

GREG ELMS / GETTY IMAGES

Guajarati chillies for sale at the bazaar in Mumbai.

bottled, over the Internet or any other way you can think of. Only the green ones are used fresh.

While chilli is a common ingredient, don't think your taste-buds will be incinerated at every meal. Chillies are used more for flavour and colour than heat, although their heat is very good for cooling the body down in hot weather. If you want to decrease the heat without compromising the flavour, remove the seeds before cooking.

Lentils and pulses

While their staples divide north and south, the whole of India — from toothless toddlers to old men — is united in its love for *daal*. The word *daal* means lentils or pulses, but mostly people use the specific name of each pulse. More often, *daal* refers to a wide range of pulse-based dishes.

From the thin *sambar* of the south to the thick *moong* (mung bean) *daals* of the north, you may encounter as many as 60 different pulses including lentils, beans and peas. Whether the legumes are cooked in the skin or husked, whole or split, changes the character of each *daal* dish. However, it's the *bhaghar* (spices tempered in hot oil or ghee which are then added to the cooked pulses) that gives each one its distinctive zip and will have your mouth watering each time you sample yet another *daal*.

Pickles, chutneys and relishes

No Indian meal — from a packed lunch to a full dinner — is complete without one, and often all, of the above. A relish could be anything from a roughly chopped onion to a delicately crafted fusion of fruit, nuts and spices. The best known is *raita* (yoghurt or curds combined with any number of vegetables or fruit, served chilled) which makes a delicious and refreshing counter to even the spiciest meal.

Beyond this familiar staple, there is a mesmerising litany of 'little bits' which can go a long way to changing the flavour of your feast. *Chatnis* (chutneys) can come in any number of varieties, from sweet to salty, and can be made from many different vegetables, fruits, herbs and spices. Most *chatnis* are made fresh and usually served in small, non-metallic bowls.

There are two standout ingredients in the gamut of Indian *chatnis*: coconut is the base for the ubiquitous coconut *chatni* in the south, and mint for the mint *chatni* in the north. Outside this division, each family will have its own favourite relishes, the recipes for which may have been passed down over generations. There are many specialised pickle stores dotted around India but many families still make their own.

Rice

Rice is the most important staple, but in a place where food and spirituality are inseparable, it is much more than simply a nutritious grain.

- India has more land dedicated to rice cultivation than any other country, and the sight of sweeping, lush paddies will stay with you long after you've returned home.
- India's yield of 90 million tonnes of rice accounts for more than half of the country's total grain production.
- Rice is integral to just about every Hindu ceremony: it's used to symbolise purity and fertility in wedding ceremonies and is often offered as *puja* (literally, respect; offering or prayers) in Hindu temples.
- On average, Indians eat almost 2 kilograms of rice a week.

A variety of rice for sale.

Rice sack carrier from the Panaji market in Goa.

Keralan-style *thali*.

Boy measuring spices at a market in Udaipur.

North and South India are often broadly divided by their most important staple; rice in the south and bread in the north. Although people in North India do eat plenty of rice, it is fundamental to the southern diet. In the south, rice turns up in every course; be it in *dosa* (a crepe of fermented rice flour and *daal*) for breakfast, *thali* (a plated meal) for lunch, and perhaps a *biryani* for dinner capped off with *payasam* (rice pudding) for a special dessert.

Spices

Spices have been important in Indian life for over three millennia, as food and as medicines in Ayurvedic cures. India supplies almost half of the world's spices and the US$420 million it receives in exports adds much colour to the cheeks of its lacklustre economy.

Cardamom is the queen of Indian spices.

- You'll find the small, green variety in savoury dishes, desserts and in warming winter *chai* (tea).
- The pods grown on the slopes of the Western Ghats are regarded as the best in the world.
- The larger black cardamom pods grown in the northeast are stronger in flavour and commonly added to meat dishes.
- Kashmiri brides traditionally wear a silver locket filled with cardamom that they give to the groom during the wedding ceremony.

Cinnamon is the inner bark of a tropical evergreen tree native to Sri Lanka, and is harvested during the rainy season when the bark is pliable. There are very few dishes that cinnamon will not enhance and it is integral to India's most popular spice blend, *garam masala*. Along with cardamom and saffron, cinnamon is a spice you'll also find in desserts.

Other important Indian spices include:

- **coriander**, seeds and leaves are both used in cooking
- **cloves**, widely used in both medicine and food
- **cumin**, an ancient spice used throughout India to give dishes a bitter edge. Most curries begin with the crackle of cumin seeds in hot oil.

Curry leaves got their name because somebody decided they smelled like curry. Which curry, we'll never know. Used mainly in the south, the leaves are freshly picked off the stem because the dried variety has only a fraction of the bitter flavour. The leaves add flavour but are not eaten; a person who is used for only one task and then discarded is likened to a curry leaf.

Saffron Spain and India are the only major producers of the flavoursome, fragile spice, saffron.

- Saffron is actually the dried stigma of the crocus bulb, grown in Jammu and Kashmir.
- The plant flowers for a couple of weeks in October, when the blossoms are plucked at dawn before the heat can wilt them. Then the delicate stigmas are dried.
- It takes more than 1500 hand-plucked stigmas to yield just one gram of saffron. Fortunately, a little saffron goes a long way.
- Saffron is widely used in savoury and sweet dishes, and just a few strands soaked in warm water or milk will infuse your dish with colour and a rich, fragrant flavour.

GREG ELMS / GETTY IMAGES

Turmeric powder from Mir Alam Market in Hyderaba

Turmeric India is the world's largest producer, exporter and consumer of turmeric. Considering its many uses, turmeric is probably India's most important spice.

- It adds colour and flavour to a wide range of dishes including meats, lentils and vegetables.
- It is used as a preservative, and is the essence of just about every Indian curry.
- You'll find it in every home as a handy antiseptic as well as a natural cure for a host of ailments including a sore throat.
- Indian women frequently use turmeric as a skin-polisher and to discourage hair growth so you'll often see them with yellow ankles, necks and faces.
- It is also held sacred by Hindus and used as a religious mark on foreheads, as well as a mark of respect between friends.
- A single line of turmeric across the threshold of a house is said to keep ants at bay.

Sweets

Indians have a mind-boggling range of *mithai* (sweets) to satisfy their voracious cravings. Most of the sweets are sickly sweet and some of the mass-produced kinds need a hazard warning. Nevertheless, sweets are an extremely effective form of *baksheesh* (tip/bribe/sweetener) and make popular gifts.

Kheer is India's favourite dessert.

- It's a rice pudding made with reduced milk to which rice is added while boiling.
- Unusual for Indian sweet things, it has a light, delicate flavour.

Sweets for *Diwali*.

Vendor and customer in a *mishti*, sweet shop.

Black cardamom for sale in New Delhi.

- Depending on where you are, your *kheer* might be flavoured with cardamom, saffron, pistachios, flaked almonds, cashews or dried fruit, but the base remains the same.
- You can bet your sweet tooth that all communal gatherings will conclude with delicious, creamy *kheer* or *payasam*, often served in earthenware cups or bowls.

Gulab jamun are deep-fried balls of milk dough soaked in rose-flavoured syrup. You'll see them in homes, restaurants, and street stalls.

Kulfi is a delicious, firm-textured Indian ice cream made with reduced milk and flavoured with any number of nuts, fruits and berries.

Jaggery Bearing in mind an unrivaled penchant for sweet things, there's no way that plain old sugar could meet all of India's sweet cravings. They extended their culinary range by coming up with another sweetening agent, known as *jaggery* (or *gur*) which is made at the first stage of sugar production. Enormous cast-iron pots of sugarcane juice are simmered for hours until the juice thickens. It's then poured into moulded trays where it turns into the hard fudge-like bricks you'll see piled up at markets and street stalls throughout the country, attracting various black and yellow insects. In West Bengal, a speciality *jaggery* is made from date juice.

Although it's sometimes used interchangeably with sugar, *jaggery* has a distinctly musky flavour of its own. *Jaggery* can be crumbled and added to lentils and sweets, and it melts down into a thick, syrupy liquid that is added to drinks. It is also slightly alcoholic and used to make liquor in central and southern villages.

Vegetables

Indian fruit and vegetable markets are mesmerising, a feast for the eyes and foreplay for the palate. With an estimated 600 million vegetarians, you'd reckon that India had something special going on in the garden, and you'd be right. Indians, even certified carnivores, love vegetables. They are served at every main meal, and *sabzi* (vegetables) is a word recognised in every Indian language. With its climatic range, India is able to grow more vegetables than most other countries.

There is no meat-and-three-veg here; vegetables play much more than supporting roles. They are rarely just boiled or steamed, instead they're generally cooked *sukhi* (dry) or *tari* (in a sauce). Within these two categories they can be fried, roasted, curried, stuffed, mashed, combined, wrapped in batter and made into a *pakora* (fritter) or a *bhaji* (vegetable fritter), or made into a *kabab* or *kofta*; whatever takes the cook's fancy that day.

- Potatoes are ubiquitous and popularly cooked with various masalas, cooked with other vegetables, mashed, spiced or fried for the street snack *aloo ki tikki*.
- Onions are fried with other vegetables, ground into a paste for cooking with meats, and used raw in relishes or as garnish.
- Heads of cauliflower are a surprising feature at the Indian market and are usually cooked dry on their own, or with potatoes to make *aloo gob*i.
- Indian carrots are small, thin and sweet, and are sometimes used in sweet snacks such as *gajar halwa* (a sweet made with carrot, dried fruits, sugar, condensed milk and lots of ghee).
- Plain okra is usually transformed into a taste sensation by being prepared dry with spices.

GREG ELMS / GETTY IMAGES

Volunteers peel hundreds of potatoes for thousands of pilgrims at the Golden Temple in Amritsar.

- Likewise, when cabbage gets the sweet and sour treatment from tamarind it is unrecognisable.
- In late summer, cobs of roasted corn emerge as a popular street snack in North India.
- Fresh green peas turn up stir fried with other vegetables in *pulaos* and *biryanis*, and in one of North India's signature dishes, *mattar paneer* (peas and fresh cheese).
- Zesty tomatoes are used across the subcontinent in salads, sauces and even soups.
- *Brinjal* (eggplant; aubergine) come in all different shapes, shades and sizes and their majestic, passionate, deep purple colour will have you swooning over them at the market.
- All over South India, white pumpkins are smashed outside homes and offices as part of the Dussehra celebrations. White pumpkin is an auspicious vegetable and their use is said to bring good luck for the coming year.
- Indians are also very fond of their *saag* (a generic term for leafy greens), which can include mustard, spinach, fenugreek, white radish and chickpeas.

SHOPPING

At the market

The market still reigns in India. It's where you can rub shoulders with the people who shape the nation's cuisine and those who converge here every day in search of the freshest produce for the least rupees. Some markets are magnificent spectacles and to enter one is to be thrust, heart pumping and head reeling into the core of Indian life. Even if you have no intention of cooking, you can't help but leave the market laden with irresistible goodies.

Green beans, eggplant and *karella* (a bitter gourd).

There are different types of markets all over India, each one with its own personality, reflecting the character, history and geography of the people who live in that area:

- Where there is a concentration of Muslims, you'll find meat.
- If you're near the coast, the markets will glisten with freshly caught fish.
- In the affluent suburbs of major cities, you'll find 'exotic' markets with edibles like mushrooms, broccoli, beetroot, kiwi fruit and grapes shipped in from mysterious lands.

The markets are often so packed with food and people that vendors spill beyond the set boundaries into surrounding streets and labyrinthine lanes, and the market just seems to blend into the rest of the city. Approaching the 'organised' section, the thoroughfares become thick with makeshift stalls.

The meat market

The meat market is always quite separate from the fresh produce, hidden away to protect sensitive eyes. Us barbarians must sneak in to fill our carnivorous desires. This is an altogether different experience, and you should brace yourself if it's your first Asian market, as no effort is made to sanitise the process. You'll smell the meat market before you clap eyes on it, and the stench of blood will have you covering your nose.

The fish market

After the grisly carnage you've just passed, the fish market looks like a picture of serenity. Silvery piles of freshly caught fish glisten on mats, some still slapping, gasping and protesting. Vendors hold them up to exhibit their freshness, and shoppers order them filleted or whole. Behind the displays,

A pushcart snack food seller in Udaipur.

GREG ELMS / GETTY IMAGES

men lop off fish heads and draw out entrails with production-line efficiency. Piles of dried fish tend to attract buzzing flies. In smaller markets, you'll see rows of women sitting behind tarpaulin mats that are spread with fish fresh from their husbands' catches.

While it's almost exclusively women who cook, many men take it upon themselves to shop. Men take pride in getting the maximum bang for the family buck and consider it an affront to their manhood to pay full price.

Roving vendors

At any time of day, market surplus is being sold on the streets; a cavalcade of fruit, vegetables, nuts, eggs and fish being pushed or dragged on rickety old carts by men happy to be out and about. Women perch baskets of fresh fruit on their heads, men hold bigger baskets packed with shining utensils that cascade over the sides. Men cycle around with fresh herbs on the carriers of their bikes and young men push ice-cream carts, tempting young children and trying the patience of mothers. Even on the beach, squint into the distance and you'll see a vendor waddling towards you with a basket of tropical fruit on their head. A peel and a chop later, the vendor has gone and the juice from the most delicious pineapple you've ever tasted is dribbling down your chin.

PREPARATION

The kitchen

If the home is shelter, the kitchen is sanctity.

Millions of Indians — traditional Brahmins and other upper castes — won't let food that's not prepared in their own kitchen pass their lips. Even those without such taboos cherish home-cooked food above all else.

Many rural homes keep livestock — 'pets' as they call them

— and any space surrounding a house is used to grow fruit, vegetables, herbs and spices.

You'll be surprised at the simplicity of modern Indian kitchens and the sparsity of poorer ones. Resources and location influence the characteristics of each kitchen more than any religious differences.

Up to 30 years ago, kitchens looked and worked the same way they had for centuries. Women prepared food while crouching on the floor and cooked in a blackened, reliable pot over an earthen fireplace in the corner of the room. Grains and spices were ground in a quern, a simple hand mill. Food was eaten while sitting on the ground in another room. Sensibly then, shoes were forbidden indoors and nobody was allowed in the kitchen before they had bathed.

Woman cooking *baati*, typical Rajasthani food.

Utensils

Little has changed for the majority of rural folk, but the kitchens of India's expanding middle class have evolved dramatically. Electricity has come to most homes, flanked by indispensable mod cons such as rice cookers, blenders and pressure cookers. Other important utensils include:

- the *karhai*, a common Indian cooking utensil, similar to a wok, for deep-frying and sautéing
- several spatulas, spoons and ladles for stirring and serving
- a *tawa*, a hot plate, for making *roti*
- *dekchis*, heavy-bottomed pots with user-unfriendly lids, of several sizes
- a *paraat,* a round base for kneading dough
- *ghada*, plastic and steel vessels for storing water; and
- *chanis*, sieves; generally plastic or aluminium but also bamboo baskets in rural areas.

Cooking pots and pans for sale at the market.

Sikh volunteers take away mounds of dirty dishes after 30,000 meals are served to pilgrims.

Making *naan* bread over a *tandoor* in Jaipur.

CLARE S RICH / GETTY IMAGES

Most cooks grind spices just before cooking; this is done with a mortar and pestle in the south, and a flat slab and rolling pin in the north. Those who can afford it have coffee grinders specifically for preparing spices.

Every South Indian kitchen has a coconut scraper, a serrated iron disc mounted on a wooden board. Customised steaming equipment designed to fit inside pressure cookers is available in the special shapes required for such foods as *idlis* (steamed cakes of fermented rice flour and *daal*).

Thalis (indented plates) are still the most popular serving dishes. Traditionally, the material they were made of — gold, silver, bell metal — was a mark of family wealth and status, but these days everyone apart from the painfully pretentious use stainless steel as it's easier to clean. The little bowls that fit in the *thali's* indentations are called *katori*.

Some Indian ways of cooking meat

Kabab is a loose term, applied to marinated chunks of meat or ground meat, cooked on a skewer, fried on a hot plate or cooked under a grill. In fact, you could use the term *kabab* to describe any small cut of meat that doesn't already have a name. The two basic forms are barbecued bits on a skewer and the Muslim specialities made with mince. Falling into the second category, *kakori kababs* are a speciality of Uttar Pradesh.

Tandoor Very few people have a *tandoor* (clay oven) in their homes but *tandoori*-cooked meats are favourite restaurant fare all over India, especially in the north. In the *tandoor*, marinated meats are cooked to make *kababs*, succulent chunks of chicken become the famous *tikka* and a whole spring chicken surrenders its head and wings in order to emerge as glowing, scrumptious *tandoori* chicken.

Korma Another North Indian speciality, *korma* is a dish in which cubes of goat, lamb or chicken are cooked in a rich, spicy sauce, usually with the addition of onions. Contemporary *kormas* are often cooked over a stove like stews but the real thing is cooked using the *dum pukht* method of steaming, in which the vessel is sealed with dough, placed over glowing embers and 'baked' slowly.

Kheema* and *koftas *Kheema* means mincemeat but is also the name given to many dishes that include mincemeat, and *koftas* are meatballs. Both are very popular methods of cooking goat, beef and lamb.

DRINKS

Sweet, milky *chai* (tea) is the drink of the nation and is the perfect antidote to the rigours of travel. Coffee provides comfort in the south and there is a tempting host of juices and dairy drinks to slake your thirst. Times are tougher for tipplers, although there is a plethora of beers as well as fine local whisky, fiery *feni* from Goa and terrifying illegal spirits.

The local brew

Tribal communities have a rich history of local alcohol production. The best-known drink is a clear spirit with a heady pungent flavour called *mahua*, distilled from the flower of the *mahua* tree. It's brewed in makeshift village stalls all over Central India during March and April, when the trees bloom. The flower ferments naturally and animals like bears, monkeys and even elephants have a ferocious thirst for it.

Rice beer is brewed all over east and northeast India. In the Himalaya you'll find a grain alcohol called *raksi*, which is strong, has a mild charcoal flavour and tastes vaguely like scotch whisky. *Raksi* is a delightful drink in cold weather.

A handful of Darjeeling tea.

Saffron-flavoured milk.

Man checking the quality of his *chai*.

Wherever you find palm trees (as in Kerala), you'll see strong, skinny men scaling them with large pots. Then you'll hear the rhythmic tapping of buffalo bone against the palm bud. These chaps are called 'toddy tappers' and if you befriend one, you'll get to taste toddy, a delicious natural wonder, straight from the source. The evening toddy is stronger in alcohol (around 15%) than the morning variety. Toddy shops usually mix the drink with water to extend it, and add cucumber, pumpkin or chemicals to preserve it.

Tea

Tea growing really took off under the British, and now India is the world's largest producer, exporter and consumer of the stuff.

There are two tea plants:

- the original *camellia sinensis* from China, cultivated in Darjeeling and the Nilgiri Hills, and
- *camellia assamica*, discovered in Assam.

And three main tea-growing regions:

- Darjeeling (in West Bengal), the 'champagne of teas'
- the Nilgiri Hills (in the Western Ghats; Nilgiris means 'blue mountains'), also produce a tea of exceptional quality
- Assam grows a strong-flavoured variety that is only really good for blending or in *chai*.

Chai

Chai is the drink of the masses. It transcends cast, creed and class, and an invitation to share it is on the first page of India's guide to hospitality. *Chai* is made with more milk than water, more sugar than you'd care to think about, and is spiced with cardamom in winter and ginger in summer. A glass of steaming

JUPITERIMAGES / GETTY IMAGES

Glasses of *falooda*, a traditional Muslim dessert drin

sweet milky and frothy *chai* is the perfect antidote to the heat and stress of Indian travel and, not only is it a tonic for body and soul, sharing *chai* provides gilt-edged opportunities to meet and befriend the locals. Even if you meet somebody away from the *chai* stand, you'll be invited to seal the acquaintance over a cup or two.

Juices

Most of India's mind-boggling range of fruit is blended into juice at some stage. Restaurants think nothing of adding salt and sugar to intensify the flavours.

The most popular street juices are made from sweet lemon and sugarcane, which is pressed in front of you by a mechanised wheel complete with jingling bells. *Jal Jeera* is perhaps India's most therapeutic and refreshing indigenous drink, made of lime juice, cumin, mint and rock salt. It's sold in large earthenware pots by street vendors but if you're not feeling game, you'll also find it served in restaurants.

The juice from the green tender coconut is a great alternative to the sometimes risky street juices. You'll find them all over the south and much of the north, and watching the machete-wielding *wallah* whop the coconut into a drink is half the fun. After you've drunk the juice, he'll whop the coconut some more, providing you with chunks of tasty coconut meat.

Milk-based drinks

Sweet and savoury *lassi* (curds drink) is popular all over India although the best are in the north. Some places give their *lassi* a little twist of their own flavour, something subtle like rose. *Falooda* is a rose-flavoured Muslim speciality, made with milk, cream, nuts and strands of vermicelli. Hot or cold *badam* (milk flavoured with saffron and almonds) is an invigorating breakfast drink.

Well-balanced fishermen at work in Sri Lanka.

NIKO GUIDO / GETTY IMAGES

Sri Lanka

Sri Lanka boasts a unique and exciting cuisine, shaped both by the island's bounty and the influence of traders, immigrants and colonisers. The island's distinctive cuisine is marked by the freshness of its herbs and spices and the methods used to grind, pound, roast, temper and combine them. An emphasis on fish and seafood provides the perfect foundation for these flavours.

CULINARY CAPITAL COLUMBO **KNOWN FOR** SPICES **IMPORTS** DUTCH AND PORTUGUESE DISHES **EXPORTS** TEA **DEVOUR** CURRY AND RICE **AVOID** *ARRACK* (ALCOHOL MADE FROM PALM TREE SAP)

Pilau, Sri Lanka's version of *pilaf*, is a common dish.

Jackfruit growing on tree.

A bicycle laden with coconuts.

CULTURE

In Sri Lanka, the influence of outsiders is never far from the menu. Muslim restaurants serve up perfect flat breads and samosas introduced by Arab traders. Celebratory cakes often have a Dutch or Portuguese touch, and deliciously sweet desserts concocted from *jaggery* (a brown sweet made from the kitul palm), coconut milk, cloves and cardamom are redolent of the influence of Malay traders from the spice islands further east.

REGIONS

Regional differences in Sri Lanka are more about availability of ingredients than ethnicity. In the north, the palmyra tree reigns, and its roots, flowers, fruits and seeds produce dishes ranging from curries to syrups, sweets, cakes and snacks. In the south, rice is considered indispensable; fish and jackfruit are popular, too. In the fertile Hill Country, there are vegetables and mutton, but fewer fish and spices.

FEASTS

As a symbol of life and fertility, rice is the food for festivities. *Kiri bath*, rice cooked in coconut milk, is a baby's first solid food, and is also the food newlywed couples feed each other.

Dumplings are popular for celebrations, and in northern Sri Lanka the revelry includes gently dropping *kolukattai* (dumplings with edges pressed to resemble teeth) on a toddler's head while the family make wishes for the infant to develop healthy teeth. Sweet dumplings, *mothagam*, are offered to Ganesh in prayer.

Ramadan ends with the breaking of the fast and the start of the *Eid-ul-Fitr* festival. Muslims eat dates in memory of the Prophet Mohammed, and then *congee* (rice soup with spices, coconut milk and meat). On *Eid-ul-Fitr*, Muslims share food with family, friends and neighbours.

Aurudu (Sri Lankan New Year) is another time for celebration. After the sacred activities, feasting begins with *kiri bath* followed by *kaung* (oil cake), a Sri Lankan favourite.

DAILY MEALS

Simple restaurants — confusingly called 'hotels' — cater to locals with a basic but utterly tasty menu of rice and curry.

Less formal places to eat include the street-side huts called *kadé* or boutiques by the Sinhalese, and *unavakam* by Tamils. The main offer here is *kotthu rotti*, a doughy pancake that is chopped and fried with fillings ranging from chilli and onion to vegetables, bacon and egg. Also available from the *kadé* and bakeries are lunch packets. These self-contained food parcels are sold all over the country between 11am and 2pm. Inside you'll usually find rice, curry (generally chicken, fish or beef, though if you're vegetarian, you'll get an egg), curried vegetables and *sambal*.

ESSENTIAL PRODUCE

Chilli

Sri Lankan food has a reputation for being absurdly spicy. If you're not deterred, some chilli-based dishes to look out for include *pol sambal* a type of dry chilli- and coconut-based condiment, and 'devilled' dishes, in which meat is infused with chilli. A great snack with a cold Lion beer is a bowl of devilled cashews.

Coconut

From the extracted oil to the grated flesh, coconut finds its way into just about every dish in Sri Lanka. *Pol sambal*, the spicy condiment made from grated coconut meat, is probably the

LONELY PLANET / GETTY IMAGES

A popular breakfast selection of *puri*, *idly* (a kind of rice cake) and the doughnut-shaped *vadai*.

most famous example of this, but you'll also find coconut milk in the island's rice dishes, breads and curries. And the liquid from young coconuts is a refreshing drink on a sweltering day.

Fish and seafood

Excellent fish and prawns are widespread in Sri Lanka, and in many coastal towns you'll find crab and lobster. *Seer*, a tuna-type fish, is a favourite. A southern speciality is the popular *ambulthiyal* (sour fish curry), made with *goraka*, a sour fruit.

Rice

Rice is a staple of Sri Lankan cuisine, and it is served at nearly every meal — plain, spiced, in meat juices, with curd (buffalo-milk yoghurt) or tamarind, or with milk.

Flour made from rice is the basis of two popular dishes: hoppers (also called *appam*), which are bowl-shaped pancakes, and *dosas* (also called *thosai*), paper-thin breads served stuffed with spiced vegetables.

Popular breakfasts include hoppers, bread dipped in curry, and *pittu*, a mixture of rice flour and coconut steamed in a bamboo mould. *Kola kanda*, a porridge of rice, coconut, green vegetables and herbs, is popular and nutritious.

Spices

Cinnamon is native to Sri Lanka. More than 80% of the world's cinnamon is still grown here. Other spices grown on the island — and used in the cuisine — include pepper, clove, nutmeg, vanilla and cardamom.

DEFINING DISHES

Hoppers

Hoppers are bowl-shaped pancakes made from rice flour and

OLIVER STREWE / GETTY IMAGES

Crab curry from a restaurant in Arugam Bay.

coconut milk. The dough is slightly fermented, often by adding toddy, giving the hoppers a subtle sour flavour, and a porous, crumpet-like consistency. Hoppers are typically eaten with *lunu miris*, a simple 'dip' based around chilli, along with curries and other side dishes. String hoppers take the form of small nests of thin, rice-based noodles that are eaten with curries. Egg hoppers are served with an egg cracked in the bottom, and are eaten on their own, often for breakfast.

Lamprais

This dish is made from rice cooked in a meat broth and served with *frikkadels* (Dutch-style meatballs), *blachan* (a dried shrimp-based 'dip'), a hard-boiled egg, eggplant, plantain and *sambal*. All of these elements are combined and steamed in a banana leaf. The dish is thought to date back to the first Dutch settlers in the 17th century, and the name allegedly comes from the Dutch words for lump (*klomp*) and rice (*rijst*).

Rice and curry

Available on almost every menu, Sri Lankan rice and curry consists of small spiced dishes made from vegetables, meat or fish, and served with chutneys and *sambal*, a condiment made from ingredients pounded with chilli.

Most curries include chilli, turmeric, cinnamon, cardamom, coriander, *rampe* (pandanus leaves), curry leaves, mustard, tamarind and coconut milk. Dried fish is also frequently used to season curry dishes.

Sambal

Sambal refers to a variety of dip-like dishes, often using fish, chili and onion, often eaten with rice or breads. The most common version in Sri Lanka is *pol sambal*, made from dried fish from the Maldives and grated coconut flesh.

Short eats

The midday joy of Sri Lankan cuisine, 'short eats' are meat-stuffed rolls, meat-and-vegetable patties (called cutlets), pastries and *vadai* (deep-fried snacks made from lentil flour and spices). You order short eats from a counter and take them away, or you can sit down if there are chairs. At some places, a plate of short eats is placed on your table, and you're only charged for what you eat.

DRINKS

Sri Lanka's heat means that refreshing beverages are an important — and vital — part of the day's consumption.

- *Arrack* is an alcoholic drink fermented and (somewhat) refined from toddy. Toddy, a drink made from the sap of palm trees has a sharp taste, a bit like cider. There are three types: toddy made from coconut palms, toddy from kitul palms and toddy from palmyras. *Arrack* can have a powerful kick and give you a worse hangover. The best mixer for it is the local ginger ale.
- Ginger beer is an old school drink — very British — but it offers refreshment with a zing. Look out for the Elephant or Lion brands.
- *Lassi*, a refreshing yoghurt-based drink, can be found in Indian restaurants and sweet shops.
- *Thambili* (king coconut) juice still in the husk is on sale at roadside stalls everywhere.

Tea

Tea came to Sri Lanka when extensive coffee plantations were decimated by disease in the 19th century. The first Sri Lankan tea was grown in 1867 at the Loolecondera Estate southeast of Kandy. Plantation owners discovered that the Hill Country

Egg hopper with *sambal*.

Hot and fresh *vadai*.

A 'three wheeler' ferries cinnamon bark to the market.

Mango *lassi*, a popular yoghurt-based drink.

PHILIPPE DESENRCK / GETTY IMAGES

combined a warm climate, high altitude and sloping terrain: a winning trifecta perfect for growing tea.

Producing tea

Tea bushes are pruned back to around a metre in height and squads of Tamil tea pluckers (all women) move through the rows of bushes picking the leaves and buds. These are then 'withered' (demoisturised by blowing air at a fixed temperature through them) either in the old-fashioned multistorey tea factories, where the leaves are spread out on hessian mats, or in modern mechanised troughs.

The partly dried leaves are then crushed, starting a fermentation process. The green leaves quickly turn a coppery brown as additional heat is applied. The art in tea production comes in knowing when to stop the fermentation, by 'firing' the tea at an even higher heat to produce the final, brown-black leaf that will be stable for a reasonable length of time.

From the time tea is picked until it is finished being processed and placed in bags for shipment takes only 24 hours.

Types of tea

The many varieties of tea are graded by size (from cheap 'dust' through fannings and broken grades to 'leaf' tea) and by quality (with names such as flowery, pekoe or souchong). Obviously, tea the same size as dust is rather inferior. Anything graded in the leaf category is considered the minimum designation for respectable tea.

Tea is further categorised into low-grown, mid-grown or high-grown. The low-grown teas (under 600 metres) grow strongly and are high in 'body' but low in 'flavour'. The high-grown teas (over 1200 metres) grow more slowly and are renowned for their subtle flavour. Mid-grown tea is somewhere between the two.

Stacks of fresh wontons in Guangzhou.

ULRIKE MAIER / GETTY IMAGES

China

China is a brimming soup bowl that should be gripped with both hands. It's the snappiest stir fry, the crispest skinned duck, the finest of dumplings and the spiciest hotpot. Visiting and tasting your way across China is the biggest rollercoaster ride any food lover can climb aboard. What's even better, you'll be riding shotgun with the locals, some of the most food obsessed of any nation on earth.

CULINARY CAPITALS GUANGDONG, SZECHUAN **KNOWN FOR** PEKING DUCK **IMPORTS** CHEESE **EXPORTS** GARLIC, APPLES **DEVOUR** *YUM CHA* **AVOID** CAMEL'S HUMP SOUP

A typical peasant breakfast in Yangshuo, consisting of hard boiled egg, vegetables, noodles and meat.

ED FREEMAN / GETTY IMAGES

CULTURE

To the Chinese, food is central to all aspects of life. It's part and parcel of religious and social life. It feeds, it nourishes, it fuels arguments, and forges bonds. Not only that, but the Chinese have an innate sense of what is good. Their mouths are finely tuned to textural differences, their palates to nuances of flavour and their sensibilities offended by food that doesn't match the high standards they set for themselves.

Food and eating, cuisine and dining are deeply linked to the culture of China. It's built up from ancient times, from ritual and ceremony, social status and codes of conduct. A meal is often seen as a way of dining with ancestors, and local traditions are perpetuated at every turn.

Most importantly, a meal is usually shared. To eat alone, unless it's a snack because you're far from home or at work, isn't considered very good form. A family will invariably gather for the nightly meal, regardless of commitments, unless making money gets in the way. A meal with guests is always an even bigger affair. Rarely will there be less than four people around a table, even in modern One-Child China.

Flavours

Chinese food is said to contain five key elements: colour, aroma, flavour, shape and texture. Along with the five basic elements, there are also the five western tastes (sweet, salty, sour, bitter and hot).

The Chinese also talk of at least two other tastes; *wok qi* (sometimes called *wok hei*), and *umami* often found in the salty, satisfying flavour of monosodium glutamate (MSG). MSG exists naturally in substantial amounts in mushrooms (particularly dried mushrooms), soy sauce, *hoisin* sauce, fermented bean pastes and seaweed.

Wok qi is best described as the life, energy or breath of the wok. It's that indefinable flavour, almost a hot iron smokiness that you get from food that is properly cooked in a wok. *Wok qi* is paramount in stir fries.

Every dish may have some aspect of each flavour, a balance, but one dish can be more sour, another hotter, another more sweet. That way the whole meal finds balance, too.

Eating for health

According to traditional Chinese medicine, all foods have a medicinal effect. When you are feeling unwell, your body is out of balance — too heated, too moist, too dry, too cold, not enough wood, metal or fire and so on. Finding the food with the right elements can help remedy and rebalance the body.

Many foods are classified as *yang* (heating, such as pepper and ginger) or *yin* (cooling, such as cucumber or bitter melon). Cooling foods can nix a sore throat, a symptom of an overheated body. A medicinal meal, *yaoshan*, is a combination of nutritious foods and therapeutic herbs such as ginseng or cordyceps. *Yaoshan* meals prevent or heal illnesses and promote longevity. The most typical are soul-warming tonics boiled for hours, rich stews with a chicken base or the sex organs of animals for virility.

REGIONS

China covers far too much territory to have a national cuisine. Here, it's all about the regional cuisines that have developed over the centuries into eight specific styles:

- *huicai* from Anhui
- *yuecai* from Guangdong
- *mincai* from Fujian
- *xiangcai* from Hunan

SURI SUN / GETTY IMAGES

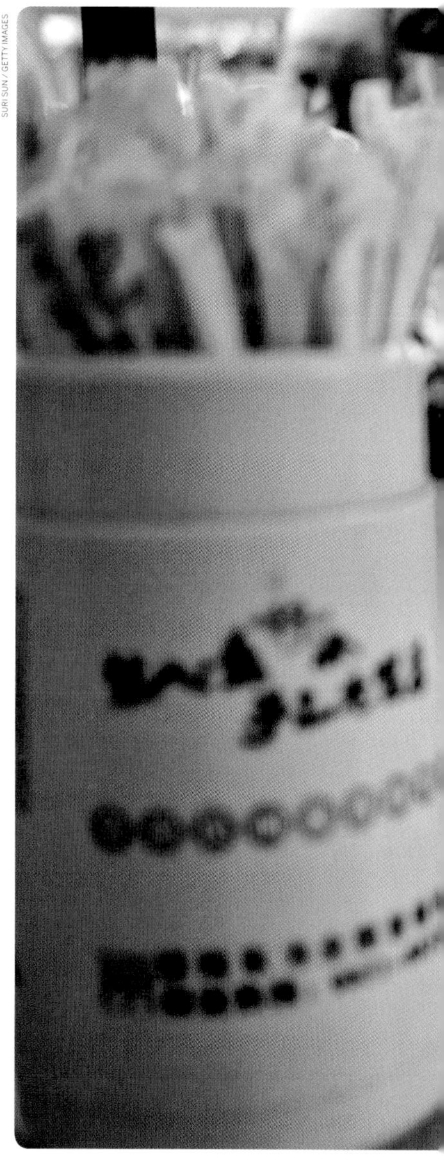

A woman eating noodles.

- *sucai* from Jiangsu
- *lucai* from Shandong
- *chuancai* from Sichuan
- *zhecai* from Zhejiang.

Each of these regionally specific styles has its own vocabulary of spices, herbs and sauces, particular to that part of the land. In fact, eating your way around China can feel like a voyage to eight different countries.

To simplify things, it helps to think of the north–south rivalry. Northerners are known as wheat eaters; southerners, rice eaters. People who eat wheat products are physically large but provincial in their outlook. People who eat rice are small and soft-willed. Or so they say about each other. The 'you are what you eat' concept is taken very seriously in China.

Northern cuisine

Particularly well suited to the harsh and hardy winter climate, northern cooking is rich and wholesome. Filling breads and dumplings are steamed, baked or fried while noodles may form the basis of any meal, particularly in Shanxi, where China's most obsessive noodle chefs can be found.

Peking Duck is the north's signature dish, and it served with typical ingredients — pancakes, spring onions and fermented bean paste.

The nomadic and carnivorous diet of the Mongolians also infiltrates northern cooking, most noticeably in the Mongolian hotpot and the Mongolian barbecue.

Guangdong cuisine

Nothing compares to the clear, light, crisp and fresh flavours of Guangdong (formerly Canton Province), China's southernmost mainland region. It's the taste of China that will be most

ULRIKE MAIER / GETTY IMAGES

Dried shark fins for sale at a market in China.

familiar to Westerners thanks to the travels of the Cantonese and the prosperity of Hong Kong.

Guangdong is the undisputed home of fresh food. Live, in fact. The markets can resemble zoos, the fish markets are full of aquarium-like tanks and the dried food shops piled high with anything and everything that can be eaten. And a few things which you might think can't.

Suckling pig is one of the masteries of the Cantonese, as is *char siu* pork, meaning literally 'held by fork over fire'. The Cantonese take credit for creating *yum cha*, tea with delicious *dim sum* dumplings. Other specialities include steamed whole fish with ginger and shallots and *congee* (rice porridge).

The Chiu Chow people from the east of the province are most famous for shark fin soup (which you probably shouldn't order because the sharks are on the verge of extinction) and bird's nest soup (ditto), but their greatest contribution to Chinese gastronomy is *lo soi*, or 'old water'. Old water is the name given to the masterstock in which poultry are braised. The spiced, lightly sweet, intense stock takes its name because in a Chiu Chow home it's never off the stove, used daily to poach chicken or ducks or pigeon. With each cooking it becomes more complex and intense.

Szechuan cuisine

The classic 'west' of China is Szechuan (Sichuan/Szechwan) province. The local cuisine is defined most by its use of the flowering (Szechuan) pepper — a pungent, mouth-numbing berry which isn't actually a pepper at all — along with fermented soy bean pastes and the ground sesame paste which isn't totally dissimilar to tahini.

Szechuan food is one of the greatest cuisines in China, where local food scholars have defined the 23 essential combinations of flavour and the 56 techniques used to cook food.

FEASTS

Spring Festival

For the Chinese, every, or nearly every, celebration or event involves food, none more so that Spring Festival (Chinese New Year). Spring Festival, which starts on a different date each year, depending on the moon but is usually between late January and late February, is a time of the greatest significance to the Chinese and holds profound social importance.

In the 15 days of the festival, houses are swept to cleanse them of bad luck and leave them open to good luck (and the brooms put away so the good luck can't be swept away). Banquets are usually held every night for at least a week, and generally serve eight or nine courses: eight sounds like the word for prosperity and nine for long lasting.

During Spring Festival:

- Tangerines are everywhere, and so are mixed nuts — the giving and receiving of both thought to bring good luck for the coming year.
- There is *yu* (fish), served at every great banquet.
- In parts of the south, they serve round rice cakes, which symbolise the unity of the family.
- Scallops and clams are served, also round to represent coins or ingots (and therefore wealth).
- Poultry and fish are served with their heads and tails or feet still on, showing a true beginning and end.
- Roast pig is served, signifying purification and peace.
- Oysters and lettuce represent good fortune and prosperity.
- Buddha's Delight is a vegetarian dish made at Spring Festival, a mix of over ten vegetables, such as gingko

Steamed chestnuts.

Dried scallops.

Tangerines are everywhere. It must be *Kung Hei Fat Choi*, Happy Chinese New Year.

Produce on display in a Chinese dried food store.

WULINGYUN / GETTY IMAGES

nuts, bamboo, lotus root, celery, snow peas, lily buds, and bean curd and water chestnuts are served in a soy based sauce.

ESSENTIAL PRODUCE

The sheer enormity of China, with its climate bordering on both the tropical and the bleak, has endowed the cuisine with an abundance of produce scarcely found elsewhere.

Great fruit and vegetables, including new world ingredients such as corn and tomatoes, abound. There's stunning seafood, there's the enormous (albeit often confronting) variety of wild foods found throughout the country such as bamboo worms, deer penis, and wild cat. Close to the Russian border in Heilongjiang province you'll be offered caviar. In the South West you may come across chilled rice noodles, cut to order from a stump-like block, or sweet potatoes grilled over coals on the street.

Dried foods

The most popular foods to dry are mushrooms. Invariably it's a way of preserving them, rather than an attempt to gain more flavour, even though a by-product of drying is a more robust, and in some ways more complex flavour. Over thirty types of mushrooms will found dried and packaged on supermarket shelves.

The dried beef of Hangzhou in Zhejiang province is truly remarkable, with a texture reminiscent of fairy floss (cotton candy) and a strong, satisfying flavour, and dried starfish are found for sale mostly around the coast.

Along with dried seafood, meats and fungus, you'll find dried vegetables, dried fruit, and sweet shops selling everything from the most wonderful fragrant little dried white figs which are the size of a thumbnail, to jujubes, apricots and snakes.

Dumplings

Dumplings are Chinese icons. The *jiaoza* of Beijing and the north are usually pork filled, fried or steamed wheat dough-coated bliss bombs. In Shanghai, the hot stock filled *xiaolongbao* are seared on one side and for sale on most traditional streets each morning. Meanwhile, in Guangdong (Canton), the worlds best dumpling meal, *yum cha*, is served for breakfast and lunch at just about every restaurant worth its Sichuan salt.

Five spice

Used extensively, five spice consists of:

- star anise — a quintessential Chinese spice with an elegant anise (liquorice) flavour
- cassia bark — a bit like cinammon, though sweeter
- fennel seeds — anise-flavoured seeds
- peppercorns, and
- cloves.

Fish and other seafood

The only thing that swims which the Chinese don't eat, a Beijing resident tells us, is a submarine. And so it is, if there's a fish, a turtle, a water beetle or something sludgy looking and edible, the Chinese will have a way of eating it. It doesn't even need to swim. Sea cucumbers are sold dried, for inordinately high prices. Fish farms dot the landscape, crabs are caught wild and farmed, lobsters are flown in daily from Australia and abalone from New Zealand. Sharks are served in Guangzhou, catfish are prized in Sichuan, freshwater shrimp drown in wine on many a table in Zhejiang, and live prawns grace the tanks at beachside dining rooms in Xiamen.

CHEN CHAO / GETTY IMAGES

Vegetables in baskets at a Shanghai market.

Fungi

Wow. If it's fungi you're into, it's China you'll love. By far the best ones to buy are fresh, and include the following:

- *Shiitake* are the most common mushrooms — choose the dark ones with cracked tops if you're buying them dry.
- Wood-ear fungus and cloud-ear fungus — crunchy fungi, the first dark, nearly black, the second pale or white.
- Monkey head mushrooms — they look like the back of a monkey's head and are the size of a child's fist.
- Oyster mushrooms — thin, pale and exquisitely subtle.
- Abalone mushrooms — fat, gently crunchy and have a vaguely abalone flavour.
- *Jizong* — meaty, flaky small things.
- The usual cultivated button and brown mushrooms you'd find at home.

Meats

China is the original home of the pig. *Rou*, meaning 'pork' in Chinese, also means meat generally. A meat dish is usually a pork dish. Pork fat, as lard, is laced through breads and pastries. It's used to moisten vegetable dumplings and seafood-filled breads in China's south, and used to fry food all through China's north.

Dining in Guangdong, there could be a wild cat on the menu or in a cage near the front door. There may be a sheepish-looking possum behind bars at the steps, seven types of snakes slithering around in cages or plastic tubs and several types of turtle nervously poking their heads from their shells. If it's edible, it's eaten.

Various types of Chinese noodles on display.

Bowl of noodle soup.

A noodle maker in Guangzhou.

Noodles

While rice has only in relatively recent times made an impact in the north, one common feature of the whole eastern half of the country is the noodle. There are hand stretched noodles from the north, where impossibly thin men twist and swirl a wheat-based dough overhead, gradually creating thin, round noodles. In the south, noodles are often made of rice flour or even mung bean or pea starch. You may see them in markets in Yunnan using grater-like cutters carving off noodles from round slabs of cooked dough and serving them cold. Glassy coloured noodles, also more favoured in the south, are made from mung bean flour, while the green ones are from peas.

Oyster sauce

The classic oyster sauce is made from a species of huge pacific oysters that can be seen being farmed off the coast of Fujian.

Pastries

Chinese pastries are among the most varied in the world. As fine and flaky as the taro dumplings in *yum cha*, the lightly chewy biscuits of Beijing and the base of egg tarts show the mastery of Chinese technique.

The *daan tad* (egg tart) you find in Guangzhou today is a derivative of the Portuguese *pasteis de natas* (custard tart) brought to the region by colonists, probably into the port of Macau. Where once a little egg was brushed over pastry, now it's the body of the dish. Abundance is leading to the redefining of old dishes, and the creation of some wonderful pastries.

Rice

It's so important that even the smell of rice is revered. Rice *hei* (breath of rice) the aroma from rice cooking — its essence and energy — must be preserved by cooking it with the lid on.

Rice, historically, has been easily divided, raw or processed, long or short grain, dark or pale. But of the several thousands of different varieties of rice, there are a few that stand out.

- Black rice is a raw, black-skinned, long-grain glutinous rice, used in China almost exclusively for sweets.
- Jasmine rice is a long-grain variety that has the subtle fragrance, if you use your imagination, of jasmine petals.
- Red rice is another version of raw, short-grained rice, mostly made into alcoholic drinks and the famous red vinegar of the eastern province of Zhejiang.

Soy beans

While China doesn't have much cheese, it does have the next best thing — soy beans; an ingredient so versatile that it can be fermented, smoked, and matured in much the same way.

From soy beans come soy milk and the resultant thickened mass, bean curd or *doufu* so commonly found in Chinese food:

- *Chou doufu* — a fermented specialty of Hangzhou.
- Bean curd — the soft, solid curd (mostly protein), staple of savoury dishes.
- Bean curd skin — the crinkly skin that forms on top of bean milk as it boils (just like milk). There is a light-coloured version used in stir fries or soups, and a darker one, used extensively in *yum cha*.
- Dessert *doufu* — with the texture of lightly set yoghurt or custard, this soft version of tofu is made fresh, and then sweetened.
- Smoked *doufu* — preserved beancurd that has been hot smoked, creating a honey coloured, resilient exterior and a pungent, smoky flavour.

KYLIE MCLAUGHLIN / GETTY IMAGES

Tofu and burnt chilli dish at a restaurant in Dongcheng.

- Dried beancurd — in *kan doufu*, the curd is pressed and dried. Normally sliced and served as a snack.
- Preserved beancurd – deep fried beancurd, which is sold in bags and used in everything from soups to *congee*.

Zhejiang versus Yunnan Ham

In China, as in Spain and Italy, there's much debate about ham. Anywhere that has more than one distinct style has the discussion: which is the best? Is it the softer, more quickly cured Zhejiang ham from the country's east, which no self-respecting Shanghainese would be without. Or the firm, salty, but incredibly fragrant hams of Yunnan in the south west?

Yunnan ham is the one that is most often recommended throughout the west. The chefs of Hong Kong discovered it and use it in everything from winter melon soups to versions of the famed XO chilli sauce. In China, it's now known as *xuanwei* (gorgeous taste) ham, distinguishing itself from the hams made in Hunan and other provinces nearby. Estimates range, but most agree that it's only been around for about the last 300 years or so and is renowned for its sweetness. Like most good hams around the world, it's prepared in winter, when the weather is better for maturing.

SHOPPING

Food shopping is still a daily occurrence for many Chinese. As many don't have fridges, and freshness is paramount even for those that do, much of the food is still bought and cooked straight away.

The traditional market is making way for the more flashy supermarket, where prices are often double those on the street outside, and the produce is better displayed, if not always better quality.

Fried scorpions, a popular market snack.

At the market

Wandering around a Chinese market is both invigorating and memorable. One minute you may see a cat being drowned in a bag for a customer, the next men crouched over a bucket of scorpions, wielding chopsticks and picking out the choicest ones to cook at home.

A market isn't just a place to buy food, it's a place to watch the Chinese at their most deft. No one wants poor produce, but price is paramount. There's plenty of argy bargy over price, and much accusing and justification going on.

Everything that's sold by weight is placed on the scales, rustic looking things with a counter weight on one end and food on a tray on the other. A chain slips from the counterweight over a fixed metal rod, which is graced with plenty of dots to mark the weight. It all means nothing, even to many Chinese, but you watch them like a hawk just the same.

Speciality shops

The old way of running shops was for everybody to be a specialist. And thankfully, just as it was in the old days in the west, the specialist still calls the shots in China. Lining the streets in most towns, you'll find:

- The tea shop — the most common speciality store, each region has it's own particular teas, and there are virtually always tiny paper cups for tasting.
- Specialist *doufu* (tofu) shops — they sell everything you can imagine could be done to solidified soy milk.
- Pickle shops — where cabbage and radish and onion and more are laid out in trays forming a kaleidoscope of red, green, purple and black.
- In the south there are famous barbecue shops — selling roast duck, suckling pig, roasted pork and chicken.

PREPARATION

Chopsticks

The Chinese not only use chopsticks for eating, they also have extra long, heatproof (usually wooden) chopsticks for cooking. They can be used to scoop out deep-fried food so it drains perfectly, to stir noodles as they cook, and to act as tongs.

Cleaver

The cleaver is the ubiquitous Chinese knife. The rectangular-shaped blade is gripped with a forefinger from the handle, and it's used for everything from peeling garlic to hacking through the bones of a duck.

Grills

Almost everywhere in the country you'll see open charcoal-fired grills. Increasingly, in cities like Beijing where air quality has reached appallingly low standards, laws forbid the cooking of food on open grills on the street.

Steamer

Then there are the fabulous steamers, ginormous metal ones used in commercial kitchens, medium-sized bamboo ones that fit inside a wok for steaming whole fish, and tiny ones for small serves of dumplings, particularly at *yum cha*.

Wok burner

No Chinese kitchen is a true place of honour without a wok burner. These are basically the equivalent of a gas stove, with multiple gas jet rings and flames. They're supremely hot and there is little, apart from a wood fire that can replicate the taste and texture of food cooked in a blackened wok over a proper wok burner.

Clean cleavers.

Dumplings, *dim sum*, in bamboo steamers.

Noodles being poured through a specially-designed strainer.

COOKING METHODS

In restaurants, preparation and timing are key ingredients. There can be five or more cooking methods employed to produce a single dish.

Curing

Curing, smoking and air-drying are fine arts, developed across the nation and most visible in the fine mahogany-skinned ducks in Guangdong, or Peking Duck. In Sichuan they smoke salt-cured ducks in tea and camphor; tofu is smoked in Shanghai and sausages smoked in the north.

Cutting

Cutting is an art; the shape of the food is intrinsically linked to how good the end dish will be. The shape influences the way flavours meld, the uptake of spice, and the release of flavour into a dish, as well as texture. Hand-shredded chicken, in Sichuan's *bang bang chicken* for instance, isn't the same dish if the poultry is diced.

Drowning

In the east, particularly around the town of Shaoxing famed for its yellow wine, drowning is the go. Crabs or prawns are immersed in a mixture heavy with Shaoxing wine, served live at the table and eaten once they stop kicking. They're called drunken crabs or prawns.

Frying

While frying is used all around the globe, the one thing that the Chinese definitely gave to the rest of the world is stir frying, where a superheated wok is drizzled with a little oil, the ingredients added in just the right quantity, at just the right time, to cook and not burn.

SAIF PHOTOGRAPHY / GETTY IMAGES

Fried squid, a popular Chinese street food.

Timing

Timing is critical. The perfectly cooked live fish is steamed so that it completes its cooking on the way to the table. Soups are simmered for a precise amount of time, so the ingredients retain the texture intended.

DEFINING DISHES

Beggar's chicken

Legend has it that Hangzhou's now famous dish has a very humble past. Once there was a beggar, a lowly man who had strayed onto the Emperor's land and was hungry enough to steal a chicken. But no sooner had he plucked, drawn and stuffed the bird than the Emperor's guards were upon him. Panicked, he wrapped the bird in lotus leaves, the closest thing at hand, and hid it in the mud. Later, when the royal guards had found nothing, he dug up the bird, still coated in mud, and decided to cook it anyway.

These days, if you're lucky, the bird is wrapped in a salt crust (or the traditional clay) to enclose the lotus leaves, but in many restaurants the crust has been dispensed with. The legendary moist and aromatic meal is delivered to the table wrapped tightly in endless layers of plastic cling film.

Hairy crab

Hairy crabs are small, green, freshwater crabs, which have hairy legs. They're a late autumn delicacy, sold alive, bound in cord, and shipped around the country.

To eat hairy crab, pull the top shell off and eat all the murky brown stuff underneath, discarding the coarse, fern-like finger gills. If it's a female, you'll find the much sought after roe under here, too. Break the crab in two through the middle, and using your fingers, tear off all but the top two legs. Now, use the

Hairy crabs for sale at Nelson Street Wet Market in Hong Kong.

Sichuan peppercorns and star anise.

A Chongqing hotpot.

two remaining legs as the handle, and take bites from the remaining crab shell, the body bits that have all those cavities containing the prized meat.

Crabs are considered a 'cooling' food, so they're served with vinegar and perhaps some ginger or garlic. Local lore says you must not drink tea, cold water or eat persimmons after tasting crabs, or your stomach will hurt.

Ma la

Eating *ma la* puts you somewhere between pain and pleasure. *Ma* means 'numbing' and *la* means 'spicy', and that is exactly what this sauce is. The Sichuan peppercorns make your lips tingle and swell, and a generous amount of chilli provokes a surge of endorphins, leaving you panting as your tongue is set on fire. No wonder the Chinese are completely hooked on this irresistible sauce.

Sichuan and Chongqing regional cuisines are famous for their *ma la* sauce, which headlines any feast there. There are flavours of fermented bean sauce, and a bouquet of star anise, cardamom and fennel provide a sweet aftertaste even as the chilli onslaught continues.

A popular way to try *ma la* is *shuizhuyu*. Slices of fish are first poached in a broth, then covered in chilli oil and heaps of bright red chilli and Sichuan peppercorns. Another crowd-pleaser is *fuqi feipian*, where slices of beef and offal are covered in a Sichuan-style chilli sauce that's particularly high on the spice metre.

A plate of *mapo doufu* will convert anyone who doesn't like tofu into an instant fan. Super-soft tofu is cooked with minced pork and a *ma la* sauce that should be powerfully hot. For those who want to take it down a notch, try the *laziji*, fried chicken pieces flavoured with Sichuan peppercorns and hidden under a mountain of red chillies. It looks intimidating but is relatively gentle.

Peking duck

If China had to be represented by one dish, it would be Peking duck. Everything about Beijing's iconic dish screams decadence, from the tableside carving of the bird to the fact that only the best parts — skin, fat and a bit of meat — are eaten. No wonder the imperial courts kept Peking duck to themselves. The recipe was developed in the Yuan dynasty, and the expertly roasted birds only made their way to the tables of China's gentry in the 1700s.

Preparing Peking duck is a lengthy, laborious craft that's testament to the genius of northern Chinese cooking.

Peking duck is made from force-fed birds, birds gorged on seed in much the same way the French and others produce *foie gras*, the fattened liver. The thin breast meat of the Pekin breed becomes impossibly tender and the flavour becomes more complex. A fattened bird is drawn and plucked, the head and most of the legs left intact. The tail end is then sewn tightly shut and the birds are filled with air. This inflation separates the skin from the meat, ensuring it can be caramelised when cooked. When deflated, the ducks are air dried. When ready to roast, they are filled with anything from water to a complex and aromatic stock. After hanging for a further 72 hours, the birds are basted with a sweetened marinade on the outside and roasted in a wood-fired oven until the flesh is fully cooked yet moist, the fat slightly rendered, and the skin glossy and gorgeous.

Red-cooked pork

Red is considered an auspicious colour in China, and the hue comes into its own with *hongshao rou* (red-cooked pork). Although more brown than crimson, and at most a mauve hue, *hongshao rou* is pork that's been slow-cooked in soy sauce, Shaoxing wine, sugar and spices. Each household has its own

Mapo doufu.

A crowd pleaser: Peking roasted duck.

Peking duck for sale at a streetside restaurant.

A variety of *dim sum* are presented at this *yum cha* meal.

LONELY PLANET / GETTY IMAGES

closely guarded *hongshao* recipe, and cooks argue over which flavour to add first, sugar or soy sauce, and whether to include star anise or chilli or keep it spice-free and mild.

Yum cha

These little steam baskets of dumplings were originally created as snacks to accompany tea, the drinking of which was the main event. Today, *yum cha* is comprised of literally hundreds of varieties of *dim sum*, tiny morsels whose name means 'to gently touch the heart' (rather than stuff the stomach). Over time, the supporting act stole the show, and while good-quality tea is still important for a *yum cha* meal, the food itself has become a fully fledged sub-cuisine particular to Guangdong and Hong Kong.

DRINKS

There's not a meal in China that is eaten without a drink. And while the drink of choice for most Chinese is tea, meals in China are often accompanied by alcohol. You'll see them drinking liquid razor wire in wee small glasses to ward off the cold in the far north east, slurping beer over dinner in Jinan, or sucking fermented milk drinks (like a loose yoghurt) from glass bottles in Beijing. That's not to mention an incomparable number of fruit drinks, soft drinks, herb- and fruit-flavoured spirits. Add them up, and you've got arguably one of the most complex arrays of beverages in the world. So *gan bei*, or drink up.

Tea

For the connoisseur, tea is as complex a topic as wine. There are at least 320 strains of the true tea plant (*Camellia sinensis*) in China, which fall into six broad categories. Within each category are the variations of vintage, harvesting method, and production — everything from double dried, fire or steam withered, rolled or not rolled.

As a rule, tea is drunk before and after the meal, except in Guangdong (Canton), where it's more likely to be drunk throughout the meal, especially if that meal is *yum cha*.

The teahouse

Teahouses are still a feature in China, particularly in the west and Shanghai. Locals gather to chat, to have their ear wax removed or endure a massage, all the while gossiping or trading jokes or playing Chinese chess. In grander places, or older places, rattan chairs dot picturesque gardens, but these days you're more likely to find white, moulded plastic to sit on, and a teabag in your cup than the finest jasmine pearls or white peony.

The teapot

A real teapot is a work of great art, and the best of the best, as everyone seems to agree across China, are the teapots made from the purplish-coloured clay of Yixing, not that far from Shanghai. Called *zi shah u*, these teapots have been prized since at least the Ming Dynasty (1368–1644) for their strength, their workmanship, but mostly for their ability to make tea taste its best and most pure. Word has it that if you make oolong tea in one of these pots for long enough, eventually all you need do is pour in hot water and what you pour out will taste like tea.

Different teas

- While black tea makes up much of the consumption of tea in China, often in the form of flavoured teas such as jasmine, there are many more kinds available.

PICTUREGARDEN / GETTY IMAGES

Green tea for sale at the market.

- Green tea, one of the closest teas to the raw leaves, is considered a good cleansing drink, popular after heavy dishes or those with thick and sweet-flavoured sauces.
- Oolong teas often smell of leather or herbs or like a heady mix of forest floor and chlorophyll.
- Shaped teas like brick teas (black or green tea pressed into blocks) are a staple of Yunnan in the south west.
- Other shaped teas are *mudan* (or *mu tan*) where long, neat whole leaves are tied at the centre and formed into a bud shape. When wet the bud opens to produce the most exquisite flower — a shape only appreciated if served in a glass cup or pot.
- *Pu-erh* tea is a double-oxidised tea also from Yunnan. It is usually formed into bricks but there is also a looseleaf variety. It's musty, almost dusty to the palate.
- White teas are so-called because of the fine, downy hair that is present on the best, young tea leaves. This is a rare tea mostly produced in Fujian province.
- Any of the above teas can be scented, and scented with virtually anything that marries with the original tea flavour. Jasmine is, of course, the most popular scent.

Fermented yogurt drinks

Many, particularly in the north, like fermented yoghurt as a morning drink. Delivered in re-useable bottles each morning, they're a great kid's drink, and a good way to introduce good local bacteria to your system when you first arrive in the country. Just remember to return your glass jar to the stand where you've bought it, or they'll harry you as you walk away.

A serving of the Kyoto classic *yudofu*, a hotpot dish.

OLIVER STREWE / GETTY IMAGES

Japan

To eat in Japan is to understand Japan, from the rigorous Zen temples to the perfect centuries-old Kyoto *ryōtei* (high-class restaurants), to the humble farmhouse kitchen. Nothing in Japanese cuisine happens by accident — every last nuance, from the garnish to the wall hanging, carries meaning.

CULINARY CAPITALS OSAKA, TOKYO **KNOWN FOR** SUSHI, *SASHIMI* **IMPORTS** FRUIT, MEAT **EXPORTS** INSTANT NOODLES **DEVOUR** *UDON* NOODLES **AVOID** *BASASHI* (RAW HORSEMEAT), *FUGU* (PUFFERFISH)

.mono-clad woman walks along a street in Kyoto.

LONELY PLANET / GETTY IMAGES

CULTURE

One can't help but feel the Japanese were predestined to be gourmands. Back in the early Jōmon period, the first residents on the islands were living it up on shellfish *sashimi*. The remnants of their early feasts of *hamaguri* (Venus clams) have been found in many coastal areas.

By 2000 BC they were hunting large fish, with their latest technical masterpiece, the toggle harpoon. Sea anemone became all the rage. Already, some 4000 years before the invention of the instant noodle, the basics of Japanese cuisine were beginning to take shape.

Rice was introduced from mainland north Asia, and towards the end of the Jōmon period the industrious folks of *Kyūsū* began to adopt a way of life markedly different from that of the northern islanders. They began wet rice farming.

Chinese influence

The next sea change in Japanese cuisine came through contact with China. By 239 AD, Japanese Queen Himiko of Yamatai was sending envoys to the kingdom of Wei in China, and soon wheat and barley were added to the list of culinary imports. Thus, some 300 years before they received Buddhism, they received the primitive versions of *udon* (wheat noodles) and *shōyu* (soy sauce).

Another Buddhist, the traveller monk Eisei, brought green tea and Zen from China at the beginning of the Kamakura period. Towards the end of the Muromachi period, *chakaiseki* (tea ceremony cuisine) was established under the patronage of tea master and culinary visionary Sen-no-Rikyū . Rikyū's legacy is a remarkable one. His *chakaiseki* saw the popularisation of *miso* and *mirin*, and from this time *shun*, or seasonality, became a core consideration in Japanese cuisine.

The shun

Take the *shun* (seasonality) out of Japanese cuisine, and it loses its soul. The Japanese are keenly aware of seasonality. It extends beyond your meal, to the choice of flowers in the *tokonoma* (recessed alcove), and indeed to the motifs at the bottom of your tea cup. Concerned gourmets perceive today's obsession with convenience, including freezing food, as a serious threat to *shun*.

Using seasonal ingredients has long been a given in Japanese cuisine, and chefs will particularly concentrate on *suimono* (a clear soup), and *suikuchi* (its topping). When the customer opens the bowl of the *suimono*, they must be able to recognise the season. This has not always been as easy as it sounds, as the only ingredient used in the clear soup garnish was *yuzu* (a type of citron). The chef would choose it according to season, when its colour would be yellow or green, or use the *yuzu no hana* (the flower of the yuzu), or even cut it to mimic the shape of seasonal imagery. Today, leaves from the *sanshō* (prickly ash pepper), and *fuki* (Japanese butterbur, a type of vegetable) buds, are commonly used.

Sakuramochi, a cherry sweet.

Instant noodles

The mixture of hard graft and invention that propelled Japan from devastation in World War II to the status of world economic power, in just decades, applied too to its domestic food industry. It was the age of the giants Kirin, Suntory and Asahi, but its undisputed champion was Nisshin Shokuhin, the company that in 1958 introduced Chikin Ramen, and thereby gave the world instant noodles. The company's success, and that of its competitors, was breathtaking. In the first year of sale, instant ramen sold 13 million units. A decade later it was shifting 4 billion packs a year.

Girl eating instant noodles.

A blossoming cherry tree in Ueno Park in Tokyo, famous for its 1200 cherry blossom trees.

Twenty-four-hour convenience stores still vend tasteless plastic dross to students working so hard in cram schools that they don't care what they eat. Yet Japan's fascination with food remains strong, with TV programs such as *Iron Chef* commanding audiences of millions, and the bookstore shelves groaning with food titles. Nearly 10,000 years after the Japanese ate their first Venus clam, they can't stop living, breathing, talking, and eating *washoku* —Japanese food.

Umami

The Chinese-derived definition of a 'perfect meal', dating back to around the 3rd century BC, demands it contains:

- the five colours — black (or purple), white, red (or orange), yellow and green;
- the five techniques — boiling, grilling, deep frying, steaming, and serving raw;
- and the five essential tastes — sweet, salty, sour, bitter and peppery hot.

The Japanese, embraced the concept, but replaced the peppery hot with their own *umami*. An echo of the peppery hot taste is only found in *shichimi-tōgarashi* (seven spice mix) and *sanshō*.

Some sources, most notably the Japanese food giant Aji-no-moto, declare that *umami* is indeed a separate basic 'taste' with its own territory mapped out on the taste buds. International opinion remains divided, but Aji-no-moto's vested interest notwithstanding, it is undeniable that the 'tastiness factor' exists. It refers to the 'tastiness' of the amino acids of MSG (found not only in canteen kitchens, but naturally in *konbu* (kelp) and fresh tomatoes), and other amino acids and nucleotides in *niboshi* (dried anchovies) and *katsuobushi* (dried bonito flakes) and the sodium guyanilate of dried *shiitake*

Sake with gold flakes.

mushrooms. While food scientists duel over theory, the populace know what they have always known. These ingredients, at the heart of Japanese cuisine, taste marvellous.

Presentation

Japanese cuisine is unashamedly visual. This applies to every meal, from humble *shokudō* (small, cheap eateries), to high-class *kaiseki-ryōrei* (restaurant serving multi-course tea ceremony cuisine). *Yosou* is the verb to 'dress up' or 'ornament' and is the formal word used to describe how food is arranged. Creating a harmony of colour, shape and texture is essential, and every element is considered from the food itself to the colour of the garnish to the shape of the dish. And in best Zen tradition, there must be *ma*, or space, that small element left forever to the imagination.

Accompanying gift-giving on the list of Japanese cultural priorities is the legendary obsession with packaging. A cultural imperative that reaches an absurd pinnacle with Lipton teabags — each bag individually wrapped, then encased in paper, then clear plastic, then wrapped and put in your humble carrier bag.

REGIONS

Osaka

Japan's second-largest city is as food-crazed as they come. Osaka's mercantile and sea-going heritage has long given it a rough-and-tough, no-nonsense image, and its industrious citizens have a reputation for partying as hard as they work. The saying goes that while Kyoto-ites will happily waste their fortunes on fine kimono, and Tokyo-ites on shoes, the Osakans have only one way to squander their riches — on food. There's even a word for it that has become Osaka's unofficial motto — *kuidaore* — the civilised practice of bankrupting oneself through sheer gluttony.

It says something about Osaka's lack of pretension, when one of its best-known epicurean delights is 'octopus balls'. They are tiny, spherical, wheat flour pancakes to which diced octopus, shredded cabbage and other vegetables are added. They are often grilled in front of the customer at *yatai* (mobile food stands), and come topped with *katsuobushi* (dried bonito flakes) and a 'secret' sauce of the owner's own invention. They are cheap, filling, fattening and seem to remain intact in one's stomach for several days following consumption. Needless to say, this does nothing to lessen their popularity, not least for a midnight stop-off between *izakaya* (traditional restaurant-cum-bar) and a *karaoke* den.

The city has also long been a *sake*-making centre, most notably Ikeda, which today still produces the excellent Seishu Goshun and Midoriichi varieties.

Osaka boasts one big culinary claim to fame, thanks to its favorite son Shiraishi Yoshiaki, who opened the nation's first conveyor-belt restaurant, Genroku-zushi, in Higashi-Osaka in the 1950s.

FEASTS

When the Japanese celebrate, it must include food and drink, and lots of it, whether it is in a rural festival to appease the rice gods (themselves not averse to the odd glass of *sake*), or in the party-hard *izakaya* of the big cities.

Celebrating life

Every Japanese person's introduction to *shoku-bunka*, the 'culture of food' comes with the *kuizome*, when a baby is given its first morsel of solid food by the eldest member of the family. This custom symbolically invokes the fates to grant the child longevity and a life free from starvation. The traditional fare at

OLIVER STREWE / GETTY IMAGES

A restaurant tucked under the railway lines in the ritzy Ginza district, the *yakitori* capital of Tokyo.

Traditional Japanese ladles dowsed in barrels of water are used in a purification ritual allowing entry to Higashi-Honganji Temple in Kyoto.

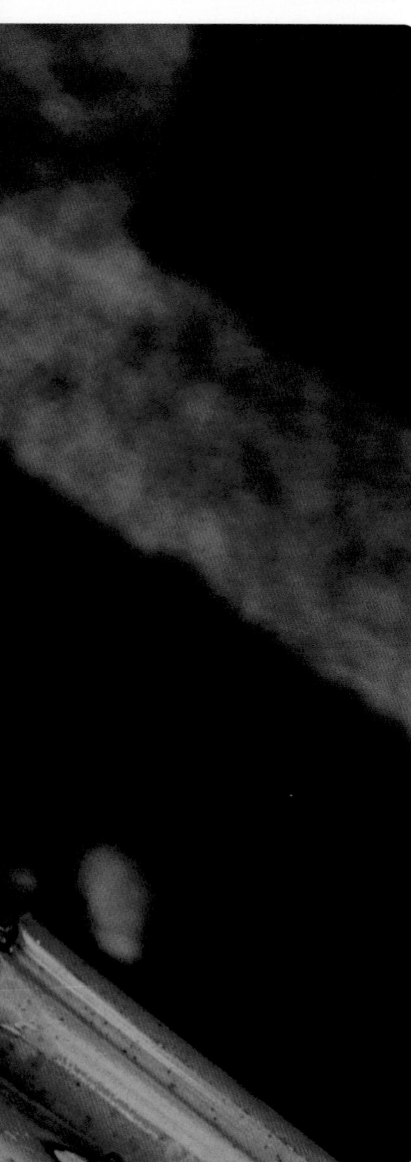

OLIVER STREWE / GETTY IMAGES

kuizome is the *tai* (sea bream). The sea bream pops up at each celebratory event and every rite of passage, most notably in the marriage ceremony, where sea bream — real or symbolic — are often presented as gifts of thanks to the wedding guests.

A month after its arrival the child will be whisked off in swaddling clothes to a Shintō shrine for the first shrine visit, which, once again, will be marked by a *sake* toast. Thus, begins a life attached to food and drink. The Japanese are born and marry Shintō, yet they die Buddhist. On the night preceding the funeral, relatives and mourners are served *butsu-ji* (Buddhist funerary cuisine). *Konnyaku* (devil's tongue), *yuba* (soy milk skin), tōfu and vegetables are the main ingredients, with meat and fish strictly forbidden.

New Year

The celebratory year begins in homes and restaurants on 1 January, with the multicourse, lavish, colourful *osechi-ryōri*. Served in four-layered lacquerware boxes, *osechi* originated primarily as a means of giving the overworked Japanese housewife three days' much-needed rest — its ingredients last well.

Not only is it practical, it also contains linguistically symbolic references. Many ingredients have play-on-word meanings derived from the homonym-rich Japanese language. *Konbu*, or *kobu* (kelp), for example, is served as it reminds one to *yorokobu* — 'enjoy'. And *Kazu-no-ko* (salted or dried herring roe), with its countless eggs, implies great fertility (*kazu* means number, or numerous; *ko* means child).

The other great New Year delicacy is *ozōni-mochi* (rice cakes served in soup). *Mochi* (rice cakes) are ever-present in religious observations, and are symbolic of New Year as *kagami-mochi*, an offertory decoration composed of two flat-bottomed rounds of *mochi*, a smaller one set atop a larger version. It is displayed with dried *konbu* and a *mikan* (mandarin orange) in homes and temples at this time of year.

If your first dream of the New Year happens to contain an eggplant, you're also in for an auspicious 12 months. A cow's pretty good too, though Mt Fuji and a hawk are preferred. If you happen to have a nocturnal encounter with a horse or a fish, you're in trouble.

ETIQUETTE

Entertaining at home

To many Japanese, entertaining guests at home is anathema. If they do discuss throwing a dinner party, it is often in the tones of someone explaining an impending bout of highly embarrassing, potentially life-threatening surgery. The reason for this is a combination of the esoteric — the cultural imperative that requires the separation of daily life and the celebratory, and the practical — most Japanese people believe they live in *usagi-goya* ('rabbit huts') that are too small, cramped and full of family to show outsiders. This, combined with the endless opportunity for eating out, makes it about as easy to get into a domestic kitchen as it is to get into the inner sanctum of the Imperial palace.

Chopsticks

Wherever you eat, you will find chopsticks — such an indelicate phrase for such elegant utensils. The long variety is used for stirring, and for transferring food from pan to plate (much as tongs are used in western cooking), and shorter versions used for eating. Traditionally, men's chopsticks were longer than women's (to fit their larger hands) and as a result, the low tables on which food was served were slightly higher for women. Even today, a his-and-hers lacquerware chopstick set is a traditional wedding gift.

OLIVER STREWE / GETTY IMAGES

Woman in a kimono drinking tea in Kyoto.

OLIVER STREWE / GETTY IMAGES

Rice garnished with prickly ash seed.

While there is a rather complex etiquette about how you hold the chopsticks, it's not worth losing sleep over. Many young Japanese adopt the casual, easiest way, and non-Japanese guests will be forgiven for doing the same thing.

There are a few no-nos, however:

- *Mayoibashi*, the 'lost and wandering' chopsticks, where you dab uncertainly at different dishes, is frowned upon.
- Passing food from your chopsticks directly to someone else's is strictly taboo, as it mimics Japanese funerary practice. As does sticking chopsticks vertically into a bowl of white rice.
- Pointing at someone with chopsticks, despite the vehemence of your conviction, is not polite. In fact, it implies, 'Do you wanna step outside?'.
- When you remove a food item to your plate from a communal bowl, it is proper to use the opposite, thick end of your chopsticks. This culinary back-hand is easy to forget, not least when you're ravenous.

DAILY MEALS

Japanese meals usually consist of a variety of separate, small dishes. The individual offerings are all generally served at once, on a single lacquerware tray or table, with only *miso* soup and rice coming later. And there's always rice.

The Japanese food day starts with *asa-gohan*, literally 'the morning rice', or breakfast. This traditional Japanese breakfast is savoury, featuring lustrous rice, fried fish and that wonderfully aromatic *miso* soup.

In the cities, women will prepare not only breakfast, but the *bentō* (lunchboxes) that their spouses and children take to the office and to school. Newlywed wives may prepare *aisai bentō*

A display of *bukkake udon*, a cold thick wheat noodle, with tempura, from the Yumadaya Udon Noodle Shop in Shikoku.

OLIVER STREWE / GETTY IMAGES

'the loving wife lunchbox', complete with a heart-shaped pickle arrangement guaranteed to cause maximum embarrassment when discovered by fellow company workers. Schoolkids dread the totally uncool poor man's *hinomaru-bentō*, plain rice with a single *umeboshi* (salted plums) at the centre, named after the Japanese flag. For *hiru-gohan* or lunch, *ramen*, *soba* and *udon* shops, company or school canteens, or even the humble convenience store are all popular alternatives.

Dinner — *Ban-gohan* — is the meal that the family is most likely to eat together. If families dine out together, it will mostly be at a *fami-resu*, the 'family restaurant' chains serving inexpensive, inexpressive, at times inedible papier mâché fare. They are at best fair, but are always handy. A popular twist of late are sushi restaurants, where each dish is a set price. A trip to a 'proper' sushi shop is reserved for special occasions. Couples without children, and young adults are most likely to head off to an *izakaya*.

ESSENTIAL PRODUCE

Beans

Given the country's Buddhist history, it's no surprise that Japanese cuisine has long been dependent on beans (*mame*) as a protein-rich food source.

Top of the Japanese bean pile is the indispensable soy bean, the *daizu* (literally, 'big bean'), which provides the raw material for *miso*, *shōyu* (soy sauce), *tōfu*, *yuba* (soy milk skin), and the infamous *nattō* (fermented soy beans).

Next is *azuki*, the adzuki bean, which is used extensively in the preparation of *wagashi* (Japanese sweets), often for the tea ceremony, and in the preparation of *seki-han* (red-bean rice) used at times of celebration and to commemorate a teenage girl's first menstruation.

The broad bean, *sora-mame*, is used as a vegetable, as a savoury garnish, and in sweets.

Eda-mame

Japan's most visible green beans are *eda-mame* (young soy beans), literally meaning 'branch beans'. They are served in the pod as an *izakaya* accompaniment to beer, especially in the summer. The pods are dusted in salt, which transfers to the beans as you pop them in your mouth between swigs of foamy ale (don't eat the pods!).

Daikon

The giant white radish, *daikon*, is an important daily vegetable. Apprentice chefs must learn how to peel *daikon* in a single unbroken strip, so as to master knife technique — and the required patience.

Eel

Unagi or eel is most auspiciously eaten during the dog days of summer, especially on a day corresponding to the water buffalo in the Chinese zodiac, when it is said to convey vigour.

Long ago, eel was grilled on a skewer. More popular now is the charcoal-grilled *kabayaki*, which takes its name from its colour, reminiscent of the *kaba* (birch tree), and is served in a *teriyaki* sauce. It is also often served as *una-don* (grilled eel on rice).

Fish

Sashimi (raw fish) is a key component in Japanese formal cuisine, not least in *kaiseki-ryōri* (a multicourse meal). It is also a regular on sushi-shop menus, and eaten at home as a small luxury. Freshness is paramount, and in the best restaurants expect to have the fish, squid or octopus fished from a tank and sliced before your eyes. *Ikizukuri* is a common way of

Tuna, sea urchin and horse mackerel *sashimi*.

Small dried fish for sale at the market in Kyoto.

Eel for sale at the Tsukiji Fish Market in Tokyo.

offering sea bream. It is laid out between the head and tail, and skewered in its death throes on an elegant porcelain dish.

More often, *sashimi* is simply arranged, with garnishes typical of the season, on a dish. Sea bream, cod, yellowtail, octopus and squid are commonly used. You dip the fish, perhaps wrapped in an *ao-jiso* (green beefsteak plant) leaf, into strong *shōyu* (often *tamari-jōyu*, a wheat-free *shōyu*) containing *wasabi* and *benitade* (water pepper), a dark red peppery garnish. Even ordinary fish deserves the best *shōyu*, and freshly grated *wasabi*.

Sashimi is not solely used to refer to fish. It also refers to thinly sliced raw meat (*a la carpaccio*), as in Kumamoto's speciality *basashi*, an abbreviation of *basashimi* (raw horse meat).

Katsuobushi

Katsuobushi is easy to spot in a Japanese fish market. It is the thing that looks least like fish — it is more like a piece of driftwood. The Japanese have been drying bonito since ancient times, when the summer fish was dried to preserve it for the winter season.

Superstition attaches itself to the humble bonito in several other ways. It is still a common gift at New Year and is given to teething babies so that they will develop perfect teeth. More often, though, it is grated either by hand (for *dashi*), using a plane (the same as a carpenter's plane), or by machine in the marketplace. Ready-shaved *katsuobushi* is convenient, but markedly less tasty.

Leaf vegetables

Na/Nappa are cultivated leaf vegetables commonly used in *o-hitashi* (where the vegetables are parboiled, then dipped immediately in cold water to retain colour, and then covered

OLIVER STREWE / GETTY IMAGES

Decorative sign in the Shibuya district of Tokyo.

with *dashi* and *shōyu*. They are also used frequently in *nabemono* (hotpot dishes). Many are also used in tempura.

Mirin

Mirin is used extensively in Japanese cuisine, and is generally referred to as 'sweetened *sake*'. It is primarily used as a sweetening agent and is preferred over sugar. This is because the inclusion of *mirin* adds depth to *dashi* (stock) and sauces. It contains around 13% to 14% alcohol, though this is often largely burned off prior to use. *Mirin* was once served as an alternative to *sake*, and the good stuff, usually called *hon-mirin*, is still sold in *sake* shops today.

Miso

Made by mixing steamed soy beans with *kōji* (a fermenting agent) and salt, *miso* is integral to any Japanese meal, where it is likely to be present as *misoshiru* (soup) or as a flavouring. It is also used in *dengaku*, where it is spread on vegetables such as eggplant and *konnyaku* (devil's tongue).

Some would argue that you can recognise a person's birthplace by their choice of *miso*. The dizzyingly salty *sendai-miso* of rural Miyagi Prefecture is a countryman's creation. A gorgeous ruddy brown, it can be kept, and indeed matures with age. *Shinshū-miso* from Nagano Prefecture in the Central Alps is less wild, less salty, with a much-praised slightly tart quality. *Edo-miso* is dark, fiery red, slightly sweet, and is as forthright and unpretentious as the *Edokko* (Tokyo-ites) who are its chief consumers.

Miso is an essential source of protein, calorie free, and packed with salt. It has also proven effective in treating radiation victims. One cannot help but wonder what thousands of Ukrainians thought on receiving hundreds of tons of the stuff from the Japanese government in the wake of the Chernobyl disaster.

Mountain vegetables

The term '*sansai*' (mountain vegetables) would imply that they are gathered from the wild, as opposed to *yasai*, which are cultivated vegetables. However, some *sansai* are grown, and some *yasai* grow wild, so the terms are not strictly exclusive. An important part of rural cuisine, their often outlandish appearance may put off first-time eaters.

Mushrooms

Japan's humid climate makes it a mycologist's dream, with over 4000 species of *kinoko* — mushrooms — and fungus (as many as there are in all of Europe). Many are edible, and they are all generally used in the same way, in *miso* soup, as *tempura*, mixed with rice as *kinoko-gohan*, or in *nabemono*.

Best known are *shiitake*. Strongtasting, and easily cultivated, they are also used to make vegetarian-friendly *dashi*.

Noodles

Japan must be the only country in the world where museums dedicated to noodles reach into double figures. Japan's noodles may not match Italy's in variety and scale, but in quality, subtlety, presentation, and sheer style, they know no equal.

There are four main types of noodles used in Japanese cuisine:

- *soba* — buckwheat noodles
- *udon* — thick white wheat noodles
- *somen* — thin white wheat noodles and
- *ramen* — yellow wheat noodles.

Octopus

Varieties of *tako* (octopus) include the Seto Inland Sea's ma-dako, best in January and February, the large *mizu-dako*, most

A bowl of *soba*, herring and buckwheat noodles.

Shimeji mushrooms.

Uzura tamago, quail eggs, are considered a delicacy and usually eaten hard-boiled.

A vendor holds up an octopus at the Ni-jo Ichiba market in Sapporo.

OLIVER STREWE / GETTY IMAGES

often taken in Hokkaidō and the small *ii-dako*. The latter 'rice octopus' gets its name for the cross-section of a sliced, mature specimen, where the ovarian tissue resembles rice grains. Superstition has it that octopus tastes better if you beat it into submission (it's already dead actually) with a *daikon* (giant white radish). Specimens from near Akashi in the Seto Inland Sea are especially prized. Octopus is rarely served raw, even in sushi, where it appears roughly, thickly chopped as *tako-butsu*. It is eaten as *sudako* with vinegar, as *nimono* (simmered), and in Osaka, as *tako-yaki* (those pancake balls with octopus filling). You can even eat it live.

Pickles

As an accompaniment to boiled rice, *tsukemono* (pickles) are present in most Japanese meals. They are also important *sake-ate* (accompaniments to *sake* and beer).

Pickles are named for the ingredient — mostly vegetables, but also fish — the length of time pickled, and the pickling base, usually either *miso*, salt, vinegar or *nuka*, a paste made of rice bran. *Nuka* was once considered such an important part of household life that daughters would include it in their wedding dowry. *Nuka-miso-zuke* (nuka pickles) which have been kneaded into a mixture of *miso* and *nuka*, and left to mature (sometimes through an entire winter), are unique to Japan.

Regional varieties and specialities abound. Kyoto is particularly renowned for its pickles, most notably the dramatic purple-hued *shiba-zuke,* which is cucumber, eggplant and Japanese ginger pickled with *aka-jiso* (red beefsteak plant).

Rice

The Japanese don't just consume *kome* (rice) all day, every day. They venerate it. Culturally, most Japanese feel a meal is simply incomplete without the inclusion of *kome*. It is the building block on which a Japanese meal is based, the heart of the Japanese culinary DNA.

Yet rice's omnipresence is not merely a dietary or culinary convention. Rice cultivation was traditionally regarded as a religious act, and even in ultra-modern Tokyo a child will often be taught to scoop a small amount of white rice from the *suihanki* (electric rice cooker) to offer to the spirits of deceased ancestors in the *butsudan* (the family's home altar).

Seaweed

Found throughout the country, *wakame*'s (a type of seaweed) anti-aging properties have long been recognised, a fact reflected in its name which means 'young woman'. Fresh it is used in *sunomono* (vinegared food), *suimono* (clear soup), and in *dashi* (stock). *Nori* (sea laver) is best known in its dried and toasted form as the outer layer of *nori-maki* (sushi wrapped in *nori*).

Stock

A great *dashi* (stock) is essential, as it is the crucial element in soups, dipping sauces, *nimono* (simmered dishes) and *nabemono* (hotpot dishes), and used for cooking fish and vegetables. Typically it is made from either *katsuobushi* (dried bonito flakes) or *konbu* (kelp). Its role in enhancing the flavour of food is paramount, and good chefs guard the precise details of their *dashi* ingredients with a zest bordering on paranoia.

Sweet snacks and desserts

It may seem as if much *wagashi*, Japanese confectionery, is designed to be looked at rather than eaten, such is its visual attractiveness. Traditional Japanese sweets are not of the Sunday-treat, cavity-inducing variety, but rather are designed for offsetting the bitter taste of the *ocha* (Japanese green tea) used in the tea ceremony.

OLIVER STREWE / GETTY IMAGES

Fresh *wasabi*, Japanese horseradish, is a luxury iter

OLIVER STREWE / GETTY IMAGES

Agedashi dofu, deep fried tofu served in a stock soup

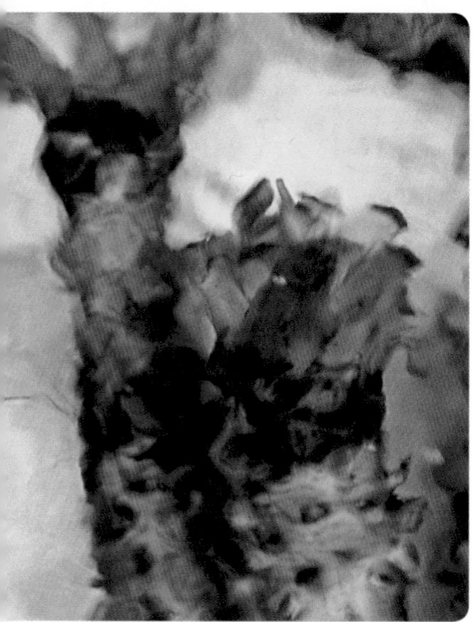

The art of *wagashi-making* reaches its pinnacle in Kyoto, most famously with higashi, an all-encompassing category of dried sweets and *senbei* (rice crackers). While these are delicately coloured, and crafted to reflect imagery appropriate to the season, a favourite *wagashi*, *uirō*, is a plain, gelatinous brick, filled with powdered tea or red beans.

No summer festival is complete without *kakigōri*. Simply a mountain of shaved ice, doused in a violently vivid syrup of shamelessly synthetic vulgarity, it is, of course, hugely popular. Equally odd-sounding is the tasty green tea and ice cream combination called *matcha-aisu*.

Tōfu

Tōfu is one of Japan's most sublime creations. Best of all is to get up with the larks, and head down to your local tōfu maker for post-dawn, freshly made, creamy tōfu that is still warm.

Tōfu is sold as the soft 'silk' *kinugoshi* and the firm *momen* (or *momengoshi*). The former is mainly used in soups, especially *misoshiru*. The latter is eaten by itself, deep-fried in *agedashi-dōfu* or used in the Kyoto classic *yudōfu*, a hotpot dish. Both momen and kinugoshi take their names from the technique when the hot soy milk is strained — if the material used is cotton, the resulting firm tōfu is *momen*; when silk (*kinu*) is used, it's *kinugoshi*.

A classic way to eat tōfu is as *hiyayakko*, cold blocks of tōfu covered with soy, grated ginger and finely sliced green onion. This is a favourite on the menus of *izakaya*.

Wasabi

Wasabi is Japanese horseradish. Fresh *wasabi*, especially the naturally cultivated variety from the pure streams of alpine Nagano Prefecture, is sublime. It is pungent and smooth. In combination with good *shōyu* or a noodle dipping sauce it is truly memorable. Recognise it by its very pale green, almost white colour, and slightly rough texture. The best *soba* shops will bring the *wasabi* itself, and a shark-skin topped wasabi grater, and you prepare your own.

A member of the cabbage family, it is extremely difficult to cultivate because it needs a constant source of flowing pure water. As a result, much is still taken from the wild.

SHOPPING

Wandering through a Japanese market, specialist shop or supermarket is a fascinating gastronomic adventure and visual spectacle in its own right. The variety is staggering, and you'll be guaranteed to find something you've never set eyes on before in your life.

Traditionally, Japan's stores were family-owned specialists, and were all gathered together in one area. Nowadays, across the country, independent stores are succumbing to the giant supermarket chains, and the ever-encroaching franchised convenience stores, yet if you take a walk down any of the remaining shopping arcades (most cities have them, built as all-weather, inexpensive retail and living space), you'll see that many of the small businesses remain.

In the supermarket

The first thing you notice as you enter the Japanese supermarket is the light — bright neon, almost surgical, illuminating every furthest corner. Then the cleanliness. Then the wall-to-wall noise. From the '*Irasshaimase*!' (welcome) to the mindlessly chattering recorded music, or taped invocations to 'Buy! buy! buy!', Japanese supermarkets are incredibly loud affairs. One recording even became a top ten hit, in which a salesman yodels in Japanese '*Yaki-niku ga tabe hoooo daaaai!*' ("Eat all the Korean barbecue beef you can

Rows of giant tuna for sale at a Tokyo market.

Twenty-four hour shopping in Shinsaibashi, Osaka.

Local white radishes, *shogoin daikon*, for sale at Nishiki-koji market in Kyoto.

Signs everywhere in an Osaka sidestreet.

OLIVER STREWE / GETTY IMAGES

buyee-hee-hee-hee!"). The noise pollution as you shop goes unheard by regular customers, who instinctively block it out.

There are no special rules for shopping in Japanese supermarkets, just bring ear-plugs, and be prepared to get bashed into by middle-aged women. The famous Japanese formality seems to disappear when bargain hunting is involved. Notice also, the near-complete absence of men.

At the market

Japanese markets, or *ichiba*, fall into two categories – the covered or arcade variety, and the less organised, usually rural, *aozora ichiba*, literally 'blue sky' markets, set in the open air.

At the latter, some farmers (or their spouses) wheel the day's fresh produce into town by cart. Both types of market allow great people-watching opportunities, and are decidedly 'interactive'. Stallholders bellow '*Rashai*!', the rough-and-tough version of 'Welcome!', and though touching the produce is frowned upon, you're very likely to be given a freebie with the invitation. Bargaining at markets is quite acceptable, as long as you don't appear to be embarrassing the stall holder with a disrespectfully low offer.

PREPARATION

The way in which food is prepared and served hasn't changed radically across the centuries.

Many families eat in the *osōzai* style, where the meal consists of several dishes, served centre table, from which the diners pick and choose. These will be accompanied by *gohanmono* (rice dishes) and *shirumono* (soups) or *suimono* (clear soup). Really traditional households will still lay on a full restaurant-style spread, but for a family of eight (not uncommon with both sets of grandparents in residence) this necessitates preparing, then washing up, around 42 dishes, so it is fast losing favour.

This labour-intensive (for mothers and daughters – fathers and sons sit around watching TV) system stems from the way in which each meal is required to contain most, if not all, the different representative forms of cooking. This includes:

- *nimono* (stewed, simmered dishes)
- *shirumono* or *suimono* (soups)
- *yakimono* (broiled, grilled or pan-fried dishes)
- *agemono* (deep-fried foods)
- *mushimono* (steamed dishes)
- *sunomono* (vinegared foods)
- *aemono* (cooked leafy vegetables, poultry or fish blended with a dressing)
- *gohanmono* (rice dishes).

No wonder, then, that the one exception to this style of eating, the *nabemono* (hotpot cuisine), is so popular.

DEFINING DISHES

Hotpot cuisine

Nabemono (hotpot cuisine) must surely be the most convivial way of eating ever invented and it's a great winter warmer. It is an age-old rustic style of cuisine that took cities by storm — today in tiny Tokyo apartment blocks families will huddle around an earthenware pot set on a calor-gas single ring stove straight out of a 1950s Boy Scout catalogue, to re-enact (on a minor scale) the great country feasts of their forebears. *Nabemono* never loses its primitive campfire feel. It's also refreshingly uncomplicated, requires little preparation, and little washing up, there's almost no waste, the natural tastes of the ingredients are allowed to come through, and, as every impoverished Japanese student

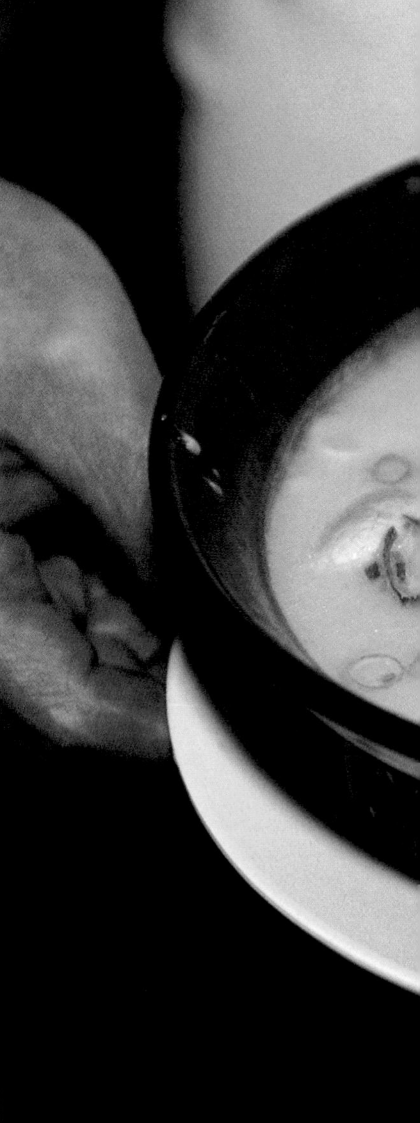

OLIVER STREWE / GETTY IMAGES

A master presents a freshly cooked bowl of *ramen*.

knows, the room gets heated as appetites get satisfied.

Cooking couldn't be any simpler. A basic stock, or in some cases just hot water, is placed in the pot, then whatever ingredients are to hand are added and brought to a simmer. Guests then fish out the vegetables, shellfish, fish or meat of their choice, dip them in a sauce (*tsukejiru*) and ... eat! The *tsukejiru* will most likely be *ponzu*, a mixture of *dashi* (stock), *shōyu*, vinegar and citrus juices.

Okonomi-yaki

*Okonomi-yak*i is perennially (and inaccurately) translated as 'a kind of Japanese pizza'. In fact, it's a discus-sized savoury pancake of wheat-flour, egg and water topped with *konomi* – 'whatever takes your fancy'. Usually this means meat, squid, vegetables and finely chopped cabbage. Often restaurant proprietors will cook it in front of you on a flat hot plate and serve it with sweet brown sauce or mayonnaise, usually garnished with dried and powdered *ao-nori* (laver seaweed,) or *katsuobushi* flakes that 'dance' as they heat up.

Ramen noodles

Ramen noodles areJapan's national-dish-in-hiding. *Ramen*'s proletarian image is probably the reason its massive impact is not so well-publicised, though the reality is that *ramen* shops are no longer solely the haunt of truckers and gangsters on the lam. These days, you're just as likely to rub shoulders with a bank manager or a student of a private girls' college.

Ramen is an interesting amalgam of the Chinese word meaning 'to stretch' and the Japanese suffix for noodles, '-men'. The stuff's popularity is enormous, with *ramen* shops galore, instant *ramen* noodles a multibillion yen business, and *ramen yatai* (itinerant street vendors), a picturesque and welcome nocturnal stop-off in all major cities.

Sushi for lunch: *nigiri-zushi* (served on rice) and *maki-zushi* (served in a seaweed roll) accompanied by pickled ginger and *wasabi*.

Man eating bowl of *miso-ramen*.

Pickles are integral to every Japanese meal.

At the heart of good (and bad) *ramen* is the *dashi*, made from chicken bones or pork bones, with the addition of vegetables, *shōyu* or *miso*. Stocks range from a light, less greasy stock, to a thick, garlicky version.

Ramen types fit into four basic categories, each with a distinctive origin: *shōyu-ramen* (soy *ramen*), from Tokyo; *shio-ramen* (salt *ramen*) and *miso-ramen* (*ramen* in a *miso* broth), both from Sapporo; and *tonkotsu-ramen* (*ramen* in a white pork broth) from *Kyūshū*.

The noodles are made from wheat flour mixed with egg. They are kneaded, left to sit, and then stretched with both hands. They are are cooked, and then served in a hot soup, with toppings such as sliced pork, bean sprouts, pickled Chinese bean sprouts, welsh onion, *naruto-maki* (thinly sliced white fish-cake with a pink, whirlpool-shaped inset) and *nori*.

Sushi

Sushi refers to anything served on, or within, vinegared rice. The most likely ingredients are fish or shellfish (mostly raw, but not exclusively so), raw vegetables or cooked egg.

It originated in China as a means of food preservation. It was essentially a pickling technique, where fish was salted and encased in rice and left to mature (some would infer 'rot') for up to a year.

Contemporary sushi falls into four broad categories:

- *Nigiri-zush*i, where toppings are pressed onto rice dabbed with *wasabi*, originated in Tokyo. Typically it is placed directly on the white wood counter, accompanied by *gari* (pickled, pinkish-red ginger), whereupon you dip it in *shoyu*: the classic way to eat sushi. It is the most elegant, visually appealing, and expensive part of a sushi menu, and the one you order first. Toppings such as raw squid and octopus;

shrimp (raw as sweet shrimp, or cooked); cod roe (raw, surrounded by *nori)* or sliced egg-omelette are favourites. Luxuries include conger-eel brushed over with *teriyak*i sauce, an exquisite crunchy-soft combination; sea urchin, and the *sake*-lover's favourite accompaniment, *kani-miso*, er, crab reproductive organs. The latter loses something in translation, but it is really rather magnificent. Imagine a kind of dark olive-green caviar-without-the-crunch.

- *Maki-zushi*, the familiar *nori*-wrapped torpedo is always the sushi shop's cheaper-end offering, but price shouldn't be confused with quality. *Shiso-ume-maki* (sour plum with beefsteak leaf) is a fabulous aromatic-meets-sour, *nori*-meets-succulent-rice delight. *Kappa-maki* with cucumber is equally humble and delicious. *Maki-zushi* is rolled in the *makisu*, a bamboo mat.
- *Chirashi-zushi* sometimes called *bara-zushi*, is traditionally eaten at celebrations. Vinegared rice is topped with *shiitake* mushrooms marinated in *shoyu*, sliced omlette, *beni-shoga* (red pickled ginger), and other ingredients, designed to be especially pleasing to the eye.
- *Oshi-zushi* is sushi pressed into a wooden mould, then sliced. It's best known form is *battera-zushi,* a strong, deliberately 'fishy' mackerel dish.

DRINKS

Green tea

During the 12th century the Chinese tea ceremony really took off. Tea became as popular as Zen. The Japanese court and aristocracy took wholeheartedly to tea, and its formalised ritual drinking. It took another half a millennium or so for the

OLIVER STREWE / GETTY IMAGES

Tonchan, a local pub or *izakaya* in Kochi.

rank and file to pick up the habit. Its popularity of *ocha* (green tea) was spurred on by the invention of a convenient, newfangled form — *sencha* (leaf tea). Since then, from exquisite teahouses purpose-built for the job, to factory canteens, to convenience stores, the Japanese have become well and truly tea-struck.

The tea ceremony

No one can dispute the influence of *sado* (the 'way of tea'), or *cha-no-yu* ('tea's hot water') on Japan's spiritual, artistic, and cultural heritage.

A traditional tea ceremony must be infused with *wakeiseijaku* — harmony, respect, quiet and solitude. At a tea ceremony guests, usually clad in kimono, assemble in a waiting room and select a member to act as the main guest. They then proceed to the garden and to the stone trough from which they ladle water to hand and mouth in order to purify themselves of worldly concerns.

They enter the teahouse, greet the host who presents the light *kaiseki* (Japanese formal cuisine), *sake*, and a *wagashi* (sweet) to offset the bitterness of the thick, green *matcha* that is to follow. Guests retire to the garden or the waiting room before re-entering the tearoom. The thick *koicha* (first brew) is passed in a single bowl from the host to a guest, who savours the strong bitter taste that slowly overcomes the sweetness of the *wagashi*, before wiping the bowl and passing it to the next person.

The host then rebuilds the coals in the brazier, and prepares the thinner *usucha*, the second brew from the same tea leaves, which he whips to a frothy consistency with the *chasen* (bamboo tea whisk), and passes to each person. Cultured conversation reigns. Then the guests depart, and the outside world seeps in. The *chaji* is over.

OLIVER STREWE / GETTY IMAGES

Mutemuka *sake* brewery in Taisho Cho.

Sake

From the first visit to a Shintō shrine at one month old, to the Buddhist funeral rites, the Japanese are accompanied by *sake*. Its place in religious life comes from its associations with rice — the food of the gods — and its symbolic purity.

It is consumed at every major rite-of-passage in a Japanese person's life. In the Shintƒ wedding ritual, the bride and groom seal the marriage by exchanging *sake* cups and drinking *sake*. This invokes the gods to intervene to help the couple, and through the sharing of *sake*, to come closer together and create a bond of friendship. *Sake* is offered to the family *butsudan*, the altar that houses the spirits of departed ancestors, and at the feast of O-bon in mid-summer (when the spirits return to this world), at family graves. It is proffered to the roadside Buddha statues that dot the countryside, and is a feature both symbolic and practical, at every *matsuri* (festival).

The five prefectures from Akita to Ishikawa and Shimane on the coastal line of the Japan Sea have the serious *sake* drinkers, to the annual tune of more than 20 litres per person.

Often termed rice wine in the west, *sake* or *nihonshu* is actually made through a fermenting process using grain, somewhat akin to beer-making. Key to the *sake*-making process are good rice, good water and the magical *kōji*, a dark greenish-yellow, fine powder fermentation agent (converting sugar to alcohol) that is added to steamed white rice.

It has an alcohol content of somewhere between 15% to 17%. *Sake*, unlike wine, does not have vintage years — its quality depends solely upon the conditions under which it is made, and foremost, the skill of the *tōji* (*sake* maker).

Steamed crab being pulled out of the pot at a night market.

FLASH PARKER / GETTY IMAGES

Korea

So you thought Korean cuisine was just *kimchi* and barbecued beef? Prepare to be blown away by the amazing diversity and spicy deliciousness of the nation's cuisine, which ranges from rustic stews and tasty street snacks to glorious royal banquets involving elaborate preparation and presentation. The leisurely sampling of soothing traditional teas and herbal infusions is also one of Korea's great culinary pleasures.

CULINARY CAPITAL SEOUL **KNOWN FOR** *KIMCHI* **IMPORTS** CHINESE CULINARY INFLUENCES **EXPORTS** *SOJU* **DEVOUR** KOREAN BARBECUE **AVOID** *BOSINTANG* (DOG MEAT SOUP)

Budae jjigae (stew) is a very common dish which is based on leftovers.

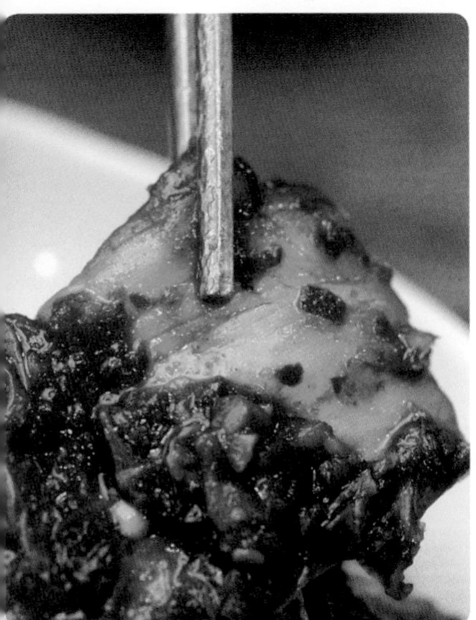

Korea's famous *kimchi*.

Mandu, Korean dumplings.

CULTURE

Perhaps the defining aspect of Korean food is preservation. Staples such as *kimchi*, fermented vegetables, or the three essential sauces — *ganjang* (soy sauce), *doenjang* (fermented soybean paste) and *gochujang* (hot red pepper paste) — were necessities during the country's long and harsh winters. Although today many Koreans have access to ingredients year-round, these items remain, and are eaten on a daily basis.

Outside influences have also shaped Korean food. Starting around the 4th century, foods such as rice, cabbage, pork and beef came from China, along with Buddhism and Confucianism. The subsequent Mongol invasion of the 13th century introduced dumplings, grilled meat dishes and noodle dishes to the Korean Peninsula. Trade with Europeans, beginning in the 16th century, led to the introduction of chillies, now a Korean staple. In more recent years, Japanese and American cuisines have come to influence Korean food; *budae jjigae* (also known as *Johnsontang*) is a unique Seoul dish that originated in the hungry years after the Korean War. At this time, tins of ham, sausages and baked beans from American army bases were bought on the black market and mixed with noodles and vegetable scraps to make a meal.

ETIQUETTE

If you're invited out to eat by Korean colleagues or friends, it's difficult or impossible to pay the bill or even contribute towards it. Arguing about who should have the honour of paying the restaurant bill is a common scene at the cashier's desk.

Meals are usually eaten communally, so dishes are placed in the centre of the table and diners put a little from each common dish in their own bowl.

At some traditional restaurants, customers sit on cushions

on the floor (the *ondol*, an underfloor heating system, is beneath). Before stepping up, always remove your shoes. A few other rules:

- Take off your shoes in traditional restaurants where everyone sits on floor cushions.
- Pour drinks for others if you notice that their glasses are empty. It's polite to use both hands when pouring or receiving a drink. Don't pour drinks for yourself (unless you're alone).
- Ask for *gawi* (scissors) if you're trying to cut something and your spoon won't do it.
- Place the chopsticks and spoon back in their original position at the end of the meal.
- Don't start eating or finish your meal before your seniors and elders.
- Don't touch food with your fingers, except when handling *ssam* (salad leaves used as edible wrapping for other foods).
- Use a spoon rather than chopsticks to eat rice.
- Don't leave your chopsticks or spoon sticking up from your rice bowl.
- Don't blow your nose at the table.

A traditional Korean meal typically consists of meat, seafood or fish served at the same time as soup, rice, and a collection of dipping sauces and *banchan*, the ubiquitous cold side dishes.

If the table is not set, there will be an oblong box containing metal chopsticks and long-handled spoons, as well as metal cups and a bottle of water or tea. The spoon is for rice, soup and any dish with liquids; chopsticks are for everything else.

Koreans tend to eat out a lot, and the most ubiquitous type of restaurant, both in and outside of Korea, is the do-it-yourself

CLAIRE-MARIE HARRIS / GETTY IMAGES

A typical Korean meal is set up to be shared.

Hotteok, a popular Korean street vendor food.

Food vendor at work.

A pile of onion *kimchi*.

barbecue. Many barbecue restaurants have a grill set into the tables on which to cook *bulgogi* (slices of beef), *galbi* (beef ribs), *samgyeopsal* (pork), *dak* (chicken) and seafood or vegetables. The server often helps out with the cooking. The inexpensive *samgyeopsal* is bacon and can be fatty. *Bulgogi*, *galbi* and *samgyeopsal* are served with a bunch of *ssam*, typically lettuce and sesame leaves. Take a leaf in one hand (or combine two leaves for different flavours) and with your other hand use your chopsticks to load it with meat, side-dish flavourings, garlic and sauces. Then roll it up into a little package and eat it in one go.

The pinnacle of Korean dining is *jeongsik* or *hanjeongsik*. Often translated as a set menu or *table d'hôte*, it takes the form of a spread of banquet dishes all served at once: fish, meat, soup, *dubu jjigae*, rice, noodles, shellfish and a host of *banchan* (side dishes). It's a delightful way to sample a wide range of Korean food in one sitting.

Korean street food runs the gamut from snacks like *tteokbokki* (rice cakes slathered in a spicy sauce) and *hotteok* (brown sugar and cinnamon pancakes), to heavier fare like *dakkochi* (grilled chicken skewers), *sundae* (sausages containing vegetables and noodles) and *odeng* (processed seafood cakes). Look out for *pojangmacha*, the tarp-covered street stalls that sell food and *soju* well into the night.

ESSENTIAL PRODUCE

Guksu

Wheat wasn't traditionally grown on the Korean Peninsula, so *guksu* (noodles) are a relatively new introduction. Some of the more popular varieties include:

- *Naengmyeon* — Buckwheat noodles served in an icy beef broth, garnished with vegetables, Korean pear, cucumber and half a boiled egg. You can add *gochujang*, *sikcho* (vinegar) or *gyeoja* (mustard) to taste. Sometimes it's served with a small bowl of meat broth, piping hot, that you can drink with your meal.

- *Japchae* — Clear 'glass' noodles stir-fried in sesame oil with strips of egg, meat and vegetables.

Kimchi

What began as a pickling method to preserve vegetables through Korea's harsh winters has become a cornerstone of the country's cuisine. With its lurid reddish hues and limp texture, *kimchi* doesn't look that appealing, but just one bite packs a wallop of flavours: sour, spicy, with a sharp tang that often lingers through the meal.

The most common type is *baechu kimchi*, made from Chinese cabbage, but there are over 180 varieties, made with radish, cucumber, eggplant, leek, mustard leaf and pumpkin flower, among others. Some are meant to be eaten in tiny morsels while others, such as *bossam kimchi*, are flavour-packed packages containing vegetables, pork or seafood.

To make *kimchi*, vegetables are salted to lock in the original flavour, then seasoned with garlic, red pepper powder, green onions, ginger, fish sauce and other spices, and left in earthenware jars to ferment for hours, days or even years. *Kimchi* can be made all year round using seasonal vegetables, but traditionally it is made in November. Many regions, restaurants and families have their own recipes, jealously guarded and handed down through the generations. High in fibre and low in calories, *kimchi* is said to lower cholesterol, fight cancer and prevent SARS and H1N1 swine flu. South Koreans eat 1.5 million tonnes of *kimchi* every year and when the country's first astronaut went into space in 2008, he took a specially engineered 'space *kimchi*' with him.

Naengmyeon noodles.

Japchae, a dish made from sweet potato noodles.

Possibly the most well-known of Korean dishes, *bibimbap*.

DEFINING DISHES

Banchan

Not a single dish per se, but rather an impressive array of side dishes, *banchan* is meant to create balance in the meal in terms of saltiness, spiciness, temperature and colour. The number of *banchan* varies greatly from three in an ordinary meal, to 12 in traditional royal cuisine, to an incredible 20 or more in *jeongsik* (set menu or table d'hôte). Besides the archetypal cabbage *kimchi*, it's common to see radish or cucumber *kimchi*, and dishes with spinach, seaweed, bean sprouts, tofu, small clams, anchovies — just about anything the chefs can concoct.

Bibimbap

Quite possibly the most famous Korean dish, *bibimbap* is a tasty mixture of rice, vegetables and minced beef often with a fried egg on top. The ingredients are laid out according to the five primary colours of Korean food — white, yellow, green, red and black — which represent the five elements. Add *gochujang* (red-chilli paste) to taste and thoroughly mix it all together with a spoon before digging in. *Sanchae bibimbap* is made with mountain-grown greens; *dolsot bibimbap* is served in a stone hotpot, the highlight of which is *nurungji*, the crusty rice at the bottom. *Boribap* is rice with barley mixed in.

Jjigae

Hearty, warming *jjigae* (stews) are a staple in Korea, and are usually served sizzling in a stone hotpot with plenty of spices. Popular versions are made with tofu (*dubu jjigae*), soybean paste (*doenjang jjigae*) and *kimchi*. *Beoseotjeongol* is a less spicy but highly recommended mushroom hotpot.

GREG THOMSON / GETTY IMAGES

Makgeolli being poured into bowl.

Hoe

Raw fish is extremely popular in coastal Korea. *Modeumhoe* or *saengseonhoe* is raw fish served with *ssam* (salad leaves), or *ganjang* (soy sauce) with *wasabi*, usually with a pot of spicy *maeuntang* (fish soup) to complete the meal. *Chobap* is raw fish served over vinegared rice. Restaurants near the coast also serve squid, barbecued shellfish, octopus and crab. More gung-ho eaters can try *sannakji* (raw octopus, not live but wriggling from post-mortem spasms) or *hongeo* (ray, served raw and fermented, or steamed — neither of which masks its pungent ammonia smell).

DRINKS

Alcohol

Drinking is the mainstay of Korean socialising, and an evening out can quickly turn into a blur of bar-hopping. The most common poison of choice is *soju*, a traditionally rice-based, distilled alcohol that is often likened to vodka.

Makgeolli is a traditional farmer's brew made from unrefined, fermented rice wine. Much lower in alcohol content than *soju*, it has a cloudy appearance and a sweetish yoghurty flavour.

Easier on the palate are a host of sweetish traditional spirits, brewed or distilled from grains, fruits and roots. *Bokbunjaju* is made from wild raspberries, *meoruju* from wild fruit, *maesilju* from green plums and *insamju* from ginseng.

Tea

Tea is a staple and the term is also used to describe drinks brewed without tea leaves. The most common leaf tea is *nokcha* (green tea); black tea is harder to find. Non-leaf teas include the ubiquitous *boricha* (barley tea), *daechucha* (red-date tea), *omijacha* (five-flavour berry tea), *yujacha* (citron tea) and *insamcha* (ginseng tea).

JERRY ALEXANDER

Beautifully-presented bowl of *kaeng khiaw waan*, green chicken curry.

Thailand

The kingdom of Thailand lures visitors with its virtually irresistible combination of natural beauty, historic temples, renowned hospitality and robust cuisine. From pulse-pounding Bangkok to tranquil villages moored along the Mekong River, Thai cooks concoct a seemingly endless variety of dishes, whether from 300-year-old court recipes, the latest in Euro-Thai fusion or simple dishes guided by seasonal and regional necessity.

CULINARY CAPITAL CENTRAL THAILAND **KNOWN FOR** *PHAT THAI* **IMPORTS** SUGAR **EXPORTS** COCONUT, RICE, GINGER **DEVOUR** SPICY SOUPS AND CURRIES **AVOID** *PLAA RÁA* (ROTTEN FISH)

Market vendor scooping fried bananas into a cup made from banana leaves.

JERRY ALEXANDER

CULTURE

Thais love to talk about their cuisine, but ask them to try to describe the essence of Thai food, and they're not likely to have a quick answer. They can be at a similar loss for words when attempting to describe their culture in general. In fact Thais don't really have a word that corresponds to the English term 'culture'. The nearest equivalent, *wátánátham*, emphasises fine arts and religious ceremonies over other aspects usually covered by the western conception of culture.

But ask what it means to be Thai, and the response is invariably two-fold: to speak Thai, and to eat Thai food. Thailand stakes its national reputation on producing a cuisine that Thai chefs and local food critics sum up with the phrase '*Rót châat phèt ráwn*' (literally, 'tastes original spicy hot'), a highly complimentary term generally applied only to Thai cooking. Other kinds of cooking, by implication, are considered *jèut* (bland) and Thais who go to visit or live in western countries often return home remarking how plain they found western cuisine.

Fresh, fast and fun

One major cultural aspect contributing to the wonderful life found in Thai food is the Thai insistence on freshness. Quick culinary techniques such as blanching, flash frying, parboiling and poaching produce dishes in which the vegetables, for example, maintain most of their just-picked freshness and flavours are effectively sealed in.

Unlike their Indian counterparts, Thai cooks assemble curry pastes and other relatively elaborate seasoning concoctions quickly from fresh rather than powdered, dried or preserved ingredients. Exceptions include the fermentation and pickling processes favoured for certain condiments and seasonings.

Quick techniques and relatively simple recipes (save for the curry pastes) also mean less time spent in the kitchen and thus more time available for enjoying the company of fellow diners, whether guests or family. It is only natural that the Thais have developed a cuisine that emphasised ease of preparation since, if any one element typifies Thai culture more than any other, it is the imperative for life to be *sanùk* (fun).

In Thailand anything worth doing — even work — should have an element of *sanùk*, otherwise it automatically becomes drudgery. This doesn't mean Thais don't want to work or strive, just that they tend to approach tasks with a sense of playfulness. Nothing condemns an activity more than the description *mâi sanùk* (not fun).

Fusion

Sanùk also comes into play when Thai cooks experiment with *tamráp kàp khâo* (formula with rice), the name given to basic recipes handed down from previous generations, traded among friends or clipped from popular magazines. Such experimentation is a tradition in a country that has long functioned as an Asian crossroads, where Indian, Arab and European traders arrived from the west, intersecting trade routes emanating from southwestern China.

Unlike China and Japan, whose cultures remained largely insulated for thousands of years, Thailand has always thrived on foreign influence. Its kitchen doors have stood wide open to admit new ideas, new ingredients and new cooking techniques. Undoubtedly one of the reasons Thai cuisine has gained international popularity comes from the fact that it successfully blends so many different taste sensations. Typically, the blend is seamless and it's almost impossible to separate the strands of influence.

This can be explained by the fact that Thais adopted and

JERRY ALEXANDER

A typical scene at Warorot night market in Chiang Mai.

adapted outside culinary influences not so much out of necessity — Thailand has always been a fertile land of plenty — but because they love to eat and they love to cook and, like great cooks and diners everywhere, they love to improvise with food.

Food plays an important role not only in the purely personal and social dimensions of Thai life, but in the ritual and ceremony of their spiritual life as well. Over 90% of all Thais are Buddhists, and one of the most important Buddhist acts is the daily feeding of the monks

FEASTS

Buddhist occasions

In a land where Buddhism and animism mix freely, feeding the household also means feeding the spirits. Next to every Thai Buddhist home stands a small dollhouse-like structure raised on a pillar known as a *sãn phrá phum* (spirit house). These receive daily offerings of rice and titbits in order to satisfy the earth spirits — and a lot more when the householder feels the earth spirits have been especially generous.

Many towns and cities in Thailand feature a *làk meuang* (city pillar), which is associated with the founding of the city and is where its guardian spirit is thought to reside. The townsfolk will leave daily offerings of food, liquor, flowers and incense at a shrine built around the *làk meuang*.

Once the *phži* (spirits) are taken care of, the worshippers' next spiritual obligation is to Buddhism. It is said that the *phži* are feared, but the Buddha is loved, and in the Buddha's honour, innumerable pots of rice, curry and other delights are regularly offered to the Buddha's direct disciples, the monks. Beyond this daily obligation to feed the monks during their dawn alms rounds, there are other occasions when cuisine intersects with Buddhist life, such as local religious ceremonies and national festivals.

JERRY ALEXANDER

Women carve fruit for a northern Thai festival.

ETIQUETTE

While Thai table manners would hardly ever be described as 'formal' in the western sense, there are plenty of subtleties to be mastered. Using the correct utensils and eating gestures will garner much respect from the Thais, who generally think western table manners are coarse.

Originally Thai food was eaten with the fingers, and it still is in certain regions of the kingdom and for certain foods such as sticky rice. In the early 1900s, Thai restaurateurs began setting their tables with fork and spoon to affect a 'royal' setting, and it wasn't long before fork-and-spoon dining became the norm in Bangkok and later spread throughout the kingdom. To most Thais, pushing a fork into one's mouth is almost as uncouth as putting a knife in the mouth in western countries. Thais do use forks, however, to steer food onto the spoon, to eat chunks of roasted meat served as *kàp klâem* and to spear sliced fruit served at the end of the meal. Even so, the fork is never placed all the way into the mouth.

Tà-kìap (chopsticks) are reserved for dining in Chinese restaurants or for eating Chinese noodle dishes. Noodle soups are eaten with a spoon in the left hand (for spooning up the broth) and chopsticks in the right.

Another exception to the fork-and-spoon routine is sticky rice (common in the north and northeast), which is rolled into balls and eaten with the right hand, along with accompanying food.

Whenever dining with Thais, it's good to remember not to touch any of the food before the host (or oldest or wealthiest person present) announces '*kin khâo*' (eat rice) often spoken quietly and informally rather than with any sort of grand gesture.

DAILY MEALS

In Thailand there are no 'typical' times for meals, though the Anglo-American influenced noon to 1 pm lunch break in urban areas tends to cluster diners in local restaurants at that hour. Even so, it's not at all unusual for a worker to order in a bowl of rice noodles mid morning, and perhaps again around 3 or 4 pm.

Nor are certain genres of food restricted to certain times of day. Practically anything can be eaten first thing in the morning, whether it's sweet, salty or chilli-ridden. *Khâo kaeng* (curry over rice) is a very popular morning meal all over Thailand, as is *khâo man kài* (sliced steamed chicken cooked in chicken broth and garlic and served over rice). Thais also eat noodles, whether fried or in soup, with great gusto in the morning, or as a substantial snack food any time of day or night.

Because many restaurants in Thailand are able to serve dishes at an only slightly higher price than it would cost to make at home, Thais dine out more often than their western counterparts. One reason eating out is so cheap is that the most common type of Thai eatery has very low overheads since the proprietor spends little on decor or presentation. Thai diners don't expect much more than great food.

Thai sweets wrapped in banana leaves.

Beer and peanuts

Any evening of the week you'll see small groups of Thais — usually males — clustered around roadside tables, in outdoor restaurants or at the back of their homes, drinking Thai-brewed Singha beer or Mekong rice liquor while picking from an array of common dishes, one morsel at a time. These are *kàp klâem*, dishes specifically meant to be eaten while drinking alcoholic beverages, often before an evening meal or while waiting for the larger courses to arrive. *Kàp klâem* can be as simple as a plate of *mét má-mûang thâwt* (fried cashews) or as elaborate as one of the many types of *yam* (a hot and tangy salad) containing a blast of lime, chilli, fresh herbs and a choice of seafood, roast vegetables, noodles or meats.

Fresh pineapple, cream and pastry dessert.

A speciality from northern Thailand, *yam phak kum* contains galangal, lemongrass, dried chilli, Thai eggplant and pickled *phak kum*.

A selection of Thai beers and snacks.

Curry pastes on display at the market.

Young girl drinking coconut milk.

ESSENTIAL PRODUCE

Coconut milk

Some newcomers to Asian cuisine mistakenly believe coconut milk (*kà-thi*) means the juice contained inside a coconut. Although this juice does make a favourite thirst-quencher in hot weather, it possesses neither the sweetness nor the thickness needed to make a good base for *kaeng* or any other dish requiring coconut.

To make *kà-thí*, the fully ripe coconut — which contains little or no juice — is husked, then split open to expose the thick white meat lining the inside of the shell. This white meat is then grated before being soaked in very hot water for around 15 minutes until the water is lukewarm. The meat is then strained through a muslin cloth to produce the *kà-thí*. The first straining is considered 'thick coconut milk' while the second is 'thin coconut milk'. One cup of grated coconut soaked in 3¾ cups of hot water will produce approximately 2½ cups of coconut milk. After the milk sits for an hour or so, it will separate (put it in the refrigerator to speed up the process). The thicker section at the top is coconut cream while the rest is coconut milk.

Dipping sauces

Naam jim and *naam phrik* are types of dipping sauce. The saucer of *phrík náam plaa* — a simple concoction of sliced fresh red and green 'mouse dropping' chillies floating in *náam plaa* (fish sauce) — is a standard condiment found on nearly every Thai table, as common as salt and pepper shakers in Europe. Often called *náam plaa phrík*, this sauce is spooned onto food whenever you feel the need for more saltiness — much like soy sauce — and for an extra kick that goes far beyond black pepper. Although Thai cooks use regular salt in the kitchen for many recipes, you will never see salt on a Thai table as a condiment.

Rows of golden-coloured smoked fish.

Squid salad.

Steamed *plaa thuu*, mackerel.

Eggplant

One of the most omnipresent vegetables in native Thai cuisine is the Thai eggplant, a member of the Solanaceae family (like chillies and tomatoes) about the size of a ping-pong ball.

- Unlike its European counterpart, the Thai eggplant has a pale green skin and a rather hard flesh.
- Thais eat them raw with various chilli dips, and in a variety of curry.
- An even smaller variety, the pea eggplant is also a popular curry ingredient.
- Thais also cook with the *má-kh ua yao*, (literally, 'long eggplant'). One of the most common dishes using this vegetable is a *yam* (salad) created by tossing a fresh-roasted long eggplant with shrimp, lime juice, ground pork, coriander leaf, chillies, garlic and fish sauce. The smoky taste of the roasted eggplant contrasts well with the bite of the chilli, lime and coriander.

Fish

Thailand boasts 2710 kilometres of coastline, much of it fringed with the beaches, islands and coral reefs that attract a massive portion of the country's tourist market. It also provides one of the nation's biggest staples, seafood.

Seafood is much more of a constant in the Thai diet than poultry, beef or pork. Virtually all Thai dishes are seasoned with shrimp paste or fish sauce, often both. Thailand's numerous rivers, streams, canals, lakes and ponds produce a huge variety of freshwater fish, the Thai favourites being:

- *plaa dùk* (catfish)
- *plaa châwn* (serpent-headed fish)

- *plaa nin* (tilapia)
- *puu naa* (field crabs)
- *plaa lãi* (freshwater eel).

Although all of these occur naturally in inland waterways, some are also commercially farmed. It's not unusual for rural Thais to dig a fish pond in back of their homes or near their rice fields for this purpose. Some people even raise fish in ceramic jars, tanks or even plastic buckets beside their houses.

One of the healthiest ways to order fresh fish in Thailand is to have it wrapped in banana leaves or foil and roasted over (or covered in) hot coals. Dip the *plaa phão* (roast fish) by the forkful into *phrík náam plaa thá-leh* and you'll experience one of the simplest and tastiest seafood dishes ever.

Fruit

In Thailand it sometimes seems as if fresh fruit (*phon-la-mai*) is everywhere you look, from the orange-hued papaya pyramids piled high on wooden shelves in market stalls and the yellow strings of bananas hanging from the eaves of *ráan cham* (sundries shop), to the panoply of cubed colours carefully stacked behind the glass panes of roaming fruit carts. During festivals and in fancier hotels and restaurants, Thailand's world famous fruit carvers fashion watermelons, papayas, pineapples and mangoes into fantastic floral, animal and even human shapes.

No discussion of Thai fruit is complete without a mention of *thúrian* (durian), dubbed the king of fruits by most Southeast Asians yet despised by many foreigners. Its heavy, spiked shell resembles an ancient piece of medieval weaponry. Inside lies five sections of plump, buttery and pungent flesh. Legions of connoisseurs as well as detractors have laboured to describe the durian's complex flavour. The durian's ammonia-like aroma is so strong that many hotels in

JERRY ALEXANDER

A dog takes a rest on pile of watermelons, or *taeng moh*.

Thailand, as well as Thai International Airways, ban the fruit from their premises.

Common seasonal fruits include the following:

- *náwy nàa*, custard-apple; July to October
- *lam yài*, longan 'dragon's eyes' — small, brown, spherical, similar to rambutan; July to October
- *má-mûang*, mango — several varieties and seasons
- *mang-khút*, mangosteen — round, purple fruit with juicy white flesh; April to September
- *má-fai,* rambeh — small, reddish-brown, sweet, apricot-like; April to May
- *ngáw,* rambutan — red, hairy-skinned fruit with grape-like interior; July to September
- *chom-phûu*, rose-apple — small, apple-like texture, very fragrant; April to July
- *lámút*, sapodilla — small, brown, oval, sweet but pungent smelling; July to September.

Hot, salty, sour and sweet

Any English-language Thai cookbook will explain how a terrific Thai dish blends themes of hot, salty, sour and sweet. What's missing from the standard four-way formula is the important role of aroma. While western cooks rarely consider smell when putting cooking ingredients together, Thai recipe books and cookery magazines always cite certain ingredients that are added for fragrance or aroma, as distinct from flavour.

Hot Much of Thai cuisine's colour and fire comes from *phrik* (chillies), which, like eggplants, tomatoes and potatoes, were unknown in Siam before the 16th century.

Surprisingly Thailand doesn't cultivate a great variety of

JERRY ALEXANDER

Preserved fruits at a market.

chillies. While contemporary Mexican markets purvey up to 90 different varieties, Thailand restricts itself to a dozen or so.

The most commonly used of all Thai chillies, *phrík chíi fáa* (literally, 'sky pointing chilli'), is long and slender (measuring about 6 to 10 centimetres) and is grown in red, green and yellow versions. Thais prize the *phrík chíi fáa* highly, and often the seeds are removed from this chilli before it's added to the mortar or wok in order to leave more room for its revered texture, colour and flavour.

The second most commonly seen chilli in Thailand is the infamous *phrík khîi nûu*, (literally, 'mouse droppings pepper'), meant as a description of its tiny torpedo-like shape. In English it is often known as 'bird's eye chilli', of which there are several varieties. Measuring only 1 to 2 centimetres, this is the hottest chilli you'll find in Thailand.

Salty At the base of all Thai cooking is the salt that spurs the eating of rice, and the main source of culinary salt for the Thais is *náam plaa* (fish sauce). *Kà-pì* (shrimp paste), which comes in a variety of grades and colours, from fresh to heavily fermented, from salmon pink to chocolate brown, is valued primarily for its deep marine flavours and sauce-thickening power more than for its saltiness.

Sour The juice of *má-nao* (lime) and the peel or leaves of *ma-krùt* (kaffir lime) impart a citrus tartness to Thai dishes often described as 'sour'. Further tartness may be achieved through the use of *má-khãam pìak*, the flesh and seeds of the husked tamarind fruit pressed into red-brown clumps. These clumps are soaked in water and the pulp strained away to produce a dark red juice with a flavour that is both tangy and savoury.

Sweet Wherever a Thai dish contains a noticeable tartness or spiciness, this must be balanced with a sweet flavour. Thai food is sweetened with cane sugar, coconut sugar or palm sugar.

Noodles

Exactly when the noodle reached Thailand is difficult to ascertain, but it almost certainly arrived along trade routes from China, since the preparation styles in contemporary Thailand are similar to those of contemporary southern China.

Four basic kinds of noodle predominate in Thailand.

Kuaytiaw These noodles are made from pure rice flour mixed with water to form a paste which is then steamed to form wide, flat sheets.

The sheets are folded and sliced into *sên yài* (flat 'wide line' noodles 2 to 3 centimetres wide), *sên lék* ('small line' noodles about 5 millimetres wide) and *sên mìi* ('noodle line' noodles only 1 to 2 millimetres wide). *Sên mìi* dry out so quickly that they are usually sold only in their dried form.

The king of Thai noodledom, *kuaytiaw* comes as part of many dishes. The simplest, *kuaytiaw náam*, is *kuaytiaw* served in a bowl of plain chicken or beef stock along with bits of meat and pickled cabbage, with *phàk chii* (coriander leaf) as garnish Probably the most well known *kuaytiaw* dish is *kuaytiaw phàt thai,* usually called *phàt thai* for short, a plate of thin rice noodles stir fried with dried or fresh shrimp, bean sprouts, fried tofu, egg and seasonings. Along the edge of the plate the cook usually places little piles of ground peanuts and ground dried chilli, along with lime halves and a few stalks of spring onion, for self-seasoning.

Khanõm jiin The second kind of noodle, popular in Southern Thailand, is produced by pushing rice flour paste through a sieve into boiling water, much the same way as Italian-style pasta is made.

Although the name literally means 'Chinese pastry', *khanõm jiin* developed its own Thai culinary genre in Southern Thailand, where it is served doused with varying curries.

Mother and child drinking at the market.

Ingredients for *phàt thai*.

Fried *ba mii* noodles.

Green mango salad in plastic bags.

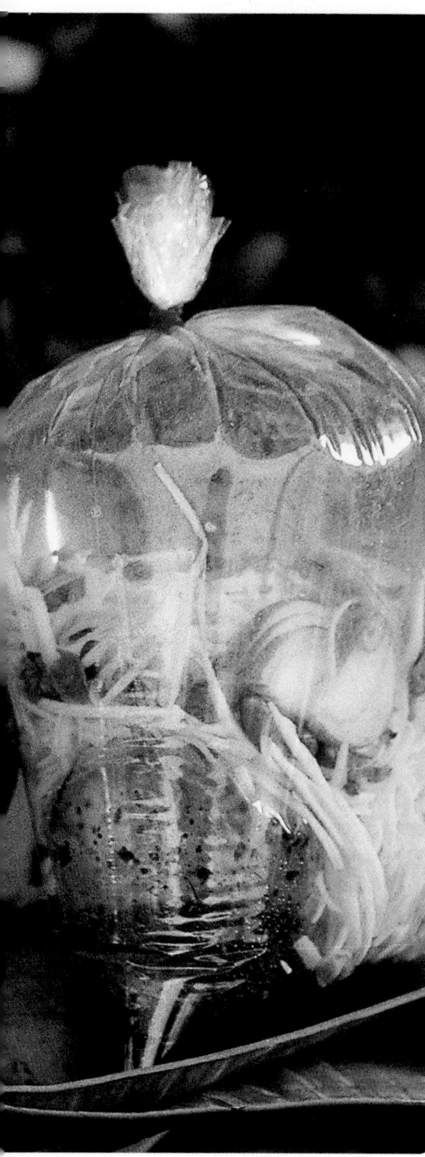
JERRY ALEXANDER

The most standard curry topping is *náam yaa*, which roughly translates as 'herbal sauce'.

Bà-mìi The third kind of noodle is made from wheat flour and sometimes egg (depending on the noodle-maker or the brand). It is yellowish in colour and always the same size, about 1.5 millimetres in diameter. It is sold only in fresh bundles and cooked immediately before serving.

Kíaw is a triangle of *bà-mìi* dough wrapped around ground pork or ground fish. These dumplings may be boiled and added to soup, or fried to make *kíaw thâwt*. One of the most popular *bà-mìi* dishes in Thailand is *bà-mìi kíaw puu*, a soup containing *kíaw* and *puu* (crab).

Wún sên Finally there's *wún sên*, a name that translates literally as jelly thread. An almost clear noodle made from mung bean starch and water, it is sold only in dried bunches, which are easily prepared by soaking in hot water for 10-15 minutes.

Wún sên is used for only three dishes in Thailand. The first and most native, *yam wún sên*, is a hot and tangy salad made with lime juice, shrimp, ground pork and various seasonings; a second appearance is in *wún sên òp puu*, bean thread noodles baked in a lidded, clay pot with crab and seasonings; and thirdly, *wún sên* is a key ingredient in *kaeng jèut*, a Chinese-influenced soup containing pork, soft tofu and vegetables.

Pandan leaves

A pointed, blade-like leaf called *bai toey* (pandan leaf), from the indigenous pandan plant is primarily used to add a vanilla-like flavour to Thai sweets. The well-known *kài hàw bai toey* (chicken wrapped in pandan leaves) uses individual pandan leaves as wrappers for chunks of chicken marinated in soy sauce, sesame oil, garlic and coriander root. The resulting packets are fried or grilled and served with a dipping sauce similar to the marinade.

Rice

Established by a people who seem to have a spiritual connection with the grain, Muang Thai (Land of the Thais) seemed destined to become the rice (*khâo*) bowl of Asia. Thailand has led the world in rice exports since the 1960s, and the quality of Thai rice, according to the perceptions of many discerning Asians, is considered the best in the world.

- Thailand's *khâo hăwm málí* (jasmine rice) is so coveted that there is a steady underground business in smuggling bags of the fragrant grain to neighbouring Malaysia, Laos, Cambodia, Myanmar.
- Rice is so central to Thai food culture that the most common term for 'eat' is *kin khâo* (literally, 'consume rice') and one of the most common greetings is '*Kin khâo láew réu yang*?' (Have you consumed rice yet?).
- All the dishes eaten with rice – whether curries, stir fries, soups, or other food preparations – are simply classified as *kàp khâo* (with rice).

Perfect white rice

Most Thais eat *khâo jâo* (white rice), which is prepared by boiling it in a covered pot. Before cooking, the rice must be rinsed. Thais rinse the raw rice grains in cold water to remove unwanted rice powder, which if left in produces sticky, starchy rice rather than the preferred slightly separated grains. Traditionally the cook rinses the rice three times in a row, the more devout Buddhists among them silently dedicating this task to the *triratana* (triple gems of the faith). Extra-finicky cooks may rinse a number of additional times until the water runs clear.

The amount of water added to the rice for boiling is crucial to the end result, although Thais don't use measuring cups as

JERRY ALEXANDER

Perfect white rice.

there's a much easier way: simply add enough water above the top of the rice to meet the first joint of your index finger. Every cook adjusts the 'rule of finger' more or less according to experience (all digits aren't of equal length, after all) and according to the age of the rice.

Most people living in Northern and North-Eastern Thailand prefer sticky rice over white rice. In fact, many dishes from these regions are always served with sticky rice, which you eat with your hands. You can easily tell uncooked sticky rice because it's much whiter – a rather opaque white – than white rice, and the grains are usually a bit shorter and more oval-shaped.

SHOPPING

At the market

Despite the arrival of shopping malls, supermarkets and department stores, *tàlàat* (traditional open-air markets) are still the most popular place to shop for foodstuffs. Such markets continue to flourish because Thai cooks value freshness above all else, and produce trucked across the country and wrapped in plastic, they reason, won't be as fresh as that found in the local grassroots *tàlàat*. It's also assumed – sometimes correctly, sometimes not – that everything found in the *tàlàat* will be less expensive than comparable goods stocked at a well-lit, air-conditioned supermarket. Discerning Thais also like to see, feel and smell the food they're buying, impossible to do when the food is covered in plastic. Pre-packaging also breaks up the marvellous displays of a traditional market — pyramids of golden mangoes, silver mackerel side by side in their bamboo steamers. It also abandons the velvety touch of traditional banana and pandan leaf food wrappers, which keep dirt at bay but allow fragrances to escape.

Traders on their boats at the floating market in Damnoen Saduak in Bangkok.

CHRIS MELLR / GETTY IMAGES

Water markets

One of the most intriguing of Thailand's many markets are the *tàlàat náam* (water markets), more commonly known in English as floating markets. These take place on the canals of Central Thailand, usually in the early morning hours, wherever a group of boats loaded with merchandise convene in one spot for the purpose of buying and selling their wares.

Local customers either paddle their own small craft alongside the market boats to make their purchases or, less commonly, squat at the canal's edge and conduct boat-to-shore transactions. In addition to boats filled with fresh produce, the typical *tàlàat náam* also features a few boats selling ready-to-eat meals such as *kʉaytǐaw* (rice noodles) and *khâo kaeng* (curry and rice).

PREPARATION

These days the outdoor kitchen is still the norm. This is so that the powerful aromas from cooking chillies, shrimp paste and garlic can escape quickly. What you will find in these kitchens in the way of tools and utensils may vary greatly, as the kitchen is an appropriation of certain things western, blended with certain things Thai. A simple kitchen will feature little more than a charcoal fire pot, a few pots and pans, ladles, spatulas and shelves for dry goods. A more elaborate set-up would include a gas cooker, refrigerator and a greater variety of utensils.

Heat

In the traditional outdoor kitchen the *tao fai* (fire pot) is still the most common heat source.

- The t*ao fai* consists of a thick-walled pot made from clay mixed with sand, rice husk and ashes.
- *Tao fai* come in different sizes, the most common

measuring about 24 centimetres in diameter at the mouth.

- Along the lip of the pot are three flanges or 'feet' that support a pot or wok while allowing the circulation of air into the fire cavity.
- A *tao fai* always sits on the ground or floor — often on an asbestos mat — so the cook must squat or sit on a low stool to fan the flames with a bamboo or palm-leaf hand fan while tending the pan.

Utensils

Full Thai meals can be prepared over one burner, whether charcoal or gas, with just three types of cookware. First and foremost is the *krà-thá*, a shallow, wide-mouthed round-bottomed pan most people know as the 'wok'. The most popular wok — and the easiest to use — has one long, sturdy wooden handle. Woks are primarily used for stir fries although some cooks also use them for curry. Whatever the dish, Thais use a *phai* (a spatula with a curved edge) to move ingredients in the wok. As essential as the wok are two *mâw* (pots), one for boiling rice and another for making curry.

Many other utensils are used throughout the country's kitchens.

- The *khrók* (mortar) and *sàak* (pestle), which come in various sizes. A smaller stone set is used to grind spices and make *khrêuang kaeng* (curry paste), while a larger earthenware *khrók* and *sàak mái* (large wooden pestle) are used for making salads such as *sômtam* (tart & spicy salad).
- The *maew khùut má-phráo* (traditional coconut grater) is also part of the traditional kitchen kit, especially in rural areas where people still grate

JERRY ALEXANDER

Chef cooking confidently with fire.

Traditional kitchen containing charcoal firepot, terracotta pot and kitchen utensils.

Woman preparing sticky rice before cooking.

Carving papaya.

their own coconut rather than buying it pre-grated in the local markets.

- The *krà-chawn* (sieve) is useful for straining liquids such as coconut milk from soaked, grated coconut meat. Very traditional households may fashion their own *krà-chawn* by piercing a halved coconut shell with small holes.
- The double-handled *krà-chawn má-nao* (lime sieve), used for squeezing lime juice, also gets a lot of use.

DEFINING DISHES

Curry

In Thai, *kaeng* refers to any dish with a lot of liquid and can thus refer to soups as well as the classic chilli-based curries like *kaeng phèt* (spicy kaeng) – for which Thai cuisine is famous. The word may also be used as a verb meaning 'to make a *kaeng*'.

The preparation of all chilli-based *kaeng* begins with a *khrêuang kaeng*. It is created by mashing, pounding and grinding an array of ingredients with a stone mortar and pestle to form an aromatic, extremely pungent-tasting and rather thick paste.

Some Thai *khrêuang kaeng* run to the consistency of fresh clay, while others are as soft as cornmeal dough. The moisture and viscosity of a *khrêuang kaeng* derives from the use of mostly fresh, rather than dried, herbs and roots, and from the inclusion of fish sauce and/or shrimp paste.

Most curries begin with the blending of the *khrêuang kaeng* into coconut cream that has been brought to a quick boil in a saucepan or wok. From here on the rest of the ingredients (meat, poultry, seafood and/or vegetables) are added one at a time, along with coconut milk to further thin and flavour the curry. A *khrêuang kaeng* should never be thinned with water, but rather with oil, coconut milk or the moisture found in other ingredients in the curry.

Some recipes will omit coconut milk entirely to produce a particularly fiery curry known as *kaeng pàa* (forest curry).

Another curry that does not use coconut milk is *kaeng sôm* (sour curry), made with dried chillies, shallots, garlic and Chinese key pestled with salt, shrimp paste and fish sauce. Cooked with *náam mákhãam* (tamarind juice) and green papaya to create an overall tanginess, the result is a soupy, salty, sweet-and-sour ragout that most westerners would never identify with the word 'curry'.

Unlike Indian curries, Thai ones do not require long cooking times. With the *khrêuang kaeng* and all other ingredients at hand, most curries are thrown together in a matter of minutes.

Soups

Most Thai soups fall into two broad categories, *tôm yam* and *kaeng jèut*, that are worlds apart in terms of seasonings.

With the predominating flavours of chilli and lime, *tôm yam* can be described as a soup-style hot and tangy salad — *tôm yam*, after all, translates as 'boiled hot and tangy salad'.

- *Tôm yam* is almost always made with seafood, though chicken may be used.
- Lemongrass, kaffir lime peel and lime juice give *tôm yam* its characteristic tang.
- Fuelling the fire beneath *tôm yam*'s often velvety surface are fresh *phrík khîi nûu* and sometimes a half teaspoonful of *náam phrík phão* (a paste of dried chillies roasted with *kà-pì*).
- Improvisation comes into play with this dish, as cooks try to out-do one another in providing a savoury soup with at least one or two 'mystery' ingredients.

JERRY ALEXANDER

Fruit market vendor sets the price of her produce.

- *Kaeng jèut* (bland soup) covers the other end of the spectrum with a soothing broth seasoned with little more than fish sauce and black pepper. Although the number of variations on *kaeng jèut* are seemingly endless, common ingredients include *wún sên* (mung bean starch noodles), *tâo-hûu* (tofu), *hua chai tháo* (Chinese radish) and *muu sàp* (ground pork).

Yam

Yam is the term used for a hot and tangy salad containing a blast of lime, chilli, fresh herbs and a choice of seafood, roast vegetables, noodles or meats. Thais prize yam dishes so much that they are often eaten on their own, without rice, before the meal has begun. Although food writers claim that the *yam* perfectly balances Thai cuisine's four basic flavours (tangy, salty, sweet and hot), the newcomer will almost certainly counter that two sensations take centre place — tangy and hot.

Lime juice provides the tang, while the abundant use of chillies produce the heat. Other ingredients vary considerably, but plenty of leafy vegetables and herbs are usually present, including lettuce (often lining the dish) and mint leaves. Lemongrass, shallots, kaffir lime leaves and *khêun chàai* (Chinese celery) may also come into play. Most yam are served at room temperature or just slightly warmed by any cooked ingredients.

On many Thai menus, the *yam* section will be the longest. Yet often when these same menus are translated into English, most or all of the yam are omitted because Thai restaurateurs harbour the idea that the delicate western palate cannot handle the heat or pungency. The usual English menu translation is either 'Thai-style salad' or 'hot and sour salad'.

DRINKS

Most Thais drink only domestically produced beers and liquors, primarily for reasons of expense. During the economic boom of the 1980s and early 1990s, the importation of foreign whiskies and wine grew feverishly among the moneyed classes. After the Thai economy began to stumble in 1997, even the 'tuppies' (Thai yuppies) returned to local tipples in large numbers.

Beer

Thai beer (*bia*), particularly Singha and Kloster, make fine accompaniments to virtually all Thai dishes. Only a few brands of beer are readily available all over Thailand. The king of Thai beer is Singha (Lion).

- Advertised with such slogans as '*Pràthêht rao, Bia rao*' (Our Land, Our Beer) and '*Pràthêht thai, Bia thai*' (Thailand, Thai Beer), the Singha label is considered the quintessential 'Thai' beer by westerners and locals alike.
- Singha's original recipe was formulated in 1934 by Thai nobleman Phya Bhirom Bhakdi and his son Prachuap, the first Thai to earn a brewmaster's diploma from Munich's Doemens Institute.
- Many international beer critics have declared the strong, hop-tasting brew to be the best beer produced in Asia.
- The barley for Singha is grown in Thailand, the hops are imported from Germany and the alcohol content is a heady 6%.
- The beer is brewed in Bangkok, and comes in brown glass bottles with a shiny gold lion on the label.
- Singha also comes in cans, and is available on tap as *bia sòt* (draught beer) in many pubs and restaurants.

JERRY ALEXANDER

Woman making *lâo khâo*, white liquor.

Rice whisky

A long-time favourite, and more affordable than beer, are Thailand's 'whiskies', which are made from sticky rice. The two major rice whisky distillers — Suramaharas Co and the Surathip Group — are locked into a two-way battle for the Thai whisky market. The first produces the famous Mekong brand, a world-famous spirit named for South-East Asia's longest river. The second company makes the slightly pricier and slightly classier (by image, if nothing else) Sang Thip.

Known simply by their brand names, both liquors have a light, slightly sweet, rum-like flavour and an alcohol content of 35%. Although Thais consume more beer by volume than they do any other alcoholic beverage, Mekong and Sang Thip run a very close second, and when the sun sets over sidewalk eateries all over Thailand you'll see table after table cluttered with the amber-coloured whisky bottles.

Lâo khão (white liquor)

Deep in the rural countryside where farming is the main activity and incomes are meagre, a colourless liquid called *lâo khão* is the beverage of choice. *Lâo khão* comes in two broad genres, legal and contraband. The legal kind, distilled from sticky rice and distributed nationwide, is commissioned by the Thai government and sold in 750 ml bottles. Sweet, raw-tasting and much more aromatic than the amber stuff, it's usually drunk neat.

Over on the untaxed, illegal side of the bar, you'll find a more interesting selection of liquors distilled from various agricultural products including sugar palm sap, coconut milk, coconut sap, sugar cane, taro, as well as sticky rice. Alcohol content varies from as little as 10% to as much as 95%. Such *lâo thèuan* (wild liquor) tends to be weaker in Southern Thailand and stronger in North and North-Eastern Thailand.

Taking ducks to market by bicycle in Hue.

GREG ELMS / GETTY IMAGES

Vietnam

In Vietnamese cuisine you are likely to encounter the wonderful and the strange, the sacred and the profane. You'll find spices that sing in your mouth, smells that trigger emotions, dishes that amaze by their cleverness and beguile with their sensuousness, drinks that surprise, fruits that will shock and creatures that will make you shriek.

CULINARY CAPITALS HANOI, HO CHI MINH CITY **KNOWN FOR** RICE PAPER ROLLS **IMPORTS** DAIRY PRODUCTS, COCA COLA **EXPORTS** RICE **DEVOUR** STEAMING BOWL OF *PHO* **AVOID** CURRIED FROGS LEGS

Portrait of an elderly man from Hanoi.

Vietnamese happy crepes, popular in Hue.

Thit kho to, or clay pot pork.

CULTURE

Historians like to say that geography is fate. Geography is also cuisine, for it determines which foods are shaped by what peoples. The topography of Vietnam presents virtually every climate and microclimate capable of yielding a crop or animal, whether tropical or temperate, from fish, rice and tea to beef, coffee and cream.

Look at the map of Vietnam. As the Vietnamese are eager to point out, it resembles a *don ganh*, a yoke, a bamboo pole with a basket of rice slung from each end. The baskets represent the main rice-growing regions of the Red River Delta in the north, and the Mekong Delta in the south. The other thing to notice on this highly symbolic map of Vietnam is its waters, comprising 2400 kilometres of coastline and innumerable kilometres of rivers and streams. Rice cultivation and the harvesting of the water world provide the cuisine of Vietnam with its two most potent symbols and substances: rice and *nuoc mam* (fermented fish sauce).

In keeping with its geography, Vietnamese cooking is heavily influenced by China, especially in methods of preparation and kitchen equipment. They share the concept of 'the five flavours', a balance of salty, sweet, sour, bitter and hot (spicy). A dish may be dominated by one or two of the five, but the others will usually play a pleasing harmony in the culinary tune. Stir fry is a common method of preparation but the Vietnamese generally use very little oil, displaying a lighter hand than the Chinese. Lightness and freshness are the goals.

Eating styles

The Vietnamese have three styles or manners of cooking and eating: comprehensive eating, or eating through the five senses; scientific eating, which observes the dualistic principles of yin and yang; and democratic eating, or the freedom to eat as you like.

In comprehensive eating, the most common form, you eat with your eyes first. Dishes must be attractively presented with a diversity of forms and colours. Then the nose follows: the Vietnamese penchant for aroma is brought to the fore, and each dish must offer pleasant odours of meat, fish or vegetables and a sauce. When chewing, take care to feel the softness of noodles, the texture of the meat, and listen to the crackling sound of rice crackers or the crunchiness of roasted peanuts. And then you taste. The cook must see to it that each dish has its own distinct flavour, and you, the diner, should take note of the differences. A dish might have all the five flavours, but none should predominate.

Scientific eating concentrates on the dualistic philosophy of yin and yang, in this case a balance between hot and cold. For instance, a fish stew would be seasoned with salty fish sauce which is yang, but balanced by the yin of sugar. Green mangoes (yin) should be taken with salt and hot chillies (yang); grilled catfish or duck (yin) must be eaten with ginger (yang). This kind of eating is said to contribute to the good health of both mind and body.

'Democratic' eating is when you eat for the sake of eating. Everybody does it, but no one wants to make a habit of it.

French influences

When the French arrived in the 19th century, they brought with them their food philosophy: an interest in and a respect for good quality ingredients and a well-developed sense of how to use them. Ruling the country for nearly a century, the French have helped enrich Vietnamese cuisine:

- They brought in the technique of sautéing, and new crops such as asparagus, avocados, corn, tomatoes and wine.

GARRETT CULHANE

Woman eating breakfast at the fish market.

- Vietnamese cooking is arguably the only Asian cuisine that can frequently admit wine successfully to the table.
- The French also gave the Vietnamese an appreciation for *baguettes*, beer, *café au lait*, and ice cream.
- Vietnamese sandwiches made of French bread, *pâté*, salad vegetables, and *nuoc mam* or chilli sauce are popular throughout the country.

REGIONS

Southern fare

The south grows a greater variety of tropical and temperate fruits and vegetables, and many varieties of spice. Hence, the south favours spicy dishes. Curries have been around since the earliest times, although, unlike the Indian originals, they are not hot but aromatic. They may be taken with noodles or rice as a family meal, or with French bread as a snack. Another Indian influence is *banh xeo*, which is akin to an Indian *dhosa*, or a large crepe filled with goodies.

Almost anything cooked in coconut milk is a typical southern dish. Southerners also use more sugar in their recipes, even the savoury ones. Sugarcane is abundant here, and besides using it in cooking, the southerners chew it for a snack, drink its pressed juice, put it in soups, caramelise it and use it as the chief flavouring agent in clay-pot cooking.

Dalat

One of the most important aspects of the varied southern diet is the existence of the mountain town and region of Dalat. With the intense light of the tropical sun, cool mountain air and rich soil, Dalat can grow just about anything from any part of the world. Long-stemmed artichokes, big fat carrots, what the Vietnamese call 'French bamboo' (asparagus), potatoes, tomatoes, cauliflower, and greens of all kinds. Watermelons,

GREG ELMS / GETTY IMAGES

Cahn chua ca, or hot and sour fish soup.

peaches, apples, avocados and white strawberries abound. Without Dalat, the south would be gastronomically impoverished.

FEASTS

Tet

Tet, the Vietnamese Lunar New Year, is considered the first day of spring and carries with it all connotations of rebirth and renewal, both physical and spiritual. The word 'tet' comes from the Vietnamese word *tiet*, literally, the knotty projection between two sections of a stalk of bamboo, an internode, a pause, a conjoining. It is a place, or time, or a means of transition between seasons or between epochs or worlds, the connection that holds all together. Officially a three-day holiday in Vietnam, it often spills over through a week.

Ancestor calling

On the first day of *Tet*, the family loads food on a prominently displayed table, the first meal for the ancestors since they have returned to the world of the living. The head of the family offers a grace, then lights three sticks of incense, kneels, folds his hands in front of his chest, bows his head and prays. He whispers the names of the deceased of the family up to the fifth generation, and invites them to partake of the feast the family has prepared for them.

This act of obeisance is known as 'ancestor calling', and is the prelude to the most important and unifying moments for the family — the sharing of a meal together, as a form of communion with their ancestors and with each other.

All over the cities, towns and villages, shops sell candies in bulk, or in assortments packaged in elegantly arranged boxes, to satisfy the sweet tooth of *Tet*. Dried watermelon seeds dyed red, or sweet green bean candies are served to visitors with their tea. To the visitor some of the most unusual treats are the sugared, dried fruits and vegetables called *mut*. Ginger, persimmons, lemons, tangerines, lotus seeds and sugared winter melons are common, as are the salted dried fruits called *o mai*.

ETIQUETTE

When sitting down for a meal, you will find yourself at the table with your bowl on a small plate, chopsticks and a soup spoon at the ready. The small plate should be used for discards and scraps. Each place setting will include a small dipping bowl at the top right-hand side of the bowl for the *nuoc mam*, *nuoc cham* or other dipping sauces, depending on the complexity of the meal. There may also be a dish of chilli sauce, as well as sliced fresh chillies or a tiny dish of salt, pepper and lime juice.

The Vietnamese eat with gusto, and noise. Slurping is not considered impolite, although belching is. Vietnamese like to interact with their food, almost to play with it. There are so many dishes that call for rolling and wrapping at the table; for adding this or that; grilling or boiling at the table; for assembling or disassembling. Dishes of crab or shrimp often require the dexterous and extensive use of fingers and little picks and other implements to shell them. It can make for a time-consuming process, but that is what the Vietnamese like, any excuse to linger over food, with friends or family.

Steamed crab in beer and herbs.

DAILY MEALS

A meal in Vietnam is composed of rice and 'something else'. If all you have is the 'something else' then you haven't had a meal, but a snack. If all you have is rice with a little *nuoc mam*, then you've had a meal. Ideally, a meal includes rice, vegetable, fish or meat, and a soup.

The Vietnamese like to eat three meals a day. Breakfast is usually simple, and may be a noodle soup such as *pho*, a rice

Bahn xeo, savoury crepe with pork and shrimp.

A grandmother sits in her roadside home in the Mekong Delta.

Bright and colourful market produce, including chillies, ginger, limes, garlic in Ho Chi Minh City.

GREG ELMS / GETTY IMAGES

gruel called *congee* with bits of seafood or meat in it, or a sticky rice cake wrapped in banana leaf and eaten on the fly. Baguettes are available at any time of day or night, and may be eaten plain with a cup of coffee, or filled with whatever is to hand.

Lunch is served at around 11 am. People traditionally go home to eat with their families, but others might remain in the office or eat at a nearby street café, or, if near the major markets at lunchtime pop in there for noodles, grilled meats or seafood with rice vermicelli. They are there not only to eat, but to chat, catch up on the latest gossip, and stay connected with friends.

Dinner is a time for family bonding. The meal is essentially a repeat of lunch, if it was a proper lunch, with all four components. Well-to-do families might add a few more items, another vegetable, perhaps two meats. Everything is served simultaneously or as it is ready. The dishes are arranged around the central rice bowl and diners each have a small eating bowl. The procedure is uncomplicated: spoon some rice into your bowl, and lay 'something else' on top of it. Take what you like, leave what you don't care for. At the end of the meal, pour a bit of the remaining soup into your bowl to wash out the remaining rice and eat it. Wasting rice is a no-no.

ESSENTIAL PRODUCE

Fruits and vegetables

After rice, fruits and vegetables make up the bulk of the Vietnamese diet. If given the choice of abandoning vegetables or abandoning meat, virtually all Vietnamese would eschew flesh and keep the veggies. And they would not be the inveterate snackers and grazers that they are were it not for the gift of fruit. Hardly anyone would go on a trip without a bag of fruit — just go down to a train or bus station and see.

Two favourite Vietnamese fruits are:

- *Buoi* (pomelo) which is like a large grapefruit. Pomelos (sometimes called *pamplemousse*) have thick skins and pith, and yield a sweeter, less acidic fruit than ordinary grapefruit. The coast of Central Vietnam produces the most prized varieties between August and November. They are often sold on the street and in train stations as a popular snack. They are often eaten with salt, or tossed with herbs to make a refreshing salad.
- *Du du* (papaya) is one of many New World crops in Vietnam; there are 45 species of papaya (also known as pawpaw). High in vitamins A and C, when ripe, the large, gourd-like fruit has a refreshing and sweet orange to red flesh, which is often taken with a squeeze of lime juice to bring out its subtleties.

Herbs and spices

While rice and *nuoc mam* define Vietnamese 'food', it is spices that define Vietnamese 'cuisine', the study, practice and development of the kitchen arts. For the building blocks of Vietnamese flavour, think mint, star anise, turmeric, ginger, chillies, sugar, coriander, basil, galangal and lemongrass.

Nuoc Mam

All along the length of Vietnam's coastline and in the deltas, people brew *nuoc mam*. Different combinations of fish and a few secret ingredients can add or change colour and flavour, and the result is many different local blends. Wherever and whatever, the process is the same.

The fish, usually small anchovy types, are layered alternately with salt. The salted fish are left in huge wooden barrels for up to three months. The liquid is drained through a tap at the base and poured back into the barrels and left for another three

GREG ELMS / GETTY IMAGES

Cha Gio, Vietnamese spring rolls.

months. It is drained off again, strained, and is then ready for sale, or it can be aged further. The flavour improves over the years, making aged *nuoc mam* like fine wine to a connoisseur.

Rice

Vietnamese have a reverence for rice. It is the 'staff of life', not only at the table but in the economy and culture. The majority of the people of Vietnam gain their livelihood by some direct involvement with its production, transport or sale. Vietnam is the world's third-largest exporter of rice, ranking only behind the USA and Thailand.

Rice noodles

While the Chinese and Europeans make their noodles with wheat, Vietnamese make them with rice.

Rice vermicelli, the thin variety (*bun*), is brittle, white, and dried in 25 cm (10 in) lengths. *Bun* are used in soups and noodle salads, and served at room temperature as a side dish to curried dishes, grilled meats and fried fish such as *cha ca*.

Banh hoi is another variety of rice noodle, which is as fine as angel hair pasta, the thinnest of all noodles. They are used primarily as an accompaniment to grilled foods.

Also made is *banh pho*, rice sticks, which are stir fried or added to soups.

Seafood

Because of Vietnam's long coastline, seafood has always been a major source of protein. Freshwater and saltwater species are common and the emphasis is always on freshness, as no refrigeration is available in most places. Crabs, prawns (shrimps), cuttlefish, clams, eel, shellfish and many species of fin fish can be bought anywhere.

Of all the items to be found in a restaurant, the most

Trussed crabs for sale at the market.

Fresh river fish at the morning market.

perishable is fish. And fish gone bad is one bad bellyache. But as a general rule in Vietnam, fish is impeccably fresh. More often than not, it is alive only minutes before it joins you for dinner. If you have a chance to see your fish before preparation, or if you are buying it yourself, check to see that its eyes aren't sunken or opaque, that the gills are ruddy, and the scales intact and adhering to the skin, not flaking off.

SHOPPING

At the market

You can get it all at the *cho*, the market. Every city and town has one. In Cho Ben Thanh in Ho Chi Minh City you will find it, like any other, divided into little territories inhabited by merchants who pay a fee for their bit of commercial real estate. A market stall may be newly occupied by its merry merchant, or it may be held by the same family for three generations, serving three generations of customers. This explains why you will often see, side by side, several stalls selling the same merchandise.

Vietnamese shoppers are not casual or impulse buyers. They generally know exactly what they want when they leave the house. Commercial transactions are personal in Vietnam, especially for such intimate things as what the family will eat. Nothing is too good for the Vietnamese housewife's family table, and she will buy her aliments from people she knows and trusts.

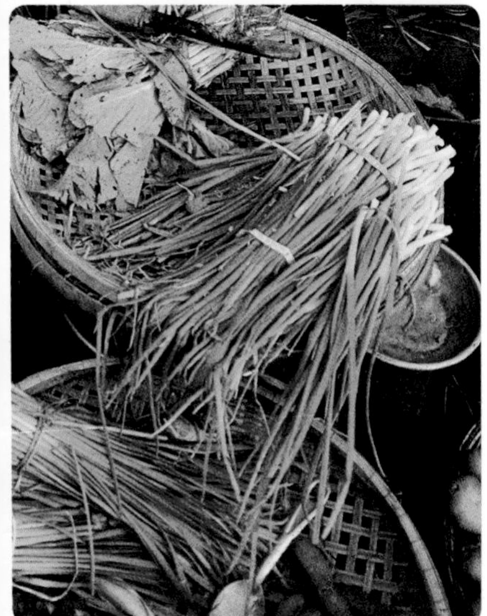

Greens at the Binh Tay Market.

Market vendors songs

One of the most delightful aspects of shopping in Vietnamese markets is the rich traditions surrounding the marketplace. There is the musical call of the *go mi*, the noodle knocker. But among the more traditional vendors there is a whole range of musical calls to buy. As you patrol the marketplace of Vietnam, listen for songs from the vendors, like this one from the female *che* vendor.

Che ... Ai An ... Bot ... Khoai ... bun tau dau ... xanh nuoc dua duong cat ong?

(Who will eat flour, potato, vermicelli, green beans, water, coconut sugar?)

Che is a sweet concoction made of green beans, lotus seeds, translucent noodles and vermicelli and Chinese cherries, cooked in a mixture of water and extract of coconut. A dish of sweet and warm *che thung* is a popular late night snack. You might not be hungry, but if the voice of the seller is lilting enough, you might change your mind. The *che* business admits no male vendor. All dealers are women.

PREPARATION

Tools and equipment

The Vietnamese cook uses lots of water, for everything must be kept clean, and boiling and steaming are common cooking methods. So the cook must have colanders or plastic mesh bowls, or simply bowls with holes to hold the washed herbs and vegetables. When turned upside-down, they are also used to protect fresh food from flies or accidents.

For cutting, the cook has an array of small, sharp vegetable knives and dangerous-looking choppers heavy enough to lop off the top of a coconut. No Vietnamese kitchen is without a mortar and pestle, which is used to grind together flavouring ingredients such as shallots, garlic, lemongrass, and chilli, as well as for making 'ground' meat and meat *pâtés*.

Traditional Vietnamese cooks generally squat on the floor while preparing much of their food. They work around the stove on a wet, tiled area, where all utensils, pots, pans and foods can be easily cleaned before and after each use.

One of the most important things in the kitchen, especially a country kitchen, is time. Vietnamese cooking is labour-

34481 / GETTY IMAGES

Serving up lunch for the family at home in Hanoi.

intensive and time-consuming. Washing baskets full of vegetables and herbs, washing dishes, pounding things in the mortar, and endless chopping and slicing, all without modern appliances, takes time.

One family member has to be on duty just to fan the flames to control the heat because most of the cooking is done over an open fire. The kitchen may not even have running water, so much of the preparation work is done outside, or at a table in a room otherwise used for sleeping or sewing.

Cooking methods

Besides boiling, deep-frying, stir-frying, and steaming, grilling over charcoal and simmering in caramel are usual Vietnamese kitchen craft.

In common with Chinese practice Vietnamese food is cut into bite-sized pieces before cooking. Meats are usually marinated in spices and *nuoc mam* for half an hour or more. Pre-seasoning in this way enhances the flavour of the food and helps to preserve the vitamins and protein in the meat while keeping it tender and juicy.

Before the Vietnamese cook puts anything other than rice on the fire, all ingredients must be ready for the pan and laid out within easy reach and in the order it will be needed. Dehydrated foods, such as dried mushrooms or cellophane noodles, have to be reconstituted well in advance of cooking. Generally speaking, the cook will spend more time at the cutting board than over the stove. Actual cooking time will be very short for most dishes.

DEFINING DISHES

Bun cha

Bun cha is grilled pork served on a bed of cold rice noodles and dressed with a few herbs. Deceptively simple. Like so much of Vietnamese cookery, you will know *bun cha* by its aroma, so

GREG ELMS / GETTY IMAGES

A delicious bowl of satisfying *pho*.

you will always be able to find it by just following your nose. The meat is always cut from a piece of well-marbled pork, and must be grilled with a pair of fresh bamboo tongs. It is marinated in a mixture of sweet, hot, sour and salty, and the resulting product tastes like none of its constituent flavours, yet more than the sum of its parts. But, like so much of the north, what gives Hanoi *bun cha* its characteristic taste and smell are the minty herbs that accompany it.

Pho

Pronounced 'fuh', this is beef noodle soup raised to the nth degree. It is Vietnam in a bowl.

A bowl of *pho* begins its Mayfly life the day before you eat it. A long, slow simmering of beef shinbones, oxtails and scraps of meat in a great deep pot brings into being a rich, clear consommé. This process alone takes about 24 hours if it is to be done right. The alchemist cooks add their herbs, their spices, their family secrets. Chief among them — and you will always know the aroma of *pho* by them — are star anise, ginger and cinnamon.

From a distance, its come-hither smell seduces and urges you to reach its source. Often it's just a little stand by the roadside, yet the aesthetics are observed.

The shopkeeper might hang a small bundle of onions wrapped in mint leaves from a string in front of the shop to scent the air. A votive offering sits on the counter, a few flowers in a corner.

The standing vendor deftly cuts rice sheets into noodles and slices meat into nearly translucent thinness. He immerses a sieve full of pre-cooked rice noodles into hot water for a moment, lifts them out, drains them with a shake, and pours them into your bowl.

Skilfully, with the eye of the florist, he arranges on top a bouquet of white onion slices, tiny yellow shavings of ginger, perhaps something green. And then, red raw beef, in slices about the size of the heel of your hand. Ladles of the simmering broth fill your bowl, its heat quickly penetrating the meat, cooking it to perfect tenderness in mere seconds.

From the garnish tray, add a squeeze of lime juice, a handful of beansprouts and a dash of chilli sauce and garlic sauce or fish sauce. Lastly, sprinkle with coriander leaves, or mint leaves, or basil. Or all of them.

DRINKS

Can

Can alcohol was long regarded as a country bumpkin's tipple. But lately, smart restaurants in Hanoi have been providing it for those who ask ahead. If you walk into a restaurant or home and see on the table what looks like a large flowerpot (*che*) holding only the wilted stems of giant flowers, it's a good bet there's a *can* party in the offing. If you look interested (or interesting) you may be handed a straw and invited to join the little suck-fest. And it is a very convivial way to drink, rather like two straws in a milkshake for a pair of lovers.

Most ethnic minorities in the central highlands make *can*, and use it for all kinds of celebrations, religious rituals, weddings, or simply for receiving guests. Its taste and alcohol content will vary, like moonshine anywhere, according to the maker and the season.

Coffee

What's this? Not a hefty mug of steaming coffee ready to drink, but a small glass tumbler with a curious little aluminium pot on top. At the bottom of your glass, half an inch of the palest yellow, sweetened condensed milk, three or four little brunette stains spreading across its surface. Another appears, fallen

ROMANA CHAPMAN / GETTY IMAGES

Vietnamese coffee: condensed milk with black coffee, served in a glass with metal filter and spoon.

Women picking tea in one of Vietnam's many plantations.

HAIPIANO NGUYEN / GETTY IMAGES

from the little top pot. Inside the pot the water is ever so lazily seeping into and through the dark-roasted coffee, ground so fine the people call it coffee powder. This is strong coffee, and your glass is still only half full. Savour each sweet sip.

Tea

The preparation, serving and drinking of tea has a social importance in Vietnam that is seldom appreciated by Western visitors. Serving tea in the home or office is more than a gesture of hospitality. Sharing tea is a ritual. It precedes the conduct of business, scholarly pursuits or meditation, meeting new people and getting acquainted. It's even a prelude to romance. Politicians and tycoons trying to ease tensions at the negotiating table will call for tea to be served, and all will halt until the rituals are performed, and calm restored.

Tea requires time. Time to prepare it, time to contemplate it, time to talk about it, time to savour it. And then time to think back upon it. It must have a good part of an afternoon, or an evening. It is to the average Vietnamese what the finest wines are to the Western connoisseur.

Gathering midnight dew

In Thai Binh Province tea is almost a cult. On moonlit nights, its devotees set out in boats on the lakes and ponds where the lotus flowers are in bloom, the air heavy with their pungent aroma. They open the about-to-bloom lotus flowers and place a pinch of tea inside each blossom, then close them with ribbon or string. Then they gather the moonlit dew from the lotus leaves. By dawn, the living scent of lotus permeates the tea, and the gatherers have enough dew to add to their teapots. After a few hours of sleep, a blissful afternoon of tea lies ahead.

The streets of Chinatown decorated with lanterns for Chinese New Year.

TOM COCKREM

Malaysia

There's no question about it. Malaysians are food-obsessed — even as they sit down at a laden dinner table they are drawn into discussing what they should have for supper. Often described as a chaos of races and languages, the colourful, multicultural traditions of the region offer the food lover a spectacular gastronomic experience like no other.

CULINARY CAPITALS PENANG, KUALA LUMPUR **KNOWN FOR** *LAKSA* **IMPORTS** DAIRY PRODUCTS, MEAT **EXPORTS** PALM OIL **DEVOUR** CHILLI CRAB **AVOID** SAGO GRUBS

Fragrant Malaysian coconut soup with tofu.

Packets of chilli sauce.

Young boy eating fried *bee hoon*.

CULTURE

Today's Malay food is the result of centuries of foreign interaction and influence, most notably from India and China. Malay culture arguably crystallised around Melaka's rise as a regional seaport and Islamic centre. The people of the coast developed a culinary style greatly influenced by visiting and, later, settling traders from Indonesia, India, the Middle East and China. Many of the basic spices and ingredients central to Malay cooking were first introduced by Indians and Arabs — including pepper, cloves and cardamom.

Rice is always the foundation of a Malay meal, and Malaysia produces its own rice. It may be steamed, boiled or fried, cooked on its own, or flavoured with coconut milk, spices and herbs. It can be *ketuput*, steamed in angular little pockets woven out of coconut fronds, or *lemang*, cooked over a charcoal fire in bamboo poles lined with young banana leaves. But whichever way rice is served, it is always customary to have it with a fish (or seafood) curry, a meat or poultry dish (or both), two or more vegetable dishes and a selection of *sambals* (chilli-based condiments).

REGIONS

Penang

Founded as an outpost of the East India Company in 1786, Penang grew to become a trading port between Bengal, Burma, the Dutch East Indies and treaty ports of China. By the next century, it was considered one of the finest islands in the world for nutmeg and cloves. The growth of the city's spice trade was accompanied by the arrival of immigrants: Malays from Kedah, Chinese from Canton, Achehnese from Sumatra, Indians from British India, Thais from across the border and Burmese. The food of Penang reflects the intermingling of these cultures and is a gastronomic highlight on any culinary tour of the area.

Penang specialties include:

- *Perut ikan* (fish stomach) — fish innards cooked in a coconut curry lightly scented with mint, presented on top of sliced beans and pineapple.
- *Char kway teow* — broad, flat rice-flour noodles stir fried with Chinese sausage and egg, topped with shrimp.
- *Nonya tok panjang* (nonya long table meal) — Peranakan festivities are celebrated at the table with an elaborate buffet-style spread. Jump in and experience one if you're lucky enough to chance upon an occasion.
- *Pong piah* — Hokkien speciality of flaky puff pastry filled with white molasses. Variations include *tau sar piah* (filled with red-bean paste) and *tambun piah* (filled with yellow-lentil paste).
- *Teh tarik* (pulled tea) — a deliciously rich, frothy and sweet tea that the coffee shops of Penang do so well.

Kuala Lumpur

Kuala Lumpur has grown from a tin-mining town into an affluent modern Asian capital. The city remains unrivalled in terms of the variety of food it offers — a melange that has been made possible by the confluence of its diverse population.

Kuala Lumpur's culinary strengths lie in the cuisines of the Malays, Chinese and Indians who dominate the population and the unique culinary inheritance that the British left behind. Savour *laksa Kedah* along one street, then tuck in to Penang-style *asam laksa* along another. Diversity also stretches to the style of dining available: you may choose to dress up and

AUN KOH

Man roasting chestnuts at his stall in the night market.

sample modern French creations with a Japanese twist one evening, and go absolutely casual the next when you eat, standing on the kerb by a satay stall on wheels.

The east coast

Compared to the more populated and industrialised west coast, the states of Kelantan and Terengganu have a far stronger sense of Malay culture, which is evident in their cuisine. This part of the peninsula was, for the most part, isolated from the rest of the country, and received few immigrants, so regional specialities remain staunchly Malay.

Both states thrive on fishing and their famous white beaches are dotted with fishing villages. In Terengganu, the locals enjoy the luxury of being able to savour seafood that's fresh from the fisherman's net and have created countless ways to prepare it, including:

- *Epok epok (*deep-fried pyramid-shaped pastries) here, are filled with fish fried with grated coconut
- *Satar*, not to be confused with satay, is a local delicacy consisting of fish, tamarind water, grated coconut, chilli, *belacan*, onion and sugar. The ingredients are blended, then wrapped in cones fashioned out of banana leaves and grilled.

Sabah

The people of Sabah (who hail from over 30 different ethnic groups) are fortunate to enjoy an abundant supply of seafood, river fish, deer, wild boar, game, wild plants, herbs and fruits from their forests.

Sabah has its own raw fish dish called *hinava* (fish marinated with lime juice and herbs). The Kadazans (Sabah's main tribal community) are famous for *hinava tongii*, a combination of fresh Spanish mackerel, chilli, ginger and shallots drenched in

AUN KOH

Char kway, or fried dough sticks.

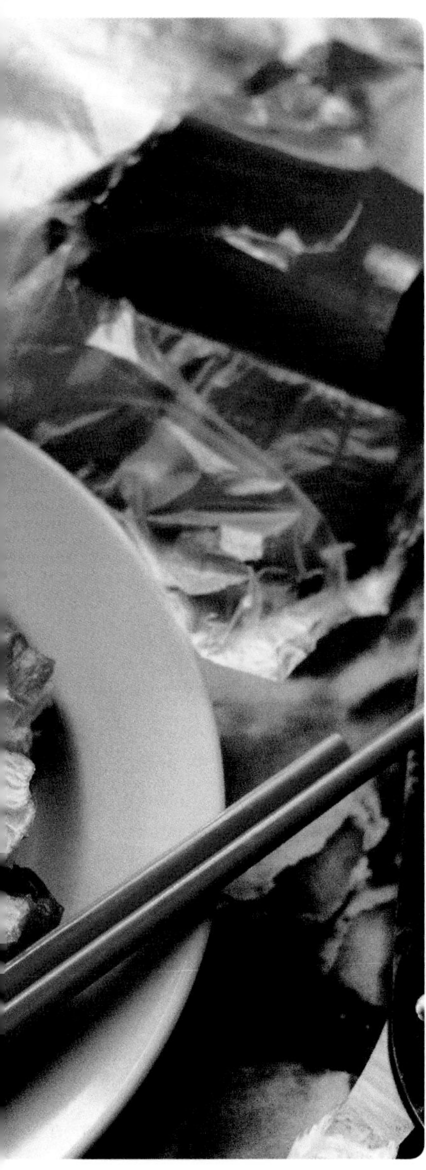

lime juice. Apparently the secret ingredient of this dish is the grated seed of the *bambangan*, a variety of mango only found in Sabah.

The Muslim Bisaya people, who live on the Klias Peninsula, make a gluey porridge with sago starch which they call *ambuyat*. The thick, sticky mixture is twirled around a chopstick and dipped into an accompanying sauce.

The Murut, who live in the hilly southwestern region of Sabah, are famous for their *jaruk*, chunks of raw wild boar or river fish packed into a bamboo tube together with salt and cooked rice. The bamboo is sealed with leaves and the contents left to ferment for several weeks or even months. It is finally eaten in small portions with rice or tapioca starch.

DAILY MEALS

Breakfast is usually bought from a roadside or hawker stall on the way to work and may consist of anything from a filling *nasi lema*k, soupy Chinese noodles, delicate *dosai* (paper-thin rice-and-lentil crêpes) or soft-boiled eggs and *roti kaya* (grilled bread with *kaya* — coconut egg jam), to a McDonald's Egg McMuffin.

By 10am, it's time for a snack — a curry puff perhaps (a deep-fried pyramid-shaped pastry), filled with a dry chicken and potato curry, and a quarter of a hard-boiled egg – and a *kopi* (local coffee sweetened with condensed milk), which helps tide over the insatiable Malaysian's need for a bite until lunchtime.

Lunch hour starts at around 12.30pm and rarely stretches over more than 90 minutes. At the numerous hawker areas dotted across urban centres, diners are focused on scoring themselves a clean table and seat. Eating is a functional (and often hot and sweaty) affair at this time of day. It is common for groups of friends and colleagues dining together to share the empty seats at their table with perfect strangers.

For busy couples and families, dinner is also often eaten at hawker stalls. Meals are more substantial, and diners tend to mix their cuisines, sometimes opting for an Indian salad, a Malay rice dish and a Chinese dessert.

Then, there's always supper. At 2am, a different world of hawker stalls serves up barbecued chicken wings, peppery pork rib soups and greasy or *luah* (oyster omelettes) to hungry night owls.

ETIQUETTE

There are no complex cutlery sets to pick your way through, and no slew of wine glasses to leave you guessing which you should drink from next. Most homes and restaurants, except the most traditional, will provide you with a fork and spoon, although few provide knives (most local foods don't require much cutting action). If your host doesn't use chopsticks or eat with his or her fingers, don't ask to do so. A fork and spoon are used all the time, not just in the presence of foreign guests.

SHOPPING

At the market

Markets play a big part in the everyday life of Malaysians. The cook of the family sets off early (around 6am) to the market armed with baskets, bags and shopping trolleys to get the best bargains and freshest produce. The market is also a meeting place, where haggling over the freshest produce becomes a social occasion. A typical market is a one-stop shop sectioned by the kinds of meat, produce and sundries sold. Lining the perimeter of most markets are shops that sell clothes, shoes and other daily necessities like brooms, mops, pails, clothes pegs, pots, pans, cutlery and crockery. Following the general rule of thumb in Malaysia, where there is human traffic, there

Malay woman cooking.

Sticky rice dumplings wrapped in leaves.

Tray of colourful breakfast *dim sum*.

Dried fish for sale at a market stall.

AUN KOH

are hawkers and food, so never far away from any market will be a hawker centre or coffee shop.

Night markets

The *pasar malam* is an open-air market which literally spills out onto the pavements at night and tempts you with the sheer variety of goods on sale. The highlight of the night market is always the food. You'll find an abundance of finger foods like grilled chicken wings, skewered fishballs, roasted chestnuts and *char dan* (braised eggs in tea), as well as desserts and sweets like *chendol* (cold coconut-milk dessert), and Malay and Peranakan *kueh-kueh* (tea cakes). Some night markets also host their own entertainment with singers crooning hits in Malay, Mandarin, Cantonese and English.

Wet markets

Wet markets are so named for their concrete floors that are washed down to clear away dirt and waste, leaving a slopping layer of water lingering on the thin aisles that separate the small stalls. Many stall keepers are decked out in gumboots or galoshes (almost always black or bright yellow), while some opt for wooden clogs.

Wet markets are usually divided into distinct sections. Fruit stalls will be located at one end, loaded with stacks of bananas, furry red rambutans, sweet-smelling pineapples, mangoes, apples, oranges and all manner of other tropical fruit. In the vegetable section, you'll find every possible variation from local spinach and *daun kari* (curry leaves) to watercress and cabbage. Another common sight in the vegetable section is a lady sifting through a pile of bean sprouts removing their dirt and 'tails'.

Not far from the vegetable section will be stalls selling freshly made noodles. These stalls also stock wonton wraps and soybean products like *silken tofu*, as well as all sorts of soy sauces and soybeans in their preserved forms. Nearby, eggs — fresh or preserved — can be bought from stalls that sell them individually or by the carton. Eggs covered in black soot are *ham dan/kiam neng* (salted eggs, usually duck), and those in flecks of dark brown sawdust are *pei dan* (century eggs).

The wettest part of the wet market is where the meat and fish are sold. If you're squeamish about raw meat and blood, you should avoid this section where great slabs of meat are hung from hooks and the occasional pig's head or a pail full of entrails share space with the butchers and their hefty meat cleavers. At the fish section, you'll find an extensive selection of the night's fresh catch. Piles of *sotong* (squid), *kupang* (mussels) and *udang* (prawns) of all sizes are readily available.

PREPARATION

Home cooking

Food is utterly central to home life in Malaysia. Rather than stick religiously to recipes, your typical home cook will be more than ready to try out her neighbour's special version, all in the name of improvement (if she can get her hands on it, that is). Whether this readiness to adapt can be traced to the migrant mindset, or wanting to add variety to the traditionally cloistered lives of female home cooks is open to debate. What's for certain is the institution of *agak* (Malay for 'estimation').

Cooking is a craft that has always been passed on from generation to generation, from mother to daughter. A familial legacy, recipes were not so much instructions set in stone as the passing down of techniques gleaned from observation. Measurements such as grams, tablespoons and cups were meaningless — learning what a small handful of this, or a generous pinch of that, could constitute helped you learn how to pick out the best from the butcher and vegetable seller, or

AUN KOH

Rambutans on display at the local market.

how to harvest the nicest leaves from the *daun kesum* (laksa leaf) plant in the backyard. You could only gauge how much you needed for your *rempah* (spice paste) when you knew the size and freshness of your lemongrass and chillies.

Seasoning the wok

A *kuali,* or wok, is an essential piece of equipment in most homes. While many latter-day variants fashioned from aluminium or stainless steel are readily available, serious cooks still insist on good old-fashioned cast iron.

A brand new cast-iron wok (available from any Chinatown) needs to be seasoned before use. To season the Malaysian way, first fry freshly grated coconut in the un-greased wok until the pulp is toasted and dry. The coconut is then discarded and the wok is rinsed. Next, the inner surface of the wok is rubbed all over with the cut side of an onion. The onion is then taken out, bruised, and fried in a few tablespoons of vegetable oil. The onion is discarded and the wok is rinsed. The wok is now ready for use — the more frequently you use the wok, the more seasoned the inner surface becomes, and the more 'nonstick' it gets. To clean after use, the wok is simply rinsed with water.

ESSENTIAL PRODUCE

Malaysian pantries are a mixed bags of tricks filled with spices, herbs, grains, sauces and many other ingredients from a host of cuisines, each continually borrowing from the other. Rather than attempt to redraw those lines, local chefs celebrate in the blurring of boundaries, creating distinctive local dishes that play with the rich food choices open to them.

Butterfly or blue pea flower

Bunga telang is a tiny, deep blue (almost violet) flower which provides the natural blue colouring for many Malay, Peranakan

Soy sauce brewing by the bucketload.

AUN KOH

and Eurasian desserts and rice dishes. It give the Kelantan speciality, *nasi kerabu* (cooked rice tossed with finely shredded herbs) its bluish hue. A handful of flowers are boiled in water and then squeezed. The water is strained and the resulting liquid is used.

Chicken

Apart from fish, *ayam* (chicken) is the most frequently consumed flesh in the region. And you can be assured that every bit of the chicken is used. The feet are marinated and served steam as a *dian xin* (dim sum) delicacy or boiled, de-boned and served cold at chicken rice restaurants as an appetiser.

Chilli sauce

There are as many kinds of *sambal* (basically a chilli sauce or relish) as there are cooks in Malaysia.

- At its most simple, the *sambal ulek/olek* is a combination of chilli, vinegar and salt blended either with a mortar and pestle, or in a food processor.
- The basic chilli paste can be served on the side with a squirt of lime or *kalamansi* (a sour lime juice) as a condiment that will add a kick to your meal.
- It's served with anything from fried Hokkien noodles and *laksa* (a spicy, soupy noodle dish), to *nasi lemak* (coconut rice with fried fish) and barbecued chicken wings.
- It can also be incorporated into curries and other spicy local dishes including barbecued fish and fried eggplant.
- By adding shallots, galangal, garlic, *belacan* (fermented shrimp paste), tamarind liquid and other ingredients at hand, different kinds of *sambal* are created, all with the essential spicy punch at their core.

Fish

Once dotted with fishing villages, today the fishing industry continues to thrive on the east coast of Malaysia. While the old days of buying live *ikan* (fish) right out of the fisherman's *sampan* (boat) are long gone in most parts of Malaysia, the variety of fresh fish available continues to be mind-boggling.

- Depending on which regional variation of *laksa* you're eating, you could be tucking into *ikan parang* (wolf herring), *tenggiri* (mackerel) or *udang* (prawns).
- *Tenggiri batang* (Spanish mackerel) is fashioned into *ikan otak otak,* spiced rectangles wrapped in banana leaves and grilled over a charcoal fire.
- *Bawal puteh* (plump silver pomfret) is delicately steamed with pickled sour plums, salted vegetable and tomato wedges, Teochew style.
- Over at the *ikan bakar* (grilled fish) stall, *pari nyiru* (grilled stingray) is the hot seller.

Malays generally prefer their fish fried whole and stuffed with spices or chopped into chunks or steaks and served in a spicy *asam* (tamarind) sauce. Chinese prefer to cook larger fish such as sea bass, grouper and snapper either steamed (this is preferred when the fish is extremely fresh), fried or braised.

Indonesian black nut

Originally from Brazil, *buah keluak* is a black, hard-shelled nut grown extensively in Indonesia. The black oily kernel has a slightly bitter taste, reminiscent of olive tapenade (without the salt) when it is cooked. The nuts need to be soaked overnight and cracked before they are cooked. Preparation is highly labour-intensive. It is loved among Peranakans and forms the focus of typical Peranakan dishes such as *ayam buah keluak* (a mildly spicy, sour chicken dish).

Rack of sauce bottles.

Basket of limes.

Fish hanging out to dry.

Ketchup

You'd be amazed at the amount of ketchup that's used by everyone in Malaysia. It appears in dishes as disparate as Hainanese pork chops (as part of the sweet-and-sour sauce), Singapore chilli crab, Indian *mee goreng* (a spicy fried noodle dish), *wonton mee* (wonton noodle soup) and *nasi tomato* (tomato-flavoured rice served with a variety of dishes). Ketchup is not to be confused with *kicap manis*, which is a thick, sweet soy sauce (sweetened with palm sugar) used in many Indonesian-influenced dishes.

Noodles

China originally introduced noodles to the rest of Asia. The noodles used in Malaysia and are made from wheat, wheat and egg, rice, or mung beans, and take myriad forms.

Instant noodles

The variety of *quai su mian (*instant noodles) available in Malaysia is astounding. You will find both wheat-flour and rice-flour varieties at most supermarkets, with flavours created to appeal to local palates. But the wackiest hawker dish around must be *Maggie mee goreng* — instant noodles (Maggie seems to be the preferred brand), softened in boiling water before being fried just like Indian *mee goreng* and topped with an egg fried sunny-side-up. You'll find this dish at Indian stalls at supper time. It's become so popular that there are even instant noodles packaged with *mee goreng* flavour sachets!

Rice

Nasi (rice) is an essential element in most meals eaten among all communities in Malaysia. Be it a simple, plain bowl of steamed rice served as an accompaniment to a spread of Malay, Chinese, Indian, Peranakan or Eurasian delights; rice

AUN KOH

Rice for *nasi lemak* in banana leaves.

steamed and then fried with other ingredients (as in the case of Malay *nasi goreng* or Chinese fried rice); grains boiled into sweet or savoury porridge; or glutinous varieties steamed and moulded into tubes or cubes, rice is invariably a major feature of local menus.

Spice paste

Rempah (spice paste) is a mix of spices created by pounding a combination of wet and dry ingredients together to form a paste. The spice mix constantly changes depending on the dish being made. Wet ingredients include shallots, lemongrass, garlic, chilli, ginger and galangal. Dry ingredients consist of items such as candlenuts, cinnamon, coriander seeds, cumin, cloves and peppercorns.

The *rempah* is considered the heart and soul of Malay, Eurasian and Peranakan curries and sauces. It thickens curry gravies and gives dimension to their flavour. Beyond pounding it into a paste, the other important technique lies in frying the *rempah*. A significant amount of oil is needed to fry it until it is fragrant, and the oil has to be hot enough before the *rempah* is added to the pan. It must be constantly stirred to prevent it from sticking to the pan. Once the oil starts to seep out of the *rempah*, the other ingredients in the recipe can be added.

Shrimps and shrimp paste

Geragau, the tiny shrimp found in the seas off the Straits of Melaka and in the waters of Penang, are used to make *cincaluk* (fermented shrimps) and *belacan* (fermented shrimp paste). *Cincaluk* — which is extremely salty — is incorporated into a *sambal*. *Belacan* is usually ground into a *rempah* (spice paste) as a flavouring in curries and other dishes.

To witness *belacan* being made is a sight to behold and a smell to be inhaled only if you have a strong stomach. The shrimp is caught at night, rinsed in sea water and mixed with salt before it is left to stand overnight. In the morning, it is spread out to dry in the sun before being put through a crushing machine.

It is then stored in wooden vats for a week before it is once again laid out to dry and put through the machine. It takes some weeks before the process is complete. The paste is finally put through a machine that shapes it into blocks that are then wrapped in a layer of tracing paper and another of brown paper. The good stuff smells of sea salt and fresh shrimp (though it does take some getting used to), while lower-grade *belacan* smells like rotting fish.

Sambal belacan.

DEFINING DISHES

Laksa

Laksa is ubiquitous in Malaysia. It's hard to walk the length of a block without being offered it. Even harder is trying to ascertain just which one to have, as every hawker seems to profess to serving the 'real' *laksa*. Hot gravy (the stock or broth), aroma, well-chosen and cooked noodles, and a crunchy and herbaceous garnish are the foundation to any decent *laksa*.

- *Sarawak laksa* — Kuching's breakfast of choice has a burnt-sienna-coloured base, its hue provided by toasted rice and coconut.
- *Asam laksa* — Very much a benchmark, this sour *laksa* strain is both loved and hated for its hefty use of tamarind that comes in moist blocks.
- *Laksa Kedah* — From the Malaysian state of the same name, this thick *laksa* uses tamarind in dried slices and has a purple appearance.

Stink beans hanging up at the market.

Young girl drying shrimp crackers.

Bowl of *laksa*.

Dried fish at a restaurant.

Man holding a plate of preserved fruits.

- *Laksa lemak* — Also known as 'curry *laksa*', this is mostly found in Kuala Lumpur and is frowned upon by some purists as 'not a *laksa*'. It lives up to its name with a generous dosing of coconut milk and curried chicken.
- *Ipoh curry laksa* — The old town of Ipoh on the west coast of Malaysia serves a curry *laksa* with bicultural tweaks that are unforgettable. Firstly the addition of Chinese barbecued roast pork, and secondly a stock made with curry leaves.
- *Laksa Johor* — Believe it or not, this is an even richer version of *laksa lemak*. It is hugely complex, with flavours of cumin, coriander seeds and turmeric, and is coconut-milk lush, with a roasted note of dry-fried shredded coconut meat. The boldest inclusion may be the use of spaghetti.

Nasi lemak

Nasi lemak is a common Malay breakfast dish, which, in its original form, consists of lightly salted rice cooked with coconut milk, topped with *sambal ikan bilis* (dried anchovies fried and mixed with a spicy *sambal* — a chilli-based condiment) and a few slices of cucumber, all wrapped up in a banana leaf. You'll find these neat little packages for sale at makeshift stalls near bus interchanges and busy thoroughfares, in coffee shops and along the streets. Long queues at the best *nasi lemak* stalls stand as testament to the popularity of this Malaysian staple.

Air Bandung. Possibly the most eye-catching drink available, this milky pink thirst quencher is made from a combination of rose syrup (a commercial product consisting of rose essence, sugar syrup and pink colouring) and evaporated or condensed milk. It makes a great accompaniment to Malay food. You should only drink this cold.

Factory workers grinding coffee in a river-powered pounder.

JERRY ALEXANDER

Indonesia

Cuisine in Indonesia is not something restricted to the kitchen. It is not tied up in rules and cooking schools. It is not the sole realm of chefs and connoisseurs. It is neither dusty nor dated. Rather, it is alive, flexible and approachable, symbolising a culture driven by interaction. You'll find the culinary life here in public places: at temples, down side streets and at markets, where food is sized up, sampled and savoured.

CULINARY CAPITALS BALI, MAKASSAR **KNOWN FOR** *GADO GADO, NASI GORENG* **IMPORTS** CLOVES **EXPORTS** PEANUT SAUCE **DEVOUR** *BEEF RENDANG* **AVOID** ROASTED DRAGONFLIES, CHICKEN CLAW

Spices, including nutmeg, tumeric, chilli, cinnamon, cloves, star anise and cumin.

A young boy from Jimbaran holds up his catch.

Urab, salad.

CULTURE

Indonesia's cuisine reflects the country's diversity. Just look at a map; here are 13,677 islands, home to at least 200 million people including 300 ethnic groups, countless cooks and a surplus of audacious stomachs. Difference is intrinsic to Indonesia's identity; the nation's slogan is 'unity in diversity' and the face of its cuisine changes depending on who you dine with and on which island.

Geography

Straddling the equator for 5000 kilometres, the islands of Indonesia promise an edible adventure. Geography has had a great bearing on the diets of the archipelago. This is a living landscape; floods and active volcanoes regularly tear up the earth and as a result, much of the land is very fertile. Cassava grows wild on the slopes of Java's Mount Merapi, papaya trees sprout like weeds on Sumatra. And then there are the surrounding seas and inland rivers with fish, fish and more fish. But there is also terrain not so characteristically Indonesian: the highlands of Irian Jaya that support little more than patches of sweet potato; the dry, craggy hills of Nusa Tenggara where corn is the staple; and the chilly, European-style gardens of Brastagi where carrots are cultivated.

Food swap

For better or worse, Indonesia has always been a centre of trade. In the name of commerce there have been kingdoms built, battles waged and cities destroyed. But underpinning the dealings has been a free exchange of foods and culinary practices. Rice, corn, curries and pineapples are just a few of the ingredients that first came here aboard trading vessels.

Indonesian cuisine is really one big food swap. Colonists, traders – even Australian Aborigines, have all influenced the inventory of ingredients and culinary practices appearing at the Indonesian table.

Merchants from Arabia, Persia and India brought goods to the coastal cities in exchange for goods from China and for local products, such as spices. Indonesia's *gulai* (coconut curry; also known as *kare)* owes its roots to Arab and Indian traders. The local curry may be different from its subcontinental counterpart, but the spices are all Indian originals: cardamom, coriander, cumin, ginger, onions, garlic. The *martabak* (crispy-skin omelette) is a *roti (*Indian flat bread) relation that can also claim Indian and Arabian heritage; the dessert version is like a pancake on steroids.

Chinese influence

Indonesia's strategic position on the sea lanes between India and China meant that trade between these two main Asian civilisations was firmly established here by the 1st century AD. The influence has been profound. China gave Indonesia many staple products, such as rice, soy beans, noodles and its national drink: tea. And it didn't stop with Chinese ingredients. China also gave Indonesia the wok and stir frying, now so integral to the cuisine. Imagine Indonesia with no stir fry, no *nasi goreng* (fried rice): it just wouldn't be the same.

REGIONS

A wonderful thing about Indonesia's regional cooking is that often you don't have to travel to a location to try its speciality. Indonesians have migrated extensively throughout their own country, thus introducing home flavours to a wider audience.

You could be wandering the laneways of Denpasar and find a *warung* (local cafe or street stall) selling *Acehnese gulai itik* (duck in coconut curry) or you might be lost in Jakarta when you smell the aroma of *sate Madura* (skewered meat cooked

JERRY ALEXANDER

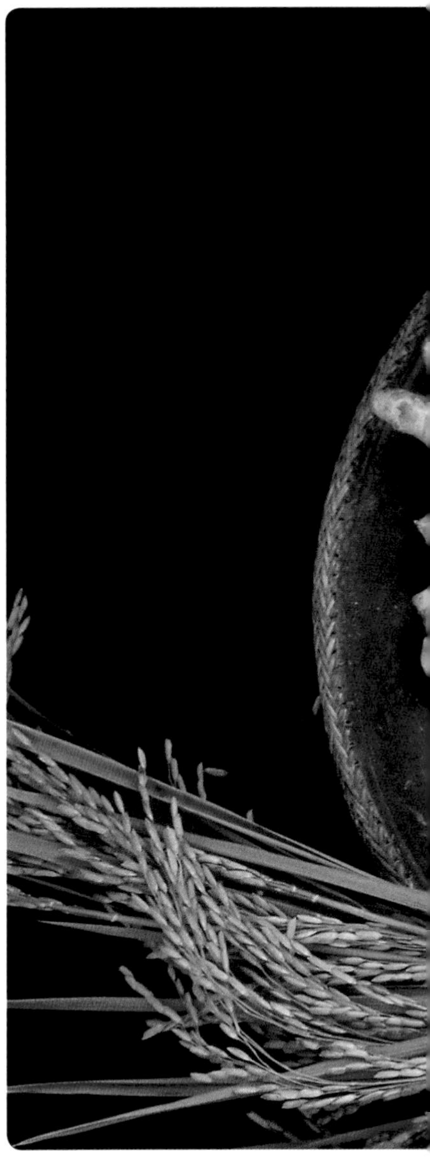

A selection of produce, including raw rice, shallots, tomatoes, garlic, ginger, onions and chillies.

Madura-style) wafting from the cart of a *kaki-lima* (roving vendor). And it's usually easy to identify the origin of a dish or cuisine by its name, as in *tahu Sumedang* (Sumedang-style tofu); *soto Lamongan* (Lamongan soup) and *pempek Palembang* (Palembang fish and sago dumplings).

Bali

The grandest Balinese dish is *babi guling* (spit-roast pig), which is stuffed with chilli, turmeric, garlic and ginger, and the skin is also smothered in turmeric. This is a long and laborious dish made for special occasions, however there are restaurants that make one *babi guling* and serve it throughout the day. Gianyar is famous for its *babi guling*, as is Ubud's Ibu Oka. And wherever you find pig in Bali (which is pretty well everywhere) you'll also find *oret* (sausage) made with offal, blood and coconut.

As well as rice, Bali's rice fields provide locals with eels and frogs. Dragonflies are another rice field-dweller up for grabs — they're caught with sticky sticks and then roasted.

The Balinese make a wide range of rice-flour snacks, including *lak lak* (a small pancake with palm sugar and coconut) and *alam* (rice flour, sugar and pandan leaf cooked in a banana leaf cylinder).

FEASTS

Whether for a marriage, business launch or just for visiting friends, food — lots of it — is an essential part of any Indonesian celebration.

A meal featuring a lot of food for many people is called a *selamatan*. Such a meal can include any combination and variety of dishes, but for special occasions a *tumpeng* will be the centrepiece. This is a pyramid of yellow rice, the tip of which is ceremonially cut off and offered to the eldest present.

Meat is always served at celebrations, often a speciality such

JERRY ALEXANDER

Yellow rice *tumpeng*, a centrepiece for celebrations.

as Sumatran *rendang* (beef or buffalo coconut curry) or Balinese *babi guling* (spit-roast pig).

ETIQUETTE

Indonesia isn't a nation of chopstickers; this is a *garpu* (fork) and *sendok* (spoon) country. Many prefer eating rice *au naturale*; it is cooked to be sticky enough to hold together, perfect for scooping in your right hand along with some of the other dishes.

Use your right hand for eating, passing things, anything — the left hand is for 'other duties'. If you're *kidal* (left handed), too bad, get used to it.

Indonesians like to use toothpicks after a meal. To tooth-pick Indonesian style, cover your mouth with your left hand and get digging with the other.

DAILY MEALS

With a population of over 200 million, you'd certainly expect a little variety in the way people fuel up during the day. One generalisation we can make is that *sarapan* (breakfast) is early – around sunrise. This is a nation of early birds, which makes sense since the morning is the coolest, freshest time of day; the best time for tending fields and walking to market or to school. But the breakfast meal varies with location, income and taste.

In the morning, cooks usually prepare a load of plain rice and three or four dishes as well as a *sambal* (chilli sauce or relish), and leave them covered on the dining table for *makan siang* (lunch), *makan malam* (dinner) or any time that hunger strikes. The cook is then free for the rest of the day and kids coming home from school can help themselves rather than wait for food to be prepared. The dishes on the table constitute the entire meal — Indonesian meals aren't served in courses, or stages.

This is a country well geared to eating out of the home; many Indonesians do just that for at least one meal of the day. A Balinese banker working in Jakarta may lunch on *nasi goreng* at her favourite *warung* (local cafe or street stall), a busker could spend his takings on a refreshing *es jeruk* (citrus juice) from a *kaki-lima* and a group of university students may break from their studies with a meal of *bubur kacang hijau* (mung-bean porridge) at the night market.

ESSENTIAL PRODUCE

Chicken

Thin, fast and loud, the average *ayam* (chicken) is an integral part of Indonesia's culinary landscape. An Indonesian village isn't a village without at least a couple pecking their way through scraps, clucking at dawn and being chased by toddlers.

To visitors' eyes, Indonesia's chickens are a tad on the scrawny side, often with a patchy plumage due to territorial disputes, and essentially don't look fit to eat. But remember this is real *ayam kampung* (village chicken), untouched by hormones and battery cages. And the proof of this is in the taste. These chickens may be skinny, but once you bite into a meal of *ayam bakar* (grilled chicken), *opor ayam* (chicken in pepper and coconut curry; or *sate ayam* (chicken sate), made with *ayam kampung*, you'll realise bigger isn't better.

One thing that may put you off your chook is the popularity of *cakar ayam* (chicken claw), which, unfortunately, is the tastiest part. We have seen adorable small children, slung on their mother's hip in a *selendang* (sling-like scarf), with a chicken claw protruding from their faces. If you see the word *cakar* on any menu item, prepare to meet the claw.

Nasi goreng with an egg on the side.

Katupat, boiled rice wrapped in coconut fronds.

Woman with chickens for sale at the market.

Cakar ayam, chicken feet, ready for delivery.

JERRY ALEXANDER

Chilli sauce

The Mexicans have salsa, the Indians chutney, but here the essential condiment is the chilli sauce called *sambal*. A table set without at least one bottle of it, at best a freshly crushed version, isn't set properly. *Sambals* come in many varieties but the base for any *sambal* is chillies, garlic, shallots and salt.

Crackers

Emping, *kerupuk* and *intip* are all crackers and Indonesia's favourite snack. Resembling lumpy chips, *emping* are made from the seeds of melinjo tree fruit, which turn an iridescent red when ripe. To make *emping*, the seeds are roasted, opened and the kernels are flattened. These are then dried and fried in oil. Packets of *emping*, either plain or coated with a sweet chilli sauce, can be bought at any supermarket or grocery.

Larger deep-fried treats such as *kerupuk* (prawn crackers) and *intip* (rice crackers) are often served as an accompaniment to *nasi goreng* or *gado-gado*. In many restaurants you'll see glass-fronted containers filled with these squiggly shaped crackers. On the containers will be written profound words such as *subur* (fertile) and *fajar* (wisdom). Many people make their own *intip* with leftover rice: you'll are likely to see stacks of these crackers drying on roofs and in front of houses.

Fish

Indonesia is surrounded by water — swimming in it. There's the Java Sea, the Makassar Strait, the Banda Sea. So much water. And so many *ikan* (fish): tuna, shark, snapper, mackerel, perch, sardines, anchovies — just to name a few.

This is the dietary constant across the archipelago. From Sabang to Merauke, there'll be *ikan* to fry, and dry, and grill. Even inland there's fish to be found. The rivers, streams, flooded rice fields and lakes play home to carp, tilapia and catfish. Being cheaper and more widely available than meat, fish is the protein hit of the population.

So what to do with all these fine finned creatures?

The most popular fishy dish is *ikan bakar* (char-grilled fish), grilled straight over the charcoal or wrapped in banana leaves.

Pepes ikan (spiced fish cooked in banana leaves) can be found all over Indonesia, the type of fish and spices depending on the region; the only constant is the banana leaf in which it is baked, giving the fish a smoky aroma.

Most often fish is cooked with no more than lime and salt and served with a fresh *sambal*.

Mango

If there is a heaven on earth it is within the skin of a *mangga* (an Indonesian mango). This sweet yet not too sweet, refreshing, gloriously sticky fruit is a native of Southeast Asia, and nowhere will you find more delectable varieties. Perhaps it's coincidental, but it makes sense that the word *mangga* also means 'you're welcome' in West Java. You'll see the welcome sight of mangoes for sale at markets, mixed into *es mangga* (mango shake) and, while still young and tart, cut into *rujak* (fruit served with a spicy sauce).

Noodles

Like rice, *mie* (noodles) came down through Southeast Asia from China and are now an essential part of the Indonesian culinary lexicon. Rice noodles, wheat noodles and egg noodles are all found here, and any may be used in the night market staple, *mie goreng* (fried noodles).

Peanuts

As far as nuts go, you can't go past *kacang tanah* (peanuts), which are the most popular nut. They:

JERRY ALEXANDER

Tropical mangosteens from Ubud.

JERRY ALEXANDER

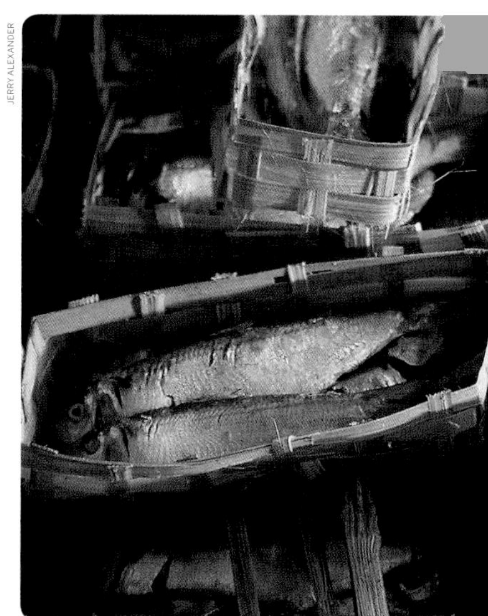

Salted fish in bamboo baskets.

- are eaten plain as a snack
- are ground and made into satay sauce
- are made into *rempeyek* (peanuts cooked within rice-flour crackers), and sweetened with palm sugar
- feature in the textural sensation, *ikan bilis goreng kacang* (fried peanuts and anchovies)
- headline in *saus kacang* (peanut sauce), which is used as a condiment, dip, or as the flavour for a main meal
- are most famous for their appearance in *gado-gado* (vegetable salad with peanut sauce).

Rice

Wherever you turn in Indonesia, rice is there shaping the landscape, growing in fields, sold at markets, hidden in sweets and piled on your plate. And as this staple is so adaptable, there's no fear of tiring of it.

A food as important as 'rice' is powerfully symbolic. Just as Tibetans have dozens of words for yak, Indonesians have many versions of our one word, rice.

In its natural state, prior to the milling that removes its husk, rice is *padi*. This word has become the English term for a rice field: paddy. But a rice paddy in Indonesian is *sawah*, at least in its flooded state; a dry rice field is *ladang*. To Indonesians, rice is *padi* only while it's in the field. Once harvested but not yet husked and milled, the rice becomes *gabah*. After it's milled but still not cooked, it's *beras*. Cooked rice is *nasi*, as in the famed Indonesian dish, *nasi goreng*.

Snakeskin fruit

As the name suggests, the skin of the *salak* resembles that of a snake. Once peeled the taste of the flesh is cooling and crisp and has a texture almost like a peeled almond. *Salak* flesh can

Fried chicken, rice and *sambal*.

Peanuts for sale at the Bedugal market.

A colourful selection of water apple and star fruit.

leave your mouth feeling dry, but this can be avoided by peeling the thin opaque skin off the interior flesh. At the centre of the fruit is a beautifully smooth seed about the size of a date.

Soy beans

Vegans rejoice. The protein-rich *kedelai* (soy bean), introduced from China, is an essential element in the Indonesian kitchen. In fact it was Indonesians who invented *tempe*, the soy bean product now eaten across the globe. To make *tempe*, the beans are washed, soaked until their skins fall off, halved, then boiled. Once drained they are sprinkled with a yeast starter, then wrapped in tubes of either banana leaf or perforated plastic. The starter grows rapidly around the beans, breaking down the properties indigestible to humans and, in two days, creating a vitamin-packed and protein-rich foodstuff.

Soy sauce

Every restaurant in the country provides their diners with a bottle of kecap, a soy sauce made from soy beans fermented in brine. Most provide two:

- *kecap asin* (salty soy sauce), which is the same as soy sauce found throughout the world; and
- *kecap manis* (sweet soy sauce), which is thicker and sweeter.

Beware that some varieties of *kecap manis* are too treacly and overpowering, but the most popular brand, ABC, produces a *kecap manis* with the perfect sweetness.

SHOPPING

At the market

The *pasar* (market) is the nucleus of Indonesia. It's where every farmer's journey ends and where every meal begins. Yes,

Indonesia's supermarkets and general stores stock many essentials, but for the serious shopper nothing can replace the fresh local produce and vibrant atmosphere of any market across the nation. In larger towns, markets are open every day (sometimes 24 hours), but smaller places will have a market day.

And if the market is too far, it comes to you. Every morning vendors wheel their carts around residential streets selling a wide range of produce, from tomatoes to *tempe*.

Supermarkets

At first glance Indonesia's supermarkets don't look like much of a cultural experience. The fluoro lights and Kenny G tunes seem more suburbia than Southeast Asia. But look a little closer at what's on the shelves. Are you in need of some durian-flavoured sweets? Have you run out of coconut jam perhaps? Or are you just craving dried fish? It's all here, as well as more familiar products you may be missing, such as cheese and chocolate.

On the streets

On the streets of Indonesia you'll also find specialist shops and stalls selling, for example, only fruit and vegetables, or perhaps just crackers. Most towns have a *toko roti* (bakery) and, although bread products aren't classically Indonesian, you will find local variations: a cheese and chocolate roll, or durian-flavoured cream cakes. Then there's the street-corner *kios* (kiosk) barely bigger than a phone booth yet stocking an incredible range of necessities. Whether you need batteries, beer or biscuits, the kiosk will provide.

PREPARATION

Traditional utensils

The real proof of the authentic Indonesian kitchen is its *cobek* and *ulek-ulek*. We could call these a mortar and pestle, but the

JERRY ALEXANDER

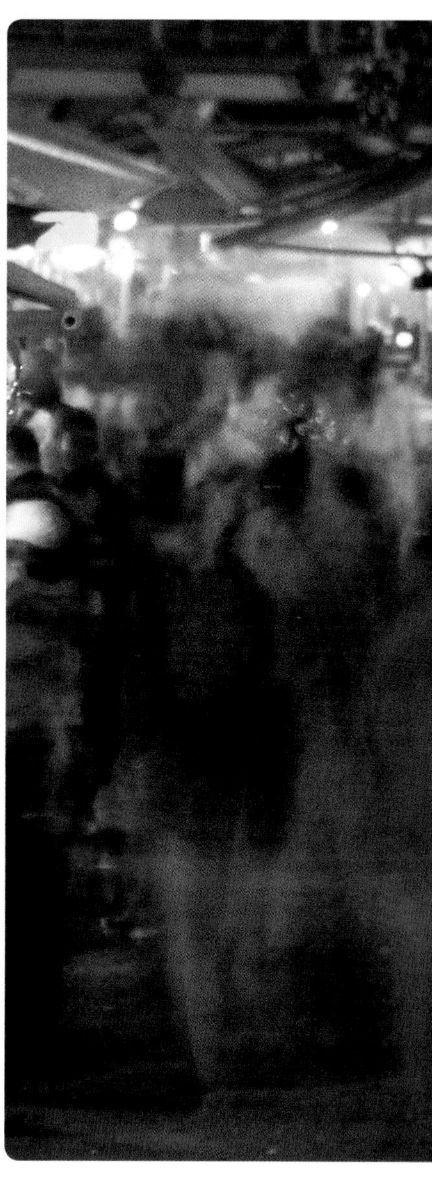

People shopping and eating at the night market.

Indonesian version is different to most. The *ulek-ulek* is shaped like an upended fat cigar and is used to push ingredients along the *cobek*, a shallow circular grinding stone. Both are made from heavy volcanic rock.

To see how a *cobek* and *ulek-ulek* should be used, look over the shoulders of vendors selling *rujak* (fruit served with a sour, spicy sauce of peanuts, sugar and chilli); they are the fastest grinders in the archipelago.

A 'natural' addition to the Indonesian kitchen is the *daun pisang* (banana leaf). Banana leaves are used to wrap food for steaming or grilling; also for wrapping soy beans and yeast to make *tempe*. What's more, the leaves can be used to wrap a packed lunch, and even as a plate.

Ways of cooking

A quick lesson in some popular cooking terms will help you to pick the street stall selling *ayam bakar* (grilled chicken) from the one selling *ayam goreng* (fried chicken) and the one selling ... you get the idea. Match the main ingredient with the cooking technique and you have yourself a meal.

- *bakar* (chargrilled)
- *gulai* (coconut milk curry; also known as *kare*)
- *goreng* (fried)
- *pepes* (steamed or roasted in banana leaves); also *pais*
- *panggang* (roasted)
- *sate* (chargrilled on skewers and served with peanut sauce)
- *asam manis* ('sour sweet'; served in a sweet and sour sauce)
- *soto* (soup); also *sop*

JERRY ALEXANDER

Fresh produce at the Sunday morning market.

DEFINING DISHES

Bakso

Bakso is the national comfort food. A homesick Indonesian wouldn't crave *gado gado*; they'd crave a steaming bowl of *bakso*, perhaps with noodles, perhaps a few beansprouts.

Whatever else ends up in the bowl depends on the *bakso* seller. Some add fried shallots, some deep-fried *pangsit* (wonton). Some add *cakar ayam* (chicken feet), just look for the word *cakar* on the signage. Every Indonesian has their favourite *bakso* seller, the one who makes 'the best bakso in Solo/ Sumbawa/Indonesia...' *Bakso* has stirred people to write songs, such is its simple beauty.

Beef rendang

As far as beefy meals are concerned, don't go past the Indonesian classic, *rendang* (beef or buffalo coconut curry). Don't be disappointed at the petite size of your *rendang* serve. The flavour and richness contained in that tasty tablet is easily enough to satisfy. What's more, eating a Texan portion will result in a feeling of fatigue at best. Let rice suffice, and *rendang* enrich. Traditional *rendang* is made with buffalo, however beef can also be used. In fact the rendang can be made with anything that won't dissolve into the liquid, such as chicken or jackfruit.

Fried rice

Nasi goreng (fried rice) is the first thing that springs to mind when you think of Indonesian cuisine. And why not? It is loved by Indonesians. Part of its popularity is the fact that it's so versatile. *Nasi goreng* can be an inexpensive meal simply dressed with crispy shallots and chillies; it can also be an extravagant dish studded with prawns and a garden of vegetables. Whatever the mix, if it contains rice and it's fried, it's *nasi goreng*. Of course other countries have their fried rice, notably China, who in fact introduced *nasi goreng* — and rice — to Indonesia. An authentic version should include shallots, chillies, *kecap manis* and — the crowning glory — a fried egg.

Sate

Sate, meat on a stick, is by no means a patentable invention, but skewered meat cooked over coals and called *sate* is an Indonesian institution.

Any meat can be used: goat, chicken, mutton, rabbit, pork, entrails or even horse and snake can find their way onto a *sate* skewer.

Cooking the *sate* over coals produces aromas delicious enough to lure a vegetarian. *Sate* is nearly always prepared with ten pieces to a serve with spicy sauce and rice or *lontong* (rice steamed in banana leaves).

DRINKS

Coffee

Indonesia produces a lot of *kopi* (coffee); in fact it's the third largest producer in the world. There was a time, after the Dutch set up their coffee estates in the 18th century that Indonesia was number one, but disease all but wiped out the valuable arabica plantations. Today the inferior robusta bean constitutes 90% of the nation's coffee crop. Nevertheless, the arabica beans still produced here are percolatable heaven, prized by caffeine freaks around the world.

So how to drink coffee, Indonesian style? Black, sweet and gritty is the nation's preferred pick-me-up. Known as *kopi tubruk*, freshly ground coffee goes straight into the glass with sugar and boiling water. It's chewy, but that's what you get. If you want *kopi susu* (coffee with milk) you'll get either

Chilies and lemons for sale in Bali.

Beef *rendang*.

Jackfruit soup.

Newly-picked coffee beans from Bukittinggi.

A street vendor serves *sate*.

Glass of *bandrek*, ginger tea.

condensed milk or non-dairy creamer (whatever that is).

There are other coffee options to be had. *Kopi jahe* is coffee brewed with ginger. Sumatrans like to start the day with *kopi telur*, coffee mixed with sugar and an egg yolk. In Tana Toraja (Sulawesi), things can get really strange; coffee is sometimes roasted with garlic. Coffee-flavoured lollies or sweets are also popular, especially the Kopiko brand.

Tea

Blanketing huggable hills, folding into clouds and camouflaging meticulous pickers, Indonesia's *teh* (tea) vies with rice for the title of the world's most beautiful crop. On the Puncak Pass in Java, you'll see lines of labourers painstakingly working their way across the slopes, filling the bamboo baskets on their backs with around 50 kilograms of loose-leaf tea in a 10-hour day.

Once collected, the leaves are sorted according to quality and left to 'wither', losing a third of their original moisture content. They are then 'curled' in a heated room of 100% humidity. Curling releases the remaining moisture in the leaves and the tea begins to ferment.

At this stage, the flavour, aroma and caffeine content are developed; so too is the variety of tea. Orange pekoe, Earl Grey, Russian caravan — all come from the same plant species: *Camellia sinensis* — tea. Once the desired flavour, colour and aroma have been achieved, the fermentation process is stopped and the tea dried, ready for the pot.

So what do you get when you order tea in Indonesia? The most popular brew is black, with varying amounts of sugar.

If you want tea without sugar, ask for *teh pahit* (bitter tea) and if you want milk, then perhaps buy yourself a cow. At many eateries, weak, sugarless tea is served free of charge. For a different take on tea, you'll find sweet *es teh* (iced tea) available at any store or restaurant.

Women checking produce at the fish market.

TOM COCKREM / GETTY IAMGES

Philippines

It's not an exaggeration to say that Filipino food has a poor reputation abroad. This perplexes Filipinos, who are convinced their home-cooked comfort food is the greatest thing in the world. The reality of Filipino food lies somewhere in-between, and although the cuisine's predominately sweet, mild flavours may not be as daring as Thai, or as diverse as Malaysian, they're satisfying and delicious, and ripe for exploration.

CULINARY CAPITALS MANILA, PAMPANGA PROVINCE **KNOWN FOR** SWEET SAVOURY DISHES **IMPORTS** RICE **EXPORTS** SAN MIGUEL BEER **DEVOUR** *ADOBO* **AVOID** *BALÚT* (DUCK EMBRYO)

Lechón, barbecued whole pig in Manila.

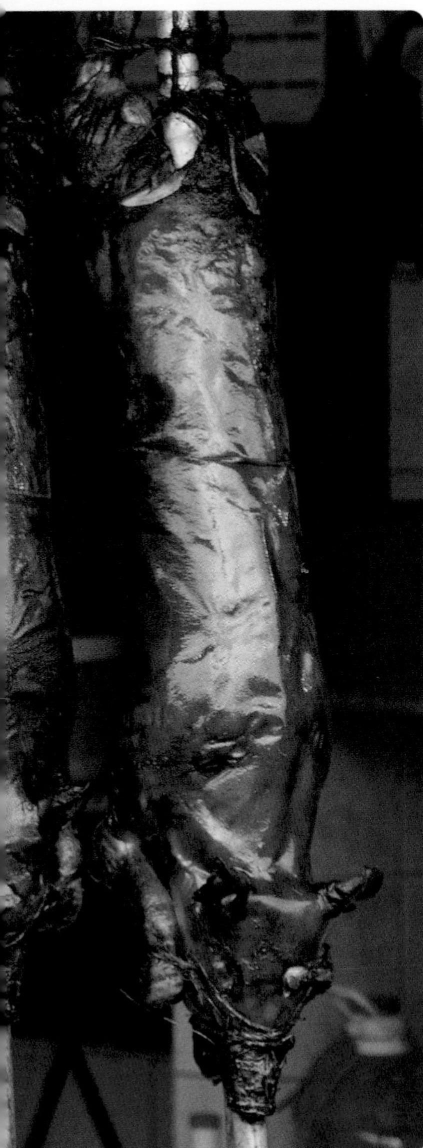
DANITA DELIMONT / GETTY IMAGES

CULTURE

On the surface, the food of the Philippines resembles that of much of Southeast Asia: a cuisine taking advantage of a vast selection of local herbs and produce, with an emphasis on fish and seafood. Unlike elsewhere in the region, where the wealth and power of royal courts led to the development of lavish, sophisticated dishes, much of Filipino food is home-based and relatively simple. In the Philippines, it was successive waves of immigration and colonialism that influenced the food.

Chinese traders were among the first foreigners to reach the Philippine islands, and they introduced ingredients such as pork and soy sauce, cooking techniques that included baking and wok-frying, and some now-emblematic Filipino dishes such as *lumpia* (spring rolls) and *pancit* (fried noodles).

The Spanish arrived in 1521 and initiated the Philippines' first wave of colonisation; a period that was to last more than 300 years. They also introduced many ingredients from their other colonies in Mexico and elsewhere in the Americas. Today, dishes such as *escabeche* (fish 'pickled' in a sweet-sour sauce) and *lechón* (roast pig), and ingredients ranging from chillies to *soursop* (an acidic fruit) are integral parts of the Filipino kitchen.

REGIONS

Manila

The Philippines' largest city, is (not surprisingly) home to the country's most progressive and cosmopolitan dining scene. It's also where the Filipinos' love for American-style fast food is most evident, and chains such as Jollibee and Max's seem to inhabit every corner.

Pampanga

Filipinos consider this province in central Luzon the country's culinary capital. The province is landlocked, so unlike elsewhere in the country, the seafood eaten here comes predominately from lakes and rivers. The region is a major producer of rice, and dishes such as *arroz caldo* (a kind of Filipino *congee*), *tamales* (which in the Philippines are made with ground rice), and *bringhe* (something of a Filipino paella made in a wok with sticky rice and chicken) can be found.

Bicol

Of the regional cuisines of the Philippines, the spicy food of Bicol is probably most amenable to Western palettes. Coconuts are an important local crop here, and work their way into several local dishes, from seafood or vegetables simmered in coconut cream to dishes seasoned with toasted coconut flesh. *Gabi* (taro leaves) are another important local ingredient; they are used to wrap dishes, or are sliced and stewed in coconut milk.

Visayas

Located in the central part of the country, Visayas is the Philippines' undisputed seafood capital. The local style of dining in coastal areas such as Cebu is known as *sutokil*, a combination of the local words *sugba* (grilling), *tola* or *towa* (boiling), and there is also *kinilaw*, a salad of raw fish or seafood. All of these, in particular *kinilaw*, require the freshest seafood.

FEASTS

Each village, town and city in the Philippines has its own fiesta, usually celebrated on the feast day of its patron saint, as determined by the Catholic calendar. Historically every household was expected to prepare food and serve it to anybody who appeared at the door. Nowadays, food is still prepared but on a greatly diminished scale, and only people

Banana cue, caramelised deep fried bananas.

Fish on the menu in El Nido.

Sweet rice cakes.

A feast of *pancit*, a local dish of noodles, meat, and vegetables.

Egg rolls with dipping sauce.

Slices of vibrant watermelon.

who have been invited show up at the buffet table. *Kaldereta* (beef or sometimes goat-meat stew), *igado* (stir-fried pork liver), fried chicken and, of course, *lechón* (roast pig) are some of the dishes you can expect to find at a fiesta. Sweet rice cakes, usually local delicacies, are served as dessert.

Birthdays and other private parties are usually celebrated with a big plate of *pancit* (noodles), though nowadays this has been widely replaced by spaghetti, the local version of which will strike most visitors as unduly sweet.

With such a deeply entrenched Catholic background, it's not surprising that Christmas is among the Philippines' most significant holidays. Christmas celebrations span six weeks, but perhaps the most important meal of the season is *Noche Buena*, when after leaving Midnight Mass on Christmas Eve, churchgoers take part in a meal that is distinctly Spanish in origin. Typical dishes include roast ham or turkey, hot chocolate (the local variety which also includes peanuts and is made with buffalo milk), and a type of cheesy brioche called *ensaimada*.

ETIQUETTE

An everyday meal in the Philippines is usually a fairly informal occasion, though it can take on the trappings of a formal Western-style dinner in the houses of the rich. Generally Filipinos eat with a fork and a spoon (no knife); many visitors find this a little hard to get used to. When eating, most Filipinos sit in Western-style chairs around a table.

The basic Filipino eatery is a *turu-turò* (literally 'point point'), where customers can order by pointing at the pre-cooked food on display, but Filipino restaurants come in many guises, from small roadside canteens to huge enterprises.

Unlike the rest of Southeast Asia, where street vendors sell complete meals, in the Philippines food carts tend to offer nothing more substantial than simple snacks, known locally as *meryenda*. Fish or squid balls are popular, usually fried in boiling oil and served on skewers, as is a sweet bean-curd snack known locally as *taho*.

DAILY MEALS

Breakfast in the Philippines typically takes the form of rice (preferably garlic rice) with a fried egg on top, and sides of *tapa* (salty beef strips), *tocino* (honey-cured pork), *bangús* (milkfish) or *longganiza* (sausages). For dessert, try *halo-halo*, served in a glass packed with fruit preserves, sweet corn, young coconut and various tropical delights topped with milky crushed ice, a dollop of crème caramel and scoop of ice cream.

It's worth noting that Filipino food tends to be long on meat and short on greens. There is only one common vegetarian dish: *pinakbét*, a tasty melange of pumpkin, string beans, eggplant, okra and other vegies, seasoned with garlic, onions, ginger, tomatoes, shrimp paste and, sometimes, coconut milk.

ESSENTIAL PRODUCE

The key defining flavours of Filipino food are sweet and sour. The sweet often comes from sugar, whether this is sugarcane from Visayas in the centre of the country, or palm sugar from Batangas, south of Manila. Sour flavours come from a variety of sources. Many dishes are made tart via a squeeze of lime, typically the slightly sweet, tiny calamansi limes. Vinegar is another essential souring agent, and is made from ingredients ranging from coconut to the fruit of the nipa palm tree. And other ingredients, such as tamarind or tart indigenous fruits such as *siniguelas* (Spanish plums) are added to soups and salads to provide a sour taste.

Squid *adobo*, a popular dish in the Philippines.

DEFINING DISHES

Balút

Much of the Philippines' poor culinary reputation probably rests on the back of this one dish: *balút*, is a boiled duck egg containing a partially developed embryo, sometimes with tiny feathers.

Adobo

If the world knows one Filipino dish, it's undoubtedly *adobo*. *Adobo* takes a surprising variety of shapes and forms, although at its most basic level, it is meat braised with vinegar, garlic and/or black pepper. *Adobo* is typically based around chicken or pork (or chicken *and* pork), but variations based around fish or squid also exist. It can resemble a stew or soup, or it can be dry. Some versions include coconut milk, and can be quite rich and oily in texture, while others are thin and soupy.

Kinilaw

A staple in Filipino homes, and quite possibly one of the country's oldest recipes, *kinilaw* is a 'salad' of raw seafood mixed with a tart, vinegar or citrus fruit-based dressing. The acidity of the dressing is said to 'cook' the seafood (often fish, but shellfish are also used), and the dish is mellowed with coconut milk and seasoned with chillies and/or ginger.

Lumpia

Spring rolls are a Chinese import and they have been irrevocably assimilated into the Filipino repertoire. Deep-fried *lumpia* are often filled with a mixture of vegetables and pork, and are served with a sweet and sour dipping sauce. Fresh *lumpia* are often stuffed with vegetables and seafood, and are served with a sweet-salty, peanut-based dip.

Hand-rolled *lumpia*.

Green mango snack.

Halo-halo, the Philippines' famous ice treat.

Pancit

Many Filipinos would be surprised to learn that *pancit*, noodles, are another Chinese import, such is their place in the local cuisine. Noodles can take various forms in the Philippines, but *pancit* usually refers to thin rice noodles fried with vegetables and seafood.

Sinigang

Although not as well known abroad as *adobo*, this tart, vegetable-studded soup is the epitome of comfort food for many Filipinos. Combining a fish or meat-based broth, a variety of largely indigenous vegetables and herbs, and the tartness of calamansi lime, the exact parameters of *sinigang* can be difficult to define, but the soup is easy to recognise and even easier to enjoy.

DRINKS

Local fruits make their way into many of the local drinks. *Buko* is a refreshing young coconut juice, while *guayabano* (soursop) juice is sweet and fragrant. And the local citrus, calamansi, is used to make a refreshing cordial or added to black tea.

Arguably the Philippines biggest culinary export is its popular San Miguel beer. The brewery dates back to 1890, making it one of Southeast Asia's oldest. Known locally as 'San Mig', the brand has 95% market share, and is available in nine varieties, including the wildly popular Red Horse 'extra strong', which has an alcohol content of 7%.

Rural alcohols include *basi*, a sweet, port-like wine made from sugarcane juice. *Tuba* is a strong palm wine extracted from coconut flowers; in its roughly distilled form it's known as *lambanog*.

An Australian tradition: chucking a few prawns on the barbecue.

JOHN WHITE PHOTOS / GETTY IMAGES

Australia

Welcome to the 'lucky country', where most Australians enjoy a high standard of living and a relaxed lifestyle. Food is often at the centre of this easygoing society. The cities here showcase diverse and cosmopolitan flavours from around the world, often using excellent local produce from the surrounding oceans and expansive land. Wash it down with a drink, because Australia's New World wines and beers are among the planet's best.

CULINARY CAPITALS SYDNEY, MELBOURNE, TASMANIA **KNOWN FOR** SEAFOOD, WINE **IMPORTS** ASIAN AND MEDITERRANEAN FLAVOURS **EXPORTS** MEAT, DAIRY, SUGAR **DEVOUR** MORETON BAY BUGS **AVOID** CHIKO ROLLS

Waterfront dining at Circular Quay with views over the iconic Sydney harbour.

Rack of lamb at a Melbourne restaurant.

Pears are produced in abundance in Australia.

CULTURE

People

Immigration has transformed Australia's culinary landscape in just over 60 years. In the 1950s, conservative flavours dominated, courtesy of colonial settlement from Britain and Ireland. Waves of immigration ensued, and Greek, Italian and Lebanese communities were followed by Vietnamese and Cambodians escaping war in Southeast Asia. From espresso coffee and Greek *souvlaki* to Vietnamese noodle soups, Australia's food scene became increasingly cosmopolitan, and Thai, Japanese, Chinese and Korean influences from nearby Asia all continue to influence the cuisine.

Land

From sheep farming to orchards and viticulture, Australia's wide-open spaces have plenty of room for diverse farming. From the warm tropical waters of northern Queensland to the cooler ocean climes surrounding Tasmania, the seas surrounding this island continent sustain many types of seafood.

ESSENTIAL PRODUCE

Bush tucker

More than 350 food plants are native to the Australian bush, but only in recent decades have Australian chefs started recognising and harnessing indigenous ingredients. Some of the most frequently used are listed below.

- Macadamia nuts — Originally from the east of Australia, and now known around the world.
- Quandongs — wild peaches known as quandongs were an important food to combat scurvy in early European settlers.

- Kakadu plums — these wild plums are the world's best source of vitamin C, and are used in gourmet pickles and chutneys.
- Wattleseed — edible seeds combining chocolate, coffee and hazelnut flavours.
- Lemon myrtle — used to flavour everything from chicken and fish through to ice-cream and aioli.
- Kangaroo and crocodile also make a regular appearance on menus.

Fruit

Australia's broad mix of geography and climate ensures a wide range of local fruit is grown throughout the country.

- In earlier years, Tasmania was known as the 'Apple Isle', and now stone fruit and cherries also are among the island state's southern mix.
- Mango, papaya and other tropical fruits grow exceptionally well in northern Queensland.

Meat

Beef and lamb are raised across Australia, with much of the best produce coming from the pristine environment of Tasmania.

- Tasmanian beef, especially from wild and windy Cape Grim, is raised in the world's finest air, blown clean by the Roaring 40s.
- Off Tasmania's northern coast, the isolated Flinders Island produces excellent lamb raised on saltgrass.
- Also from Flinders Island, wallaby is favoured by top urban chefs in Melbourne and Sydney. Kangaroo is also eaten, but there is a certain reticence from the

Macadamia nuts are an important crop.

Backhousia citriodora, or lemon myrtle.

Kangaroo fillets for dinner at an Adelaide Hills restaurant in South Australia.

Australian public in eating one of the animals on the country's coat of arms.

Seafood

Almost 90% of Australians live within 50 kilometres of the ocean, so briny produce is consumed with gusto across the country.

- Tasmanian oysters from Bruny Island or Freycinet are plump and sweet. NSW rock oysters are also highly regarded.
- Stanley on Tasmania's rugged northwest coast has Australia's best crayfish. Balmain bugs and Moreton Bay bugs are smaller slipper lobsters, while freshwater crustaceans include yabbies and marron.
- Tasmania's inland lakes and rivers are a mecca for salmon and trout flyfishers.
- An iconic Australian ingredient, prawns are grilled on a barbecue, or dressed up with Southeast Asian or Mediterranean flavours.
- The prized ocean fish, barramundi, comes from the north of Australia.

SHOPPING

Supermarkets reflect the wide variety of food cultures that have made Australia home. For more local and regional offerings, consider the following.

- Farmers markets — An increasingly important part of the Australian food scene, with more being launched every year.
- Providores — Delicatessens, often dubbed 'providores' in Australia, are a good place to source local products.

ANDREW FURLONG / GETTY IMAGES

Risotto with green beans and Moreton Bay Bugs.

- Farmgates — Explore the back roads of rural Australia for fresh fruit. Tasmania's Huon Valley has apples, cherries and strawberries, and in the Barossa Valley in South Australia, grapes and seasonal stone fruit feature.

DEFINING DISHES

Barbecue

A laid-back and much-loved cross between meal, cooking method and social occasion, the barbecue is one of Australia's quintessential dining experiences. In earlier decades, the emphasis was firmly on salads, snags (sausages) and grilled steaks and seafood, but now an Aussie barbecue is just as likely to incorporate Asian and Mediterranean flavours. If you are invited to one, it's good manners to take along a bottle of wine or a few cold beers.

Cakes and biscuits

New Zealand also claims historical ownership of Aussie–Kiwi desserts like lamingtons (chocolate-iced and coconut-dusted sponge cakes) and pavlova (a crisp plate-sized meringue with a gooey centre, topped with fruit).

Anzac biscuits (made with oats, golden syrup and coconut) celebrate the two countries' shared military history in WWI.

Pies

More evidence of Australia's British heritage, pies are another culinary touchstone that have had a makeover from Australia's waves of immigration. Still beloved are meat pies at the 'footy' (Australian Rules Football) in Melbourne.

Vegemite

This salty, dark brown paste — a yeast extract that is a by-product of brewing beer — is definitely an acquired taste for visitors to Australia. Most Australians love it though — especially smeared on warm toast with butter — and more than a few Australian backpackers take it along when heading to Europe for their extended 'OE' (Overseas Experience). It's also loved across the Tasman Sea in New Zealand.

DRINKS

Beer

With a colonial history partly predicated on hard-drinking gold miners and convict immigrants from Britain and Ireland, beer and pubs have long been an integral part of Australian society. Mainstream brands like 'VB'(Victoria Bitter), Tooheys and XXXX still have the biggest market share, but craft beer is growing in popularity. Most state capitals now have multiple craft beer pubs where the emphasis is on quality over quantity.

- With more than 30 craft breweries across the state, Victoria is the country's leading producer of more interesting brews.
- Hops have been grown in Tasmania's Derwent Valley since the 19th century, and the island state has six craft breweries. Originally opened in 1824, Hobart's stately Cascade Brewery is Australia's oldest operational brewery.

COFFEE

Scratch a respected café owner in London, and you'll probably discover an ex-pat Australian, evidence of the authority the Australian coffee scene now enjoys overseas. Australian cities are dotted with chic and funky cafes, and throughout the country, coffee-making standards are uniformly high.

Lamingtons, coconut-covered spongecake squares.

Every kid's favourite: Vegemite on toast.

Man dresses up a simple snag (sausage) with tomato sauce at a barbecue.

Vineyard in Margaret River, Western Australia.

PATRICK EAGAR / GETTY IMAGES

Wine

Australia's wine production began in the Hunter Valley in NSW in the 1820s, and most Australian states now nurture established wine industries. Vineyards large and small feature cellar door sales and wine-tasting, and many larger operators also have excellent cafes or restaurants.

- New South Wales — The lower Hunter Valley is known for Shiraz and Semillon, while the upper Hunter wineries specialise in Cabernet Sauvignon and Shiraz.
- Victoria — The Yarra Valley and the Mornington Peninsula both produce excellent Chardonnay and Pinot noir, while Rutherglen wineries craft good fortified wines and Shiraz.
- Tasmania — Key areas include the Pipers River and Tamar Valley region in the north, and the Coal River Valley in the south. Sparkling wine, Chardonnay, Riesling and Pinot noir all feature.
- South Australia — Cabernet Sauvignon from Coonawarra, Riesling from the Clare Valley, and Shiraz from the Barossa Valley and McLaren Vale are all internationally regarded.
- Western Australia — Margaret River produces excellent Cabernet Sauvignon and Chardonnay, while the Pemberton region specialises in Pinot noir, Chardonnay, Merlot and Sauvignon Blanc.

Try **Tasmanian oysters** from Bruny Island or the Freycinet Peninsula. Devour them at the source fresh from the shell with a dab of Tabasco and a squeeze of lemon, or buy from the seafood punts around Hobart's Constitution Dock.

A mussel farm in Kenepuru Sound, Waitaria Bay on the South Island.

ROLF HICKER / GETTY IMAGES

New Zealand

New Zealand is one of the world's most isolated nations, but its compact population of just 4.4 million has an innovative and interesting food culture. International flavours are embraced, and excellent local produce is often infused with the culinary influences of Pacific and Asian neighbours. Closer to home, ingredients originally used by New Zealand's indigenous Maori people are growing in popularity.

CULINARY CAPITALS HAWKES BAY, CENTRAL OTAGO **KNOWN FOR** LAMB, WINE **EXPORTS** CRAYFISH, KIWI FRUIT **IMPORTS** PACIFIC RIM FLAVOURS **DEVOUR** BLUFF OYSTERS, CRAFT BEER **AVOID** *PAUA* FRITTERS

Kai moana (seafood) platter at a restaurant in Moeraki on the South Island.

A little lamb on Papamoa Hills.

Manuka honey.

CULTURE

People

New Zealand's indigenous Maori arrived from Polynesia around 800 years ago, followed, from the 1830s onward, by the first British settlers. The new colony's culinary focus remained conservative until European immigration following World War II. Further immigration from the Pacific Islands, Asia and the Middle East from the 1980s increased culinary diversity, and New Zealanders returning home from overseas travel also demanded more interesting food.

Auckland has the world's biggest Polynesian population, and the city incorporates and celebrates communities from Samoa, Tonga, Niue, the Cook Islands and Fiji. Visit the annual Pasifika festival to experience Polynesian cuisine.

Land

Agriculture and proximity to the sea are key drivers of New Zealand's cuisine. From the country's earliest days, lamb and dairy products have been vital exports, and the Maori's love of *kai moana* (seafood) is shared by all New Zealanders.

ESSENTIAL PRODUCE

Fruit

Buying fresh fruit from roadside stalls is one of the pleasures of exploring New Zealand independently by car.

- Apricots, nectarines, peaches, plums and cherries abound in Central Otago from November to March.
- Originally from China, but now known around the world as a thoroughly New Zealand product, kiwi fruit, as well as their juice and wine, are widely available.

Indigenous produce

New Zealand chefs have recently become interested in traditional herbs and spices, many sourced from local forests or shorelines, and used in earlier centuries by Maori.

- *Horopito* is a zingy bush pepper.
- *Kawakawa* translates as bush basil.
- *Pikopiko* are green fern fronds with a taste between a pea and fresh asparagus.
- *Manuka* was dubbed 'tea tree' by 18th century British explorer James Cook. The tree's wood is used to smoke fish and meat, and *manuka* honey has significant anti-bacterial properties.

Meat

Cattle, sheep and venison munch on lush pastures year-round, producing meat that's lean and sustainably grown.

- New Zealand's best lamb comes from the Canterbury Plains in the shadow of the Southern Alps.
- Farmed venison is showcased at many high-end restaurants, and wild venison is a favourite of recreational hunters.
- *Titi* is also known as the mutton bird. Seasonal harvesting is restricted to local Maori around Foveaux Strait, but mutton bird is occasionally on offer in South Island restaurants.

Seafood

New Zealand's meandering coastline of 15,134 kilometres is the 10th longest in the world. Many freshwater rivers and lakes also punctuate the landscape.

- Bluff oysters are world-renowned, as are other shellfish

LASTING IMAGES / GETTY IMAGES

Kina, or sea urchins, on a rock.

including green-lipped mussels, scallops, *tuatua* (clams) and *paua* (abalone).

- Local rock lobster is rich and sweet, and *koura* are smaller freshwater crayfish.
- Fly-fishing for brown and rainbow trout in lakes and rivers is popular.
- New Zealand's finest ocean fish is the blue cod, which is best eaten when freshly caught from the waters surrounding the isolated Stewart Island.
- Whitebait are netted from September to December and these tiny fish are the juvenile spawn of the *inanga* and *kokopu* species.
- *Kina* are sea urchins much prized by New Zealand's indigenous Maori.

Vegetables

Local vegetables include several varieties originally harvested by the Maori people in earlier centuries.

Kumara is a variety of sweet potato originally introduced by the earliest Polynesian settlers. *Kumara* fries are a tasty local variation of fried potatoes.

Taewa are traditional Maori potatoes; they are small and coloured dark purple.

Maori boil up the green leaves of *puha*, a wild prickly thistle, with pork, mussels and mutton bones.

DEFINING DISHES

Desserts and sweets

Lamingtons (chocolate-iced and coconut-dusted sponge cakes) and pavlova (a crisp plate-sized meringue with a gooey centre) are both claimed by Australia and New Zealand, but

The popular pavlova, this one topped with cream, strawberries and kiwi fruit, is claimed by both Australians and New Zealanders.

A handful of freshly caught whitebait.

Flat white: the New Zealand take on a latte.

another treat New Zealand definitely owns is hokey pokey ice-cream, which is packed with chunks of honeycomb toffee.

Hangi

This is a traditional Maori form of cooking where meat and vegetables are steamed slowly on hot stones in an underground earth oven.

Sunday roast

New Zealand's British colonial roots are evident in the country's love of a good old-fashioned Sunday roast. Many pubs serve up roast lamb with all the trimmings through winter.

Whitebait fritters

These tiny fish can only be caught for a limited time, and are best in a simple batter and served on white bread with a squeeze of lemon juice.

DRINKS

Coffee

New Zealanders take their coffee very seriously, and many local roasters are small batch operators with a fairtrade focus.

- Flat whites are made with espresso coffee and steamed milk, and served in a cup.
- Long blacks are double espressos with water, served with a robust *crema* on top.
- Short blacks are concentrated and served in a smaller cup — what the rest of the world refers to as an espresso.

Beer

In recent years, many craft breweries and independent brewpubs have opened, and innovative local brewers are putting a Kiwi stamp on beer styles as diverse as Russian stouts, American Pale Ales and Belgian Saison brews.

- Wellington, the country's capital, is the also the nation's craft beer capital with an ever-expanding number of bars catering to the city's population of hipsterish beer geeks.
- Aromatic hops from the Nelson region are in demand with brewers around the world, and local craft brewers include some of the country's best.

Wine

New Zealand's first vines were planted in the 19th century by French Catholic missionaries, but the country's international reputation was established by Marlborough Sauvignon Blanc in the 1980s. New Zealand Pinot noir is also world-renowned, but the country's diverse terroir supports many different varietals. Around Auckland, Waiheke Island and the Hawkes Bay, Chardonnay and intense red wines are exceptional, and North Canterbury has excellent Riesling and Pinot gris.

- Zesty and aromatic, Sauvignon Blanc from the Marlborough region grabbed the world's attention in the 1980s, but in recent years the style has become more complex with greater use of oak.
- The finest examples of New Zealand Pinot noir come from Central Otago — especially around the barren and arid hills of Bannockburn — and the Martinborough region north of Wellington.

This citrus-flavoured fizzy drink **L&P** (Lemon & Paeroa) is the taste of a Kiwi childhood. Established in the town of Paeroa in the North Island in 1908, the iconic beverage is now owned by Coca Cola, but is still "world famous in New Zealand" as the infamous advertising slogan goes.

MARC ROMANELLI / GETTY IMAGES

The beautiful coastal view from the top of the hill at Te Whau Winery on Waiheke Island, North Island.

Cheeky restaurant signage.

PETER PTSCHELINZEW / GETTY IMAGES

USA

Outside the US borders, American food is represented by the worst of American exports — fast food chains and sugary beverages giving the country's cuisine something of a bad name internationally. But within the 50 states you'll find a diversity and depth of cuisine arguably unrivalled in the Western world. From Tex-Mex to Cajun, Southern to soul food, American cuisine is a vast, bright tapestry of colours, flavours and ethnic traditions.

CULINARY CAPITALS NEW YORK, THE SOUTH **KNOWN FOR** HAMBURGERS, COCA COLA **IMPORTS** MEXICAN FLAVOURS **EXPORTS** FAST FOOD CHAINS **DEVOUR** COUNTRY COOKING **AVOID** SUGAR-LADEN SODAS

eat me
113

Chilli and cornbread.

MICHAEL MAES / GETTY IMAGES

CULTURE

People

Although America encompasses peoples of many cultures, creeds and origins, its regional and ethnic cuisines remain intact and distinct. Many of the foods enjoyed by Native Americans — cornbread, berries, turkey — are still eaten country-wide, and native cooking techniques like barbecue have had a deep influence on later cuisines. In New England, the Puritan culture of the earliest colonists means simply, hearty food: fresh seafood, dense chowders, homemade ice cream from local dairies. Down South, the West African influence of plantation slave cooks remains evident in dishes like fried chicken, stewed okra, and candied yams. In the Southwest, Mexican-Americans bring their flavours to the table — tacos, burritos, chilli, rice and beans. German and Scandinavian immigrants populated much of the Midwest in the 1800s, which means hearty casseroles, sausages and, of course, beer. The French-speaking Cajun and Creole people who settled in Louisiana in the early days of the Colonies brought their Franco-inflected cuisine to the party, making New Orleans a culinary highlight.

REGIONS

Make no mistake: America is massive. You could drive from Lisbon to Moscow, passing through eight separate countries, faster than you could drive from San Francisco to New York. So it's no surprise that the regions of America can feel as distinct as different nations.

The Northeast

The Mayflower ship full of English Pilgrimsmade landfall in Massachusetts in 1620, making the Northeast the first region to be permanently settled by Europeans. Those Pilgrims probably wished they'd hit the coast a bit further south, as the weather in this region is notoriously harsh. This harshness has shaped the culinary tradition of the region, especially in the states of Massachusetts, Connecticut, Rhode Island, Vermont, New Hampshire and Maine, which collectively are known as New England. Local cuisine is full of simple dishes that take advantage of the limited local produce and abundant seafood: creamy clam chowder studded with potatoes, boiled beef and cabbage, fried cod, heavy kettles of baked beans. Further south, the New York–New Jersey region is an epicentre of immigration and, therefore, culinary diversity. Try Italian-influenced but wholly 'New York-style' pizza, nosh on the bagels and lox of the Eastern European Jews, slurp the dumpling soup of Chinatown, or down a *dosa* in Manhattan's 'Curry Hill'.

- In fishing-centric Maine, lobster is king. Crack into a whole steamed one, or have a lobster roll sandwich.
- The Jewish delicatessen, or 'deli', is classic New York, serving cold cut sandwiches, salads and pickles. Try a towering pastrami (a type of smoked beef) sandwich on rye with mustard, *never* mayo.

Clams, popular in New England.

The South

The steamy South offers up one of America's richest — and most fattening! — culinary traditions. Heavily agricultural and historically poor, many of the region's most delectable dishes are born of the ingenuity that comes from disadvantage and rural living. Traditional Southern home cooking might mean fried chicken or pork chops, 'greens' such as collards or turnip greens cooked with a ham hock, sweet potatoes, fried okra, biscuits, fruit pies and towering coconut layer cakes.

In antebellum East Coast cities such as Charleston and

Okra for sale at a farmer's market.

The classic New York deli sandwich, pastrami on

Savannah, 'lowcountry cooking' reflects the diverse influences of French traders, upcountry Scots-Irish and West African slaves, so you'll find she-crab soup with sherry, *benne* (sesame seed) wafers and hoppin' John (black-eyed peas with rice and bacon). In the bayou country of Louisiana, Cajun food marries native spices like sassafras and chilli pepper with provincial French cooking, while the Creole food of New Orleans is more citified — shrimp *remoulade*, crawfish *étouffée* and *beignets*.

- 'Barbecue' is both a noun and a verb in the South, and means different things in different regions. In North Carolina, it's pulled pork in vinegar sauce, whereas in Memphis it can be ribs in sweet-sticky red sauce.
- Frying is the South's favourite way to cook. Must-try delicacies include fried chicken, fried okra, hushpuppies (fried balls of cornmeal), and green tomatoes.

The Southwest

Two ethnic groups define Southwestern food culture: the Spanish and the Mexicans, who controlled territories from Texas to California until well into the 19th century. While there is little actual Spanish food today, the Spanish brought cattle to Mexico, which the Mexicans adapted to their own corn and chilli-based gastronomy to make tacos, tortillas, enchiladas, burritos and other dishes made of corn or flour pancakes filled with everything from chopped beef to poultry to beans. Texas's cattle industry means tons of barbecued brisket and meaty chilli con carne, Arizona's chewy slabs of fry bread are a Native American staple, and don't leave New Mexico without trying the state's beloved spicy green chilli, which tops everything from eggs to burritos to bagel sandwiches.

'Texas-style' chilli means meat, meat and more meat, topped with cheese served up in diners, drive-ins and backyards.

Chicago-style deep-dish crust pizza.

The Midwest

Throughout the Midwest they eat big and with plenty of gusto. Portions are huge — this is America's farm country, and people here need fuel to get through their daily labour. Influenced by the heavy cuisines of the German, Eastern European and Scandinavian pioneers who settled here during America's westward expansion, Midwestern food is big on starchy noodle casseroles, potato dishes and meat-filled pastries. Chicago, a hard-working multi-ethnic city, has a large Italian element, and Chicago-style deep-dish pizza is in continuous rivalry with New York's thinner slices. Meat is big, literally and figuratively, with steaks, *bratwursts* and 'loose meat' sandwiches (ground meat on a bun) served up to satisfy. Everything is washed down with plenty of beer — mass-produced American brews like Miller, Budweiser and Pabst Blue Ribbon all hail from the Midwest, and have lately been joined by a myriad of craft brews.

- The state of Michigan grows the vast majority of America's cherries, and fresh-baked, flaky-crust cherry pie is one of the Midwest's prime summertime treats.
- Wisconsin is America's great cheese-producing state, and its sharp cheddar cheese is a delight. But the most beloved dairy treat in the upper Midwest is the humble cheese curd, a byproduct of the cheese production process — fresh ones should squeak when you bite into them.

FEASTS

Americans love a good feast, and nearly every holiday on the calendar has some food-related tradition attached.

- Thanksgiving, celebrated the fourth Thursday in November, is the biggest secular American food holiday. Families gather together for the traditional gut-busting spread: turkey and gravy, stuffing, sweet

Pancakes with bacon, banana & syrup.

Sliced pumpkin pie with whipped cream.

4th July is honoured with a hotdog and a beer.

potatoes, cranberry sauce, and pumpkin and pecan pies. The holiday commemorates the first meal between the English Pilgrims and the Massachusetts Wampanoag Indians back in 1621, but these days is all about eating, watching football, and hanging out with family.

- Christmas is celebrated with gusto in the United States. The traditional Christmas dinner, eaten on Christmas Day afternoon, includes ham or roast goose, mashed potatoes, roast vegetables and various pies and cakes. Prettily decorated Christmas cookies, chocolate fudge, bags of caramel popcorn, and peppermint candies are popular food-related gifts.
- Jewish Americans celebrate the winter holiday of *Hanukkah* with fried potato pancakes called *latkes*, homemade jelly doughnuts, and other fried treats.
- The 4th of July, American Independence Day, is honoured with backyard barbecue blowouts of hamburgers, hot dogs, watermelon and ice cream.

DAILY MEALS

Americans favour 'three squares' a day, with plenty of snacks in between. There are really no rules here: an American might eat a full breakfast of eggs, pancakes or waffles, and bacon, or simply grab a smoothie or granola bar to go. Even the smallest towns these days have a chain coffee establishment to satisfy the national love for sweet coffee drinks like caramel mochas. Busy Americans often eat lunch on the run or at a desk. Dinner tends to be earlier here than in Europe — 6 or 6:30 pm in smaller towns, and 7 to 8 pm in bigger cities. If you're feeling peckish during non-meal hours, nearly everywhere in the US sells food — gas stations, pharmacies, office supply stores — so you'll never go hungry.

Fast food is extremely popular — about one quarter of adults eat fast food every day, though fast food can mean anything from a to-go taco to a Subway sandwich to the classic burger and fries. So-called 'fast casual' restaurants offering higher quality food at high speeds are growing in popularity. Most are chains, offering a variety of cuisines from noodles to burritos to fully-loaded salads. Buffets, especially all-you-can-eat buffets, are a sometimes-mocked American speciality. Common buffet cuisines include Chinese, Indian, pizza, Southern and seafood. You'll also find a full gamut of fine dining options, from stylish bistros to molecular gastronomy restaurants with $200 tasting menus. Long gone are the days when Indian restaurants were viewed as suspiciously 'foreign' — even small towns tend to have at least one Indian, Chinese, Thai and sushi restaurant — and Mexican food is nearly as common as pizza.

INTI ST CLAIR / GETTY IMAGES

ESSENTIAL PRODUCE

Bread

Americans love their carbs, but, until several decades ago, bread choices were, well, less than sophisticated. But the US has come a long, long way from the days of bagged white Wonder Bread, and now proudly offers local specialities to rival France. Add to that the country's various ethnic breads and bread-like products, and you'll be in a carb coma before noon!

- Biscuits — When a Brit or Aussie says 'biscuit', they're talking about what Americans call a 'cookie'. When an American says 'biscuit', they mean a small, savoury, flaky bread risen with baking powder rather than yeast, which is a staple of Southern cooking.
- Cornbread — A Native American staple, this quick bread made from ground cornmeal is often cooked in a cast-iron pan.

Basket of french fries with cheeseburger.

- Sourdough — A San Francisco speciality, this chewy bread gets its slightly sour taste from naturally occurring *lactobacilli* bacteria.
- Tortilla — A staple of Southwestern and Mexican-American cooking, these flat pancakes can be made from flour or corn, and are used for scooping up meat or beans or eggs, or filled to make tacos or burritos.

Dairy

With its millions of acres of grass prairie perfect for grazing, America is a dairy-loving nation. And don't think all American cheese is *that* kind of American cheese: the country has an increasingly robust and diverse cheese-making industry.

- Buttermilk — True buttermilk is the liquid left behind after churning butter, but most modern stuff is simply soured milk. It is ubiquitous in American baking recipes (buttermilk pancakes, buttermilk biscuits) and for soaking chicken before frying.
- Cheese — Wisconsin and California make 50 percent of American cheese, but artisan cheese-makers are everywhere. Some names to look out for: Rogue Creamery (Oregon), Cowgirl Creamery (California) and Cypress Grove Chevre (California). Indigenous cheese varieties include mild Colby and Monterey Jack, farmstead hoop cheese, and crumbly Wisconsin brick cheese.
- Cream cheese — Famously associated with Philadelphia, this smooth spreadable cheese tops bagels nationwide.

FRUIT

There is an incredible range of fresh fruit available across the country. What grows abundantly in Florida wouldn't last a

Freshly-baked biscuits.

Bagel and cream cheese.

Hands clasping a large stack of handmade tortillas.

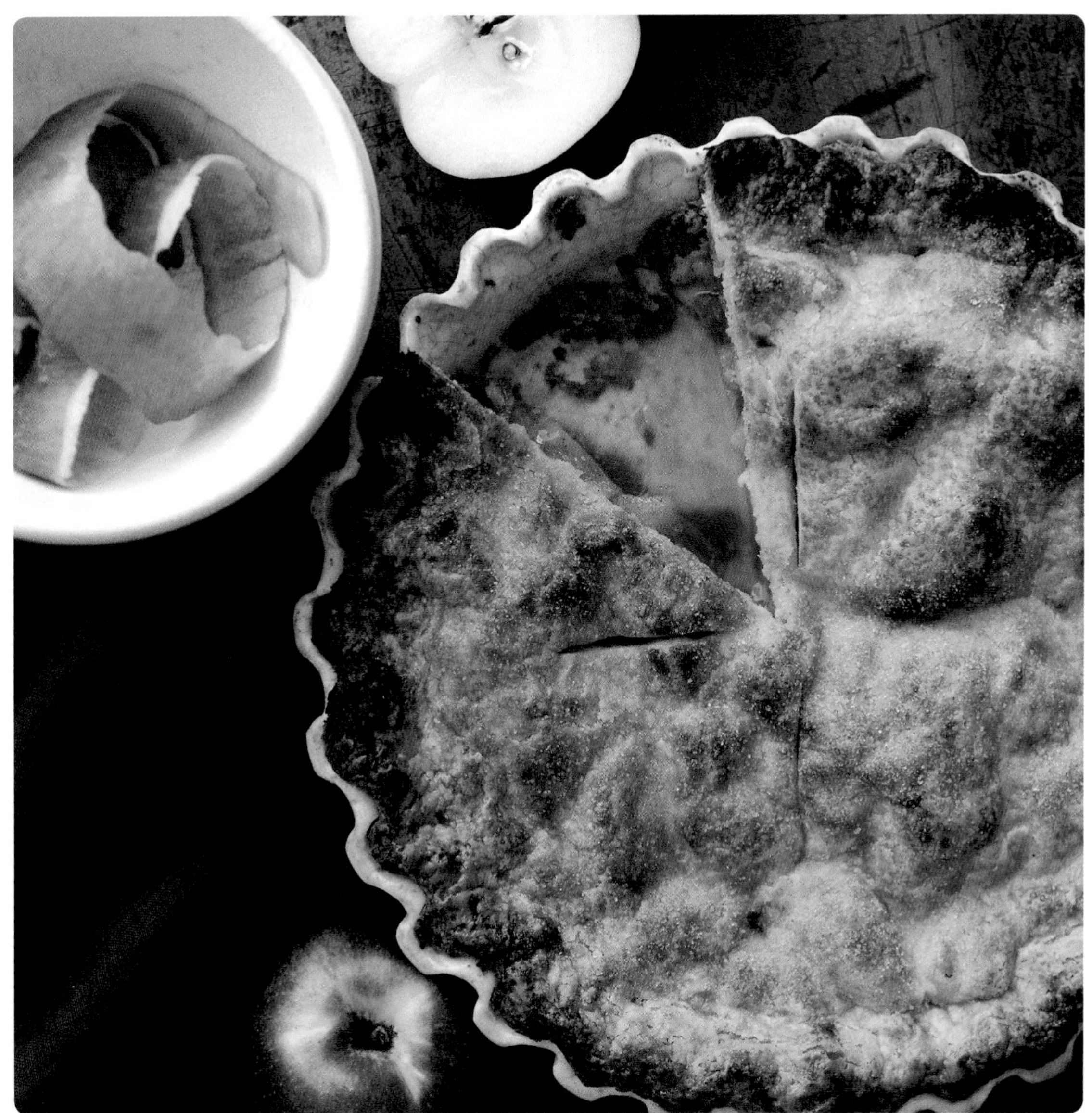

American as apple pie with a flaky butter crust.

Peaches for sale.

Harvested and boxed cherries.

minute in Montana, and vice versa, giving America a beyond-amazing variety of fruits.

- Apples — Native favourites include the crisp Cortland (New York), sweet Cameo (Washington), the soft, best-for-canning Golden Delicious (West Virginia), sweet-sour Jonagold (New York), tart and firm North Spy (New York), bland-but-popular Red Delicious (Iowa), balanced Winesap (Virginia), and sweet-crunchy Honeycrisp (Minnesota).
- Georgia and South Carolina battle it out for the 'America's best peaches' title. Michigan is tops for cherries, Florida oranges and other citrus fruits ship nationwide. Florida and California both grow creamy avocados, Southern rhubarb fills pies every spring, and Southern watermelons quench thirst all summer long.
- Sweet-tart blueberries, native to New England, come up in mid-summer and are fantastic in pies, smoothies or raw. Cranberries, another New England fruit, are incredibly sour and usually used for cranberry sauce. Thick-skinned Muscadine and Scuppernong grapes are Southern specialties, while Massachusetts's Concord grape is good for jellies and jams. Black cherries, native to eastern North America, are a common flavouring for sodas, candies and ice cream. Huckleberries, from the Pacific Northwest, are similar to blueberries.

Grains, legumes and nuts

The Midwest is America's breadbasket, growing the vast majority of the country's grains. Grains and legumes make up the bulk of the country's agricultural output, especially corn, soybeans and wheat.

- Corn, when eaten as a grain, can be ground into grits,

which are similar in texture to Italian polenta, or into finer cornmeal, the base of cornbread and corn tortillas.

- Black-eyed peas are common in Southern cuisine, pintos and black beans in Southwestern and Tex-Mex, and Great Northern beans in the food of New England.
- Peanuts, technically a legume, grow across the South and are ground into peanut butter, roasted for snacking, or, in the Deep South, boiled while still green and served hot.
- Local nut species include black walnuts, pecans (often used in candies and pies), the Southwest's pinyon pine nuts, and Hawaii's macadamias.

Meat and poultry

America is a capital of factory farming, but it's also the centre of a heritage breed renaissance, in which long-forgotten types of meat animals are being revived by small farmers. The country's farmers' markets are a good place to look for locally raised beef, pork, chicken and more. Be brave and try only-in-America exotic meat and game: alligator, rattlesnake, bison.

- Beef — Most standard American beef cattle are corn-fed, but foodies and environmentalists go for grass-fed, which has become increasingly common in recent years. Popular American cuts include the brisket, which is often used for barbecue, the ribs, and the chuck, the source of the venerable hamburger. For steaks, the T-bone and ribeye cuts are tops for their hearty flavour.
- Game — America's populous white-tailed deer plague drivers by dashing across the road. Fortunately they're also tasty. Elk, populous in the Great Plains, has a similar flavour. Bison (colloquially called 'buffalo'), once wild, is now cultivated for its juicy beef-like meat.

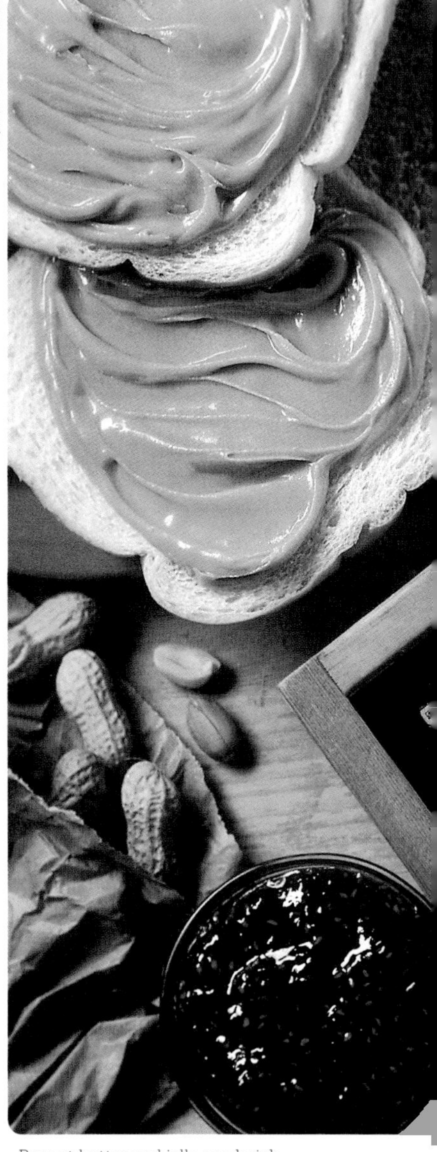

Peanut butter and jelly sandwich.

Oddities such as rattlesnake, alligator and squirrel will show up on the occasional menu, usually as a hyper-regional novelty.

- Pork — Berkshire hogs are among the tastiest and most common heirloom varieties in the US. In the South, the rare Ossabaw is the platinum standard for pork.
- Poultry — Chicken is big, of course, fried, barbecued or nugget-ed, but for a unique taste of America, try turkey (Benjamin Franklin's choice for the national bird). Though often relegated to Thanksgiving, you can find smoked turkey legs at county and state fairs. Duck is less common: the most common American breed is the pekin, from Long Island, New York.

Seafood

With around 20,000 kilometres of coastline touching two different oceans, the US has a wealth and variety of seafood seen in few other countries. Many coastal communities still rely on fishing for their livelihoods, and any number of classic American dishes are based on seafood: fish tacos in Southern California, clam chowder in Boston, lobster rolls in Maine, shrimp n' grits in coastal South Carolina, and *cioppino* (a type of seafood stew) in San Francisco. America's 20 landlocked states don't miss out on the fun either, chowing down on freshwater mountain trout and fried catfish.

- Catfish — Sometimes known as the mudcat, this freshwater bottom-feeder is popular in the South.
- Crabs — Blue crabs are a delicacy in the mid-Atlantic states, especially Maryland, while Dungeness crabs are a treat on the West Coast in the winter. Stone crabs are a Florida speciality, and massive Alaskan king crabs are shipped nationwide.

- Crawfish — Aka 'crayfish' or 'crawdads', these lobster-like river crustaceans are an integral part of Cajun and Creole cooking.
- Lobster — *Homarus Americanus*, aka the Maine lobster, is found from New Jersey all the way up to Canada. It's greenish-brown while alive, bright red once cooked.
- Oysters — Try Apalachicolas in Florida, Kumamotos in Washington, or Wellfleets in Massachusetts, to name a few of the dozens of oyster varieties in the US.
- Salmon — Varieties of this pink-fleshed fish can be found on both coasts, but the wild salmon of Alaska and the Northwestern states of Oregon and Washington is the most prized.

VEGETABLES

After years of canned green beans and frozen peas, Americans are finally learning to eat their veggies properly. And, oh, what a wonderful variety of veggies there are. From Southern fried green tomatoes to the ephemeral onion-like 'ramps' of the East coast, to the fiddlehead ferns of the Pacific Northwest, farmers' markets are filled to the brim with local bounty.

Leafy greens

- In the South and many rural parts of the US, the word 'greens' typically refers to peppery collards, spicy mustard greens, or the leafy tops of beets or turnips.
- While iceberg lettuce is still the base of many a tasteless cafeteria salad, look for more flavourful varieties like Bibb, lamb's lettuce, red leaf, and dandelion greens.

GENE KREBS / GETTY IMAGES

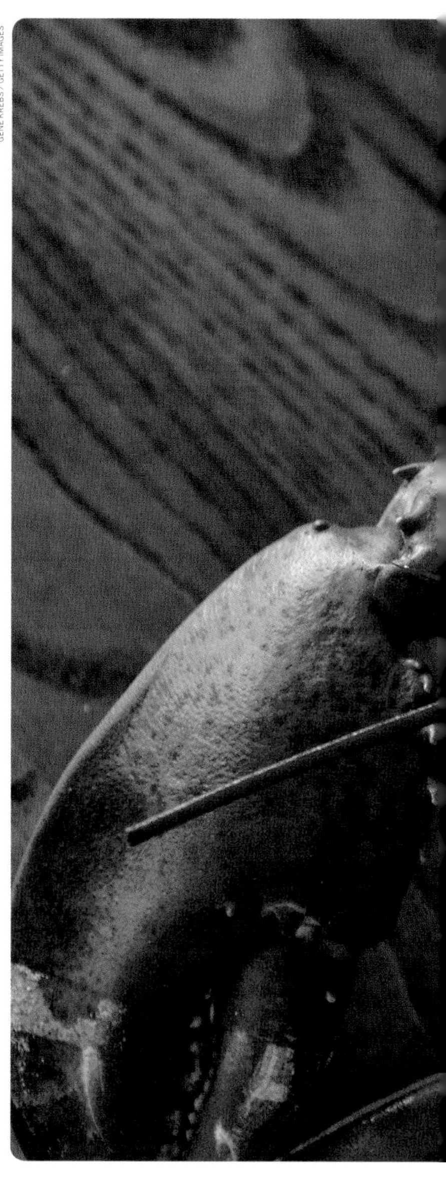

Boiled lobster and chips for dinner in New England.

Root vegetables

That internationally ubiquitous root veggie, the potato, is native to the Americas, and root vegetables form the backbone of many regional cuisines.

- Potatoes — Russets fluff up nicely for mashed potatoes, yellow-fleshed Yukon golds are good for almost anything, waxy little red potatoes are best boiled, while purple potatoes make a colourful potato salad.
- Sweet potatoes — While 'yams' and 'sweet potatoes' are botanically unrelated, the sweet tubers look and taste similar and the terms are often used interchangeably, especially in the South.
- Other root vegetables include crunchy jicama, usually eaten raw, earthy sunchokes, sweet turnips, parsnips and rutabagas.

I Love Me Some Greens.

Native species

- Native to the Americas, squash include starchy 'winter' varieties — butternut, Hubbard, acorn, delicata, and various types of pumpkin – and juicy 'summer' varieties such as zucchini, pattypan and crookneck.
- Ignore flavourless supermarket tomatoes in favour of tastier 'heirloom' varieties such as Brandywine, beefsteak, Early Girl and Green Zebra.
- Chilli peppers are integral to Southwest, Tex-Mex and Cajun cuisines. Notable varieties include New Mexico's mild Hatch green chillies, spicy tabascos and cayennes from the South and Southwest, hot datil peppers from northern Florida, and uber-spicy Scotch bonnets, common in Caribbean cuisine.
- Corn, the dominant crop in the United States, is both

Roasted purple and red potatoes.

Gourds, pumpkins and squash at a farm stand.

Mature corn crop on an Illinois farm in the late afternoon sun. Illinois is the country's second largest grower of corn, trailing only Iowa.

Young man grilling burgers outdoors.

Fried green tomatoes.

a grain and vegetable. Sweet corn varieties like Silver Queen and Sugar Pearl are eaten fresh.

SHOPPING

Since the middle of the 20th century, most American shopping has taken place in the refrigerated and somewhat sterile environs of chain supermarkets. Today, even big box stores like Wal-Mart have added grocery sections. Speciality stores like butchers, fishmongers and dairies are less common than in many countries, though they're experiencing a bit of a renaissance in larger cities. Farmers' markets are also increasingly popular — there are some 7800 today, compared to a mere 1700 in 1994. In spring and summer, look for local farm stands along rural highways or parked in vacant lots outside cities.

PREPARATION

Technique

- Deep frying is especially common in Southern cuisine.
- Barbecuing (aka 'grilling' or 'cooking out') on backyard grills is popular during the summer months across rural and suburban America.
- 'Clam bakes' are a summertime New England occasion, wherein seafood is covered in seaweed and steamed by hot stones. A copious amount of beer is generally involved. 'Seafood boils', where large amounts of shellfish are cooked in a pot and dumped out on brown paper to feed a crowd, are a Southern take on the same tasty tradition.
- Various types of hog roasts include the Southern 'pig pickin', the Hawaiian *luau* (featuring kalua pig, cooked

in a pit in the ground), the New Mexican *matanza*, the South Florida Cuban-America *caja china* fiesta (in which a pig is cooked in a special *caja china, a* Chinese box). Hog roasts are central community activities, common at weddings or church picnics.

- Baking, especially pies, cakes and cookies, is particularly popular in the US.

DEFINING DISHES

Apple pie

They don't say "as American as apple pie" for nothing. An import of early English settlers, this tender-crusted dessert can be found behind glass cases at roadside diners and cooling on windowsills nationwide. Typically baked using crisp, sour apples like Granny Smiths, the pies are often spiced with cinnamon, allspice, nutmeg and/or ginger, the combination of which is sold commercially as 'apple pie spice'. Crusts may contain butter, shortening or lard for flakiness. When served with ice cream, the dish becomes 'apple pie a la mode'. In the Midwest, apple pie is sometimes served with a wedge of sharp cheddar cheese.

Burger and fries

Though the origins of the hamburger remain shrouded by time and myth, most people agree on this: German immigrants brought 'Hamburg steak', a ground beef dish, to the United States in the 1800s and it gradually appeared, in modified form, on restaurant menus in the late 19th and early 20th century. Various towns, restaurants and lunch counters claim the invention of the modern hamburger on a bun with ketchup, and the genesis of the cheeseburger is equally disputed. Either way, the burger and its classic accompaniment, French fries,

SVARIOPHOTO / GETTY IMAGES

Famous New England clam chowder.

have become an iconic American meal, exported globally thanks to the US's far-reaching chain restaurants.

- Regional variations on the hamburger include the green chilli cheeseburger (New Mexico), the pepper-laced pimento cheese burger (South Carolina), the butter-fried 'butter burger' (Wisconsin), and the coleslaw-topped Carolina Burger (North Carolina).
- A patty melt is a burger between two slices of griddled bread, a slider is a small burger with chopped onions, and a Luther burger (a carnival speciality) is a burger served between two Krispy Kreme doughnuts as buns.
- McDonald's (in)famous Big Mac is two burger patties with American cheese, lettuce, onions, pickles and mayo-based 'special sauce' on a sesame seed bun.

Clam chowder

The pilgrim settlers of New England found a rocky coast teeming with clams, and various types of clam soups and stews soon followed. Clam chowder is eaten as a hearty lunch or comforting dinner up and down the Eastern Seaboard.

- New England clam chowder is cream-based and studded with chunks of potato and bits of softened onion. It's usually served with oyster crackers (so-called because of their shape) for sprinkling on top.
- Manhattan clam chowder is tomato-based, thanks to the Italian and Portuguese immigrants of the late 1800s.

Fried chicken

One of the most beloved Southern dishes, fried chicken originated as a fusion of the Scottish immigrant taste for fried foods and the spices and cooking techniques of West African slaves. Though recipes vary widely, chicken pieces are often

Fried chicken and waffles.

LAURI PATTERSON / GETTY IMAGES

soaked in buttermilk, milk or salted water overnight, then breaded with flour and seasonings and either deep-fried or pan-fried in a cast-iron pan. Variations include:

- chicken and waffles, wherein a piece of fried chicken is served atop a waffle with syrup
- upstate New York's sauce-splashed 'Buffalo wings' served at sports bars nationwide, and Nashville's cayenne pepper-spiked 'hot chicken'.

Barbecue

In the American South, otherwise sane people will come to blows about which regional version reigns supreme. The definition of barbecue depends on where in the country you are, but the best versions are often served in the dumpiest and most remote of smokehouses. A barbecue expert is known as a 'pitmaster'.

Here's a rundown of the four main barbecue zones:

- The Carolinas — In North Carolina, barbecue means succulent, slow-cooked pork. Chopped or shredded, it's drowned in a tangy vinegar sauce ('Eastern-style') or a sweeter, ketchup-spiked sauce ('Western-style'). In South Carolina, the pork is doused in a yellow, mustard-based sauce. It's usually served as a sandwich, with coleslaw on a squishy white bun, or as a platter, which generally comes with slaw and hushpuppies (fried balls of corn meal dough). The classic North Carolina barbecue event is called a 'pig pickin', wherein an entire barbecued pig is 'picked' clean by the crowd.
- Tennessee — The city of Memphis is as beloved for its barbecue as it is for its blues music. Here, barbecue comes in two varieties: pulled pork or ribs. The pulled pork is smothered in sweet tomato-based sauce, while

the ribs can be 'wet' (coated in the same sweet sauce) or 'dry' (rubbed with a herb mix).

- Texas — In cattle country, the quintessential barbecue is slow-cooked beef brisket, but nearly any kind of meat goes — chicken, sausage, ribs, even goat. Though you'll find the occasional side dish of potato salad or pinto beans, it's all about the meat here. Some of the Lone Star State's most iconic establishments serve their barbecue with nothing but slices of fluffy supermarket white bread.
- Kansas City — All sorts of meat are slow-smoked then smothered in the thick, sweet, tomato-based sauce you typically think of when you hear 'barbecue sauce'. Here, 'burnt ends' (which are exactly as the name suggests, the burned ends of the brisket) are considered a delicacy, served alone or in a sandwich.

DRINKS

Beer

The Midwest is dotted with big breweries started by German immigrants, such as Budweiser, Pabst Blue Ribbon and Miller, which mostly produce insipid American lager. But the microbrewery revolution of the 1990s means most regions have their own local specialties. Popular born-in-America brews include light American Pale Ale, hoppy IPA, and light golden cream ale.

Soft drinks

Americans adore their sugary sodas: the average American drinks more than 165 litres (yes, really) per year! Favourites are Coke and Diet Coke, Pepsi, cherry-cola flavoured Dr Pepper, lemony Sprite, and orange Fanta. Every region has their own

JESSICA BOONE / GETTY IMAGES

A stack of sweet and soft chocolate chip cookies.

classic micro-sodas: North Carolina's reddish Cheerwine, Maine's bitter Moxie, Detroit's fruity Faygo.

Wine

The US is the fourth largest wine producer in the world. California has by far the largest output, and is best-known for its Cabernet Sauvignon, Zinfandel, Sauvignon Blanc, Chardonnay and Pinot Noir. The Napa Valley, northeast of San Francisco, has become a mecca of wine tourism; Washington and Oregon also have notable wine industries.

CHOCOLATE CHIP COOKIES

Ingredients

2 ¼ cups flour
1 teaspoon baking powder
1 teaspoon salt
1 cup butter
¾ cup sugar
¾ cup brown sugar
1 teaspoon vanilla extract
2 eggs
2 cups chocolate chips

Method

Preheat the oven to 190°C. In a small bowl, combine the flour, baking powder and salt.

In a large mixing bowl, beat together the butter, sugar, brown sugar, and vanilla extract until creamy. Add 2 eggs, one at a time, beating well after each addition.

Gradually mix in the flour mixture then stir in 2 cups chocolate chips.

Drop rounded teaspoons directly onto un-greased cookie sheets and bake for 9 to 11 minutes or until golden brown.

A pumpkin field in autumn, Prince Edward Island.

THOMAS KITCHIN & VICTORIA HURST / GETTY IMAGES

Canada

Canadian cuisine doesn't get a lot of international airtime. Often dwarfed by its southern neighbour, this notoriously nice nation of 35 million isn't the type to brag either. But take note: from the homey food of the Alberta prairies to the French-inflected bistros of Montreal and the seaside seafood stands of British Columbia, Canada has plenty to offer the gastronomic tourist.

CULINARY CAPITALS MONTREAL, VANCOUVER **KNOWN FOR** MAPLE SYRUP, *POUTINE* **IMPORTS** AMERICAN FOOD **EXPORTS** GRAINS, SALMON **DEVOUR** QUÉBECOIS CUISINE, FRESH SEAFOOD **AVOID** SEAL BLUBBER

Poutine, Canada's favourite comfort food.

Punnets of raspberries, blueberries and red currants.

A French import, *coq au vin*.

CULTURE

The First Nations people native to these lands fished, hunted bison, and gathered native berries. Further north, the Inuit relied on fatty sea animals like seal, whales and walruses, and foraged roots and tubers. Settled largely by the British and, in Québec and the Maritimes, the French, Canada's cuisine is influenced by both cultures: roast beef and Yorkshire pudding sit alongside *tourtière* (a type of hearty meat pie). German and Eastern Europeans populated many of the Prairie Provinces, bringing their schnitzel, dumplings and heavy pastries. Jews brought bagels and smoked meat to Montreal, while the Chinese have made *dim sum* a Vancouver staple.

REGIONS

Québec

With its French heritage, Québec prides itself on its gourmet sensibilities. Parisian-styles bistros serving French classics like *coq au vin* (chicken cooked in wine) and steak *frites* abound, while heartier French-Canadian specialties like *tourtière* (a type of meat pie) and *cretons* (a fatty pork spread) are home-cooked favorites. *Poutine*, French fries topped with gravy and fresh cheese curds, is the ultimate Canadian comfort food. It is much tastier than it looks.

The Maritimes

The Eastern seaboard provinces of New Brunswick, Nova Scotia, and Prince Edward Island are famous for their salt air and saltier inhabitants. The sea defines the cuisine: fresh lobster, oysters and clams, *dulce* (a type of seaweed), and fish and chips.

Poutine râpée, a gelatinous ball of grated potato filled with pork and topped with blackstrap molasses, is the acquired taste specialty of French-speaking New Brunswick.

The West Coast

Vancouver, the largest city of the western province of British Columbia, is one of Canada's most international cities. The large population of Cantonese-speaking Chinese (nearly a third of the city's inhabitants are of Chinese origin) make *wontons* and soup noodles as Canadian as maple syrup. Going out to eat *dim sum*, the Cantonese 'small bites' of dumplings, buns and egg tarts, is a classic Vancouver weekend event. Seafood, unsurprisingly, is also big.

Baskets of *dim sum* in Toronto.

ESSENTIAL PRODUCE

Seafood and meat

With thousands of miles of sea coast touching both the Atlantic and Pacific oceans, seafood is a major part of the Canadian diet. The Maritime provinces mean lobster, while Prince Edward Island's Malpeque oysters are internationally renowned, and the salmon of the West Coast appears on tables country-wide. With some 64,000 cattle farms, beef is a huge part of the national cuisine as well.

Fruit and vegetables

Canada's cold climate limits the growing season, but, come spring, watch out. The country bursts forth with produce unrivalled by the rest of the world, much of it wild.

- Fruit — The climate is perfect for apple growing, making it the country's biggest fruit crop. Blueberries and cranberries are second only to the US, while blackberries and raspberries grow rampant in the summer forests.
- Vegetables — Corns, beans and sweet peas are a dietary staple, and winter veggies like cabbage and kale also do well. Rarer treats include fiddlehead

Oysters with a squeeze of lemon.

A fisherman displays two lobsters caught in the waters near Prince Edward Island.

ferns, which have a short spring season in the east, sea vegetables like *dulce* and purple laver, and tangy greens like salsify, foraged in the Pacific Northwest.

DEFINING DISHES

Butter tarts

Perhaps the most-loved Canadian dessert, this humble tart is a flaky pastry shell filled with butter, sugar, eggs and raisins. Everyone's grandmother has their own version, and will battle anyone who says it's not the best.

Maple syrup

Québec produces three-quarters of the world's maple syrup, the golden sap of certain maple trees. Maple syrup is a

MAPLE SYRUP PIE

What's more Canadian than maple syrup? Perhaps a slice of sweet, gooey maple syrup pie.

Ingredients

1 ½ cups light brown sugar
2 eggs
½ cup cream
⅓ cup maple syrup
2 teaspoons of melted butter
1 x 20 cm shortcrust pie case

Method

Preheat the oven to 180°C. Whisk together the sugar and eggs until light and creamy. Add the cream, maple syrup, and melted butter and whisk until smooth. Pour the filling into the shortcrust and bake for 50-60 minutes. Allow the pie to set and cool down.

Mayple syrup, Canada's golden nectar.

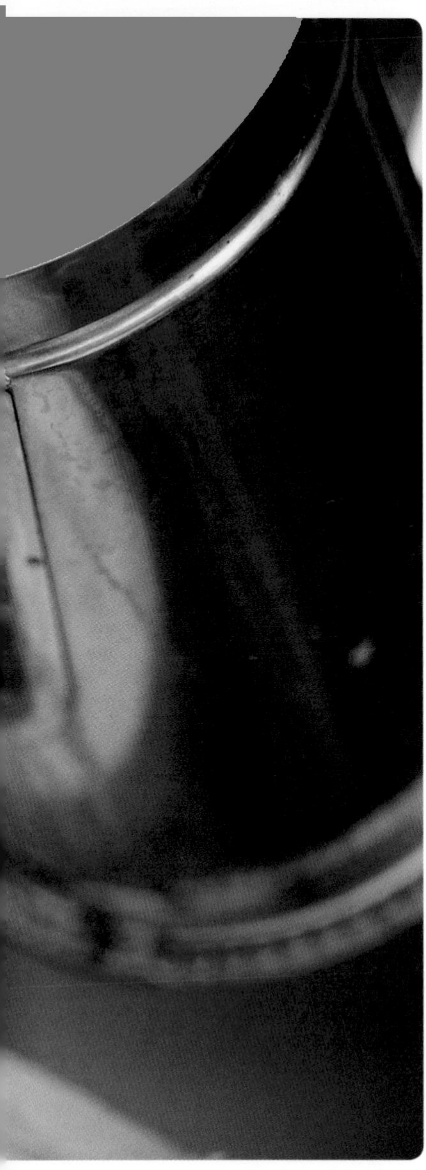

quintessential part of many Canadian treats, from maple syrup ice cream to maple syrup candies to salmon with a maple glaze.

Poutine

We've already mentioned this fries-topped-with-gravy-and-cheese curds dish, Montreal's favorite post-beer snack. But it bears emphasis: even the McDonald's in Francophone Canada serve their own version. Upscale chains riff on *poutine* by adding caviar, smoked salmon, bison sausage and other incongruous items.

Smoked meat

A specialty of the Jewish delis of Montreal, this slow-smoked and sliced brisket is the kind of thing people travel hours to taste. Choose lean, medium, or fat cuts, served on rye bread with mustard. Smoked meat worth its salt is always sliced by hand, as a slicer would damage its delicate texture.

DRINKS

Beer

Canadians, by and large, love nothing more than a tall cold brew. Top commercial beers include Coors Light, Labatt and Molson, though connoisseurs will go for microbrews — and there are plenty. 'Ice beer', which has undergone a special freezing process, is a high-alcohol Canadian invention.

Coffee and tea

The French influence in Québec means coffee is taken seriously. Look for Parisian-style *café au lait* (coffee with milk) and *café noisette* (an espresso with just a little steamed milk). The Canadian doughnut chain Tim Hortons is well-loved for its (decent and cheap) brew. The nation's English heritage means black tea with milk or lemon and sugar is Canada's favorite afternoon drink.

Red hot *chile de arbol* for sale at Libertat Market in Guadalajara.

GREG ELMS / GETTY IMAGES

Mexico

Mexican cuisine is a fiesta, a celebration of the senses; a window to a past of conquest, colonisation and revolution. It is the rich aroma of a *mole* simmering on the stove. It is the bubble and pop of frying *tortillas* at a street stall at night and the chatter of hungry customers. It is fresh fish grilled to perfection and served with a wedge of lime, and a cold beer or a rich hot soup, filled with the ingredients of a vast and varied land.

CULINARY CAPITALS MEXICO CITY, OAXACA, PUEBLA **KNOWN FOR** *TAMALES, TORTILLAS* **IMPORTS** CORN **EXPORTS** FRUITS AND VEGETABLES, COFFEE **DEVOUR** *TORTILLAS* **AVOID** *PAN DE MUERTO* (BREAD OF THE DEAD)

Woman selling Oaxacan cheeses at Juarez Market in Oaxaca City.

GREG ELMS / GETTY IMAGES

CULTURE

Food in Mexico has a significance which transcends mere nourishment. It is a medium of pleasure, a focal point for social gatherings and special celebrations, and a badge of identification. For years, the principal concern of Mexico's greatest thinkers has been la Mexicanidad. What is Mexico? Who are Mexicans? Before the 1910–17 Revolution, the answers seemed clear. Mexicans were descendants of either Spanish or Indians. The division was not entirely a product of skin colour but as much to do with dress, wealth, where you lived and what you ate.

The Revolution revealed to Mexicans what should have been evident all along — Mexicans are Spanish and Indian, not one or the other. When the Mexican looks to his past, he looks as much to Madrid, Seville and Granada as to Tenoctitlán, Chizen Itza and Zempoala.

These Mexicans are drinkers of Indian chocolate with Spanish *leche* (milk) who readily pour a chilli-based *mole* (savoury sauce with chocolate) over a *puchuga de pollo* (breast of chicken). These dishes, and many others that combined elements of Spanish and indigenous cooking, have existed for centuries. But it is only since the Revolution that they were embraced as part of a national cuisine.

Acceptance of the tortilla

The fusion of Spanish and indigenous cuisines yielded mixed results. Chocolate was adopted enthusiastically into the Spanish diet and chillies turned up in several Spanish dishes and preparations including *chorizo*, the spicy sausage. Likewise, the natives discovered *manteca* (pork lard) as a cooking agent. Following Independence, recipes for *chiles en nogada* a truly *mestizo* (mixed) dish appeared.

But other foods were resisted by both sides. The most famous example being wheat bread versus corn tortillas. Wheat bread was essential to the European table while corn tortilla had been a staple in the mesoamerican diet for the previous two thousand years. The final acceptance of the tortilla paralleled the acceptance of other features of new nationhood. Led by the likes of artists, Diego Rivera and Frida Kahlo, educator Jose Vasconcelos and President Lazaro Cárdenas, Mexico came into its own as a nation. Indigenous identities were revisited and embraced. Food was no exception.

Street food

Step off any intercity bus and you will be struck immediately by the smell of meat, onions and garlic, drifting from a cluster of *puestos* (semi-permanent street stalls) catering for hungry travellers. But *puestos* aren't only for transients — the culture of eating in the street is firmly entrenched in the Mexican gastronomic psyche and some *puestos* become neighbourhood institutions.

The most common *puestos* are no more than 2m high by 2m wide, made of thin sheets of metal with shutters serving as sun screens by day and security by night. Depending on the speciality a *puestos* may have a counter, a chopping block, a deep frying pot, a large *comal* (flat grill pan), and refreshments nestling among large blocks of ice.

In a tiny, makeshift kitchen, you can expect to see cooks rushing to construct *guarachos*, tortilla shells piled high with *chorizo*, *carne*, potato, coriander and chilli salsa. Other places sell *tacos* of every variety, *quesadillas*, golden *flautas* (flour tortillas wrapped around a filling and fried), *hamburguesas*, stubby hot dogs wrapped in bacon, overflowing *tortas* (flat bread), *gorditas* stuffed with ground seasoned meat or melted cheese, or *sopes* (tortillas topped with beans and vegetables),

Iced fruit drink from the market in Tepoztlan.

Mexican man in Guelavia.

A good old-fashioned barbecue with *tasajo*, steak and *chorizo* sausages.

homemade *tamales* (corn-based tortilla that have been stuffed and baked in plaintain or other leaves), and even corn on the cob.

Puestos do not limit themselves to hot *antojitos* (popular snack foods). Another popular item is the *chicharrón*. This is a large flat square of puffed corn which is then topped with *palanquetas* which are made of the same stuff but shaped like petrified spaghettis. This deep-fried delight is then liberally topped with lime juice and bottled *salsa picante* (spice sauce). There's very little to them and they are not much more than textured vehicles for yet another way to take lime and salsa.

On the coast, you will find *puestos* selling *nieves* (snow) drinks made from ice; they are easily recognisable by the colourful jars of fruit syrup displayed across the top counter.

Jugos (juices) are also popular street items, often supplied from a push cart equipped with a citrus squeezer bolted to its platform and a basket of oranges to the side. More complicated juice *puestos* advertise themselves by lining the entire stand with the myriad of fruits on offer. In addition to a citrus squeezer, these places may have a pulveriser for juicing carrots, beets and other hard vegetables.

Hot food is also served in the dirt-cheap *comedores* (restaurants). Unfortunately, you often get what you pay for but these are good places to find out the regional preferences: for example, a Guadalajaran *comedor* is bound to serve *birrias* (a spicy meat stew), chocolate in Oaxaca, or *atoles* (a corn masa drink, sometimes translated as gruel) in Mexico City.

Many visitors are woken by the sound of a loud-speakered voice invading their dreams, then growing louder, until it fills the room from the street below. The loud speakers are attached to a cart or a bicycle or a hybrid of the two and enthusiastically announce that the rider is in possession of fine pistachios, *tamales*, roasted peanuts or some other product you might argue you didn't need to be woken for.

GREG ELMS / GETTY IMAGES

Spices are the key ingredients for cooking *birria*, a speciality of Jalisco.

REGIONS

While some ingredients — beans, corn and chillies in particular — are found in kitchens from Tijuana to Tuxtla Gutiérrez, Mexico's cuisine remains highly regionalised. The country's geography is rugged, marked by two mountain ranges that cut it in three parts from north to south. Before the advent of air travel, going from one state to another was a major journey. As a result, regional cuisine developed in relative isolation, using what was readily and locally available.

Climate also contributed to regionalisation as Mexico offers virtually every climatic condition save Arctic Tundra. The north is dry and dominated by the deserts, which offer little in the way of edible vegetation. In the south and on the Yucatán peninsula, Mexico is subtropical with lush, overgrown forests characterising the landscape. In the centre, temperate highlands get enough rainfall to sustain a family farm, and there are low-lying coastal plains with temperatures that delight beach-goers and provide for a variety of tropical fruits.

Puebla

The city of Puebla in Central Mexico stands above all other Mexican culinary centres. Two dishes in particular, *mole poblano* and *chiles en nogada*, both products of Puebla kitchens, are testament to its superiority.

Mole poblano, whether served with *pavo* (turkey) or *pollo* (chicken) is an indescribable wonder, a complex mixture of up to 100 ingredients including several kinds of chilli, spices, sesame seed, broth and chocolate — the final item in the list characterises the *mole poblano*. Despite the work that must go into every batch, *mole* is widely available in local restaurants. To come to Puebla without having *mole poblano* is to come in vain.

GREG ELMS / GETTY IMAGES

Distinctive Yucatecan food, *conchinita pibil* in salsa.

Chiles en nogada, Puebla's other notable dish, is a source of not only culinary pride, but also evokes patriotic sentiment among Mexicans. The origins of the dish go back to 1821 and the signing of the Treaty of Córdoba, which formalised Mexico's independence from Spain. Soon after, one of the leaders of the new republic, Agustin de Iturbide, was passing through Puebla. Municipal leaders decided to celebrate the occasion with a lavish banquet. Despite the lavish spread, Iturbide did not eat. The man who would eventually name himself emperor of Mexico had many enemies and feared that one would somehow manage to poison his food. So as the platters of roasted meats, seafood cocktails, fresh fruit and pastries passed him, he took nothing. It wasn't until he was presented with a plate of *chiles en nogada*, the sumptuous green chillies stuffed with a stew of beef and fruits, topped with *nogada*, a white almond-chestnut cream sauce, and adorned with red *semillas de granada* (pomegranate seeds), that the general's resistance broke down.

FEASTS

The *fiesta* is another great Mexican institution with food and drink at its foundation. The word translates literally as 'party' and, as such, has snuck into the global lexicon. But in Mexico, a *fiesta* refers to much more than that. Mexico is one of the most celebratory societies in the world and each month, it seems, has its own holiday or fiesta. Some, like the Day of the Virgin of Guadalupe on 12 December, Constitution Day in February and Independence Day on 16 September are national celebrations but each town and village also has its own day to commemorate local patron saints.

Such fiestas are marked by parades and ceremonies, shouts and cheers, fireworks and pistol shots in the air, singing and dancing. They are times to mourn death and celebrate new life,

Papaloapau dancers doing *Flor de Pitra* (pineapple dance) in Oaxaca City.

GREG ELMS / GETTY IMAGES

to end stale romances and begin new ones. Rigid social conventions and the established order are cast aside and chaos reigns for a brief, impossible moment. The prohibited becomes permissible: macho men dress as women, political authority is reduced to a joke, the rich and poor mingle without hierarchical convention, and masks — both real and imagined — are worn everywhere.

In anticipation of a fiesta, women will spend entire days preparing *tamales*, *tortillas* and *guisos* (stews). The most humble families will save for years to throw their daughter a proper wedding party. And for those without the cash, an ancient system of bartering exists, where ingredients are swapped or labour is offered in exchange for food.

Drinking goes on late into the night and delivers the licence necessary for a *fiesta* to truly become a *fiesta*. Beer, brandy, *tequila*, *mezcal*, and *pulque* will all be consumed in generous portions and contests break out to see who can drink the most. And when it's all over, everything returns to normal for a year.

Day of the Dead

On the surface, *Dia de Muertos* celebrations are not remarkably different from other national parties: there is *mole*, drink, music and general revelry. But when you consider that *Dia de Muertos* translates to Day of the Dead, the festivities take on a decidedly ironic edge. The origins of the holiday reach back to the Aztec month of Miccailhuitontli, which was named for the goddess Mictecacihuatl, the Lady of the Dead. Offerings of food and drink were left to supply the departed with nourishment on their journey through the nine tunnels, which conducted them to the world beyond.

Celebrations — and they *are* celebrations — include food and drink. Candies made with marzipan and shaped into skulls with hideous, toothy grins are gobbled up by children. Women spend 1st November making the favourite dishes of their recently deceased. If there has been a death in the house in the previous year, the day is especially important and relatives and friends gather to eat and drink with the visiting spirits.

An altar to the dead, decorated with bright flowers, ribbons and coloured candles, is erected in one corner of the house. Plates of *tamales*, *pan de muerto* (bread of the dead — a heavy loaf made with egg yolks, fruits and tequila or *mezcal)* are left so that the dead feel welcome on their return.

Outside, vendors pass among the crowds selling candies and sweetbreads as memorial processions make their way to cemeteries, where people leave bunches of marigolds on the graves of their loved ones.

The Northern asado

In Northern Mexico, celebrations — birthdays, anniversaries, graduations, family reunions — are marked by *asados*, a word loosely translated as barbecues. These are whole-day, whole-family occasions with every generation participating.

Any good *asado* begins with the *leña* (wood for cooking) which in this case must be *mesquite* in order to infuse the meat with a distinctive flavour. The meat is either beef or *cabrito* (kid or baby goat), prepared prior to cooking in the kitchen with a simple combination of seasoning: salt, pepper and lime (according to the proportions in the family recipe.)

Men prepare the *leña* and the grill while the women season the meat. The *leña* must burn for a time, until the visible flames are diminished and all that remains is a bed of glowing embers. Generations come together, with the old ones teaching young ones the secrets of the great *asado*: selecting the meat, proper seasoning, and the family recipes for side dishes.

Meat is the star of the show, but the *asado* also includes *guacamole*, vegetables, potatoes and wheat *tortillas*. Kid goats

Tamales and *tamales dulce* in Puebla.

are grilled virtually whole, split at the ribs and spread like giant butterflies over the grill. It is a fatty meat and the drippings cause frequent flare-ups that burn the skin crisp. In the north, where goat and cattle herding were a fundamental part of the region's economic formation, the *asado* has special, sentimental meaning. Even the most urban families will discuss the quality of the meat — it's fat content, the texture, the aging process — as though they had been raised on a ranch.

An *asado* will last the whole afternoon. Many will sneak off to one of the bedrooms for a little siesta.

ETIQUETTE

There are no hard and fast rules regarding eating and drinking in Mexico and those that do exist are more about common sense than anything.

Food is served in casseroles or on platters and you are expected to serve yourself. Plates are laid out on placemats along with the requisite utensils: fork, knife and spoon. A salt and pepper shaker and napkin dispenser may be the only other non-food items on the table. Because many Mexican foods are eaten with the fingers, everyone goes through several napkins in a single sitting.

There is a certain sloppy quality to eating because so many meals begin with a *tortilla* which is filled with spoonfuls of whatever meat, fish or vegetable is featured. With practice, you will become skilled at knowing just how much your *tortilla* can take, and the ways to fold it so that you don't leave one end open and ready to spill the contents.

DAILY MEALS

The kind of *desayuno* (breakfast) eaten depends on how busy the rest of your day is. On the go, it may consist of nothing

A buffet-style lunch with guacamole and refried beans washed down with a cold Corona in Mexico City.

Horchata, a rice- and mezcal-based drink.

Birria, a goat meat dish from Jalisco.

more than a cup of coffee and a sweet roll or doughnut. For those who did not have enough at breakfast, there is the late morning *almuerzo* (brunch - sometimes translated as lunch). There is nothing formal about this meal, which really amounts to a glorified snack: a quick plate of tacos or a sandwich will do.

The average Mexican's day is centred around the *comida*, the multi-course meal taken between 1:30 pm and 4 pm. A businessperson might spend these hours at a restaurant with associates, discussing deals as though they were in a boardroom. In smaller cities and towns, the *comida* is a time for the whole family to come together, before returning to work or school. The truly civilised among them will carry on one of the most pleasant Mexican traditions, the *siesta*.

While the *comida* is the main meal, workers usually have it in restaurants these days. School-aged children still go home for *comida* but the main family meal is the evening *cena*, often the leftovers of the afternoon meal. It tends to be smaller than the suppers eaten by North Americans or northern Europeans.

Outside the cities, *comida* is still most important. Entire towns shut down from about 2 pm to 4 pm; businesses lock their doors, taxis seem to disappear and noise from the street subsides until late afternoon when it all starts up again.

In-between meals

Antojitos are the original take-anywhere food experience. The word is translated as 'little whimsies', although they are much more than simple snack foods, and include *tacos*, *quesadillas*, *sopes* (soups), *totopos* (a black bean and maize tortilla), *tamales* and *tortas*. You can pick up a couple of *tacos* on from a street stall to bridge the gap between meals, or order a plate of *tacos de pollo* (chicken tacos) at a restaurant, enjoy them with a beer, decide you'd like something else and order *tacos arabes* (tacos made with slightly thicker wheat bread). And if you're still not satisfied, you can choose something else and your 'little whimsy' has turned into a big meal. *Almuerzo*, the disappearing institution of brunch, consists almost invariably of *antojitos*. But *antojitos* can be eaten at anytime of the day or night, up to the wee hours of the morning after an evening of dancing and music.

ESSENTIAL PRODUCE

Some foods emerge as staples because alternatives are scarce, as is the case in Mexico with corn, beans and rice. But what makes a cuisine is what is done to these staple ingredients, and that's what separates Mexico from its Central American neighbours.

Beans and rice

Beans and rice have been listed together because they serve as a staple food for so many Mexican diets. Beans provide the protein and rice the carbohydrate content.

The most common way to eat rice is steamed. It can serve as a side dish or be mixed with meat and vegies to make a casserole. Beans are most often eaten *refritos*, first cooked then crushed or pureed then refried with *manteca* (pork lard) and spice. Virtually every *entrada* (appetiser) in a Mexican restaurant will come accompanied by a large spoonful of this brown paste, sometimes topped with crumbled *queso fresco* (a creamy white cheese) and a few *totopos* (a black bean and maize tortilla). Refried beans are generally made with red kidney beans. Black beans are also used widely including in a popular Veracruz dish which also includes onion, bacon, jalapeño chillies and cheese. There is even a tasty dish made in the Yucatán and on the Gulf Coasts which combines white rice with black beans and goes by the decidedly tasteless name *moros y cristianos* (Moors and Christians).

Chicken stand at the Juarez Market in Oaxaca City.

Beef

Mexicans are big meat eaters, especially when dining out. The most popular tacos are *al pastor* or *bistec*. *Bistec* is thinly sliced beef which is chopped and fried before being stuffed into a hot *tortilla* shell. *Tacos al pastor* is an all-day preparation, where a pile of beef is stacked with onions and seasoning on a vertical spit and then slow roasted, rotating before a hot element. The idea is that the meat cooks at the same rate as customers demand it so everyone gets juicy meat in their taco but often you'll end up with overdone, dry meat — another reason to stick to busy places.

Cheese

A wide variety of cheeses are available at supermarkets and speciality shops in municipal markets, but for the most part, Mexicans use just two varieties of cheese in their cooking: *quesillo*, a stringy goat's milk cheese from Oaxaca and *queso fresco*, a light creamy white cheese made with cow's milk. In the north, the Mennonite communities produce several varieties which are stamped with a seal of authenticity and are renowned throughout the country.

Mexican cheeses are mostly mild in taste and do not have the heavy creaminess associated with high fat-content cheeses. One exception is *queso añejo*, a hard, aged variety with a sharp flavour similar to parmesan.

Chilli

Put simply and without exaggeration: there would be no Mexican food without chilli.

The first chillies were cultivated around 3000 BC and have remained a part of Mexican cuisine ever since. They are used as a seasoning with eggs, beans, meats and fish; as a basis for salsas or as a main dish itself, as in *chiles en nogada* or *chiles*

Dried corn on the cob.

rellenos. While most chillies used aren't particularly *picoso* (hot), the penetrating spiciness can be the undoing of even the most steel-gutted foreigner. Yet to a native, the chilli is nothing less than the flavour of Mexico.

Natural diversification and bio-technology have given Mexico 300 known varieties of chilli. They range from the fist-sized *chilli poblano* to the miniature *chilli pekin.* They range in colour from orange to red to yellow to green. They can be eaten fresh or preserved by drying in the sun. Cooks will chop or grind them raw as an addition to a salsa, stuff them, dip them in egg batter and fry them, roast and pickle them. In markets, there is no mistaking the section where carefully stacked chillies emit a rich, pungent aroma that only hints at the full flavour potential.

Corn

According to legend, using both white and yellow corn, raw and ground, the Mayan gods fashioned the great race which has flourished in south-eastern Mexico and Guatemala, despite years of attempted assimilation and extermination. To sustain themselves, it was only natural that their diets should be based on corn.

Anthropologists say that the first corn was planted in the Valley of Mexico between 5000 and 3500 BC. At the time, the Indians, who inhabited the region, called it *toconayo* meaning 'our flesh'. Babies were referred to as 'maize blossoms' and young girls were called 'tender green ears'. The 'Lord King Cob' was a strong and able warrior. Corn made the indigenous people what they were and was treated with due respect. Not a kernel was wasted and many societies used corn as the principal offering to their gods.

Over the years, experimentation propelled the many uses for corn: from movie-house popped corn, to the dough used in *tamales* and *atole* (a corn masa drink, sometimes translated as gruel), and to corn roasted on the cob and served on a stick. But by far and away, the most popular use of corn is the *tortilla*, which serves as the basis for so much Mexican food.

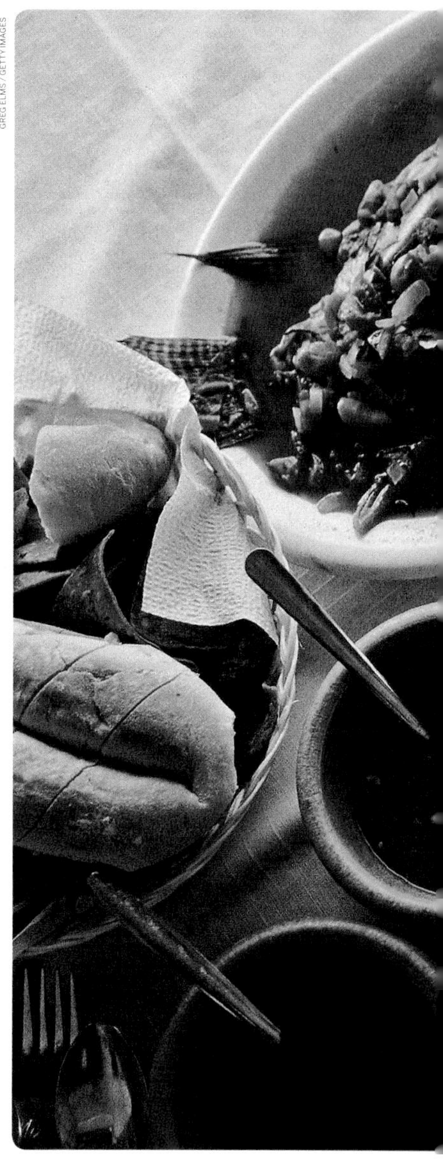
GREG ELMS / GETTY IMAGES

Salsas

Walk into virtually any restaurant in Mexico and you will see a bowl of salsa waiting on each table. It is the most common condiment in Mexico, meant to be splashed onto every dish on the menu. Almost all are home-made and each restaurant will have their own unique salsa, varying in spiciness and flavour.

A basic salsa will include the following ingredients: chilli, tomato (either green or red), *cebolla* (onion), *ajo* (garlic), *jugo de limón* (lime juice), and *agua* (water). This simple combination gets complicated when you consider that any of the vegetable ingredients may be roasted first to bring out a smoky quality and that there are well over 300 kinds of chillies in Mexico and some salsas require many different ones.

- The most common salsas are the tomato-based *salsa verde* (green tomatoes) and *salsa rojo* (red tomatoes). The texture of each will depend on how aggressively they are ground.
- The chunkiest of the salsas is *salsa bandera*, so-called because its tomatoes, onions, chillies and coriander carry the three colours of the Mexican flag.

Salsa is served with every meal:

- At breakfast, an order of *huevos rancheros* will get you scrambled eggs topped with a red chilli sauce.
- *Chilaquiles,* another common breakfast meal, consists of day-old *tortillas* smothered in the same chilli sauce and sprinkled with cheese.
- You may wish to sauce up a *torta* (flatbread) sandwich at brunch or drizzle a spoonful into your soup at dinner.

Traditional food of Veracruz: shrimp soup, octopus in its own ink, fresh prawns, spicy baked fish and condiments.

Hanging out at the fish market in Puerto Veracruz.

Crabs at the market.

Bag of *charal* at the market in Mexico City.

It's perfectly acceptable to have salsa with everything, to dip bread into the bowl at the table, or even to spread a spoonful on a fresh *tortilla* and roll it into a *taquito*.

Seafood

Mexico's two coasts are blessed with a wide variety of *pescado* (fish) and *mariscos* (shellfish). The lakes and rivers of the interior also provide many fresh-water species, although increased levels of pollution have raised questions about the safety of eating these.

The most common varieties of fish are *huachinango* (red snapper) and *rabálo* (sea bass). On menus, when you see the word 'fillet' under the *pescado* section, you can assume that you will be served some sort of white fish. Dried, salted cod, called *bacalao*, is a popular fish when chopped and added to soups.

Shellfish is for the most part a delicacy although *ceviche* is common. This is a sort of cocktail with shrimp, oysters or crab mixed with *escabeche*, a sauce made with lime, onion, salt, tomatoes and bottled salsa.

Soup

Much of Mexico is at high altitude and in these conditions a hot *sopa* is the perfect evening meal. Pre-Hispanic cultures knew this method of staying cosy, using vegetable, fish and turkey *caldo* (broth). Most soups today are made from chicken or beef broth and can include an infinite variety of ingredients.

In Mexico City's Mercado de la Merced, there are stacks of *tripa* (tripe), bought in large quantities to use as a flavour base for huge pots of soup. Restaurant chefs and others who cook for a lot of people will come in early to buy stacks of the stuff, along with other cuts that don't have so much table appeal: intestines, head, *patas* (hooves) etc.

Perhaps the best known soup is *pozole* which, while made all over the republic, is the pride of the state of Jalisco. There, the *pozole* is white and includes kernels of *elote* (hominy), chicken, *garbanzos* (chickpeas), shredded cabbage, and radish. It can be taken as an appetiser in small bowls or served as a full and hearty meal. In Michoacán, the *pozole* is made with pork or beef broth. Red chillies add colour and spice. It is possible to get both versions throughout the country and at least one restaurant chain, Potzollcalli, specialises in p*ozole* as a meal.

*Sopas secas i*s a dry soup and *sopas aguadas* liquid. *Sopa seca* refers to rice and pasta dishes such as *risotto*, or anything that was cooked in water or a reduced broth.

Although eaten across classes, soup has traditionally been very important in peasant diets as it provides an excellent source of protein and a means of stretching a little meat a long way. Virtually every *comida* begins with a *sopa* and many suppers consist of nothing more than reheated soup with a stack of *tortilla*s.

Tortillas

There may be nothing better (or more Mexican) than the taste of a hot corn *tortilla*, straight from the grill, almost too hot to touch. A fresh *tortilla*, cooked until slightly crisp on the outside, almost melts in your mouth, filling it with the taste of corn.

The *tortilla* is the single most important food in Mexico. It is the main source of nourishment for many Mexicans, especially those in rural regions.

Simultaneously a food and a utensil, it serves as a receptacle for stews, grilled meats, vegetables, *guacamole*, potatoes, rice — virtually anything that will fit in the cradle it forms when folded in two.

In traditional *tortilla* making the following process occurs:

- Kernels of corn are cut from the husk and then soaked

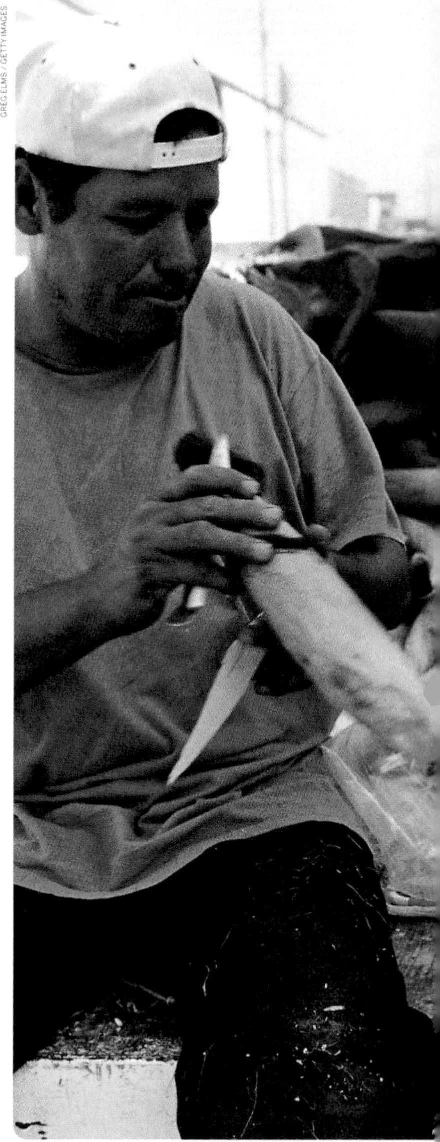

GREG ELMS / GETTY IMAGES

Vendor husking corn in Tequila.

in a mixture of warm (but not boiling) water and *cal* or mineral lime.

- The corn is soaked for at least 5 to 7 hours, usually overnight.
- The next morning the corn is rinsed and drained then ground into a masa.The process of turning corn into masa is laborious, requiring the cook to kneel in front of the *metate* (large flat grinding stone) using the *mano* (a kind of stone rolling pin) to grind and roll.
- The masa has to go through the whole process three times to achieve the proper consistency for making *tortillas*.
- A hunk of masa, the size of a golf ball, is first pressed flat and then passed from palm to palm with each stroke making the *tortilla* a little flatter until, after 30 or 40 slaps, the *tortilla* is the right thickness.
- It is then placed on the *comal,* a flat, iron pan which has no rims, allowing the cook to get close to the surface.
- After about a minute, the *tortilla* is flipped and cooked on the other side. Vigilance is important, for burning a *tortilla* is considered bad luck. The result is a slightly crisp yet chewy *tortilla* that is best eaten right away.

SHOPPING

At the market

City markets have always been important in Mexican society, not only for commerce but also as a place where friends and acquaintances meet and discuss the issues of the day.

Markets are reflections of the regions and cities they serve. Each small town market has a day or two in the week designated as a *día del mercado* (market day) when fresh

Pan dulce (sweet breads) in the window of a bakery in Puebla.

GREG ELMS / GETTY IMAGES

produce is trucked in. On those days, shoppers come early, eager to get to the best stuff before it is sold out. The rest of the week, a sort of languor prevails.

You'll know without prompting when you've entered the meat section. The smell of raw flesh is accompanied by the sound of chopping cleavers and electric slicers preparing fillets for sale. Mexicans are frugal about meat, using every part of the slaughtered animal. As a result there are stacks of tripe, buckets of intestines and skinned pigs heads hanging from hooks that look like props from a production of William Golding's *The Lord of the Flies.* There are chains of *salchichas* (frankfurters), giant heaps of *chorizo* (sausage), and sheets of dried beef called *machaca*.

There are stalls which sell all types of grocery items from honey to bottled salsas, spices to packed sweets and dried tea blends which can alleviate any ailment.

Cake shops

Pastelerias are cake shops. Although when you see a window display with a metre-high white frosted wedding cake, you'll figure that out. In addition to wedding cakes, a *pasteleria* may offer *pastel de tres leches,* a very heavy cake made with, as the name indicates, three kinds of milk: evaporated, condensed and evaporated cream. Try one of the small cookie-like nibbles called *pastel margaritas*, which may be made with almond marzipan or various fruits. Some even venture into fruit turnovers and eclairs, covered with chocolate and almonds.

PREPARATION

In the kitchen

Virtually every kitchen will have a large, blue bottle of purified drinking water. In some it will stand alone to be poured into pitchers cooled in the fridge, while others will be inverted and popped into a stand-alone cooler. Because it is so essential, delivery trucks pass on a daily basis, driving slowly up and down streets calling '*Aaaaagua*!' from a loud-speaker as boys jump from the truck to deliver new bottles and take away empties.

The *estufa* (top of the stove) is used much more than the *horno* (oven) in Mexican cookery. In fact, in some homes, the oven serves as nothing more than a space to store stove-top pots and pans. In houses where there is space out the back, there is likely to be a *brasero*, a charcoal-burning barbecue used for grilling meats and giving roasted chillies a special, smoky flavour.

Vulve a la vida, seafood and snail cocktail.

Special utensils

The *molcajete* is a bowl of thick clay, baked to hardness and enamelled, which stands solidly on three stubby legs. The surface is heavily textured, some with engraved multi-directional lines, others with a sort of stucco. The texture allows salsa ingredients to be mixed with greater ease.

The *chimolera* is a textured pestle. It comes in a variety of shapes with the common feature being the round head.

In some families, *molcajetes* are passed down from generation to generation and it is said that, with use, they become seasoned and the salsas made in them are better for it.

*Tortilla*s taste best when they are made fresh and cooked immediately. Having a *prensa para tortillas* helps. It is a simple utensil consisting of two hinged metal plates. Dough is rolled into a ball, flattened slightly by hand and placed between two sheets of wax paper before being pressed flat and cooked on the *comal*.

Man cutting agave plants for tequila.

DEFINING DISHES

Mole

Mole (a savoury sauce with chocolate) is one of the dishes that defines Mexican cuisine. It is used on all festive occasions and

Girls share a smile as they squeeze oranges at a juice stand at the market in Tepoztlan.

Salsa roca, red chilli sauce, and *mole*, a spicy chocolate sauce.

GREG ELMS / GETTY IMAGES

each region, even each family, has their own variation, from the very simple to a very complex combination of ingredients and precise preparation.

The first *mole* is said to have been created by a Dominican nun, Sor Andrea de la Asunción, who discovered the magical, indescribable flavour that the addition of chocolate gave to her *guiso* (stew) of puréed roasted chilli, clove, cinnamon, pepper, cilantro, sesame seeds and turkey broth.

A *mole* must be tried at least once, as it is a unique experience. What makes the *mole* so important to the Mexican identity is its reliance on the fusion of the native and the Spanish ingredients to make a single, homogeneous sauce to be served with turkey or chicken or even fish. It is a truly *mestizo* dish and has therefore been embraced by patriotic Mexican foodies for centuries.

Tamale

The word *tamal* (plural: *tamales*) comes from the nahuatl (the most common language in pre-Hispanic Mexico) word *tamalli* and refers to anything wrapped up. Their design is very pragmatic, with the *hoja de platano* (plantain leaves) serving as both plate and insulator, keeping the ingredients inside warm while allowing for portability. They may be considered the Americas very first take away food.

A *tamale* essentially consists of three elements: the leaf, the *masa* (corn-based dough) and the *relleno* (filling). The leaf is generally the massive *hoja de platano*, which is then wrapped around the filled *masa*. Sometimes the *relleno* must be cooked first, sometimes the ingredients are cooked within the *tamale*. Perhaps the only kind of meat never used is the *chivo* (goat) which has given rise to an expression, '*hagan de chivo los tamales*' (make *tamales* of goat) which refers, somehow, to a spouse's infidelity.

The most common cooking method is *a vapor* (steamed) using a large double-boiler with the *tamales* sitting atop a *tapesco* or bed of plantain leaves. They can also be cooked underground, in the same sort of apparatus that is used for softening *maguey* (fleshy-leaved agaves) plants for *mezcal* (poor man's tequila). Others are roasted on a *comal* or fried in fat.

DRINKS

Mexico's warm climate has been the inspiration behind the creation of a wealth of drinks, both alcoholic and non-alcoholic. Serious drinking has long been a part of Mexican culture and can be considered a sub-culture all of its own.

Beer

Mexican *cerveza* (beer) seems to have been precisely engineered to go with Mexican food. With a few exceptions, it is light and well-carbonated, perfect for dousing the spiciness of a chilli sauce and cutting through the grease of a *cabrito asado.*

The Aztecs had a kind of beer called *sendecho*, which was made with corn as opposed to barley and flavoured with *tepozán*, a vegetable with curative qualities. The Mayans also had a brew made with juice extracted from corn stalks. The Spanish introduced European-style beer to the Americas soon after the conquest, but it wasn't until the end of the 19th century that brewing really took off in Mexico.

The time-honoured practice of plunking a wedge of lime in the mouth of a bottle of Mexican beer is not as common in Mexico as it is elsewhere. Legend has it that the practice began as a means of keeping the flies from your beer and developed into an essential part of the beer drinking experience. With the lighter, crisper beers like Corona or Montejo, the squeeze option may actually improve the taste, but the best Mexican beers require nothing more than a bottle opener.

GREG ELMS / GETTY IMAGES

Tamales and *tamales Oaxaquenos* (in banana leaves

Tequila

The Spanish brought sophisticated distilling techniques and the tequila industry was born. The same process is used today:

- The *jimador*, the man responsible for the initial stages of the tequila-making process, first prepares the *piña* (heart) of the mature blue agave (only the blue agave is used) by removing the leaves and stalk.
- The plant is then steamed for up to 36 hours to soften the fibres and release the *aguamiel* (must).
- The next stage, mashing, separates the fibre from the thick, dark juice with the liquid funnelled into large tanks for fermentation.
- It is then distilled, sometimes twice, and pumped into barrels for aging.

The length of the aging process determines the colour, taste, quality and price of the tequila. The basic, common *blanco* is aged least, followed by *reposado*, aged for 2 to 12 months, and *añejo* which has a dark, whiskey-like colour. The most common fine tequila, Don Julio, named for the founder of the Tres Maguey, is aged well over a year. Some *añejos* remain in their barrel for up to 12 years and sell for over US$200 a bottle.

There was a time in Mexico when tequila was the exclusive tipple of testosterone-driven machos. Tequila has grown up and is now regarded as a more refined drink. On a wine list the price of a shot of tequila can rival that of an imported single malt whiskey, and is taken much the same way, neat in a small glass, enjoyed with pleasure in tiny sips.

The turn back to tequila is being led by young people, whose enthusiasm has given rise to a new breed of mixed drinks to join the margarita. A Bloody María substitutes tequila for the vodka of a Bloody Mary. A tequila martini, with a drop or two of dry vermouth, is available at trendy bars in Mexico City.

Selling clusters of *guinep* fruit on the beach at Bluefield.

JERRY ALEXANDER

Jamaica

Fresh fish plucked from the rich, blue Caribbean waters, tropical fruits growing wildly in the verdant mountains of the interior, killer-spicy pepper sauce, the hot home of iconic jerk chicken, washed down with an ice-cold can of Red Stripe: Jamaican food is a party on a plate.

CULINARY CAPITAL KINGSTON **KNOWN FOR** JERK CHICKEN **IMPORTS** ALMOST EVERTHING **EXPORTS** BANANAS, GINGER **DEVOUR** PATTIES, RUM CAKE **AVOID** TOO MUCH RUM

The fruit and vegetable market in downtown Willemstad.

JERRY ALEXANDER

CULTURE

Jamaica is a culture of immigrants and migrants, a place where people have been arriving and leaving since the Arawaks began their northward island-hopping some 2000 years ago. It is a culture that reaches beyond the azure seas and touches nearly every part of the globe. Food plays a major role in this amorphousness. It serves as a bridge to the homeland for the many Jamaicans who have travelled abroad, and as a cultural handle for those who have never set foot on Caribbean soil.

Of all the Caribbean countries it is in Jamaica that a truly national cuisine has developed. When you get to Jamaica, it only takes a trip away from the tourist drags to realise that Jamaicans love to eat. Every city block has a few chimneys where smoke rises continuously throughout the day as a signal that something delicious is under roof.

So where to begin? Ask any Jamaican and they will not hesitate to answer *ackee* and saltfish. It is practically a national dish, for no other place in the New World grows the *ackee,* the fruit that originally arrived from West Africa with Captain Bligh in the HMS Bounty. To make *ackee* and saltfish, salted cod is soaked for several hours to reduce the salt content, after which the flaky fish is stewed with the ackee along with onions, peppers and thyme.

Thanks to the East Indian influence, curry spice is an important part of Jamaican cooking, and curried goat is an essential dish at any important event. Likewise, *roti* is as popular in Jamaica as anywhere.

When it comes to meat, chicken is king. In some cities, you can't throw a rock without hitting a place that serves fried chicken, roast chicken or, best of all, pan chicken. The best pan chicken is cooked over hot coals in an old oil drum that has been cut in half and designated for a higher calling than transporting crude around the world.

What did Marley eat for breakfast?

To most of the world, Jamaica means reggae music and a dreadlocked Bob Marley encased in a thick cloud of smoke as he tokes from an enormous spliff. The music, the hair and the marijuana are, of course, all icons of Rastafarianism. But just as important is *Ital* cooking, a culinary philosophy that sets down the guidelines for what a Rastafarian can and cannot eat.

The word *Ital* means 'vital' and the foods are characterised by their life-giving qualities. Meat, for example, is to be avoided as a dead animal does not have vitality. Similarly, foods that are preserved, processed or salted are rejected for their unnatural qualities. Instead, the Rasta diet is dominated by fresh fruit and vegetables, and fresh (not dried) herbs and spices. Herbs, in this case, definitely includes marijuana, and Rastafarians will often add a bit of ganja to baked goods and stews. The most ardent among them will not even use utensils that have been forged by a machine, but rather will eat from clay dishes or cups made from coconut shells.

ETIQUETTE

The first rule of etiquette in Jamaica is common sense. The sort of rules your mother tried to teach you as a child apply here: no chewing with your mouth open, no throwing food. Nevertheless, Caribbean meals have a casual air and no one will make you feel as though you are dining with the royal family. People enjoy their food, and enjoy the opportunity to sit, dine and chat with friends and family.

While most things tend to move a little slower than in western countries, meals are not one of them. People here love to eat. So food is dispatched speedily and devoured before everyone retires to the front porch to shoot the breeze and enjoy the rest of the evening together.

Etiquette in restaurants depends entirely on the type of

A colourful array of cocktails in Montego Bay.

Jamaica's favourite food, *ackee* with saltfish.

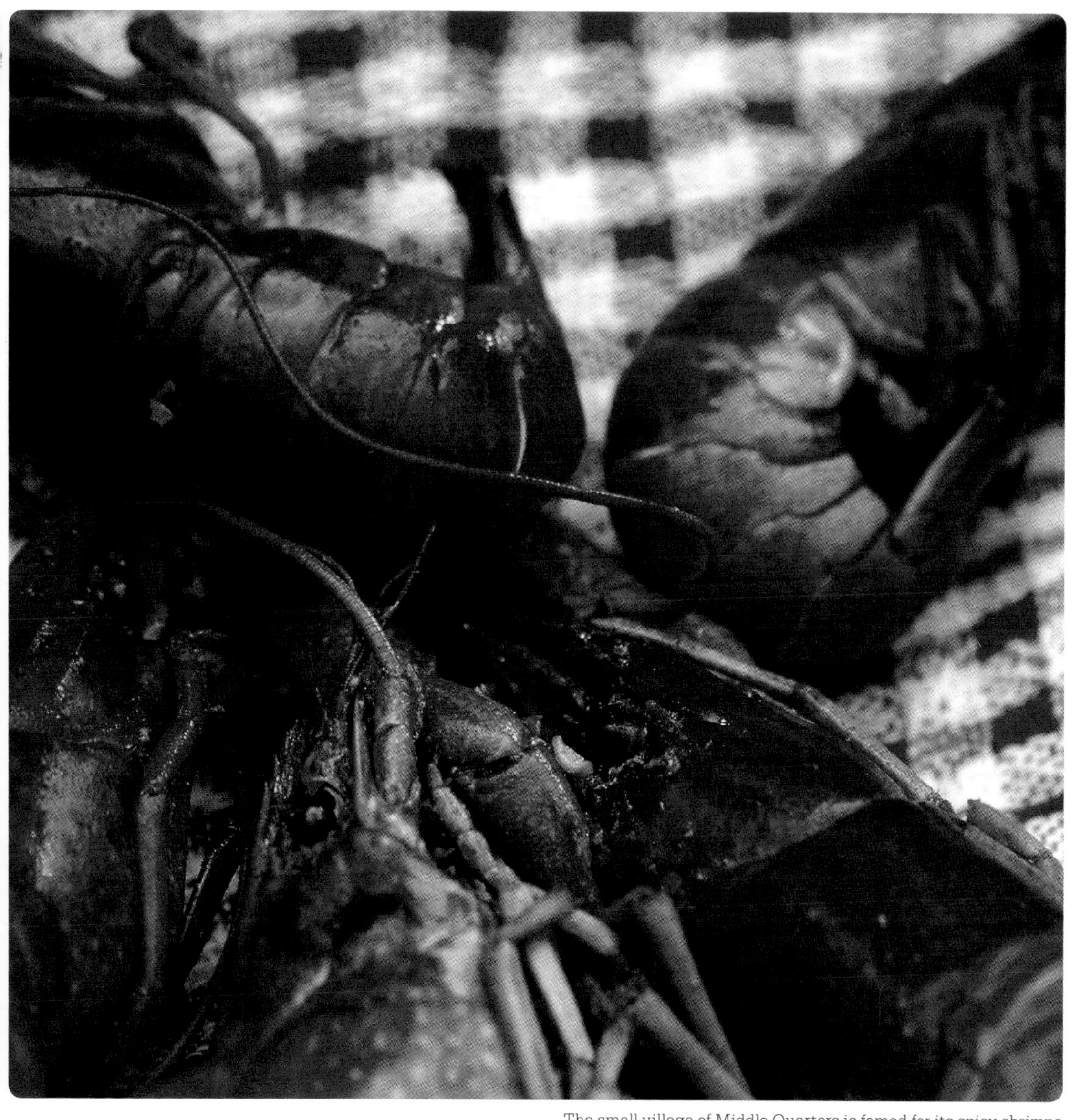

The small village of Middle Quarters is famed for its spicy shrimps.

place. Upscale establishments will follow the same rules as in North America and Europe. As you move down the ladder, however, the atmosphere changes; diners get a little louder, eating with your hands is more acceptable and beckoning waiters with a sharp 'psst' is the norm.

DAILY MEALS

For everyday eating it is safe to say that the lighter, quicker breakfast (sometimes nothing more than a cup of coffee or tea) is the preferred option. You may find a small bakery that sells pastries and breads – look for Johnny cake, sweet bread that is served hot with creamy butter. Or what about combining your fruit and bread by indulging in a freshly baked roll filled with currants, or a pastry made with shredded coconut.

Lunch is a much more serious affair and in many parts it is still the main meal of the day. But as elsewhere, its prominence is being squeezed by the pressures of the work day. As a result, the long, lazy multi-course lunches are becoming an exception.

And so it falls to the evening meal to provide the culinary highlight of the day. Caribbeans tend to eat dinner late. Even in homes, dinner is not served until after sunset, perhaps in the hope that the heat will not be as strong. Meals at home are big and boisterous; plates of food are laid out with oversized spoons for heaping portions onto your plate.

ESSENTIAL PRODUCE

A diverse history and ethnology has had a major influence on what is eaten across the islands of the Caribbean. However, the sharing of seas and soils, and common links to Africa and the Amerindians, has also created a culinary cohesion. This can be seen — and tasted — everywhere in Jamaica.

JERRY ALEXANDER

Green bananas being prepared for market.

Allspice

Allspice (also known as pimento or Jamaican pepper) is not technically a spice, but rather a berry that grows on the indigenous pimento tree. Its flavor is strong and distinctive, so you don't need much allspice to get the pimento point across. Even so, allspice does not mask other flavours, and so makes an excellent part of the seasoning for any stewed meat, and is one of the key ingredients in Jamaican jerk.

Bananas and plantains

Although a native of Southeast Asia, bananas are now synonymous with the Caribbean landscape and diet. Banana trees exist throughout the islands, either covering hillsides with their palm-like leaves or individually on roadsides and in backyards. One of its most successful export crops, bananas can be cut green from the tree and so are ripe when they arrive at an overseas market.

The much-loved plantain (cooking banana) is larger than other bananas with more distinct edges. Perhaps the tastiest preparation is to slice the fruit into long flat pieces and then fry gently in oil over a slow flame until the natural sugars caramelize and the slices gain a golden-brown crust. They are then dried on a paper towel and lightly salted. Usually served as part of a larger dish, but they are delicious solo.

Fruit

When driving in Jamaican cities, look out for the dare-devil street vendors who hock their juicy produce on major intersections (at great risk — Jamaicans are notoriously reckless behind the wheel).

A must-try item is *guinep*, a small green fruit that grows in bunches like grapes. To get to the flesh, which is a little tart, peel the skin and suck on the pip (careful not to choke!) until you get all the good stuff off. People in Jamaica eat them like nuts, munching down on one while opening the next. If you've ever eaten fresh lychee, you'll find the *guinep* similar, both in taste and texture.

Ackee, the fruit used in the ever-popular *ackee* and saltfish dish, is about the size of a pear. It is related to the mango and has the same red-orange skin that protects a black shiny seed and three yellow pods. The pods are the edible bits of the fruit (although not raw) but they cannot be eaten until the fruit splits open to reveal them — otherwise, the *ackee* is poisonous. In Jamaica, children are taught from an early age never to pick an *ackee* until it has split, indicating that it's safe to eat.

Ginger

There are those who claim that Jamaica produces the best ginger in the world, and as a consequence much of it goes to the export market. Locals use it in drinks (tea and wine) as well as in breads and curries.

Peas and rice

It is difficult to mention rice in a Caribbean culinary context without also mentioning peas. The ever-present side dish of peas and rice is found everywhere, and the peas in this dish can be almost anything. Some will use *garbanzos*, others go for kidney beans or regular green peas. In Jamaica, peas and rice are cooked in coconut water.

Peppers

Peppers have always been an important part of the Caribbean diet. Cooks in Jamaica will tell you that the hottest pepper is the bird pepper, which derives its name from the fact that the only way it seems to grow is when the seeds are eaten by birds and then deposited in the soil, together with natural fertilisers.

JERRY ALEXANDER

Ackee is a tree grown fruit native to Africa and eaten in Jamaica as a staple breakfast.

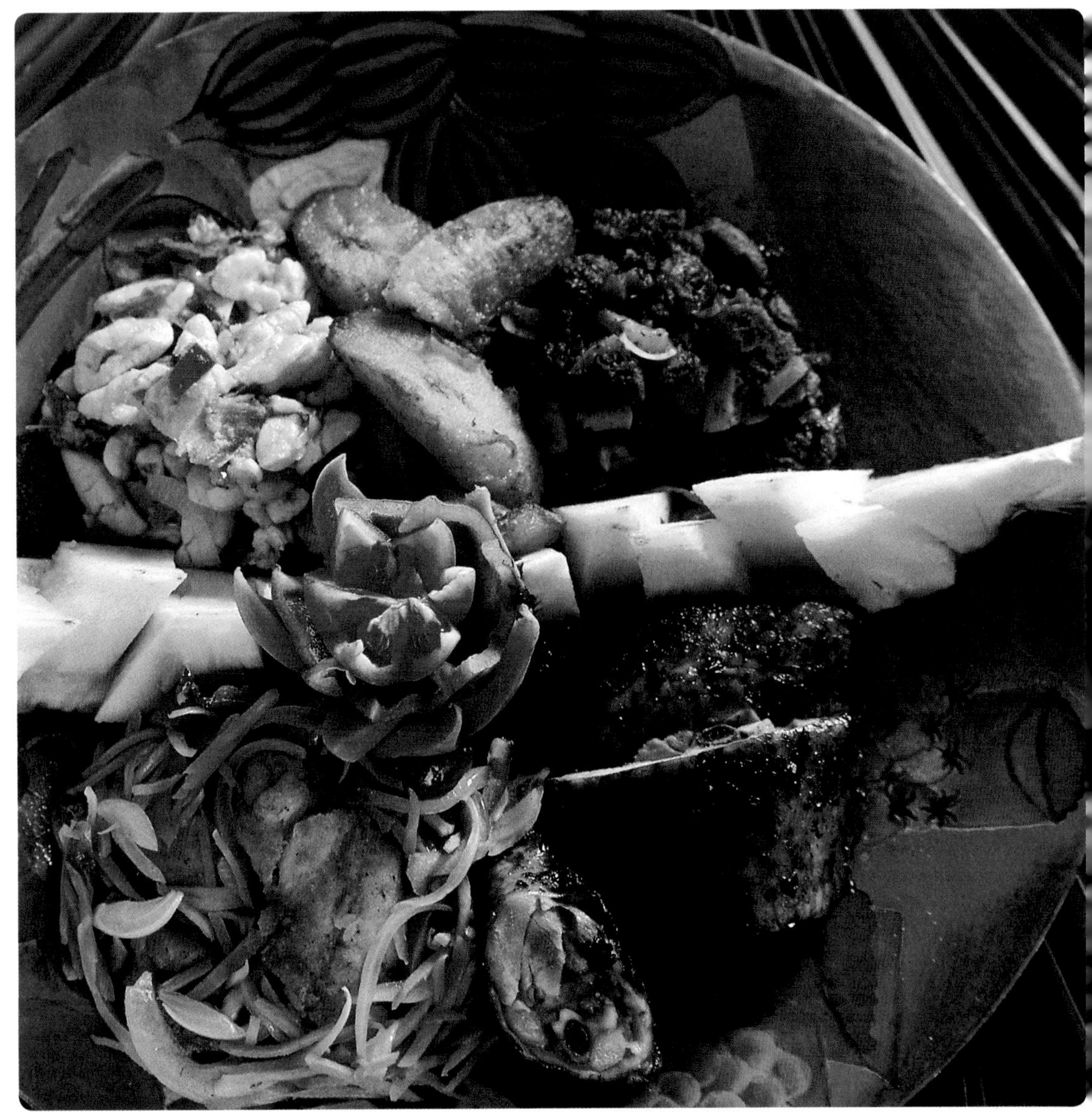

Boonoonoo (plentiful) serving of food at a popular Jamaican restaurant.

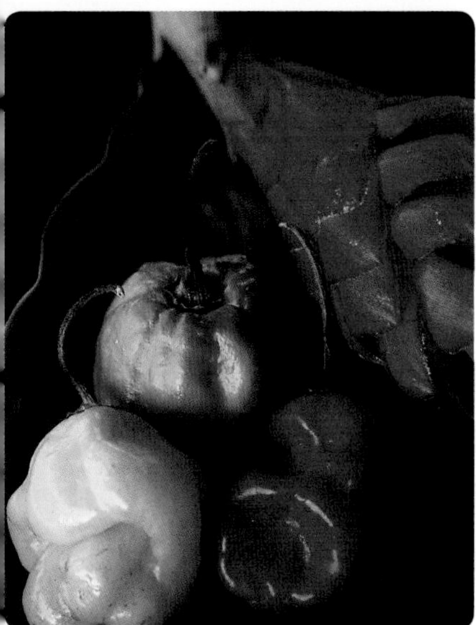
Scotch bonnet pepper and red ginger flower.

Red snapper caught locally at Knip Bay.

But don't be frightened by the likelihood of biting into a local dish and burning your face off. The hottest peppers are rarely hidden in dishes. Instead, they are made into pepper sauce and served as a condiment. Pepper sauce generally consists of pureed peppers with vinegar and salt.

Seafood

Grouper, snapper, mahi mahi (dolphin fish), conch, shrimp, lobster, shark, marlin, flying fish, crab and tuna all make their home in the coastal waters surrounding Jamaica. Red snapper is a favourite, coveted for its perfect white flesh and subtle flavor. A delicate grilling and squeeze of lime makes fish sing. Jamaicans indulge on fish without restraint, and the favored preparation is whole – head and tail included (in fact, the head is the best bit).

Shellfish

The mighty conch, used by the castaways in Golding's *Lord of the Flies* as a symbol of political power, is today one of the most recognisable symbols of the Caribbean. You're no doubt familiar with the conch's shape, with its sun-bleached outer shell, spiny body and pearly pink underbelly. But for locals, it is the meat inside that is the real treasure. Conch is one shellfish that needs extensive preparation — you need to pound it, and pound it good — otherwise, eating conch is like chewing on a bike tire. Once pounded and marinated in lime juice, it can be prepared in a variety of ways.

Vegetables

In Jamaica tropical roots and tubers are staple foods. Tubers will grow under all sorts of soil and climatic conditions, and are easy to prepare. As a result, they became a mainstay in the diets of the Amerindians, as well as plantation workers. Today, few Jamaican meals come without some form of starch, and tubers are the usual choice:

- Of all the roots, the most popular is the potato, which is most often prepared as French fries.
- Cassava (also called yucca), with its brown, fibrous skin and white interior is found stacked high in most markets.
- Sweet potatoes are another common carbohydrate hit.
- Pumpkin is boiled, made into fritters, used in soups and as fillings for pastries. Caribbean pumpkins have a green and white exterior and a rich, sweet orange interior.
- *Quimbombó* (okra) is a prominent ingredient throughout the Caribbean, a fact not surprising given that it originates from the same area of Africa that the slaves came from.

SHOPPING

At the market

The history of markets in the Caribbean goes back to early colonial days when slaves were allowed to grow some excess foods in their own gardens and then take them to market in the nearest town on Sunday. This could be quite a lengthy and difficult journey. Much of the selling was done by women, a fact that remains the case in Jamaica today. Female sellers were called *higglers*, a name that survives in its verb form: *to higgle* is to bargain. A vendor at a Jamaican marketplace expects to barter and may initiate it without a moment's hesitation. Jamaica's Montego market, off the main tourist path, is a bustling mecca complete with *higglers* dressed in peacock-hued calico dresses, who compete at charming the dollars out of your pockets with their cries.

JERRY ALEXANDER

At this roadside stall, the house speciality is peanut

DEFINING DISHES

Goat curry

A popular meat is goat, which has a similar taste to lamb but is greasier. No party menu in Jamaica is complete without a big steaming pot of goat curry. Often, the head of the goat will be used to make a soup called mannish water.

Jerk

Jerk is pure Jamaica. Locals line up at their favorite jerk pit to get their daily fill of pork, chicken or, in some instances, seafood and the wonderful mixture of spices that permeates every cell of the meat. Intense, brash, unforgiving, smoky, it tastes like ... rebellion. The jerk pit joins the church and the rum shop as the three fixtures in every small town and village across Jamaica.

The unique blend of spices used to make jerk was developed from the need to preserve meat. Your first bite of jerk may lead you to believe that hot pepper is used by the bowlful. However, the most essential ingredient is allspice.

The intensity of flavour is not only due to the ingredients of the jerk marinade itself, but also from the fact that you must leave the meat in the marinade for a long time. In the case of pork, this means at least 24 hours, but results are better if you can leave it for 48. Purists will tell you that the only way to do real jerk is to cook the pork on slats of still-green pimento wood over a pimento-wood fire.

Today, jerk is moving into uncharted territory. A fast-food chain called Island Grill offers a jerk burger, while Norma's, one of Jamaica's best known restaurants, serves a jerked chicken penne pasta. Given the extent to which Jamaican's love their jerk, this can only be the beginning.

Handmade sign advertises jerk three ways.

Barbequed corn served with lime juice.

Jamaica Patty's shop in Savanna-la-Mar.

Patty

Other islands serve patties, but in Jamaica it's the lifeblood of local cuisine. At one location of Tasty Patty in midtown Kingston, the lunchtime line up is 10 deep, even though it has only one item available.

Patties consist of flaky, buttery pastry rolled into a circle and folded around a meat filling. Traditionally, the filling is ground beef, which is browned with finely chopped onions and other spices. The patty has evolved to include other fillings such as chicken, cheese, fish or even lobster. It's then baked in an oven and served piping hot with pepper sauce.

At some of Jamaica's patty places, you can buy coco bread, soft, white bread that is folded before baking and comes to you piping hot. The idea is to split the coco bread and then insert a whole patty. It sounds like a lot of carbohydrate and it is. A better way to enjoy it is to have a meatloaf patty, where spiced meatloaf is slipped between an unfolded loaf of coco bread.

Rundown

Jamaicans are also fond of a dish called rundown. This is a fish stew made by simmering coconut milk so it reduces, then adding fish (mackerel, snapper or swordfish), chopped onion, thyme and other seasonings.

Rum cake

Desserts in Jamaica tend to be served warm, as in the case of bread pudding or bananas in rum and cinnamon. Rich, sweet dishes such as flan with caramel sauce or candied guava with cheese are also popular. But the Caribbean dessert of choice has to be rum cake. There are many ways to make it, but the rum should always be dark as this provides the richest flavor. If you're lucky, it will be covered in a sweet icing that makes for a winning combination with the rummy cake.

Souse
Souse is another iconic Jamaican dish. There are many different ways of preparing it, but the end result is generally a sort of stew with a thick, gravy-like sauce. Fish is the usual main ingredient, but souses can also be made with conch, chicken, pork or tongue. It is a dish with a heritage that stretches back to the days of slavery, when it was a preparation of whatever was left over from the plantation owner's kitchen.

DRINKS

The culture of the Caribbean is tightly wedded with booze. Economically, the rum trade has generated billions of dollars for island distillers. Culturally, alcohol fuels the bacchanalian madness known as Carnival. And socially, cracking the seal on a bottle of rum can herald the beginning of a long, languid evening of conviviality and conversation.

Beer
The undisputed king of beers in the Caribbean is Red Stripe, a full-flavored lager. Red Stripe is a cultural institution in Jamaica, sponsoring sporting events, reggae festivals and maintaining its status with an omnipresent advertising campaign. Red Stripe is even available in vending machines!

For the most part, beers in the Caribbean tend to be light lagers. The notable exception is Guinness. In Jamaica, Guinness is rivalled by the sweet and malty local, Dragon Stout. Part of the reason for stout's popularity is its alleged ability to improve stamina in the sack.

Rum
As the world's largest producer of sugarcane for centuries, it is only natural that the Caribbean should give the world rum. For

JERRY ALEXANDER

A Jamaican woman eyes a colourful cocktail.

many years, however, it was virtually unknown outside the region. Europe's first rums were made in Barbados in the mid 1600s. The current name is derived from 'rumbullion', a word used to describe the rumbustious behavior exhibited by those under its spell.

This crude original rum was lethal in excess. Made from a boiled sugar water left to turn sour and then distilled twice, it produced a highly flammable spirit. Soon the concoction became a favorite among slaves and marauding pirates who yo-ho-ho'd their way from port to port, wreaking havoc.

It wasn't that good rum couldn't be made. It was simply more expensive, requiring more time and better ingredients. Jamaican distillers, J Wray & Nephew, took home medals in the 10-, 15- and 25-year-old rum classes at the 1862 London exhibition, and eventually developed the iconic Jamaican Appleton brand, whose V/X label and 21-year-old rums are still favoured among connoisseurs.

White rum remains the most popular, but aged rum can be pure art, especially when aged anywhere from three to 21 years. This is a darker rum (taking on the colour of the oak barrel in which it ages) that exhibits a classic mellowness that makes mixing unnecessary. A good seven-year old, or *añejo* rum needs only to be poured over ice, perhaps with a lime twist. But not all dark rums are aged. There are dark or spiced rums that take on their colour when caramel or colouring is added after the distillation process.

Sno-cone

One other drink that needs mentioning is the sno-cone, which is served from battered trailers, often attached to bicycles, which are pushed through the streets by hot and haggard-looking men. To make a sno-cone, a block of ice is scraped until there are enough shavings to fill a paper cup. Some cherry-

JERRY ALEXANDER

Roadside drinks and coconut jelly stand in St Andre

flavored syrup is poured over the ice until each glistening crystal has turned red.

Tea and coffee

Tea is one strong legacy left by the English. Many people in Jamaica will have nothing more than a cup of tea for breakfast, adding plenty of cream and sugar to the mix. The standard tea is orange pekoe, but some shops stock specialty teas.

Jamaicans have been growing coffee for nearly 300 years. From humble beginnings, Jamaica became the world's largest coffee producer and remained so until the mid-19th century when the current world leader, Brazil, launched its industry.

There are an estimated 60,000 coffee farmers in Jamaica, of which Jamaica's Blue Mountain coffee enjoys the best international reputation. Getting to the Blue Mountains will make you shake as much as if you swallowed seven consecutive espressos. Nevertheless, the scenery is striking: birds fly low over hills covered with banana palms. The highest peak, for which the range is named, is shrouded in clouds.

JAMAICAN CRAWLER

Ingredients

30 ml (1 fl oz) light rum
30 ml (1 fl oz) melon liqueur
90 ml (3 fl oz) pineapple juice
1 splash grenadine

Method

Combine rum, melon liqueur and pineapple juice with ice. Stir well and top with grenadine.

Dried beans and seeds at ground level at Antigua market.

JEREMY WOODHOUSE / GETTY IMAGES

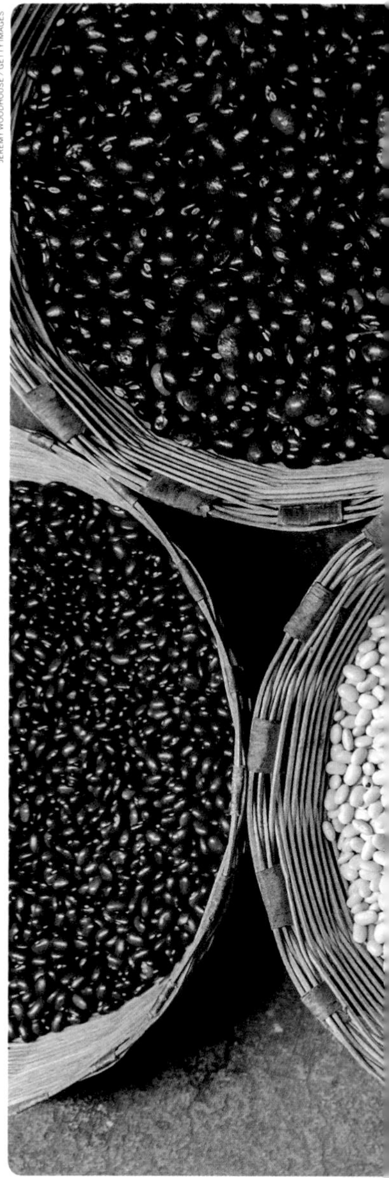

Guatemala

All hail the Mayans: no other country has a cuisine so strongly influenced by this once-mighty people. Far from that being the end of the world for Guatemalan gastronomy, this could be the beginning. Long overshadowed by neighbouring Mexico's daunting array of flavours, Guatemala is now having its ancient recipes flaunted by TV chefs — and it's the indigenous element that is gaining Guatemalan food its distinction.

CULINARY CAPITAL ANTIGUA **KNOWN FOR** COFFEE BEANS, **IMPORTS** AFRO-ARAWAK PANACHE **EXPORTS** COFFEE **DEVOUR** *PEPIÁN* **AVOID** MAYAN MOONSHINE

Freshly-picked coffee beans.

Pollo campero, or fried chicken, at the market.

CULTURE

Ancient Mayans dining today in Guatemala would recognise many of the same kitchen staples consumed 1000 years earlier: the beans around which most meals are based, the turkey in traditional *kak'ik* soup, and the maize eaten in all forms from on-the-cob to the ubiquitous tortilla. The most notable Spanish imports are the chicken, pork and beef, the rice, and the avocados Guatemalans devour with relish.

Slavery brought West Africans over to the Caribbean coast, and they mixed with the native Arawaks and Caribs to form today's Garifuna population. That wasn't the only mixing: exotic Caribbean produce got worked into dishes, particularly when banana plantations got established in the 19th century. Around the same time, German immigrants set to work on the coffee plantations, helping to make coffee become Guatemala's most highly regarded culinary product.

Crunchy corn tortillas.

REGIONS

Guatemala is a small country. Culinary regions can, at best, be defined as the Mayan-influenced interior and the Garifuna-influenced Caribbean seaboard.

Highlands and jungle

From the Petén jungle southwest to the rearing highlands, the Mayan legacy is strong: food preparation has altered little in centuries. Quintessential Guatemalan dishes like *kak'ik*, Cobán's turkey and chilli soup, or stews *subanik* and *pepián* hail from here. It's Guatemala's main produce and coffee-growing area.

- Antiguan candies — Milk, honey and local fruits boiled into sweets like *canillitas de leche* (with cinnamon).
- *Jocón* — Green sauce of coriander, *tomatillos* (tart green Central American fruits) and seeds, served over meat.

Caribbean coast

It's a small region but, thanks to settlement by African slaves who mingled with the indigenous population, Guatemala's Caribbean makes use of its bananas and coconuts to cook up novel, often seafood-themed dishes. For example, *tapado* is Guatemala's own *bouillabaisse* and contains shrimp, crab, squid or red snapper thrown together with coconut milk and plantains.

DAILY MEALS

Breakfast is substantial, bolstered by beans, eggs and rice. Guatemalans often have a mid-morning drink of *atole*, a maize-based drink, lunch is the main meal, and dinner is taken about 7 pm. Stews and soups dominate. *Relleno* (meaning stuffed) is a popular method for serving anything from bananas to potatoes.

Guatemalans dine informally: street food is big and sit-down restaurants are for tourists, with the exception of fast food chains like Pollo Campero.

ESSENTIAL PRODUCE

Maize remains the staple for most Guatemalans; black beans, served either whole or mushed into paste, are everywhere too.

Chicken

Pork is popular and turkey is utilised for special dishes but *pollo* (chicken) is *numero uno* meat. It's invariably chopped or shredded into a soup or stew such as *pollo con loroco*, a chicken stew enhanced by potent *loroco* vines.

Maize

Maize makes the tortillas, lends the *tamales* their beautiful gooiness, thickens the stews, and gets smeared in cheese, chillies and mayonnaise to be devoured in 'corn-on-the-cob'

Tightly-wrapped crabs.

The ubiquitous beans, rice and plantain.

Mayan women cooking tortillas at the market.

form. The maize husk wraps more food in Guatemala than plastic does and often contributes to food flavours.

Spices and seeds

The highland Verapaces region is a key cardamom producer; the spice frequently flavours Guatemalan coffee. Cinnamon is sprinkled on desserts and the sweet breads called *bunuelos*. Chillies spice up most meals, although rarely to the intensity of some Mexican dishes. Seeds, usually pumpkin or sesame, often bulk up sauces.

DEFINING DISHES

Stews

The lynchpins of Guatemalan cuisine are the Mayan meat-and-vegetable medleys of *pepián* and *subanik*.

- *Pepián* is chicken and pork blended with toasted seeds, chillies and tomatoes.
- *Subanik* uses beef or chicken combined in a *tomatillo*, onion, sweet pepper and chilli sauce.
- Watery stews are *caldos*; thicker stews are *recados.*

Tamales

Guatemala's *tamale* diversity probably exceeds any other country. This leaf-wrapped meal with a meat-and-*masa* (sticky corn dough) filling is popular across Latin America but the Guatemalans have a few special modifications. Banana or *mashan* leaves are more common than maize husks as the wrapping for the snack.

- *Chuchitos* — Guatemala's husk-wrapped *tamale* is served with hard white Zacapa cheese.
- *Tamales Colorados* — Coloured red by the hot *achiote*

MICHAEL DEFREITAS / GETTY IMAGES

Tamales for sale at an outdoor market.

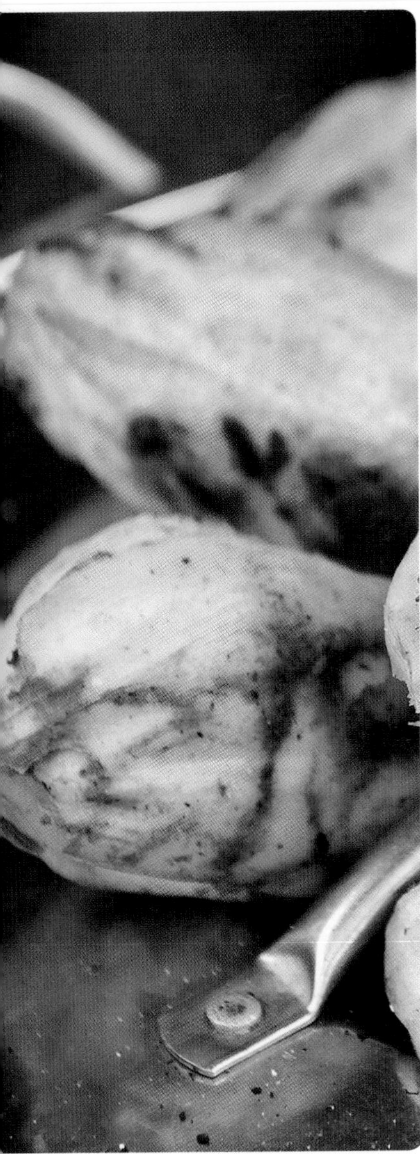

seeds and tomato *recado* used in the filling, along with olives, capers and chicken.

DRINKS

The flavourful Gallo is the main beer; Rum is also popular.

- *Licuado* — A soft fruit like papaya is blended with milk.
- *Atole* — A sweetened corn *masa* and cinnamon drink.
- Ron de Zacapa — A dark rum from the homonymous eastern Guatemalan town, is an award-winning drink with a taste influenced by a maturation method traditionally used for sherry.

ELOTES

Ingredients

4 ears corn, shucked
3 tablespoons fat-free mayonnaise
2 teaspoons fresh lime juice
2 tablespoons grated cheese (parmesan best)
½ teaspoon chili powder
¼ teaspoon ground red pepper
¼ teaspoon ground cumin
¼ teaspoon salt
Cooking oil

Method

Mix mayonnaise and juice in a bowl. Combine cheese with the chilli powder, ground red pepper, ground cumin and salt.

Place corn, coated in thin quantity of cooking oil, on a grill; grill each ear of corn for 10-12 minutes or until tender, turning frequently.

Remove corn from grill; brush with mayonnaise mixture and then sprinkle with cheese mixture. Serve immediately.

Chef grilling meat in the kitchen.

ANDREA PISTOLESI / GETTY IMAGES

Brazil

Brazil is big: diners in southern states might never visit the Amazonian north. Historically, this geographical immensity meant Brazilian food was disparate, but economic boom-times have brought many Brazilians back from overseas armed with innovative approaches. New restaurant influences, from indigenous to Japanese, are in, and Brazilians are dining out more than any other nation.

CULINARY CAPITAL SÃO PAULO **KNOWN FOR** *CAIPIRINHA* **IMPORTS** WHEAT, MILK **EXPORT** FRUITY SUPERFOODS **DEVOUR** *FEIJOADA* **AVOID** JAMBU LEAVES (THEY NUMB YOUR MOUTH)

Sugarcane plantations near Sao Paulo.

Buriti fruit for sale at morning market.

Brazilian *bolinhos de bacalhau*, or codfish cakes.

CULTURE

It was the Portuguese that came, saw and conquered in Brazil. Unlike the Spanish, they found no significant mineral wealth upon arrival in the 16th century and turned to sugarcane production for commerce.

This still-flourishing industry created the Brazilian sweet tooth but also, notoriously, contributed toward a society divided between the excessively privileged and the desperately poor. The wealthy adopted more European-style eating habits, while the impoverished majority kept to a diet of beans and jerky which, with the additions of slightly improved meat, rice and government-subsidised wheat, still serves as the basic diet today.

Indigenous food (fish, fruit, pulses and the *manioc* root) didn't initially enthral the Portuguese, although they later added their rice, beef and pork to native tribal staples. Nor was the available indigenous workforce sufficient to meet Portuguese labour needs. The colonists shipped in slaves from Africa to make up the shortfall on the plantations and in the kitchen. African culinary creativity, as slaves strove to concoct leftover ingredients into tasty dishes, became the most distinctive influence on Brazil's food, and it is still recognisable today in the reddish *dendê* oil, derived from African palms, which is the signature Afro-Brazilian cooking fat. The national dish *feijoada* (black beans, *manioc* flour and beef/pork trimmings) is the African development of a Portuguese dish using indigenous ingredients: a cultural fusion food, if ever there was one.

Sugar plantations dominated the northeast, but the south, influenced by the *gaucho* culture of Argentina and Uruguay, became cattle-raising territory. The *churrasco*, or Brazilian grill-up, was born here, and has become the nation's best-known dish overseas.

In the 19th century, with Brazil a new republic, the switch from slave to wage labour saw the city of São Paulo's rise as a prime agricultural area, particularly for coffee. At the government's invitation, waves of Italian, German and later Japanese immigrants settled here to man the coffee plantations. The Germans also became pork or dairy farmers, bringing with them brewing techniques and several sweet cakes. The largest Japanese community outside Japan is in São Paulo, where sushi is ubiquitous and Brazil's version of a *wonton* is a popular street food.

REGIONS

Northeast

Most people believe Brazil's culinary heart is in this hot, drought-prone region, dominated historically by the Africans who came to work the sugar plantations, and topographically by stunning coastline. The centre of culinary creativity is Afro-Brazilian Mecca, Salvador, where alluring seafood dishes theme the cuisine. Inland in the arid, inhospitable *sertão*, sun-dried meat (*charque*) and tubers like *manioc* are popular, and indigenous cuisine, with the rainforest not so far away, (and incomers preferring the more fruitful coastline) holds more sway. *Feijoada*, the Brazilian national dish, comes from the Northeast. Local specialties include:

- *Vatapá* — Paste of shrimp, coconut milk, peanuts and dendê oil.
- *Queijo Coahlo* — Northeastern cheese often eaten on a skewer, with molasses.
- *Mocoto* — Cow's foot stew.
- *Moqueca* — The Northeast's famous seafood stew.
- *Caruru* — Okra paste with onions, shrimp, malagueta

NICO TONDINI / GETTY IMAGES

Feijoada, a traditional Brazilian stew.

peppers and *dendê* oil, often with cashews or peanuts added, often served with sea fish like *garoupa*.

- *Jaggery* — Date palm-and-sugar sweet.

North

The North's Amazonian cuisine retains the strongest links to pre-colonial food. Fruits and fish, and the much-devoured *manioc* lend the dishes their special character. A hot chilli-based sauce is much-loved as an accompaniment to dishes.

- *Acaí* — Violet-hued, caffeine-rich berry now renowned as a superfood. It's a staple in Rio's juice bars but in the Amazon *acai* is eaten fresh, either salted or sweet with tapioca or honey, and served in gourds called *cuias*.
- *Pirão* — *Manioc* flour cooked with meat/fish stock to form a kind of polenta.
- *Pato no tucupi* — Duck dish boiled in the *manioc's* yellow broth; served with rice and the mouth-numbing *jambu* leaves.
- *Surubim* — Endemic Amazon fish commonly gracing plates in Northern Brazil; served with *pirão* and rice.

THE MENU

With Brazil's cuisine as multi-faceted as its ethnic make-up, there's a plethora of different, and endearingly Brazilian, types of eating establishments to try.

- *Botecos* — Bars as famous for their bar snacks as their alcohol; the southeastern city Belo Horizonte has more *botecos* per capita than any other city in the world. *Boteco* cuisine includes unusual snacks like *figado acebolado* (liver with onions).
- *Churrascarias* — Barbecued meat-eating houses;

GINA SABATELLA / GETTY IMAGES

Salting beef at a Brazilian *churrascaria*.

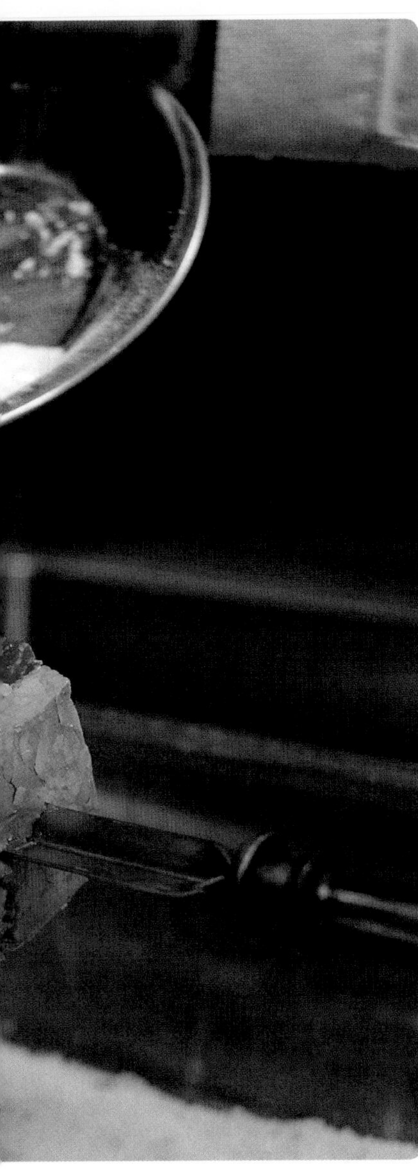

serving is via the *rodízio* system, with servers coming round and offering more (and more) until you're full.

- *Lojas de sucos* — Juice bars.
- *Lanchonete* — Snack bar; snacks are termed *petiscos* or *tira-gostos*.

ESSENTIAL PRODUCE

Beef

Beef is Brazilian cuisine's most defining meat, whether cut up for the grill in the South's fabled *churrasco* (barbecue) or dried, often in the sun, to form what Brazilians call *charque* ('jerky' in English). It's also cut up for simmering in stews and soups, including *feijoada*.

Cheese

Minas Gerais is Brazil's cheese-producing capital. *Frescal* (fresh cheese) is usually served within a week of being made and is tender like mozzarella. *Meia cura* is the partially-matured version and *curado* (mature) is a white-yellow in colour, more granulated and ideal for use in cooking.

- *Requeijão* — Brazilian cream cheese.
- *Romeo e Julieta* — Generally a Minas *queijo frescal* (fresh Minas cheese) with guava paste.
- *Pao de queijo* — Popular bread made with Minas *curado* cheese.

Chillies

Chillies play an interesting role in Brazilian cuisine. They come in an impressive range of sizes and colours yet are used far more sparingly in dishes than in, for example, Peru. They're often presented pickled in vinegar as condiments.

- *Malagueta* — Fiery red or green chilli-pepper common in northeastern cuisine.
- *Pimenta biquinho* — Pointed red chilli named for its likeness to a bird's beak.

Fish

If you ate a different Amazonian fish every day in Brazil, it would still take you years to get through all the possibilities. A quintessential Amazonian preparation method is to sun-dry the fish. In the Northeast, simmering shellfish together in a pot to create one of the region's beloved *moquecas* (stews) is preferred. Smoking or flame-grilling are other popular methods or, in São Paulo's Japanese-influenced society, sushi is common.

- *Na brasa* — Translating as 'flame-grilled'; this is a favoured way of serving a fish like the *surubim* (Braziliian catfish).
- *Casquinha de carangueijo* — stuffed crab with *manioc* flour.
- *Tacacá* — Indigenous dish of sun-dried shrimp cooked with *jambu* leaves, peppers and *manioc*.

Fruit and vegetables

Acaí steals the fruit show, and it's delicious when served in the syrupy sorbet *Acaí na tiegla*, but all that Amazonian fruit has given Brazil some bizarre drink and ice cream flavours. As often as not, it's eaten raw. Fresh green vegetables have a

Acaí na tiegla, meaning '*açaí* in the bowl', is made with the purple superfood fruit that hails from the Amazon. It is served chilled in southern Brazil, with a medley of tropical fruit, granola and caffeine-rich *guaraná* syrup.

Moqueca, fish with tomatoes, garlic and lime juice.

Cashew nut fruit for sale at the market.

Açaí in baskets.

Manioc, or cassava, for sale at a Brazilian street market.

DANIEL BARBOSA / GETTY IMAGES

rather scant role in the cuisine: distinctive vegetables include African-introduced okra, and heart of palm, which is drizzled in oil or served in salad.

- *Acerola* — Tart, bright red berry; makes a great juice, and also a version of *caipirinha* (famed Brazilian cocktail).
- *Guaraná* — Amazon-native berry with twice the caffeine levels of a coffee bean; used to flavour soft drinks nationwide.
- *Cupuaçu* — Sweet, creamy Amazon fruit; the pulp is used in juices and sweets.

Manioc

Used by Brazil's indigenous peoples for millennia, this long, tapered tuber also goes by the name of *yucca* and cassava across the continent. Most South Americans love them, but no nation utilises *manioc* like the Brazilians. It's ground into flour called *farinha*, which bulks up sauces, soups and dish fillings and is bludgeoned into a meat stock. The hardy *manioc* can grow almost anywhere, adding to its universal popularity.

- *Farofa* — *Farinha* which has been toasted on the stove with butter.
- *Polvilho doce* — Sweet *manioc* starch.
- *Polvilho azedo* — Sour *manioc* starch.
- *Tucupi* — Broth remaining after the manioc has had its starch removed. Then poisonous, *tucupi* must be boiled for several hours to become safe to eat. It's then used in a sauce for food, seasoned with salt and the basil-like *alfavaca*.
- *Beiju* — *Manioc*-based tapioca gets griddled pancake-style with coconut.

PREPARATION

Sealable clay pots are commonly used for Northeastern *moquecas* (stews) and barbecue tools for southern *churrascos*. In Brazil, the following cooking styles are important.

- *Comida mineira* — In addition to *baiana* (cooking typical of Bahia and the Northeast) and the South's *churrasco*, this is a specific cooking style that uses pork (including pork fat in which many dishes are cooked), collard greens, abundant preserved fruits and Minas cheese.
- *Nova cozinha brasileira* — A recent, São Paulo-focused cuisine where chefs, often influenced by European fusion, develop modern takes on Brazilian culinary traditions.

DEFINING DISHES

Acarajé

A peeled black-eyed pea bread and speciality of the north-eastern state of Bahia, this snack, which originated in Nigeria, is indicative of Brazil's street food, and of its African heritage. It is particularly iconic because of how it is sold — by Salvadoran women who serve *acarajé* dressed in their white *baianas de tabuleiro*. Both these clothes and the food are representative of Candomblé, an Afro-Brazilian religion that is a fusion of African deities and Catholic beliefs. Black-eyed pea-based dough balls are deep-fried in African palm oil *dendê*, then invariably munched with a prawn and peanut/cashew nut paste called *vatapá*.

Caipirinha. Brazil's signature cocktail is now easily recognisable world-wide: take *cachaça* (a sugar-based liquor) and blend with lime, sugar and crushed ice. *Caipirissima* is the same but with Bacardi rum rather than *cachaça*, *caipirosca* the same, but with vodka.

STEVE OUTRAM / GETTY IMAGES

Iced *caipirinha* and a bowl of shrimps and chicken.

Churrasco

Southern Brazil's gaucho grill-up, the *churrasco*, was the staple of the cattle-herders-of-yore in Rio Grande do Sul region — a means of roasting meat cuts by the campfire. It may be Brazilian cuisine's poster boy overseas but *churrasco* doesn't quite have the popularity that its equivalent, the *parrilla*, does in Argentina. Still, it's a Sunday tradition, and entails a basted slow roast with some Brazilians favouring just salt as a seasoning and others using milk, honey or *cachaça* (sugarcane-based liquor) as marinades.

Feijoada

Take the ancient tribal staple of black beans and *manioc* flour, add the scraps of Portuguese-introduced pork or beef (traditionally feet, ears and tail) that were left for the African plantation slaves to cook into something palatable, and you have the foundation for *feijoada*, the culinary representation of Brazil's mixed cultural origins. This is served as a stew.

Moqueca

One of Brazil's most vivacious dishes, *moqueca* uses Brazil's African culinary heritage to conjure seafood into a delectable bouillabaisse. Octopus, lobster or perhaps prawns are stewed in a clay pot sealed to retain those essential flavours, with coconut milk as a thickener and *dendê* oil, yellow onion, tomato, coriander and green peppers to assail all the senses.

DRINK

Tea is only important in the gaucho-influenced South; elsewhere *cafezhino* (coffee) is the thing, with amply-sweetened espresso popular. Cold drinks — *sucos* (juices) or soft drinks known as *refrigerantes* or *guaraná* — often out-sell hot in these tropical climes.

Guarana, a berry native to the Amazon and used to flavour drinks.

Coconut milk ready to drink.

Assorted pulses: pinto, black-eye and chick peas.

The South is the spot to drink beer, much of it developed by the strong German influence. But the radiant talisman of tipples is *cachaça*, a variant of the *aguardiente*, or strong sugarcane-based liquor common to many Latin American nations. Evolved from Brazil's important sugarcane industry, its roots date back to the 16th century, and it appears in all forms from the dirty and cheap to the refined and pricey. It's Brazil's most common distilled drink, and forms the base for many cocktails.

ACARAJÉ

Makes approx 16 balls

Ingredients

2 x 400 g tins black-eyed peas
1 clove of garlic, finely chopped
1 onion, roughly chopped
1 small chilli, deseeded and finely chopped
1 to 2 tablespoons *manioc* flour (or replace with *tapioca* flour)
salt and pepper
palm oil

Method

Drain the black-eyed peas and place in food processor.

Add the garlic, onion and chilli, and process until a paste forms.

Add the flour, a little at a time, adding a little water if required to produce a smooth but firm consistency. Season with the salt and pepper.

Divide mixture into approximately 16 balls and fry in 2 to 3 centimetres of palm oil over a medium–high heat until brown.

Drain on paper towels, then serve.

Vineyards in the fertile fields of Argentina.

CRISTIAN LAZZARI / GETTY IMAGES

Argentina

All that beef and wine: how could a meal in Argentina go wrong? It doesn't, often. The infectious pride of the Argentines about their food, and the time spent chatting over meals, sets the stage for some special eating experiences. But gone is all that typical South American spice: food is served *au naturel* here. Culinary critiques may call the cuisine conservative, but it's more that Argentines like what they know, and know what they love.

CULINARY CAPITALS BUENOS AIRES, SALTA **KNOWN FOR** *CHIMICHURRI* **IMPORTS** ITALIAN CUISINE **EXPORTS** LARGE CUTS OF BEEF **DEVOUR** *ALFAJORES* (COOKIE SANDWICHES) **AVOID** (EATING) LLAMA

Mate: Argentina's favourite cup of tea.

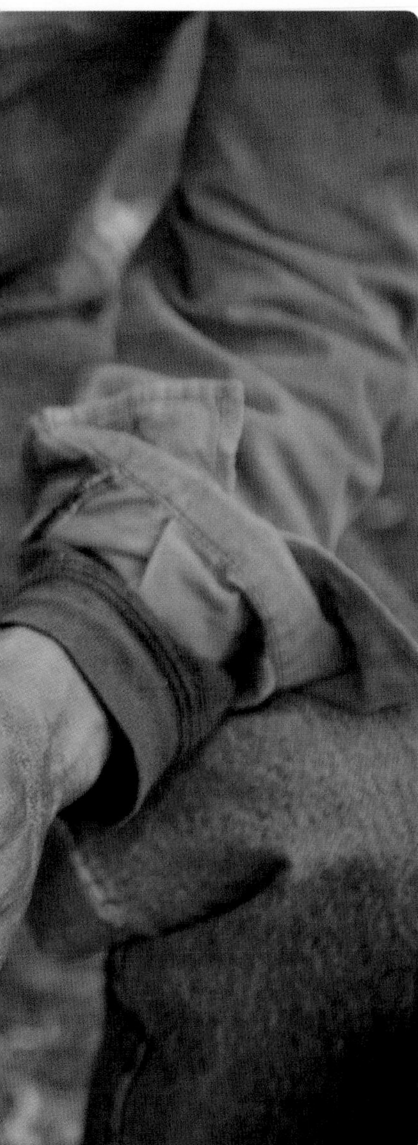
CRISTIAN LAZZARI / GETTY IMAGES

CULTURE

Indigenous peoples still hold cultural sway in Argentina, but only in furthest reaches of the land. In the Northwest, elements of their typical diet remain in today's cuisine: grains, squashes, and the Argentine take on the Andean *pachamanca* cooking method, *guatia*. This is a slow roast over hot stones in an oven set in a hole in the ground; the ingredients are wrapped in leather.

In the Northeast, European expansion across the continent spread the culinary influence of the Guaraní people, who inhabited the frontier lands of what was to become Argentina and Paraguay. Their main contribution was *yerba mate*, infusion tea served in a gourd, which had reached central Argentina by the 17th century and is now sipped everywhere. But 1536 was a significant year in the history of the nation's food: this was when the Spanish introduced cattle to the fertile lowland pampas, and changed the diet here for good.

Later European incomers garnered some well merited culinary praise. In the 19th century, Italian immigrants introduced their gastronomic talents, and over time a unique Argentine brand of Italian food developed, primarily in and around Buenos Aires where they began experimenting with a whole new kind of pasta. Italian influence also made pizza and ice cream national favourites.

Other nationalities headed further south. In the Argentine Lake District town of Bariloche, Swiss-German settlers started arriving around 1900, and had soon made the place Argentina's chocolate capital. Welsh settlers also wove themselves into the fabric of Patagonia, where they took to sheep farming and spreading their traditional cultural preferences for tea and fruitcake.

REGIONS

A landscape that alternates between sizzling jungle and chilly hill ranges has paved the way for Argentina to become a major agricultural player, with some intriguingly illogical results. Dry Northwestern valleys produce plentiful quantities of some of the best wine in the world, but Argentines have historically kept this mostly for their own consumption; conversely, lush central-Argentinean farmland provides a fifth of the planet's soybeans, but the crop plays little part in national diet.

Northwest

A warm, dry, high-altitude, low-humidity region, yet with plentiful water supplies channelled off the Andes mountains, the Northwest is Argentina's wine capital. But it's the high indigenous population that keeps Northwestern food so distinct. The food has elements of the cuisine of the Quechua/Aymara people of Ecuador, Peru and Bolivia: evidenced by a multitude of *cazuelas* (stews). Salta is the culinary hub, most famously giving its name to one of South America's most classic snacks: the *empanada*-like *salteña*.

- *Salteña* — Perfected in Bolivia, the *salteña* was originally Salta's delicacy and it is the ultimate *empanada*, only the meat filling is combined with a sauce or *recado*. They are distinguished by the bumpy, ridged, central fold in their pastry coat.
- *Locro* — A stew of beans, *chorizo*, and chunks of beef jerky or pork prepared with pumpkins or squash and corn or wheat.
- *Cazuela salteña* — Chicken stew served with onion, raw eggs, and potatoes on rice and, unusually for Argentine food, quite spicy.

Making *empanadas*.

Medialuna croissants.

Typical meat from the *asado*.

Central Argentina

This is the nation's big, beefy heart. It probably wasn't until the 19th century that the cattle industry really thrived here, and beef burgeoned onto the scene courtesy of its bumpkin ambassador the *gaucho*. This Argentine cowboy would herd the cows to market, then cut off the least-favoured cuts for himself (which led to the birth of the *asado* or grill-up, a national phenomenon) and trade them for the tobacco and *mate* tea they loved.

Patagonia

Topography gets wilder and cooler down south and in creeps the influence of lamb, venison and boar, which in some instances dominate beef on menus. A typical menu item might be roast rack of lamb with berries from Neuquén Province (also a source of apples, pears and other fruit). *Ahumados* (smoked) meats are particularly common. Down at Tierra del Fuego, shellfish has an impact on dishes.

Bariloche

This gastronomic anomaly of a city in western Patagonia serves up fondues and great chocolates and lets you wash them down with beer, all courtesy of the Swiss-German settlers' impact on cuisine.

MENU

Isn't this just like Paris? Or Rome? Such rhetorical questions are common in Buenos Aires and while the answer is 'no', dining does follow more recognisably European patterns — leisurely meals out for business and pleasure, restaurants favoured over street food, less buzz about the spice and more about the ingredients.

ASHOK SINHA / GETTY IMAGES

Patagonian lamb roast.

Dine out at the:

- *Parrillada* — The most Argentine of Argentine eateries, where *parrillas* (grilled meat dishes) are served.
- *Cafetines/Bodegones* — Bars where you can often pick up *picadas* (tapas-style plates of diced ham or cheese) as snacks and *minutas*: quickly-prepared dishes, that are a crossover between a snack and a meal.
- *Confiteria* — This is a café and a socialising point throughout the day and into the evening.

DAILY MEALS

A light breakfast is usually focussed around an espresso, classically served with a *medialuna* (small croissant) or tea. Lunch is the big meal and Argentines take the opportunity of a siesta until mid-afternoon. *Picadas* (tapas-style plates of diced ham or cheese) help hunger-bust come early evening, until you finally get dinner (anything from 10 pm until midnight).

ESSENTIAL PRODUCE

Beef

Beef dishes exhibit the undeniable quality of Argentina-reared meat, juxtaposed with the surprising simplicity of its preparation: the seasoning is rarely more than salt and pepper. Ask for your beef to be *jugoso*, (very rare), *a punto* (medium rare) or *bien cocido* (well done). The cuts are usually thicker than elsewhere in the world.

- *Bife a Caballo* — 'beef on horseback', crowned by a fried egg.
- *Bife de lomo* — lean, fillet steak.
- *Milanesa* — breaded fillet.

- *Bife de chorizo* — similar to the US rib-eye steak, often on the bone, and more flavoursome than *lomo*.
- *Bife de costilla* — T-bone steak.
- *Vacio* — Fatty, juicy; often the cheapest cut available.
- *Matambre* — Thin but fatty cut of flank steak, this term is also used to describe a *relleno* (stuffed) beef dish with a filling of vegetables and egg.
- *Parrilla and asado* — These are two confusingly similar, but distinct terms relating to the Argentine grill-up of meat. The *parrilla* refers to the cooking process where the meat is cooked on a flat griddle and turned. The *asado* is an event as much as it is a process, similar to a barbecue. As a cooking term, *al asador* means cooking the meat on a raised stand, above the fire, allowing flames to rise and cook all parts of the meat.

Beef rib *asado*, a traditional Argentinian dish.

Cheese

Argentina's cheese is exceptional by South American, if not by European, standards, and is a legacy of French, Italian and Spanish influences. Stand-out cheeses are:

- The hard Sardo, often used when preparing salads or soups
- Reggianito, a cousin of Italian Parmigiano Reggiano, with a particularly grainy consistency, and;
- La Capilla, a Manchego-like cheese. There is a version effused with Argentine Malbec.

Cheeses from La Pampa.

Pasta

It's Italian, yet it's not Italian: Argentines have some novel ways of dealing with this classic carb fix, although spaghetti, *fettuccine* and *cannelloni* are all popular. Sauces can be

A variety of local cheese for sale.

Flouring the tops of *malfatti*, ricotta and spinach dumplings.

Chorizo sausage.

Alfajores cookies.

tomato-based but are often creamier, in *béchamel* style.

- *Sorrentinos* are ginormous circular ravioli filled with ham, mozzarella and ricotta; from the seaside resort of Mar del Plata.
- *Malfatti* are spinach gnocchi.
- *Fainá* gives Argentina its own eclectic pizza: a chickpea dough covers the pizza topping.

DEFINING DISHES

Asado

It's not just a meal. It's a cultural initiation. Few things are as quintessentially and fundamentally Argentinean as the *asado*, or barbecue. This typical family get-together over grilled meat can last half a day or more. If you're invited and you're new to *asados*, show up early to come for the full experience, which firstly involves going along to the butcher to choose the cuts of meat, then setting up the grilling arena, and then mingling with other guests over smaller snacks and plates, called *picadas*, whilst waiting for meat to cook.

Grilled fare typically involves *achuras* (offal), *morcilla* (blood sausage) and maybe *provoleta* (a provolone-like cheese especially designed to be barbecued). This is followed by *choripán* (spiced sausage), *entraña* (innards), *mollejas* (sweetbreads) and all the regular beef cuts. Argentines have none of the frequent European squeamishness over less

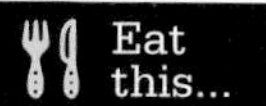

Alfajores are cookie sandwiches, usually glued together by *dulce de leche*. They're found elsewhere in South America, but Argentina's penchant for them is unrivalled: they're coated in dark or white chocolate or *al nieve* (snow), made with egg whites and sugar.

desirable cuts. Fernet is an aromatic aperitif commonly drunk at *asados*. *Cabrito al asador* (roast goat) is a popular variation on the *asado* in Córdoba province.

Chimichurri

Argentines prefer rather conservative food preparation, then add on sauces separately made with a complexity that would otherwise be absent from their meals. *Chimichurri* is the most ubiquitous flavour, using a base of olive oil, vinegar, parsley and garlic. Herbs vary regionally, and include oregano, cumin and thyme. It's a feature of a classic Argentine *asado*.

Dulce de Leche

This thick, caramel-like sauce is concocted by slowly boiling milk and sugar, spices such as vanilla, and an agent like bicarbonate of soda. As the milk evaporates, the sweet brown sauce remains. Argentines don't need much excuse to get out the *dulce de leche*. It's a spread for bread, *croissants* and *brioches* and it's the favoured cake filling too.

DRINKS

Argentines make good coffee, although *yerba mate* (infusion tea) is, if not more popular, the more distinctive beverage.

Submarino is another non-alcohol Argentine classic: a glass of steamed milk with a chocolate bar melted into it.

Argentines are so addicted to *yerba mate* that they often carry it with them on journeys: hence the *mate* (hollowed gourd) receptacle the tea is drunk from, usually with a *bomba* (straw). *Yerba mate* is normally drunk in a social setting, with everyone in the group using the same *mate* and *bomba*.

JUANMONINO / GETTY IMAGES

Chimichurri, the classic Argentinian sauce.

Beer is increasingly popular, with Quilmes the main brand, but wine, national drink since 2010, is what Argentines like to quaff most, with the Mendoza province producing the majority. Conditions have conspired to make Argentine wine free from most of the bugs that plague other wine-growing regions.

- Malbec, the grape introduced by the French produces Argentina's most famed wines. The highest-quality Malbecs come from Mendoza province's high-altitude valleys, and are heralded by some as the world's best.
- The second-most productive region after Mendoza is the San Juan wine region. It has a hotter, drier climate and produces sherry-style wines.
- *Torrontes* is a white, distinctly Argentine grape which grows well in Salta's cooler drier climate.

CHIMICHURRI

Ingredients

1 bunch parsley
8 cloves garlic, chopped
¼ lemon, juiced
1 tablespoon diced red onion
170 ml extra virgin olive oil
60 ml red wine vinegar
1 teaspoon oregano
1 teaspoon ground black pepper
½ teaspoon salt

Method

Finely chop the parsley and place in a food processor.

Add remaining ingredients and process until well incorporated.

Use half the sauce for a marinade and serve the other half with the dish.

Tuber used for making potato flour sold by Quechua Indian women at the market in Cuzco.

HUGHES HERVE / HEMIS.FR / GETTY IMAGES

Peru

Simple is sublime in today's culinary reckoning and while Peru's cuisine still pivots around its markets and street-side snacks, food pride is filling the streets with fancy restaurants opening and celebrity chefs launching foodie festivals. The sleeping gastronomic giant has awakened onto the world stage.

CULINARY CAPITALS LIMA, CUZCO **KNOWN FOR** *CEVICHE* **IMPORTS** CONQUISTADOR CUISINE **EXPORTS** *CEVICHE*, COFFEE, *PISCO SOUR* **DEVOUR** *LOMO SALTADO (BEEF DISH)* **AVOID** AMERICAN FAST FOOD

Woman basting *cuy*, guinea pig.

Dish of *ceviche*.

Mate de coca.

CULTURE

Peru possesses the ultimate fusion food: it's a blend of indigenous preparation methods and the influence of Spanish conquistadors.

Pre-colonial peoples worked with a diet of root vegetables like potatoes and squashes, a plethora of chillies, maize and guinea pig, alpaca or fish. Most cooking was done on smouldering stones in a hole, the *pachamanca* method that's a hallmark of Andean Peruvian cooking today. Marinades are also key, especially in the country's celebrated fish dish, *ceviche*.

When the Spanish invaded in the 16th century they brought beef, pork, chicken, rice, limes, garlic and the like. But the influx of ingredients did not replace indigenous cuisine, it just enhanced it.

Ditto with subsequent waves of immigration: 19th-century African slaves had a knack for turning leftovers into delicacies such as *tacu tacu*, an omelette made with old rice and beans. The Chinese replaced Africans in many manual labour jobs and Peru began using more ginger and soy sauce.

The Japanese forged diplomatic relations with Peru before they did any other Latin American country, and immigration from the Far East added zest to Peruvian food by the 20th century: most notably by expanding Peru's citrus-marinated fish repertoire.

REGIONS

Peruvian culinary styles can seem poles apart because of its three topographical extremes. Coastal desert (where fish-based food predominates) is backed by 6000-metre plus Andean peaks (where links to ancient Incan cooking techniques are strongest), which are flanked, in turn, by the Amazon rainforest (where wondrous fruit, plants and river fish enrich the feasting).

COAST

Peru's Pacific coastline stretches nigh-on 2500 kilometres down the western edge of the country, abutted by a desert landscape that creates a sizzling, dry, dusty climate. It's unsurprising Peru's hallowed national dish, *ceviche* — a cooling citrus-marinated fish dish — originated here. Fish has been in the coastal diet since Peru's seaboard-dwelling Moche people started preparing *ceviche* almost two millennia ago.

Now Peru's seafood has a wider spectrum, thanks as much to African, Japanese and Chinese immigrants (who mostly settled near coastal ports) as Peruvians. *Camarones* (shrimps) and the white fish *corvina* (similar to sea trout) have most influence on meals. Favoured dishes include:

- *Chaufa* — China's guiding hand in Peru's food evolution: Peruvian seafood rice with ginger, squid and mussels.
- *Chupe de camarones* — shrimp chowder.
- *Shambar* — flying the flag for Africa's influence on Peruvian food, *shambar* is a soup from Trujillo made with leftover pork rind, beans (indigenous origin) and wheat/onions (Spanish origin).
- *Tiradito* — similar to *ceviche* but without onions it has a marinade of feisty *aji amarillo* (yellow pepper) and ginger: typifies Japanese culinary influence.

Coastal living also created a thirst for alcohol. The port of Pisco produces the homonymous grape brandy. The Ica region yields some fruity white wine — Peru's best.

Inca Kola, Peru's home-grown soft drink, is the world's only brand to out-sell Coca-Cola as a nation's number one soda. With an amber-yellow hue and a creamy bubble-gum taste, it's bottled national pride.

Tiraditos, Peruvian dish of raw dish.

Glass and bottle of Inca Kola.

Mashed potato, shrimps and peppers.

Andes Mountains

The Central Andes massif has a hefty impact on the nation's cuisine. It's remote, and Spanish influence has had less opportunity to tamper with old Inca methods of food preparation: here mountain meat like *cuy* (guinea pig) or llama might be roasted *pachamanca*-style within hot coals in a hole in the ground. Freshwater lake fish such as trout dominate on menus: often baked in clay to seal flavours. This region is almost certainly where potatoes originated. Potatoes, other roots like cassava, and energy-boosting grains like *quinoa* bulk up the hotter, heavier, meatier dishes popular in the Andes to combat chilly temperatures. Some common dishes are:

- *Papas a la Huancaína* — yellow potato salad dowsed in creamy white cheese sauce originating from the highland culinary hub of Huancayo.
- *Rocoto relleno* — Arequipa city's signature dish of fiery chillies stuffed with beef, olives and eggs, cooked in a cheese sauce.
- *Sopa de quinua* — hearty amber-coloured soup packed with 'wonder-grain' *quinoa*, squash, beans and other Inca ingredients.

Amazon Basin

With the long river trip, comes the meal wrapped in a jungle leaf. Many foods are served thus in Peru's rainforest for portability. Lighter meats like chicken or one of several river fish take precedence. The array of fruit here, with bright delights like Vitamin C-rich *camu camu* or *cherimoya* (Peruvian custard apples) contribute to a huge variety of juices and desserts. Bananas and peanuts star in meal preparation, and the *ceja de la selva* (eyebrow of the jungle; transition zone

LEW ROBERTSON / GETTY IMAGES

Bowls of *camu camu*.

between Andes and Amazon) fosters ideal conditions for Peru's coffee industry to flourish. A dish often served here is *juanes*: meat and rice boiled together in the leaf of an Amazonian plant like the *bijao* or banana.

DAILY MEALS

Peruvians are early risers and eat big breakfasts to help give workers an energy boost. Lunches are light to suit the afternoon heat, and dinner is eaten later, with 10 pm the standard time.

Peruvians are not great lingerers over their meals: no-nonsense eating with gusto is the norm. Much emphasis is placed on street food, and Peruvians are more likely to be chowing down on this — using their fingers — than in restaurants.

- *Cevicherias* are eating houses specially tailored to serve Peru's national dish, *ceviche*. (They open at lunchtime only).
- Chifas are Peruvian-Chinese restaurants.

ESSENTIAL PRODUCE

Chicken

Chicken (*pollo*) is the meaty king of the kitchen in Peru.

- *Pollo a la brasa* is Peru's favourite way to take chicken — the meat is basted in soy sauce, peppers and cumin, and cooked on charcoal.
- *Aji a la gallina* is a chicken stew made with condensed milk and *aji amarillo*, thickened with leftover bread.

Chilli

Wondering what gave your Peruvian meal that 'unlike anything

I've had before' taste? It is the chilli. Peru's chillies are the country's original seasoning, and some are rarely found outside its borders.

- *Aji amarillo* is a floral, fiery yellow chilli endemic to the Andes; described by celebrity chef Gaston Acuario as Peruvian cooking's most important ingredient.
- *Aji rocoto* are red, green or yellow, shaped like peppers and used in dishes like *rocoto relleno* (stuffed rocoto).
- *Aji limo* is used to flavour *ceviche* and other seafood.

Homemade chicken soup.

Grains and pulses

Now Incan super-foods are in health-food stores worldwide, but the Incas have waged wars fuelled by vitamin-laden grains and pulses like *quinoa* for centuries. For most Peruvians, grains, which are most commonly used in soups, provide a key source of nutrition. Beans are a Peruvian staple, and are cooked with garlic to add, with rice, to meal bases. Maize is the traditional crop in Peru and is incredibly influential on the cuisine here.

- *Kaniwa* is *quinoa*'s little-known cousin: a nutty seed with all *quinoa*'s nutrition but a taste deemed superior by many.
- *Pallar* is the Lima or butter bean, common in soups and salads.
- *Tarwi* are the seeds from Peruvian lupins that are used to thicken Andean stews and soups.

Quinoa, the grain of the Incas.

Potatoes

Peru could rightly be called 'kingdom of the potato' as it was here in the isolated highlands near Lake Titicaca that the earliest evidence of their cultivation was discovered. There are some 4000 types of potatoes currently grown in Peru.

Native Peruvian potatoes.

Street food vendor in Cuzco.

Plates of breakfast pastries and boiled eggs.

Plastic bags of soup for sale.

Two common ones are:

- *Papas amarillas* — soft, grainy yellow potatoes perfect for mashing and used for the Lima specialty, *causa* (citrus- and chilli-infused mashed potato with onions, olives and eggs).
- *Papa canchan* — are pink flavoursome potatoes used to make *papa rellena* (stuffed mashed potato) and *pachamanca* cooking (over hot stones in a hole).

SHOPPING

Everything happens at the market: and it happens early, with the trading action and best produce gone by 6 am. Markets have grown in popularity as tourist attractions.

- Mercado de Belén, Iquitos, is best for seeing the weird-and-wonderful foods of the Amazon being vended.
- Mercado Mayorista, Huancayo is one of the most vivid and friendly fruit and vegetable markets.

PREPARATION

Peruvian food is ancient in origin and still utilises Incan techniques, but it can also be thoroughly contemporary.

- *Pachamanca* — Dig a hole in the ground, make a fire hemmed in by rocks and when the rocks are baking hot, you have your *hutia* (oven) ready for *pachamanca*. *Cuy*, pork or chicken is then basted in spices and cooked over the *hutia* with potatoes and chillies.
- Clay pots are the classic Peruvian cooking apparatus: porous pots that allow unnecessary moisture content to evaporate, thus preserving flavours.
- *Novoandina* takes ancient ingredients and uses

contemporary cooking technique to give them a haute-cuisine image shake-up, as with *quinotto* (*risotto* made with *quinoa*). *Novoandina* was the reason Peruvian food become the next big thing in the 1990s.

DEFINING DISHES

Anticuchos

Nothing better represents the 'waste not, want not' approach to Peru's cooking than this use of the less-desirable cuts of meat. *Anticuchos* uses cuts such as beef heart or chicken gizzards devilled up with spices then griddled on skewers. The practice was derived from the need to use the meat wealthy Peruvians did not want to eat, and so left for their slaves. Seasonings include anything from chilli to lemon juice to beer.

Ceviche

The Moche people of Peru's northern coast started making it about 2000 years ago; conquistadors added essential ingredients and Peruvian-Japanese chefs helped perfect it: *ceviche* is Peru's national dish, and the epitome of its multicultural culinary history.

The indigenous method was to marinate fish in a fermented beverage, which helped preserve it in hot climes. They would also have used their ubiquitous stash of chillies in the marinade, and consumed the dish with sweet potato just as it is consumed today. The Spanish introduced the lime juice that became the marinade of choice in the 16th century, along with the onions, another key ingredient in the marinade.

Marinating times for the fish vary, and were traditionally anything from overnight down to a couple of hours. But Japanese-Peruvian chef Dario Matsufuji reduced marination time down to a few minutes in the 1970s, and

NATALIE WINTER / GETTY IMAGES

Rows of dried maize in a '*chicha*' house.

that method is used in many *cevicherias* in Peru still today.

The fish used in *ceviche* should be white, but varies according to the region. The coast often uses *corvina*, the mountains *trucha* (trout) and the Amazon *dorade* or *paiche*.

Lomo saltado

One of Peru's most popular dishes, and indicative of the impact of the Far East on Peruvian cuisine, *lomo saltado* is strips of beef (*lomo*) marinated in soy sauce and vinegar. The beef is then mixed together with French fries and red onions, and served on a bed of rice.

DRINKS

Of the milder beverages, *mate de coca* (*coca* leaf tea) is among the most popular, and a combatant of altitude sickness. Markets are great places to sample juices, which are as varied as Peru's fruits.

The battle between Cuzco (which makes the malty Cusqueña) and Arequipa (making Arequipeña) as to whose beer is best will rage forevermore.

Peru's wine industry is gaining momentum, but strong liquor is more the thing.

- *Chicha* is made with maize or *manioc* root. *Chicha morada* is a sweet soft drink concoted with purple maize and spices — the alcoholic version is the archetypal poor man's booze, with maize chewed in the makers' mouths to initiate fermentation.
- *Pisco Sour* is the world-famous cocktail that was perfected in Lima using Pisco (grape brandy) combined with lime juice, egg white, syrup, Angostura bitters and ice.

Empanadas cooking in oil over fire.

DANITA DELIMONT / GETTY IMAGES

Chile

Three times a day just isn't enough for the Chileans: they indulge in four meals instead. The nation's relationship with food developed out of a culture that prioritises family ties: *once* (teatime) is a good excuse for a gossip and an *asado* (barbecue) is foremost a family get-together. Neighbouring Peru and Argentina may get the culinary publicity, but the Chileans are most likely laughing.

CULINARY CAPITAL SANTIAGO **KNOWN FOR** *ASADO*, WINE **IMPORTS** GERMAN SWEET TREATS **EXPORTS** WINE **DEVOUR** *EMPANADAS* **AVOID** COFFEE

Stomping on the grapes, a vintage tradition.

Plum kuchen, courtesy of German immigrants.

Pisco sour cocktail.

CULTURE

The Spanish influence spread across Chile in the same way as elsewhere in South America, only here opposition from indigenous peoples was comparatively subdued. As a result, the cuisine is more akin to European fare: with the exception of the food of the Mapuche people from the Chiloé archipelago; they fiercely resisted colonisation, and to an extent preserved their culinary traditions. Chiloé treats include the seeds of the *araucaría*, the Chilean monkey-puzzle tree — ingredients indicative of that native tribe's foraging culture.

Spaniards introduced the olives and beef in Chile's famed *empanadas* and the grapes producing Chilean wine. During the 19th century French grape varieties were also introduced.

In the 19th century, German immigrants brought their penchant for sweet staples like the now-ubiquitous *kuchen* (German cake). The British had a gastronomic role too: during their 19th-century tenure of Chile's mines, the culture of *once* (teatime) took off.

REGIONS

The proximity of coastline in Chile — it stretches the length of the country — defines the food so fish and seafood dominate, but with this gangly country spanning 35° latitude and some of the world's wettest and driest climatic zones, there are significant culinary variations.

North

The arid north is, livestock-wise, the domain of goats and llamas; sub-tropical climes have also fostered distinctive fruits. These include the acidic Pica lemons that sharpen up Chile's *Pisco Sour* (a cocktail), and endemic, mango-like *caricas*.

Chumbeque is a triple-layered sweet from Iquique sandwiched with either *manjar* (a caramel-esque spread) or Pica lemons.

Central Valleys

The verdant valleys around Santiago are as Mediterranean as Chile gets. Cue the olives (starring in Chile's meat turnovers, *empanadas*), the avocados (blended into delicious condiment sauces) and, of course, the vineyards.

Pebre is the default Chilean condiment that originates in Central Chile, comprising onions, garlic, coriander and chillies; it accompanies almost anything.

South

Wild, and very wet, southern Chile is a prime dairy area. The region rears plentiful salmon, and colder Pacific waters allow unusual seafood to thrive. Chile's most distinctive culinary region, Chiloé, is here, as are its German immigrant communities.

- *Crudos* — German-influenced steak tartares from Valdavia.
- *Charquican* — Mapuche potato, meat, corn and pumpkin stew: augmented in Chiloé by seaweed.
- *Curanto* — Chiloé seafood-and-meat dish stewed with *chapaleles* (dumplings), the ingredients are covered in *nalca* leaves (a plant similar to rhubarb).

ESSENTIAL PRODUCE

Chilean food is often dubbed 'lack-lustre' as, despite the nation's name, there's less spice than other Latin American cuisine and, ostensibly, less creativity in the prep. But the natural flavours speak for themselves.

Meat

Beef and pork are most popular: chicken is often considered inferior. Sausages assume a greater role than in other South

A selection of grilled meats.

Caldillo de congrio, a traditional fish stew.

Girl enjoying one of Chile's favourite foods, the hot dog.

American nations. Meat is often served in a stew (*cazuela*). *Bistek el pobre* (poor man's beef) features the ubiquitous loin cut with eggs and fried onions/potatoes.

Seafood

What steak is to Argentina, seafood is to Chile. Fish dishes often get cooked up with wine: Chileans are passionate about what fish goes with which vintage. Seafood is served as *chupe* (broth) or *paila marina* (whitefish-and-shellfish stew). *Ceviche* (lime-marinated fish) is popular; Easter Island produces a rare take on *ceviche* using yellowfin tuna. Other favourites include:

- *Centolla* — King crab, a speciality of Punta Arenas.
- *Loco* — A sea snail that is often served with mayonnaise is one of several rare Chilean molluscs.
- *Corvina* — Chilean sea bass; used in Chilean *ceviche*.

DEFINING DISHES

Caldillo de Congrio

Chilean poet Pablo Neruda loved *caldillo de congrio* so much he wrote an ode to it. It's a fishy broth with conger eel, boiled with carrots, onions, garlic, potatoes and coriander.

Completos

One of the Chilean's biggest food obsessions is the hot dog, supposedly imported from the US. Traditional *completos* are bigger than the American version, with tomatoes, mayonnaise

Chile has the odd precedent of naming sandwiches after Presidents. Try a ***'Piñera'*** (salmon/rocket/cream cheese) or the grilled cheese-and-meat fest, *'Barros Luco'*.

JAMES STRANGE / GETTY IMAGES

The ever-popular seafood dish, *ceviche*.

and sauerkraut. A *completo Italiano* features tomatoes, avocados and mayonnaise — the colours of Italy's flag.

Empanadas

The filling and superior size of these Latin American fried/baked pastry snacks set the Chilean version apart; *empanadas* have 'national dish' status. Take minced beef, olives, egg, onions and raisins and you have the filling, known as *pino*. Seafood *empanadas* might have mussels or sea snails as fillings.

DRINK

Tea-drinking culture was probably derived from Paraguay's Guaraní people. German immigrants introduced decent beers, but as Latin America's main wine exporter Chile has had wine flowing through its veins since the 16th century.

The Andes provide natural irrigation and combined with the balmy central Chilean climate, it makes for wonderful wine-growing conditions. Chilean wine has higher-than-average antioxidant content due to mountain air currents causing sharp night-time temperature drops.

- The Maipo Valley produces Cabernet Sauvignon.
- The Maule Valley produces the largest quantities of Chile's most traditionally-grown grape, *Pais*.
- Concha y Toro's Casillero del Diablo is the best-known Chilean wine.

Colo de mono or 'Monkey's tail' is a sweet eggnog-like drink traditionally served at Christmas, combining coffee, *aguardiente* (firewater), milk, cloves and cinnamon.

Farmer walking with cows in a field at dusk.

ANDREW HOLT / GETTY IMAGES

Ethiopia

Ethiopian cuisine is an astounding departure from that of of its neighbours. The complex food of this diverse and proud nation juggles a flavour-bomb of hot, spicy and sour. Wrapped up in ancient ritual and ceremony, customs in Ethiopia can be as intricate as the food itself. At its simplest though, food here is all about sharing. With a simple '*enebla*' (please join us) even complete strangers are invited to the table.

CULINARY CAPITALS ADDIS ABABA **KNOWN FOR** *INJERA*, COFFEE **EXPORTS** VERY LITTLE **IMPORTS** WHEAT, SORGHUM **DEVOUR** *MINCHET ABESH* (SPICY STEW) **AVOID** *TRIPPA WAT* (TRIPE STEW)

A very significant food crop, *enset*, for sale at the weekly market.

Frying lamb on an open fire.

Fragrant local honey for sale in a pottery jar.

CULTURE

Ethiopia's unique cuisine evolved out of isolation. Treacherous mountain terrain cut off the normal influence of neighbouring cuisines, creating a national diet quite unlike the rest of Africa. More inquisitive and courageous traders did make it through though and brought the spices of the Far East to the Ethiopian larder. These new flavourings provided the key to the pungent and spicy dishes of Ethiopia today.

The Italian occupation of Ethiopia from 1935 to 1941 shook up the food landscape. The occupying soldiers and settlers introduced spaghetti and pizza, now found commonly throughout the country, and made the *macchiato* a standard way to serve coffee.

In modern Ethiopia, the daily menu continues to be dictated by religion. Ethiopian Orthodox Christians account for around 45% of the population and the rigorous and complicated schedule of fasting proscribed by the church has seeped into the diet creating an entire subset of fasting foods.

Restaurants serving traditional Ethiopian food are known as 'national food' restaurants. Some specialise in preparing the local dish of raw meat, *tere sega*. You'll see the butcher busily hacking off meat from the animal carcasses swinging in plain sight of the restaurant entrance. Others serve only *kitfo*, raw ground beef marinated in red chilli powder and clarified butter.

ESSENTIAL PRODUCE

Bread

Injera is an Ethiopian flatbread that forms the basis of every meal. It is traditionally made from *teff* (a native cereal, high in iron and fibre). The *teff* flour is mixed with water and fermented for several days. When the mixture is ready, it is poured over a clay plate and baked over an open fire. The resulting bread has a spongy, crepe-like texture and vinegary taste.

- Today in lowland areas where *teff* production is inadequate, wheat flour or corn flour is substituted.
- The standard way to serve an Ethiopian meal is to use the *injera* as the plate, with food heaped on top of the bread. Pieces of *injera* are then torn from the edge and used to scoop food, removing the need for cutlery.
- *Kotcho* (also known as *enset*), another bread-like staple, is made from the starchy root and leaf sheaths of the false banana plant. Usually served with *kitfo*.

Meats and poultry

Ethiopian dishes make extensive use of meat. *Bege* (lamb) is common in highland areas, while *figel* (goat) is used more often in the lowlands. Due to its relative affordability, *doro* (chicken) is prevalent everywhere.

The most everyday way to serve meat is in a *wat* (stew) but raw meat is a national delicacy.

- *Tibs* — slices or strips of pan-fried meat.
- *Kitfo* — minced meat, served warm but uncooked, with butter and the popular *berbere* spice.
- *Tere sega* — raw meat served with condiments.

Pulses

Chickpeas and lentils are used in dishes for traditional Ge'ez (fasting) periods when no animal fats can be consumed.

- *Kik Wat* — red lentil curry spiced up by *berbere*.
- *Messer Wat* — yellow lentil curry with turmeric and garlic.
- *Ful* — a puree of fava beans and butter introduced to Ethiopia from Egypt and Sudan.
- *Shiro* — a bean or chickpea puree.

TIM WHITE / GETTY IMAGES

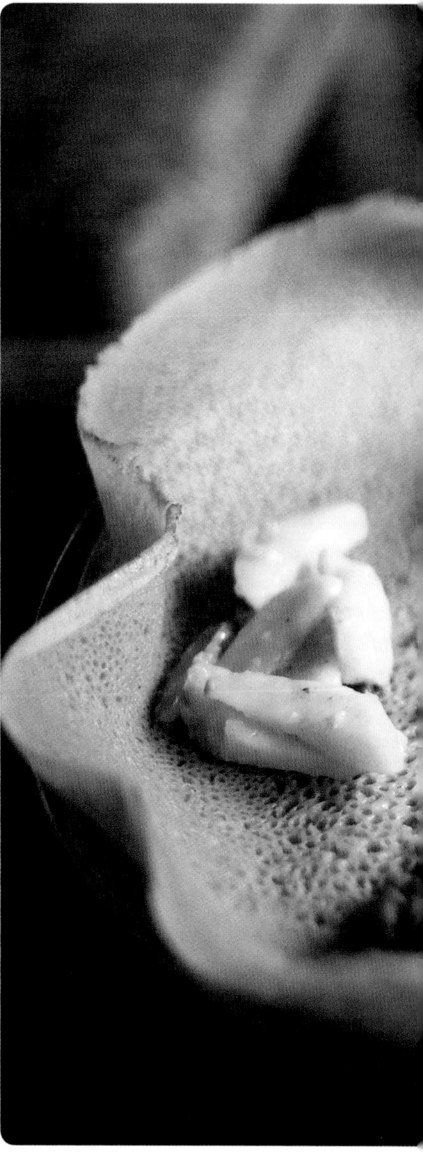

Injera bread dish.

Vegetables

The Ethiopian diet doesn't have an abundance of vegetables. *Gomen* (collard greens), potatoes, carrots, and *kai iser* (beetroot) are the most common. They are often incorporated as ingredients in a *wat* or sautéed in the pan with *tibs*.

DEFINING DISHES

Berbere

The essential ingredient in almost every Ethiopian meal is *berbere*. This pungent powdered spice dominates the nation's flavours. The ability to prepare a good *berbere* mix is highly regarded and valued above any other culinary skill. 'The woman with the best *berbere*', an old Ethiopian saying goes, 'will get the best husband'.

A basic *berbere* powder is made from a ground-down mix of dried hot chilli peppers, garlic, ginger, basil, fenugreek, *korarima* (also known as Ethiopian cardamom), rue, *ajwain* (also known as bishop's weed), and nigella. A good *berbere* powder can contain up to 16 different spices.

Berbere is used extensively in *wat* sauces. *Kai sauce* (the basis of *kai wat* and *minchet abesh*) is pungent and fiery red in colour because of liberal helpings of *berbere*.

It's also served in powder form as a condiment to be sprinkled, or heaped, on *kitfo* and *tere sega*. It's even commonly used at breakfast time. *Yinjera fir fir*, which makes use of leftover *injera* with onions, butter and spice, and *genfo*, a kind of porridge, are two morning dishes that both include *berbere*.

Doro wat

Doro wat, or chicken stew, is Ethiopia's most common dish. Chicken drumsticks and wings are stewed in a sauce of butter, onions, chilli, cardamom, and *berbere*, and the dish is topped with hard-boiled egg.

FRANCES LINZEE GORDON / GETTY IMAGES

Filling bags with *berbere*.

Dulet

Minced tripe and liver are stir-fried in butter and flavoured with onions, chilli, cardamom and pepper in this dish, which, not for the faint-hearted, is also commonly served raw.

Minchet abesh

This thick stew of minced meat is smothered in a spicy red sauce made from *berbere* and topped with hard-boiled egg.

Yinjera fir fir

This popular breakfast fare consists of torn-up *injera* pieces mixed with butter and *berbere*.

DRINKS

Coffee

According to legend, coffee was first discovered by an Ethiopian herder who noticed his goats behaving oddly after chewing the berries of a certain shrub.

The traditional Ethiopian coffee ceremony begins with an incense burner being lit and freshly-cut grass scattered on the ground while the coffee beans are roasted in a pan. A pestle and mortar is used to grind the roasted beans before brewing. The coffee is served in tiny cups, with large helpings of sugar. At least three cups must be accepted and drunk before the ceremony can end. The third cup is called the *berekha* (blessing cup), because drinking it is thought to bestow a blessing.

Tej. This honey wine is Ethiopia's tipple of choice. Leaves and stems of the gesho (shiny-leaf buckthorn) plant are boiled and the juice is extracted, mixed with honey and given time to ferment. Despite the sweet taste it packs a powerful alcoholic punch.

HEIN VON HORSTEN / GETTY IMAGES

Harvesting tomatoes in Limpopo Province.

South Africa

Take a little black magic, a dash of Dutch heartiness, a pinch of Indian spice and a smidgin of Malay mystery and discover an amazing array of cultures all simmering away in the *potjie* (pot) of culinary influences that is South African cuisine. In recent years this has matured and can now be considered as a cuisine in its own right, marrying all the cultural influences that abound in South Africa.

CULINARY CAPITALS CAPE TOWN, WINELANDS **KNOWN FOR** WINE **IMPORTS** VEGETABLE OILS, RICE, WHEAT **EXPORTS** WINE, FRUIT, FISH **DEVOUR** *BILTONG* (CURED MEAT) **AVOID** *MAMPOER* (HOME BREW)

Biltong, cured meat.

Masala curry powder in a Durban spice shop.

Malay cooking: *waterblommetjie* and celery *bredie*.

CULTURE

The earliest inhabitants survived on animals hunted for the pot, seafood and vegetables. When passing ships needed fresh vegetables and fruit, the Dutch inhabitants planted a culinary garden. Their rich cuisine was infused with nutmeg, cinnamon and cassia, as well as rice from their colonies in the east. Malay slaves from Madagascar, Java and Indonesia added to the mix, providing spicier accompaniments to the bland fare on offer.

While the Cape was the birthplace of South African cuisine, KwaZulu-Natal is important too, as there were black tribes who migrated from other African countries, British settlers, and Mauritians who planted exotic fruits and introduced their spicy tomato sauces. When the Indian indentured labourers arrived in the mid-19th century, they brought their spices with them.

- African staples of maize and sorghum porridge were served with vegetable or meat sauce.
- Afrikaners had dried foods to suit their trekking habits: *biltong* (dried strips of salted meat), rusks, *boerewors* (sausage) and dried fruit.
- Indians brought curries, *breyanis* and *samoosas*.
- Cape Malay introduced *bobotie* (gently spiced minced meat with an egg custard topping) and *bredies* (vegetable stews, sometimes with meat).

REGIONS

Geography and climate differ greatly in this vast country. While the Western Cape's Mediterranean climate provides perfect conditions for growing wine grapes, the dry Karoo lends itself to sheep farming. KwaZulu-Natal is subtropical, while the Free State is wheat and cattle country.

- Mpumalanga, Gauteng and the north-east have trout farming, wheat, sunflowers, soy beans and *mealies* (corn cobs).
- Free State has venison, beef, cherries and wheat.
- KwaZulu-Natal has avocados, pineapples, mangoes and papaya; Durban is famous for its Indian curries.
- Karoo offers lamb and mutton.
- Eastern Cape grows sugar beet, aloe ferox and pineapples.
- Western Cape grows grapes, apples, pears, citrus fruit, olives and has a fishing industry. It is well known for its Cape Malay cuisine, and the heartland of South African cuisine in general.

Traditional Karoo lamb *sosaties*, or kebabs.

DAILY MEALS

In a country where there is such disparity in income, it is difficult to generalise about what people eat on a daily basis. Those living on a small amount of money will subsist on *samp* (crushed maize kernels) or *pap* (maize porridge) and beans with small amounts of meat in their diet. At the other end of the scale, in many white farming communities, meat is considered a staple and is eaten at every meal.

The diversity of South Africa's cuisine allows for many different types of restaurants. While there are the usual chain restaurants in most towns, it is worthwhile experimenting with local fare.

- Fine dining — the Winelands have the most innovative chefs in magnificent surroundings. Summer-time picnics are often available at the wineries, too.
- Cape Malay cuisine is at its best in the Bo-Kaap district of Cape Town.

Lunch at a vineyard in Boschendal.

Drying apricots at a farm in Barrydale.

- A highlight of visiting a township is experiencing some family-style cooking in a bed and breakfast and sipping the local brew in a *shebeen* (unlicensed bar).

ESSENTIAL PRODUCE

Fish

Considering the fact that South Africa is surrounded by two oceans, it has a remarkably modest reputation as a seafood-lover's destination. Yet there are some delicious fish dishes such as lightly spiced fish stews, *snoekbraai* (grilled snoek), mussels, oysters and saltwater crayfish. Pickled fish is popular in Cape Malay cuisine.

Meat

Local meat is excellent, particularly steak and Karoo lamb or mutton. Meat from springbok, kudu, warthog and ostrich are very popular. *Boerewors* (farmer's sausage) can be made from any of these meats by adding vinegar, coriander and other spices. It is often *braaied*, and is also available dried (*droewors*). *Biltong* is dried strips of preserved meat and the quintessential South African snack.

DEFINING DISHES

The Braai

The national pastime and the main food-centred social event across South Africa is the *braai* (barbecue). Even the public holiday officially known as Heritage Day (24 September) has been re-branded National *Braai* Day. The *braai* fire can be made in a steel drum sawn in half, at a *braai plek* (fire place) in a national park or in a fancy kettle barbecue. Wood, charcoal or vine off-cuts are used, and when the coals are glowing and there are no flames, they are ready for cooking.

PETER BROOKS / GETTY IMAGES

Barbecued *boerewors*, sausage, and *sosaties*, kebab.

On the barbecue you may see:

- Meat — karoo, lamb chops, steak, venison and ostrich.
- *Sosaties* — lamb pieces skewered with small onions and dried apricots, in a Cape Malay marinade of curry spices, vinegar and apricot jam.
- Poultry — chicken pieces, kebab or butterflied chicken, marinaded in *piri-piri* sauce or lemon and herb dressing.
- *Boerewors* farmer's sausage, usually made from beef, spiced with coriander seeds.
- Fish and shellfish — Snoek is a favourite fish, brushed with apricot jam and butter before cooking. Prawns and crayfish are excellent cooked over the coals.
- *Skilpadjies* are not really little tortoises as the name suggests, but lamb's liver wrapped in caul fat and *braaied* until crisp.
- Vegetables *mealies* (corncobs) are a favourite, as are sweet potatoes and ordinary potatoes baked in their skins in the coals.

Braai etiquette means you must:

- Take along a bottle of wine or some beer.
- Dress casually — the atmosphere is relaxed.
- Do *not* poke the fire or pick up the tongs if you are female — men do the cooking, beer in hand, while women make the salads.

Waterblommetjie bredie

A great tradition in the Western Cape, this stew of Afrikaans origin features lamb with *waterblommetjies* (also known as *Aponogeton Distachys*), flowers that grow in dams and ponds. The flowers are gathered in spring, but may be found tinned at other times of year. The stew is flavoured with wild sorrel, green chillies, fresh ginger, onions, potatoes and spices such as cloves, nutmeg and allspice. Red wine, stock and tamarind or lemon juice make up the sauce. The *bredie* is even better if left to mature overnight. It is served with rice.

Potjiekos

Cooked over a slow fire in that most African of cooking vessels, the three-legged cast-iron pot, *potjiekos* (small pot food) contains layers of vegetables and meat moistened with beer or old brown sherry.

Black tribes migrating into South Africa hundreds of years ago learned the use of this cast ir on pot from Arab traders. The pot retains the heat well and needs only a small amount of fuel. With the lid on, steam circulates inside which means that extra stock is not necessary for a tender stew. This is the perfect pot for a nomadic lifestyle and was adopted by the Voortrekkers who hooked it under their wagon while travelling, then added ingredients when they reached camp.

There are a couple of rules to *potjiekos* cooking:

- Layer the ingredients — The meat usually goes in first and is browned in oil, and then the vegetables are added in the order of their cooking time: potatoes then carrots at the bottom, followed by onions, pumpkin and sweet potato.
- Do not stir! This is the most important rule.

Grilled crayfish. Also known as a rock lobster, the saltwater crayfish is a great delicacy in South Africa. Served simply with lemon or garlic butter, they are best eaten at an open-air restaurant with your toes in the sand of a West Coast beach.

Potbrood, pot bread.

Crayfish with lime and herbs.

Kitchenware, including a *potjieko*, inside a typical mud hut on the Wild Coast of South African's Eastern Cape Province.

Woman stirring the pot in the creation of traditional South African home brew.

LAUREN BARKUME / GETTY IMAGES

- *Potjiekos* is generally served with *potbrood* (pot bread), which is also cooked over the coals in a straight-sided cast-iron pot.

DRINKS

Beer

Beer is the national beverage. The world's largest brewer, SAB Miller, is based in Johannesburg, so there is no shortage of brands, with Castle and Black Label the best-sellers and Peroni a stand-out favourite. Ciders are also popular, as are cocktails and shooters. Craft micro-breweries are in vogue, including Triggerfish, Jack Black and Darling Brewery.

Wine

South African wine debuted in 1659. Since then, it has had time to age to perfection, and is both of a high standard and reasonably priced. Wines are all certified and labels reflect their estate, vintage and origin.

- Dry white — Sauvignon Blanc, Riesling, Colombard and Chenin Blanc are particularly good.
- Red — Cabernet Sauvignon, Pinotage, Shiraz and Pinot noir.
- Makers of sparkling wine use Chardonnay and Pinot noir blends and the *méthode champenoise*.
- Fortified — sherries, ports and brandy are widely produced in South Africa. *Mampoer* or *Witblits* is a very strong home-distilled peach brandy.

Drink this...

Pinotage is a uniquely South African grape developed from a cross of Pinot noir and Cinsaut (Hermitage). The resultant wine is a full-bodied red with fruit flavours and a distinctive spiciness.

Jostling for position: food sellers at the street market.

TOM COCKREM / GETTY IMAGES

Mozambique

With a coastline of almost 7000 kilometres, it is not surprising that Mozambique's cuisine is especially noted for its seafood. Dishes have a pizzazz that distinguishes them from those of neighbouring countries, with liberal use of coconut milk and *piri-piri*, which is made from red chillies and means 'spicy-spicy'. For Mozambicans, the meal takes centre stage at all family celebrations and women spend days preparing the food.

CULINARY CAPITALS MAPUTO, ZAMBEZIA PROVINCE **KNOWN FOR** PORTUGUESE INFLUENCE **IMPORTS** MAIZE, RICE **EXPORTS** PRAWNS, CASHEW NUTS **DEVOUR** *PIRI-PIRI* CHICKEN **AVOID** *NIPA* (A LETHAL LOCAL BREW)

A low-key street market.

Fish sliced open and hanging to dry.

Doughnuts cooking in hot oil.

CULTURE

Mozambique produces tropical fruit such as mangos, papayas, pineapples and coconuts, and fish is plentiful in the sea, rivers and Lake Niassa. However, meat is often too expensive for many Mozambicans, and is saved for special occasions such as birthdays and holidays. As in the rest of Africa, staples of rice, *upshwa* (cassava) and *xima* (maize) are served with fish, vegetables or beans. In more rural areas, this type of food (together with grilled chicken and chips which is found almost everywhere!) is the main option. What sets Mozambique apart is its history of Arab and Indian traders plying the coast and setting up trading posts, and its Portuguese former colonial masters: they all brought a touch of spice to the traditional African cuisine.

- Arab merchants sailing their *dhows* along the coast and trading in slaves and produce introduced salt, pastries and doughnuts, onions and garlic, coriander, maize and rice.
- Indian traders and workers from Goa introduced Indian cuisine: *caril* (curry) dishes are common, as are *chamusas* (samosas — triangular wedges of fried pastry, filled with meat or vegetables). Coconut milk is widely used in Mozambique, just as in Goa.
- The Portuguese were the colonial rulers of Mozambique for more than 500 years and they introduced the highly spiced *piri-piri* dishes, bread rolls, cassava, cashew nuts and wine. Much of their inspiration came from their other colonies in India and Brazil.

Specialities to watch for include *matapa* (cassava leaves cooked in a peanut sauce, often with prawns) in the south, and *galinha á Zambeziana* (chicken with a sauce of lime juice, garlic, pepper and *piri-piri*) in Quelimane and Zambézia provinces.

FEASTS

While only about 30% of Mozambicans are Christian, there is a strong Roman Catholic influence here. Hence meat is often avoided on Fridays, and Christmas, also known as Family Day, is an important event. Special food is prepared to celebrate, such as:

- *bolo polana* — a cashew nut and potato cake, and
- *filhos de Natal* — Christmas deep-fried fritters made with yeast, honey, eggs and flour and often flavoured with brandy.

THE MENU

For the first course, Portuguese soups are popular: Salads are served with the main course, which consists of a starch plus fish, meat or poultry. On the side condiments such as *piri-piri* sauce, cashews and coconut milk are commonplace.

Fresh fruit salad and *malasadas* (doughnuts) are common desserts. *Sobremesa de Abacate* is the quintessential Mozambican dessert: just a couple of ripe avocados mashed with the juice of three tangerines with sugar stirred in to taste, served sprinkled with cinnamon.

DAILY MEALS

Mozambicans usually have little more than a roll or an egg sandwich and coffee for breakfast.

In rural areas, lunch (*almoço*) is the main meal of the day. In cities, this is often taken on the run from road-side food stalls called *barracas*, which serve a selection of take-away meals. Favourite lunches include:

- *Prego* rolls, which contain a thin slice of steak in *piri-piri* sauce on a soft, round, white roll.

ARIADNE VAN ZANDBERGEN / GETTY IMAGES

Piri-piri, hot chilli sauce, is the local speciality.

- Chicken and chips.
- *Xima* (maize porridge) or *upshwa* (cassava porridge) and a sauce of beans, fish or meat.
- Toasted cheese sandwiches.

For city-dwellers, dinner (*jantar*) is more likely to be the main meal of the day. Often diners are seated in chairs at the dinner table set with cutlery, which illustrates the European influence on the culture.

ESSENTIAL PRODUCE

Fish and seafood

As Mozambique has such a long coastline, a large lake (Lake Niassa) and several of the most important rivers in Africa running through it (the Limpopo, Zambezi, Lugende and Save), seafood is plentiful with fish, shellfish, calamari, octopus and crabs inexpensive and easy to find and so fish are a crucial element of the diet. The most popular river fish is the *chambo*.

Fruit and nuts

Tropical fruits and nuts are abundant in Mozambique and contribute to the nutrition of the people as well as being important exports.

- Cashews are often ground and used to thicken sauces.
- Coconuts are grated to extract the 'milk' which is used in sauces to counteract the fiery chillies of *piri-piri* sauce.
- Fruits such as pineapples, lichis, mangos, bananas and papayas often feature in a tropical fruit salad dessert.

Starchy staples

The African tradition of using starchy vegetables to make a porridge which is then served with a sauce of meat, fish or

JAMES BAIGRIE / GETTY IMAGES

Woman preparing *ugali*, made with cassava or maize

beans is no different in Mozambique. What might differ is the use of chillies to give the fairly bland starch a more zingy flavour.

- Cassava and maize are used for making porridge.
- Bread is soft and white in the Portuguese-style and fresh rolls are available every morning at bakeries.
- Rice is very popular and often served with curries and with prawns or chicken.

DEFINING DISHES

Bolo polana

This dessert cake of Portuguese origin is made with mashed potato and cashew nuts, flavoured with citrus zest. It is served at Christmas and other festive occasions.

Frango Zambeziana

Coconut milk is a typically Goan ingredient in this chicken curry, which is spiced with *piri-piri* chillies, tamarind or lime juice and a spice masala of cardamom, nutmeg, cumin, cloves and cinnamon. Served with rice, this dish is popular in the central Zambezia Province.

Matapa

Matapa is a rich, flavourful dish from the south, made with cassava leaves (or any other greens such as cabbage or kale), ground peanuts, coconut milk and garlic. Sometimes onions, tomatoes, grated green papaya and *piri-piri* chillies are added. Long cooking — up to five hours — enhances the flavours. *Matapa* is served with grilled or sautéed seafood and white rice.

Piri-piri prawns

Large, succulent prawns, still in their shells, are opened out 'butterfly' style, basted with *piri-piri* sauce and grilled. Served with more *piri-piri* sauce, white rice or bread rolls, a mixed salad and crisp Portuguese wine, this is the simplest yet most delicious Mozambican dish.

DRINKS

Beer and wine

Mozambicans love their *cerveja* (beer) which is available almost everywhere. Outside the major cities, it might not be served cold.

- Local brands include Dois M (2M), Manica and Laurentina, which are sold by the bottle or can.
- South African and Namibian beers are easy to find: Castle, Black Label, Amstel and Windhoek Lager among them.

Portuguese *vinho* and South African wines are found in supermarkets in larger cities and in hotels.

Local brews

Local brews are popular at weddings and other celebrations and include:

- *Nipa,* made from cashew nuts, cassava, mango and sugar cane, can be very strong.
- *Sura* is a palm wine common around Maputo and in the south and west. It is not as strong as *nipa.*

According to tradition, ***ukanhi***, a southern Mozambique traditional brew made from the fruit of the sacred *canhoeiro* (marula) tree, should never be sold, but given away.

Piri-piri prawns with rice.

2M, the most popular beer in Mozambique.

Women selling cashew nuts in Inhambane city.

Woman with an abundance of oranges at a market in Ghana.

ULRIKE MAIER / GETTY IMAGES

Ghana

With a reputation as Africa's friendliest country, Ghana certainly possesses a joy for life. Celebrations are a big part of the culture here. The geography and climate dictate regional food specialities: fish is widely available in the coastal and Volta areas, the south and interior have rich agricultural land, while further north towards the Sahel is drier. Ghana's food is representative of the best of West Africa.

CULINARY CAPITALS ACCRA, KUMASI **KNOWN FOR** *RED-RED* **IMPORTS** OIL, NUTS **EXPORTS** COCOA, PINEAPPLES **DEVOUR** *JOLLOF RICE* **AVOID** TURKEY TAILS

Friends and family gathering at Kejetia Market.

Fermented and dried cocoa beans.

Kola nuts for sale.

CULTURE

Ghana's 24 million people belong to dozens of ethnic tribes. Of these, 44% are Akan, which includes the Asante from the Kumasi region, and the Fanti, who fish the central coast and farm its near hinterland. Favourite dishes include:

- *Oto*, the sacred dish of the Akan and Ga people, features hard-boiled eggs, mashed yam and palm oil. It is served at a baby's naming ceremony or at harvest celebrations.
- *Fante-Fante* is a fish dish in a light tomato sauce and comes from the Fanti people.
- *Fetri desti* is an okra dish, originating with the Ewe people of the Volta region.

Cocoa is one of Ghana's most important crops. Kuapa Kokoo (meaning 'good cocoa farmer') is a union of small farmers, 28% of them women, supported by the Fairtrade Foundation. They supply cocoa for hundreds of Fairtrade chocolate products all over the world.

WHERE TO EAT

Local eateries known as 'chop bars' serve traditional dishes, usually with daily specials. Street food in Ghana is rewarding. A good selection is found in areas where people eat on the run, such as markets and bus stations. You will often find:

- *kelewele* — cubes of plantain fried with ginger and spices
- *kyinkyinga* — kebabs of beef, goat or pork sprinkled with a spices
- ice cream or frozen yoghurt sold in plastic bags, and
- rice and stew wrapped in banana leaves.

DAILY MEALS

For breakfast, Ghanaians eat bread and different types of porridge, often with ginger, sugar and cloves. Try:

- iced *kenkey* — a fermented corn dough crumbled into iced water, with evaporated milk and sugar
- *kooko*, a millet and corn porridge, or
- *tom brown*, a roasted maize porridge.

Lunch or dinner consists of a starch served with sauce. A light, stock-based sauce that always features onion, pepper and tomato is called a 'light soup', and contrasts with the heavier sauces that are thickened with groundnuts, *gari* (cassava) or *wele* (smoked cowhide).

Ghanaians love spices and 'hot' food. Most main meals contain fresh red chili peppers, garlic, onion and ginger. Shrimp powder and *wele* (smoked cowhide) round out the flavours.

Spices for sale in Kejetia Market.

ESSENTIAL PRODUCE

Bread

An important staple, Ghanaian bread is white, soft and sweet. Although made with wheat, cassava flour is sometimes added to improve texture.

Sugar bread is very soft and extremely sweet, tea bread less sweet, milk bread slightly richer and cinnamon bread is as its name suggests.

Palm oil

Ghanaians eat chicken, guinea fowl, pork, beef, tilapia, shellfish and a variety of beans, but an essential part of traditional cooking is the extensive use of vegetable oils, particularly palm oil. *Dzomi* is a palm oil infused with spices, including ginger. The red oil gives colour as well as flavour.

Popular foods, *red-red* and fried plantains.

Fufu, a mix of steamed plantains and cassava root being pounded using a wooden bowl and long stick.

Starchy staples

Vegetable starches are essential to Ghanaian cuisine.

- *Kenkey* is a fermented corn dough steamed in corn husks or banana leaves.
- *Fufu* dumplings are made from yam, cassava, *cocoyam* (taro) or plantain.
- *Tuo zaafe* from northern Ghana is a thick porridge made from millet, sorghum, cassava or corn that can be soft or thick enough to slice.
- *Gari* is dried and roasted cassava not unlike *couscous*.

DEFINING DISHES

These well-known foods are eaten all over Ghana.

- *Jollof rice* is found all over West Africa. This one-pot meal is reminiscent of paella and includes meat, poultry, fish or vegetables.
- *Palm nut soup* is a rich soup containing goat's meat, smoked fish, a cream made from pounded palm nuts, tomatoes, garden eggs (eggplants), okra and habanero peppers. It is served with *fufu* or *omo tuo* (rice balls).
- *Red-red* is a black-eyed pea stew with smoked fish, flavoured with ginger, garlic, powdered shrimps and herbs. Fried plantain is served alongside. Palm oil, tomato paste and red chilies contribute to the red colour.

A nice cuppa in Ghana is served in a huge mug with lots of evaporated milk and heaps of sugar. In summer, you might prefer a glass of ***bissap***, a delicious hibiscus flower iced tea.

BRIAN D CRUICKSHANK / GETTY IMAGES

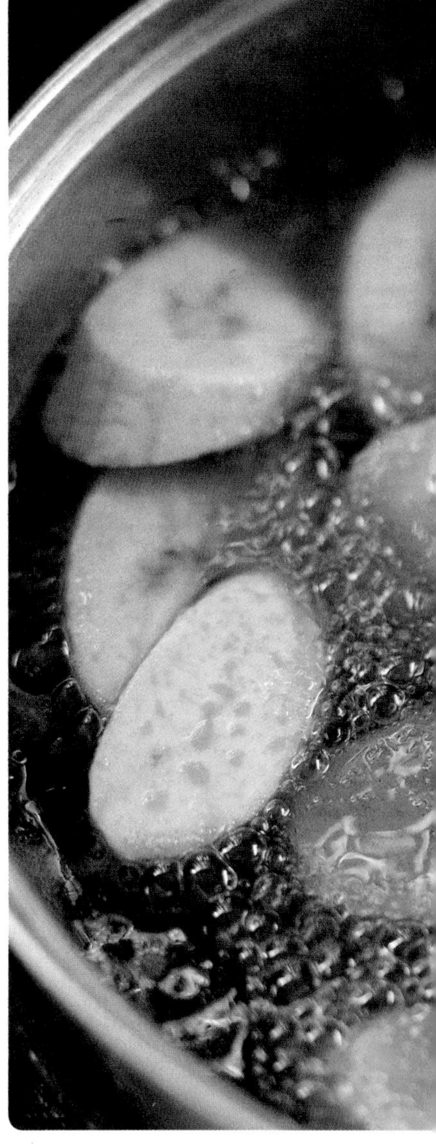

Plaintains frying in palm oil.

DRINKS

Bars in Ghana are often referred to as a 'spot'.

- Beer is widely available; brands include Star, Club, Gulder and Guinness. *Pito* is a millet beer popular in the north.
- *Palm wine* is the preferred tipple in the south.
- You could try *Akpeteshie*, a fiery local spirit.

KELEWELE

Plantain chips known as *kelewele* are versatile: eat them for breakfast, as an all-day snack, or serve as a side dish.

Serves 4

Ingredients
4 to 6 ripe plantains, peeled and diced
2 centimetre knob of fresh ginger
1 teaspoon salt
5 garlic cloves, peeled
1 teaspoon cayenne pepper
¼ small onion
palm oil or vegetable oil

Method
Grind together the fresh ginger, salt, garlic, cayenne pepper, onion, and 2 tablespoons of water in a mortar and pestle or small food processor.

Toss the diced plantain in the mixture and coat thoroughly.

In a deep pan, heat enough palm or vegetable oil (approximately 4 cm) to allow the cubes to float. Add the plantain and fry in batches, turning once, until golden on all sides. Drain on absorbent paper and serve immediately.

Authors

The following authors contributed to these chapters:

John Ashburne
Japan

Brett Atkinson
Australia, New Zealand

Carolyn Bain
Denmark, Norway, Sweden

Robin Barton
British Isles

Austin Bush
Korea, Philippines, Sri Lanka

Joe Cummings
Thailand

Matthew Evans
China, Italy

Steve Fallon
France

Bruce Geddes
Jamaica, Mexico

Will Gourlay
Iran

Catharine Hangar
Morocco

Martin Hughes
India, Ireland

Jessica Lee
Egypt, Ethiopia, Lebanon

Emily Matchar
Canada, USA

Sheema Mookherjee
India

Helen Ranger
Ghana, Mozambique, South Africa

Lynelle Scott-Aitken
Portugal

Karen Shimizu
Georgia

Richard Sterling
Greece, Spain, Vietnam

Su-Lyn Tan
Malaysia

Dani Valent
Turkey

Mara Vorhees
Hungary, Poland, Russia

Luke Waterson
Argentina, Brazil, Chile, Guatemala, Peru

Nicola Williams
Belgium, Germany, Switzerland

Patrick Witton
Indonesia

Index

Kk

Ll

Mm

Nn

Pp

Rr

Ss

Tt

Uu

Vv

THE FOOD BOOK

A Journey Through the Great Cuisines of the World

Published in December 2013 by

Lonely Planet Publications Pty Ltd
ABN 36 005 607 983
90 Maribyrnong St, Footscray,
Victoria, 3011, Australia

www.lonelyplanet.com

Publishing Director Piers Pickard

Publisher Ben Handicott

Commissioning Editor Robin Barton

Project Manager Bridget Blair

Art Direction & Design Mark Adams

Designer Leon Mackie

Image Researcher Kylie McLaughlin

Pre-Press Production Ryan Evans

Print Production Larissa Frost

Book Production by Captain Honey
www.captainhoney.com.au

Thanks to Yvonne Bischofberger, Katherine Marsh, Clara Monitto, Virginia Moreno, Wibowo Rusli

Front cover images Getty Images (second from left); iStockphoto

Spine image iStockphoto

Back cover images Greg Elms (first left); Jerry Alexander

ISBN 978 1 74321 949 2
Printed in China

10 9 8 7 6 5 4 3 2 1

Paper in this book is certified against the Forest Stewardship Council™ standards. FSC™ promotes environmentally responsible, socially beneficial and economically viable management of the world's forests.

Lonely Planet Offices

Australia
90 Maribyrnong St, Footscray, Victoria, 3011
Phone 03 8379 8000
Email talk2us@lonelyplanet.com.au

USA
150 Linden St, Oakland, CA 94607
Phone 510 250 6400 **Toll free** 800 275 8555
Email info@lonelyplanet.com

United Kingdom
BBC Worldwide Media Centre, 201 Wood Lane, London, W12 7TQ **Phone** 020 8433 1333
Email go@lonelyplanet.co.uk